Freedom, Determinism, and Responsibility

Readings in Metaphysics

Neil Campbell

Wilfrid Laurier University

Prentice
Hall

Upper Saddle River, New Jersey 07458

Library of Congress Cataloging-in-Publication Data
Freedom, determinism, and responsibility: readings in metaphysics / [edited by] Neil Campbell.
p. cm.
Includes bibliographical references.
ISBN 0-13-048517-9
1. Free will and determinism. 2. Responsibility. 3. Metaphysics. I. Campbell, Neil

BJ1461.F76 2003
123–dc21   2002035460

VP, Editorial Director: Charlyce Jones-Owen
Acquisitions Editor: Ross Miller
Assistant Editor: Wendy Yurash
Editorial Assistant: Carla Worner
Production Liaison: Fran Russello
Project Manager: Marty Sopher/Lithokraft II
Prepress and Manufacturing Buyer: Brian Mackey
Art Director: Jayne Conte
Cover Designer: Bruce Kenselaar
Marketing Manager: Chris Ruel

This book was set in 10/12 Times Optima by Lithokraft II
and was printed and bound by Courier Companies, Inc.
The cover was printed by Phoenix Color Corp.

© 2003 by Pearson Education, Inc.
Upper Saddle River, New Jersey 07458

Printed in the United States of America

10 9 8 7 6 5 4 3 2 1

ISBN: 0-13-048517-9

Pearson Education Ltd., *London*
Pearson Education Australia, PTY. Limited, *Sydney*
Pearson Education Singapore, Pte. Ltd
Pearson Education North Asia Ltd, *Hong Kong*
Pearson Education Canada, Ltd., *Toronto*
Pearson Education de Mexico, S.A. de C.V.
Pearson Education—Japan, *Tokyo*
Pearson Education Malaysia, Pte. Ltd
Pearson Education, *Upper Saddle River, New Jersey*

Contents

Preface

I was once asked to prepare an outline for a course on freedom, determinism, and responsibility. I searched long and hard for a suitable textbook but came up empty-handed. The books I found were either out of print, out of date, or contained no original works by important philosophers. This struck me as strange, for few topics excite undergraduate students as much as the issue of whether or not human beings are free. It is one of those fundamental questions in which there is a great deal at stake. My goal in editing this book is to fill this serious gap in undergraduate philosophy textbooks.

The shape of this collection was determined by three concerns. First, I wanted the book to expose students to some of the core writings on the topic by some of the most influential philosophers to shape our thinking about the concepts of freedom, determinism, and responsibility. Second, I wanted to avoid an historical approach and give students a sense of the breadth of the work in the area by including a number of contemporary contributions. These often draw on the historical background of the core works, but also provide new and different ways of conceiving of the problems, and sometimes suggest novel solutions. Third, it was important that this text be flexible enough to be useful to first-year undergraduates as well as senior students in philosophy. Most of the selected texts are written in quite accessible language and few of the readings in this anthology are highly technical. To help students who are new to philosophy, I have also made a special effort to write clear and accessible guides to the readings that precede each section. These should help students identify the central ideas in each of the readings and provide a solid grounding for lectures and for discussion of the material. Despite these measures, the readings themselves are subtle and complex enough to challenge senior students and provide the basis for broader discussions about the nature of determinism, of human agency, about the relationship between determinism and science, and between psychology and science, to name a few examples.

I would like to thank Frances Brennan and several anonymous referees for very helpful comments on both the general form of this book and the introductions to the readings. Grant money from Wilfrid Laurier University is also greatly appreciated, as is the work of Keitha McNab, who helped me track down and contact the owners of the copyrights to the selections that appear in this book. My thanks to the various publishers and authors who generously agreed to allow me to include their works in this volume.

I also want to express my gratitude to the following reviewers for their intelligent and helpful suggestions: Lou Lombardi, Lake Forest College, Daniel Silber, Florida Southern College, James Swindall, John Carroll University.

Introduction

There is an almost universal conviction in the idea that for anything that happens there is a cause for it happening. Indeed, the natural sciences use this notion of cause as their very foundation. When you go to the doctor you do so with the hope that the physician will be able to identify the cause of the ailment and prescribe a treatment. It probably never occurs to you to think that your illness happened for no reason at all. If we thought that diseases were uncaused, we would not bother spending billions of dollars on medical research and treatment. We would just sit back and hope for the best.

Science is often described as the search for causes and the quest to discover the universal laws that govern causal relationships. This search for causes is not limited to the world of inanimate matter, but also includes human beings. We, too, are objects of scientific study. Over the past few hundred years our understanding of our selves from the points of view of sociology, psychology, biology, neurology, and anatomy has increased tremendously. As our knowledge increases, we see that we are as much a part of the natural world as anything else, and hence, that we are also subject to the laws of nature. For example, we know that the colors of our hair and eyes are the result of the genetic material passed down to us from our parents, that they received this genetic material from their parents, and so on back through the generations. We also know that when we raise an arm, its motion is caused by the expansion and contraction of muscles, which are in turn caused by electrochemical impulses sent through the nerves from the brain. While it is true that we cannot yet identify all the causal origins of such an action, due to the tremendous complexity of the brain, we nevertheless believe there are such causes to discover and that they form but a small part of a long and seamless chain of causes and effects receding ever farther into the past. The implications of this idea are tremendous. It would appear as though we have as little control over our behavior as we do over our eye color. The color of our eyes was determined by causal forces that were at work long before we existed, and the same is true of our actions. Any action we perform has causal origins that can in principle be traced back in time to a point long before we ever existed.

Isn't there an importance difference, though, between the color of your eyes and the fact that you raised your arm? Although it is undoubtedly true that your eye color is determined by forces out of your control, raising your arm seems to be different. True, raising your arm involves a vast number of complicated neurophysiological processes, but these processes are not without a beginning. They start with your decision or choice to raise your arm. I think we can all agree that when we act intentionally or do something with a purpose our action is (at least in part) the result of our choosing. But choosing doesn't happen in a vacuum. When we decide to do something, we have reasons for doing it. Perhaps you decided to raise your arm because you wanted to ask a question in class. Your choice, then, is caused (at least in part) by the fact that you wanted to ask a question. Once we start looking for explanations for our decisions or choices we will be led to the same conclusion reached earlier. For, once again, your wanting to ask a question must have been caused by something (perhaps your inquisitive nature), which itself has causes (perhaps the way your parents raised you), and so on. It makes little difference whether we talk about the purely physical causes of our bodily movement or about the reasons we have to make the choices we do. In either case, there is a chain of causes and effects connected with your actions that reach back to a point that is beyond your control.

This, in broad outline, is the doctrine of determinism. Its details can be expressed in a number of different ways depending on the kinds of laws and causes one is interested in. One might say that our behavior is determined by physical laws, by biological laws, or by psychological or sociological laws, to name but a few. Whichever causes one chooses to focus on, the end result is the same: everything that happens, including everything we do, is the product of causal forces that are beyond our power to manipulate.

Despite the almost universal acceptance of the thesis of causal determinism, we have an equally strong conviction that at least some of our actions are the product of free choice. That is, we believe there are occasions when we perform the actions we do for no other reason than the fact we chose to perform them. Sure, your parents might have tried to influence you to go to university, and their arguments about the advantages of a university education were compelling, but they didn't make you go to university. You decided to go, and it was equally within your power to decide not to go if that is what you wished. Most of the choices we make seem to have this characteristic: we could have done otherwise, even if the situation were no different. That is, it was equally possible for you to decide not to go to university even if your parents still made all the same arguments, and even if you remained the same inquisitive person.

There are, of course, occasions when we do not make free choices. If your parents threatened to torture and murder you if you didn't attend university, we would likely say that your going to university was not a free choice, but was coerced. If a madman chained you up in his basement and escape was impossible, then you were certainly not free to go to university. These are the exceptions rather than the rule. Most of the time, it seems, these kinds of obstacles or coercive forces are not at work. Usually, we are the masters of our own fate.

This idea is behind our belief in moral responsibility. We do not hold the kleptomaniac responsible for stealing because stealing is a compulsion the kleptomaniac cannot resist. Similarly, we do not blame the spy who betrays state secrets to the enemy when tortured to a point beyond human endurance. If I make a large donation to a charity only because the life of a loved one is threatened if I refuse, I should not be praised for my act of generosity. Only if the element of coercion is missing, if the action is a product of free choice, does it seem appropriate to hold a person responsible for what they do. The idea of merit, of praise and blame, appears to make sense only on the assumption that we act freely and could have acted differently.

If the thesis of causal determinism is true, then it seems that anything we do, including all the choices we make, are just as inevitable and beyond our control as our eye color. A natural tension exists between the idea that our actions are determined and the claim that, at least sometimes, we act freely and are responsible for our actions. The subject of this book is the nature of and relationship between these ideas. Through the various selections that comprise this text, we will explore the issue of freedom, determinism, and responsibility.

Philosophers who debate this topic tend to divide themselves into certain philosophical camps. It will be useful to mention these briefly. The central division among philosophers is between compatibilists and incompatibilists.

The incompatibilist thinks freedom and responsibility are not consistent with a belief in causal determinism. According to the incompatibilist, then, if one accepts causal determinism, one must reject freedom and responsibility as illusions. Alternatively, if one accepts freedom and responsibility as the truth, then one must reject determinism. The view that determinism is false and that human beings are free and responsible beings goes by the name *libertarianism.* The other position, holding that determinism is true and that freedom and responsibility are illusory, is called hard determinism.

A compatibilist is someone who thinks causal determinism is true and that we are nevertheless free and responsible beings. In their view, there is a way to reconcile determinism with freedom and responsibility. Usually this involves reexamining the concept of freedom and defining it in a way that is consistent with causal determinism. The compatibilist position often goes by the name *soft determinism: Determinism* because of the belief that all events are causally determined, but since the view advocates notions of freedom and responsibility, the determinism in question is softened or relaxed in comparison to hard determinism. Hence, *soft determinism.* As you read the selections in this book, you should ask yourself which camp best describes the author and consider whose arguments are the strongest.

This book is divided into four chapters. Each chapter explores one element of the freedom-determinism debate. Chapter 1 is dedicated to the thesis of causal determinism and examines various ways in which this thesis can be understood and defended. The selections are intended to show that there are a number of different ways to express the idea of causal determinism and that each way has its own merits and shortcomings. Chapter 2 explores the concept of free will in similar detail and includes attempts to ground freedom in ideas as diverse as existentialism and quantum mechanics. Chapter 3 examines various arguments for and against compatibilism, generally focusing on the relationship between determinism and moral responsibility. In the final chapter, which contains the most advanced readings, we explore different approaches to compatibilism that are founded in a branch of philosophy sometimes called action theory. Of central concern here is the way our explanations of human behavior function and their relationship to causal laws. The selections in each chapter do not necessarily agree with one another. In fact, they often reflect important philosophical disagreements. You should regard the selections as providing contrasting views with one another and as providing the ground for discussion about the most productive ways to discuss the issues.

CHAPTER 1
Determinism

In the first part of this book, we examine the concept of causal determinism and the threat it poses for our sense that human beings are free and responsible beings. In general, the causal determinist claims that everything that happens could not have happened differently. This is because what happens now is the result of events in the past in conjunction with the laws of nature. All events are therefore the inevitable product of things that happened in the past. Of course, this is a very broad characterization of causal determinism. The readings in this section provide more details about what it is for an event to be causally determined and explain how human actions are subject to causal determination.

Pierre Simon de Laplace (1749–1827), a mathematician and philosopher, is generally regarded as the writer who gave the thesis of causal determinism its modern formulation, and he associates with this thesis a number of ideas that have been both influential and controversial. He wrote at a time in which there was much interest and progress in the natural sciences. Human beings used to think that celestial events, such as passing comets, were supernatural phenomena controlled by an intelligent force to warn or punish them for bad deeds. By Laplace's day, however, we knew better. With the development of astronomy as a science, we developed the ability to understand and to predict such events as natural occurrences. We no longer need to think that some form of intelligence guides a comet's trajectory; we can explain and predict its movements by appealing to physical laws.

Laplace writes optimistically that the kind of understanding that was developing of celestial phenomena can (at least in principle) extend to all things, even down to the level of molecules. He regards science as an expanding enterprise that will eventually encompass all things, including human behavior. The principle of sufficient reason (the claim that everything has a cause), then, is true not only of nonliving matter, but of humans as well. Just as gravitational forces determine the trajectory of Halley's comet, motives determine our actions. The entire universe is, for Laplace, a seamless sequence of events, each stage being determined by the events coming before. If we could know all the relevant facts about the distribution and orientation of all the matter in the universe, and if we could know all the laws of nature, then we would, he claims, be able to predict with perfect accuracy everything that will happen in the future. In this short passage from Laplace, then, we see the association of causal determinism with science, with scientific method, and with the concept of predictability.

The next selection, by Brand Blanshard, aims to undermine three arguments in support of indeterminism. In responding to these arguments, Blanshard develops his own characterization of determinism, which differs in several significant ways from Laplace's.

The first argument for indeterminism comes from our feeling of being free. When we act, we do so on the basis of making choices, and we have an awareness of it being up to us what choices we make. The future appears to be open in this respect: the choices we choose are made by us and picked from a realm of infinite possibilities. This means that although the behavior of other things in the world may be deterministic, our acts of choosing are not (for example, your choice to attend university).

Blanshard responds to this by dismissing the feeling of freedom as an illusion. Yes, he agrees, we *feel* free, but that doesn't mean we *are* free. This sense of freedom, the conviction that we choose our own choices, stems merely from our ignorance of the causes of our actions. Choosing is, as the indeterminist suggests, a future-directed activity, but because of this, we are blind to or ignore the events in the past that determine these choices. The feeling of freedom, then, is just that: a feeling and nothing more.

The second argument Blanshard considers draws on the connection between determinism and science that we see in writings by Laplace and many others. This time there is an interesting twist. The suggestion is that science has recently changed its mind about the behavior of matter at its most fundamental level. Thinkers such as Heisenberg, Eddington, and Born have claimed that subatomic particles behave indeterministically. This is not simply a matter of appearance. The indeterminism is not merely a reflection of our own ignorance of the relevant laws controlling the behavior of electrons. These scientists claim there are no such laws at work on this level. Since the ultimate nature of matter is indeterministic and we are, at least in part, made up of matter, it is likely that this indeterminism percolates up to the physical processes involved in making choices. Hence, our choices inherit the indeterminism of the microphysical processes on which they depend.

Blanshard points out, by way of response, that indeterminism in science is still a contested issue, but claims that this is no matter. Even if it is true that subatomic particles are fundamentally indeterministic, it does not follow that our choices are similarly undetermined. The problem is that the argument is guilty of a fallacy of composition. The form of the fallacy is to assume that because the parts of something have a certain characteristic, the whole possesses that characteristic too. The reason this is a fallacy is that the conclusion does not necessarily follow. Consider a feather. A feather is light. It does not follow that any collection of feathers is also light. If I made a *really big* pillow that contained millions of feathers it would be very heavy. Similarly, Blanshard argues that conglomerations of subatomic particles do not inherit the indeterministic behavior of their parts. Billiard balls are made up of subatomic particles, but billiard balls behave deterministically. Since making choices depends not on individual subatomic particles, but large collections of them, there is no reason to expect that choosing inherits the indeterminism of those subatomic particles.

The third and final argument Blanshard considers for indeterminism is the moral argument. If determinism is true, then it completely undermines all of our moral concepts. Notions of praise and blame, responsibility, and especially duty have no real meaning in a deterministic world. Since these concepts do have meaning, determinism must be false.

Blanshard's reply to this argument depends on a distinction he draws between different levels and kinds of causation. The sort of causality at work in the physical world and in our bodies, he claims, is different from the kind of causality that happens in our minds, as when one idea causes another. The causality between prejudice and habit in belief or action is also different from the causality of moral action. Each level of causation has its own form of determinism, and morality is no different. When we act out of a sense of duty we are not acting freely, we are instead compelled by moral necessity. Blanshard likens this kind of determinism to the sort of determinism that can control the actions of an artist. At times an artist may claim that his or her work has taken over and controls the artist's brush, relieving the artist from making aesthetic choices. When we act out of a sense of duty, something similar is happening: our actions are determined by a special sort of moral causality. What this shows, in Blanshard's view, is that our moral concepts are not necessarily undermined by determinism, but have a kind of determinism of their own.

Richard Taylor's "Fate," explores the idea that the future is fixed and unavoidable; that whatever we do we cannot escape the particular outcome that fate has determined for us. From his perspective, any consistent, thoroughgoing determinist should also be a fatalist, though a belief in fatalism is possible independently of whether or not one accepts the thesis of causal determinism. Taylor outlines three possible sources of fatalism: divine omniscience, causal determinism, and the law of excluded middle.

Divine omniscience refers to the kind of knowledge that God is thought by many theists to possess. To be omniscient is to know everything that can be known, to know every truth about the past, present, and future. If God is omniscient, then God must know about all of my future actions, and this foreknowledge implies that my future actions are fated. If God knows what I am going to do before I do it, then it seems I don't really have a choice. I am going to do what God foresaw all along.

If one is a causal determinist, then one believes that the future is determined by the past. Since it is not, and never was, in our power to change the past, it follows that it is beyond our power to change the future. All of our actions and all of our choices were set in motion long before any of us were born. Hence, what will happen is inevitable and thus unavoidable.

Using "The Story of Osmo," as an illustration, Taylor argues that if one accepts the claim that there exists a body of truths about every aspect of one's life, including events that have not yet happened, then one should become a fatalist. In his view, it does not matter whether or not these truths are written down. All that matters is that they exist. Given a principle of logic called "the law of excluded middle," he argues, they must exist, so fatalism is true. The law of excluded middle states that for any proposition that can be formulated, that proposition is either true or false. There is no middle ground between truth and falsity. Taylor's understanding of this principle is that such truths are eternal; they are not bound by time, for otherwise there would be propositions that are neither true nor false but that *become* true at some point. These truths constitute an unwritten biography for each of us. Just as there is a true statement about the moment and circumstances of my birth, there is a true description of the moment and circumstances of my death. It does not matter that no one knows, in advance, this truth about my death. The fact that this truth exists, and has always existed, means that the time and circumstances of my death are unavoidable. One cannot change what is true into what is false.

To close chapter 1 is Michael Ruse's "Darwinism and Determinism." In this article, Ruse explores the relationships that freedom, determinism, and morality have with Darwin's theory of evolution. His general aim is to show that although evolutionary theory leads to a form of determinism, it nevertheless leaves room for morality and freedom if we understand these ideas in a particular way.

Evolutionary theory tells us that we are heirs to "epigenetic rules." Since we are the products of evolution, it has bestowed upon us innate rules that guide the way we process information and, in many cases, how we act. The built-in obstacles to incest are a prime example of such rules. Since evolution is often described as the survival of the fittest, one gets the impression that among these epigenetic rules there should be a powerful drive toward selfish behavior. However, Ruse argues that this is a mistake. In fact, evolutionary principles can predict and explain forms of altruism. Morality itself, he argues, should be regarded as a product of evolution that helps us to coexist peacefully and securely with one another, thus improving our chances of survival. Morality, then, should be regarded as a sociobiological mechanism rather than as an abstract body of truths.

If our very natures are the result of evolution, then is causal determinism true? Here Ruse distinguishes between straightforward causal determinism and what he calls "biological" and "control" determinism. Causal determinism in the ordinary sense, he claims, must be true if we are to accept evolutionary theory, for causal determinism is required for science itself. Without the idea that there are objective regularities or laws of nature, science is simply impossible, for science relies on observed regularities and seeks to discover laws of nature. Biological determinism is also true, he claims, but we must be careful to understand what this means. We are the products of evolution and biology, but we are also the products of our environment. It would be a mistake to insist, for instance, that biological determinism entails some form of eugenics, according to which certain racial groups are disposed toward certain forms of behavior. Biological and environmental factors function together in extraordinary complexity to fashion the kind of people we are.

Finally, Ruse speaks of control determinism. Here the question is whether causal and biological determinism render us mere puppets without free will. Are we in control of our actions or is something else? Ruse argues that we do have control understood as freedom from constraint. If I am bound in chains I am constrained and hence, unfree to run around as I please, regardless of my causal and genetic ancestry. A key element in being unconstrained, Ruse argues, is that we be able to control our emotions. When we are able to direct our desires to (often) moral goals, we are free. When our emotions get the better of us, we are constrained.

Evolutionary theory, then, has tremendous implications for the philosophical issue of freedom, determinism, and morality. It gives special meaning to, and evidence for, the truth of determinism, and it explains how morality and freedom can be understood in a way that is consistent with determinism.

PHILOSOPHICAL ESSAY ON PROBABILITY*

Pierre Simon de Laplace

All events, even those which because of their small scale do not appear to keep to the great laws of nature, arc just as necessary a result of those laws as are the revolutions of the sun. In ignorance of the ties which bind these events to the entire system of the universe, people have made them depend on final causes,[1] or upon chance, depending on whether they happen and recur with regularity, on the one hand, or in an apparently disorderly way, on the other. But these imaginary causes have been gradually pushed out of the way as the boundaries of our knowledge have increased, and they would completely vanish in the face of sound philosophy, which sees in them only the expression of our present ignorance of the true causes.

Present events have a connection with previous ones that is based on the self-evident principle that a thing cannot come into existence without a cause that produces it. This axiom, known under the name of the *principle of sufficient reason*, extends even to actions which people regard as indifferent.[2] The freest will is unable to give birth to them without a determinate motive. Take two situations characterized by exactly similar circumstances; if the will were to act in the first case and refrain from acting in the second, its choice would be an effect without a cause—so it would be, as Leibniz puts it, a case of the 'blind chance' which the Epicureans talk of. Believing in such uncaused events is an illusion of the mind, which loses sight of the elusive reasons underlying the will's choice in "indifferent" situations, and convinces itself that the will is self-determined and motiveless.

We must therefore regard the present state of the universe as the effect of its preceding state and as the cause of the one which is to follow. An intelligence which in a single instant could know all the forces which animate the natural world, and the respective situations of all the beings that made it up, could, provided it was vast enough to make an analysis of all the data so supplied, be able to produce a single formula which specified all the movements in the universe from those of the largest bodies in the universe to those of the lightest atom. For such an intelligence, nothing would be "uncertain", and the future, like the past, would be present before its eyes. The human

---

*Translated by John Cottingham. From *Western Philosophy: An Anthology*, ed. John Cottingham (Oxford: Blackwell, 1996). Reprinted with the kind permission of Professor Cottingham and Blackwell Press.

mind, in the perfection which it has been able to give to astronomy, presents a feeble shadow of this intelligence. Its discoveries in mechanics and geometry, added to that of universal gravity, have brought it within reach of including within the same analytical formulae all the past and future states of the world system. By applying the same method to various other objects of its knowledge, it has managed to reduce the observed phenomena to general laws, and to predict the results which must be generated by any given set of circumstances. All the efforts of the human mind in its search for truth tend to bring it continually closer to that vast intelligence we have just imagined; though it will always remain infinitely far removed from it. This onward tendency, peculiar to the human race, is what makes us superior to the animals; it is progress in this area which distinguishes nations and epochs and is their true glory.

Let us recall that in former times, still not so very far away, a heavy rainfall or prolonged drought, a comet trailing a very long tail, eclipses, the aurora borealis, and in general all out of the ordinary phenomena, were regarded as so many signs of celestial anger. Heaven was invoked in order to avert their dire influence. No one prayed to heaven to stop the courses of the planets and the sun; observation had soon made people see the futility of such prayers. But because these unusual phenomena, appearing and disappearing at long intervals, seemed to contravene the order of nature, men supposed that heaven created and altered them at will to punish crimes done on earth. Thus the comet of 1456, with its long tail, spread terror throughout Europe, already appalled by the rapid successes of the Turks, who had just overthrown the Lower Empire. But for us, now that four successive revolutions of the body in question have elapsed, it has aroused a very different interest. The knowledge of the laws of the world-system acquired during the interval had dissipated the fears produced by ignorance of the true relationship of man to the universe; and Halley, having recognized that the appearances of 1531, 1607 and 1682 all related to the same comet, predicted its next return for the end of 1758 or the start of 1759. The learned world impatiently awaited this return, which was destined to confirm one of the greatest discoveries ever made in the sciences, and fulfill the prediction of Seneca when he said, speaking of the revolution of those stars which come from an enormous distance: "The day will come when studies pursued over many centuries will reveal in all clarity things that are now hidden, and posterity will be astonished that we had failed to grasp such clear truths." Clairaut then undertook to analyze the perturbations which the comet had undergone as a result of the action of the two great planets, Jupiter and Saturn; after vast calculations he fixed its next passage at perihelion towards the beginning of April 1759—which was quickly confirmed by observation. There is no doubt that this regularity which has been demonstrated by astronomy in the movement of the comets also obtains in all other phenomena. The curve described by a simple molecule of air or vapor is determined in just as certain a manner as that of the planetary orbits; there are no differences between the two cases, except those which are a function of our own ignorance.

NOTES

1. Explanations referring to the end state or goal towards which a process or action is apparently directed.

2. i.e., actions where I seem to have an entirely "open" choice between two options. In traditional terminology, someone was said to possess "liberty of indifference" when entirely free and undermined as to which of two courses of action to select.

THE CASE FOR DETERMINISM*

Brand Blanshard

I am a determinist. None of the arguments offered on the other side seem of much weight except one form of the moral argument, and that itself is far from decisive. Perhaps the most useful thing I can do in this paper is explain why the commoner arguments for indeterminism do not, to my mind, carry conviction. In the course of this explanation the brand of determinism to which I am inclined should become gradually apparent.

But first a definition or two. Determinism is easier to define than indeterminism, and at first glance there seems to be no difficulty in saying what one means by it. It is the view that all events are caused. But unless one also says what one means by "event" and "caused," there is likely to be trouble later. Do I include among events not only changes but the lack of change, not only the fall of the water over the cataract's edge, but the persistence of ice in the frozen river?

The answer is "Yes." By an event I mean any change or persistence of state or position. And what is meant by saying that an event is caused? The natural answer that the event is so connected with one preceding event that unless the latter had occurred the former would not have occurred. Indeterminism means the denial of this. And the denial of this is the statement that there is at least one event to which no preceding event is necessary. But that gets us into trouble at once, for it is doubtful if any indeterminist would want to make such an assertion. What he wants to say is that his decision to tell the truth is undetermined, not that there is no preceding event necessary to it. He would not contend, for example, that he could tell the truth if he had never been born. No, the causal statement to which the indeterminist takes exception is a different one. He is not saying that there is any event to which some namable antecedents are not necessary; he is saying that there are some events whose antecedents do not make them necessary. He is not denying that all consequents have

*From Sydney Hook, ed., *Determinism and Freedom in the Age of Modern Science* (New York: New York University Press, 1965). Reprinted with the kind permission of the estate of Sydney Hook.

necessary antecedents; he is denying that all antecedents have necessary consequents. He is saying that the state of things just before he decided to tell the truth might have been exactly what it was and yet he might have decided to tell a lie.

By determinism, then, I mean the view that every event *A* is so connected with a later event *B* that, given *A*, *B* must occur. By indeterminism I mean the view that there is some event *B* that is not so connected with any previous event *A* that, given *A*, it must occur. Now, what is meant here by "must"? We cannot in the end evade that question, but I hope you will not take it as an evasion if at this point I am content to let you fill in the blank in any way you wish. Make it a logical "must," if you care to, or a physical or metaphysical "must," or even the watered-down "must" that means "*A* is always in fact followed by *B*." We can discuss the issue usefully though we leave ourselves some latitude on this point.

With these definitions in mind, let us ask what are the most important grounds for indeterminism. This is not the same as asking what commonly moves people to be indeterminists; the answer to that seems to me all too easy. Everyone vaguely knows that to be undetermined is to be free, and everyone wants to be free. My question is rather, When reflective people accept the indeterminist view nowadays, what considerations seem most cogent to them? It seems to me that there are three: first, the stubborn feeling of freedom, which seems to resist all dialectical solvents; second, the conviction that natural science itself has now gone over to the indeterminist side; and, third, that determinism would make nonsense of moral responsibility. The third of these seems to me the most important, but I must try to explain why none of them seem to me conclusive.

One of the clearest heads that ever devoted itself to this old issue was Henry Sidgwick. Sidgwick noted that, if at any given moment we stop to think about it, we always feel as if more than one course were open to us, that we could speak or be silent, lift our hand or not lift it. If the determinist is right, this must be an illusion, of course, for whatever we might have done, there must have been a cause, given which we had to do what we did. Now, a mere intuitive assurance about ourselves may be a very weak ground for belief; Freud has shown us that we may be profoundly deceived about how we really feel or why we act as we do. But the curious point is that, though a man who hates his father without knowing it can usually be shown that he does and can often be cured of his feeling, no amount of dialectic seems to shake our feeling of being free to perform either of two proposed acts. By this feeling of being free I do not mean merely the freedom to do what we choose. No one on either side questions that we have that sort of freedom, but it is obviously not the sort of freedom that the indeterminist wants, since it is consistent with determinism of the most rigid sort. The real issue, so far as the will is concerned, is not whether we can do what we choose to do, but whether we can choose our own choice, whether the choice itself issues in accordance with law from some antecedent. And the feeling of freedom that is relevant as evidence is the feeling of an open future as regards the choice itself. After the noise of argument has died down, a sort of intuition stubbornly remains that we can not only lift our hand if we choose, but that the choice itself is open to us. Is this not an impressive fact?

No, I do not think it is. The first reason is that when we are making a choice our faces are always turned toward the future, toward the consequences that one act or the other will bring us, never toward the past with its possible sources of constraint.

Hence these sources are not noticed. Hence we remain unaware that we are under constraint at all. Hence we feel free from such constraint. The case is almost as simple as that. When you consider buying a new typewriter your thought is fixed on the pleasure and advantage you would gain from it, or the drain it would make on your budget. You are not delving into the causes that led to your taking pleasure in the prospect of owning a typewriter or to your having a complex about expenditure. You are too much preoccupied with the ends to which the choice would be a means to give any attention to the causes of which your choice may be an effect. But that is no reason for thinking that if you did preoccupy yourself with these causes you would not find them at work. You may remember that Sir Francis Galton was so much impressed with this possibility that for some time he kept account in a notebook of the occasions on which he made important choices with a full measure of this feeling of freedom; then shortly after each choice he turned his eye backward in search of constraints that might have been acting on him stealthily. He found it so easy to bring such constraining factors to light that he surrendered to the determinist view.

But this, you may say, is not enough. Our preoccupation with the future may show why we are not aware of the constraints acting on us, and hence why we do not feel bound by them; it does not explain why our sense of freedom persists after the constraints are disclosed to us. By disclosing the causes of some fear, for example, psychoanalytic therapy can remove the fear, and when these causes are brought to light, the fear commonly does go. How is it, then, that when the causes of our volition are brought to light volition continues to feel as free as before? Does this not show that it is really independent of those causes?

No again. The two cases are not parallel. The man with the panic fear of dogs is investing all dogs with the qualities—remembered, though in disguised form——of the monster that frightened him as a child. When this monster and his relation to it are brought to light, so that they can be dissociated from the Fidos and Towsers around him, the fear goes, because its appropriate object has gone. It is quite different with our feeling of freedom. We feel free, it was suggested, because we are not aware of the forces acting on us. Now, in spite of the determinist's conviction that when a choice is made there are always causal influences at work, he does not pretend to reveal the influences at work in our present choice. The chooser's face is always turned forward; his present choice is always unique; and no matter how much he knows about the will and the laws, his present choice always emerges out of deep shadow. The determinist who buys a typewriter is as little interested at the moment in the strings that may be pulling at him from his physiological or subconscious cellars as his indeterminist colleague, and hence feels just as free. Thus, whereas the new knowledge gained through psychoanalysis does remove the grounds of fear, the knowledge gained by the determinist is not at all of the sort that would remove the grounds for the feeling of freedom. To make the persistence of this feeling in the determinist an argument against his case is therefore a confusion.

The second reason, I suggested, why so many thoughtful persons remain indeterminists is that they are convinced that science has gone indeterminist. Well, has it? If you follow Heisenberg, Eddington, and Born, it has. If you follow Russell, Planck, and Einstein, it has not. When such experts disagree it is no doubt folly for the layman to rush in. But since I am discussing the main reasons why people stick to indeterminism, and have admitted that the new physics is one of them, I cannot afford to be quite prudent. Let me say, then, with much hesitation that, as far as I can follow the argument, it provides no good evidence for indeterminism even in the physical world, and that, if it did, it would provide no good evidence for indeterminism in the realm of will.

First as to physical indeterminism. Physicists now tell us that descriptive statements about the behavior of bodies are really statistical statements. It was known long ago that the pressure that makes a football hard is not the simple quality one feels in pushing something: it is the beating on the inner surface of the football of millions of molecular bullets. We now know that each of these bullets is a swarm of atoms, themselves normally swarms of still minuter somethings, of which the proton and the electron are typical. The physicist admits that the behavior of an enormous mass of these particles, such as a billiard ball, is so stable that we may safely consider it as governed by causal law. But that is no reason, he adds, for assigning a like stability to the ultimate particles themselves. Indeed, there is good reason, namely the principle of indeterminacy, for saying that they sometimes act by mere chance. That principle tells us that whereas, when we are talking about a billiard ball, we can say that it has a certain momentum and direction at point B as a result of having a certain momentum and direction at point A, we can never say that sort of thing about an electron. Why? Because the conditions of observation are such that, when they allow us to fix the position exactly, they make it impossible to fix the momentum exactly. Suppose that we can determine the position of a moving particle with more accuracy the shorter the wave length of light we use. But suppose that the shorter the wave length, the more it interferes with the momentum of the particle, making it leap unpredictably about. And suppose there is no way of determining the position without in this way leaving the momentum vague, or of determining the momentum without leaving the position vague. It will then be impossible to state any precise law that governs the particle's movement. We can never say that such-and-such a momentum at point A was necessarily followed by such-and-such a momentum at point B, because these statements can have no precise meaning, and can be given none, for either antecedent or consequent. Hence to speak any longer of nature as governed ultimately by causal laws—i.e., statements of precise connection between antecedent and consequent—is simply out of the question.

This argument, as Sir David Ross has pointed out, may be interpreted in different ways. It may be taken to say that, though the particle does have a certain position and momentum, we can never tell, definitely and for both at the same time, what they are. Many interpreters thus understand the theory. But so taken, there is of course nothing in it to throw the slightest doubt on the reign of causality. It is merely a statement that in a certain region our knowledge of causal law has limits. Secondly, the theory might be taken to mean that electrons are not the sort of things that have position and momentum at all in the ordinary sense, but are fields, perhaps, or widespreading waves. This, too, has no suggestion of indeterminism. It would not mean that general statements about the nature and behavior of electrons could not be made, but only that such statements would not contain references to position and momentum. Thirdly, the theory might mean that, though these particles do have a position and a momentum, the position or momentum is not definitely this rather than that. Even laymen must rise at this point and protest, with all respect, that this is meaningless. Vagueness in our thought of a position makes sense; vagueness of actual position makes none. Or, finally, the argument may mean that, though the particle does have a definite position and momentum, these cannot even in theory be correlated with anything that went before. But how could we possibly know this? The only ground for accepting it is that we do not know of any such correlates. And that is no reason for denying that any exist. Indeed, to deny this is to abandon the established assumption and practice of science. Science has advanced in the past precisely because, when things happened whose causes were unknown, it was assumed that they had causes nevertheless. To assume that a frustration of present knowledge, even one that looks permanent, is a sign of chance in nature is both practically uncourageous and theoretically a *non sequitur*.

But let us suppose that the Eddingtonians are right and that what has been called "free will among the electrons" is the fact. Would that imply indeterminism in the realm that most nearly concerns us, the realm of choice? I cannot see that it would. The argument supposed to show that it would is as follows: Psychical processes depend on physical processes. But physical processes are themselves at bottom unpredictable. Hence the psychical processes dependent on them must share this unpredictability. Stated in the abstract, the argument sounds impressive. But what does it actually come to? We are told that, even if there is inconstancy in the behavior of single particles, there is no observable inconstancy in the behavior of masses of them; the particles of a billiard ball are never able to get together and go on a spree simultaneously. Eddington admitted that they might, just as he admitted that an army of monkeys with a million typewriters might produce all the books in the British Museum, but he admitted also that the chances of a billiard ball's behaving in this way were so astronomically remote that he would not believe it if he saw it.

The question of importance for us, then, is whether, if acts of choice are dependent on physical processes at all, they depend on the behavior of particles singly or on that of masses of particles. To this there can be but one answer. They depend on mass behavior. An act of choice is an extremely complex process. It involves the idea of one or more ends, the association of that idea with more or less numerous other ideas, the presence of desires and repulsions, and the operation of habits and impulses; indeed, in those choices for which freedom is most demanded, the whole personality seems to be at work. The cortical basis for so complex a process must be extremely broad. But if it is, the great mass of cells involved must, by the physicist's admission, act with a high stability, and the correlated psychical processes must show a similar stability. But that is what we mean by action in accordance with causal law. So, even if the physicists are right about the unstable behavior of single particles, there is no reason whatever for translating this theory into a doctrine of indeterminism for human choice.

We come now to the third of the reasons commonly advanced in support of indeterminism. This is that determinism makes a mess of morality. The charge has taken many forms. We are told that determinism makes praise and blame meaningless, punishment brutal, remorse pointless, amendment hopeless, duty a deceit. All these allegations have been effectively answered except the one about duty, where I admit I am not quite satisfied. But none of them are in the form in which determinism must troubles the plain man. What most affronts him, I think, is the suggestion that he is only a machine, a big foolish clock that seems to itself to be acting freely, but whose movements are controlled completely by the wheels and weights inside a Punch-and-Judy show whose appearance of doing things because they are right or reasonable is a sham because everything is mechanically regulated by wires from below. He has no objections to determinism as applied by physicists to atoms, by himself to machines, or by his doctor to his body. He has an emphatic objection to determinism as applied by anyone to his reflection and his will, for this seems to make him a gigantic mechanical toy, or worse, a sort of Frankenstein monster.

In this objection I think we must agree with the plain man. If anyone were to show me that determinism involved either materialism or mechanism, I would renounce it at once, for that would be equivalent, in my opinion, to reducing it to absurdity. The "physicalism" once proposed by Neurath and Carnap as a basis for the scientific study of behavior I could not accept for a moment, because it is so dogmatically antiempirical. To use empirical methods means, for me, not to approach nature with a preconceived notion as to what facts must be like, but to be ready to consider all kinds of alleged facts on their merits. Among these the introspectively observable fact of reflective choice, and the inference to its existence in others, are particularly plain, however different from anything that occurs in the realm of the material or the publicly observable or the mechanically controlled.

Now, what can be meant by saying that such choice, though not determined mechanically, is still determined? Are you suggesting, it will be asked, that in the realm of reflection and choice there operates a different kind of causality from any we know in the realm of bodies? My answer is: Yes, just that. To put it more particularly, I am suggesting (1) that even within the psychical realm there are different causal levels, (2) that a causality of higher level may supervene on one of lower level, and (3) that when causality of the highest level is at work, we have precisely what the indeterminists, without knowing it, want.

1. First, then, as to causal levels. I am assuming that even the indeterminist would admit that most mental events are causally governed. No one would want to deny that his stepping on a tack had something to do with his feeling pain, or that his touching a flame had something to do with his getting burned, or that his later thought of the flame had something to do with his experience of its hotness. A law of association is a causal law of mental events. In one respect it is like a law of physical events: in neither case have we any light as to *why* the consequent follows on the antecedent. Hume was right about the billiard balls. He was right about the flame and the heat; we do not see why something bright and yellow should also be hot. He was right about association; we do not understand how one idea calls up another; we only know that it does. Causality—in all such cases means to us little if anything more than a routine of regular sequence.

Is all mental causation like that? Surely not. Consider a musician composing a piece or a logician making a deduction. Let us make our musician a philosopher also, who after adding a bar pauses to ask himself, "Why did I add just that?" Can we believe he would answer, "Because whenever in the past I have had the preceding bars in mind, they have always been followed by this bar"? What makes this suggestion so inept is partly that he may never have thought of the preceding bars before, partly that, if he had, the repetition of an old sequence would be precisely what he would avoid. No, his answer, I think, would be something like this: "I wrote what I did because it seemed the right thing to do. I developed my theme in the manner demanded to carry it through in an aesthetically satisfactory way." In other words, the constraint that was really at work in him was not that of association; it was something that worked distinctly against association; it was the constraint of an aesthetic ideal. And, if so, there is a causality of a different level. It is idle to say that the musician is wholly in the dark about it. He can see not only that *B* succeeded *A*; as he looks back, he can see in large measure *why* it did.

It is the same with logical inference, only more clearly so. The thinker starts, let us say, with the idea of a regular solid whose faces are squares, and proceeds to develop in thought the further characteristics that such a solid must possess. He constructs it in imagination and then sees that it must have six faces, eight vertices, and twelve edges. Is this association merely? It may be. It is, for example, if he merely does in imagination what a child does when it counts the edges on a lump of sugar. This is not inference and does not feel like it. When a person, starting with the thought of a solid with square faces, deduces that it must have eight vertices, and then asks why he should have thought of that, the natural answer is, Because the first property entails the second. Of course this is not the only condition, but it seems to me contrary to introspectively plain fact to say that it had nothing to do with the movement of thought. It is easy to put this in such a way as to invite attack. If we say that the condition of our thinking of *B* is the observed necessity between *A* and *B*, we are assuming that *B* is already thought of as a means of explaining how it comes to be thought of. But that is not what I am saying. I am saying that in thinking at its best thought comes under the constraint of necessities in its object, so that the objective act that *A* necessitates *B* partially determines our passing in thought from *A* to *B*. Even when the explanation is put in this form, the objection has been raised that necessity is a timeless link between concepts, while causality is a temporal bond between events, and that the two must be kept sharply apart. To which the answer is: Distinct, yes; but always apart, no. A timeless relation may serve perfectly well as the condition of a temporal passage. I hold that in the course of our thinking we can easily verify this fact, and, because I do, I am not put off by pronouncements about what we should and should not be able to see.

2. My second point about these causal levels is that our mental processes seldom move on one level alone. The higher is always supervening on the lower and taking over partial control. Though brokenly and imperfectly rational, rational creatures we still are. It must be admitted that most of our so-called thinking moves by association, and is hardly thinking at all. But even in the dullest of us "bright shoots of everlastingness," strands of necessity, aesthetic or logical, from time to time appear. "The quarto and folio editions mankind" can follow the argument with fewer lapses than most of us; in the texts of the greatest of all dramas, we are told, there was seldom a blot or erasure; but Ben Jonson added, and no doubt rightly, that there ought to have been a thousand. The effort of both thought and art is to escape the arbitrary, the merely personal, everything that, casual and capricious, is irrelevant, and to keep to lines appointed by the whole that one is constructing. I do not suggest that logical and aesthetic necessity are the same. I do say that they are both to be distinguished from association or habit as representing a different level of control. That control is never complete; all creation in thought or art is successful in degree only. It is successful in the degree to which

it ceases to be an expression of merely personal impulses and becomes the instrument of a necessity lying in its own subject matter.

3. This brings us to our last point. Since moral choice, like thought and art, moves on different causal levels, it achieves freedom, just as they do, only when it is determined by its own appropriate necessity. Most of our so-called choices are so clearly brought about by association, impulse, and feeling that the judicious indeterminist will raise no issue about them. When we decide to get a drink of water, to take another nibble of chocolate, to go to bed at the usual hour, the forces at work are too plain to be denied. It is not acts like these on which the indeterminist takes his stand. It is rather on those where, with habit, impulse, and association prompting us powerfully to do *X*, we see that we ought to do *Y* and therefore do it. To suppose that in such cases we are still the puppets of habit and impulse seems to the indeterminist palpably false.

So it does to us. Surely about this the indeterminist is right. Action impelled by the sense of duty, as Kant perceived, is action on a different level from anything mechanical or associative. But Kant was mistaken in supposing that when we were determined by reason we were not determined at all. This supposition seems to me wholly unwarranted. The determination is still there, but, since it is a determination by the moral necessities of the case, it is just what the moral man wants and thus is the equivalent of freedom. For the moral man, like the logician and the artist, is really seeking self-surrender. Through him as through the others an impersonal ideal is working, and to the extent that this ideal takes possession of him and molds him according to its pattern, he feels free and is free.

The logician is most fully himself when the wind gets into his sails and carries him effortlessly along the line of his calculations. Many an artist and musician have left it on record that their best work was done when the whole they were creating took the brush or pen away from them and completed the work itself. It determined them, but they were free, because to be determined by this whole was at once the secret of their craft and the end of their desire. This is the condition of the moral man also. He has caught a vision, dimmer perhaps than that of the logician or the artist, but equally objective and compelling. It is a vision of the good. This good necessitates certain things, not as means to ends merely, for that is not usually a necessary link, but as integral parts of itself. It requires that he should put love above hate, that he should regard his neighbor's good as of like value with his own, that he should repair injuries, and express gratitude, and respect promises, and revere truth. Of course it does not guide him infallibly. On the values of a particular case he may easily be mistaken. But that no more shows that there are no values present to be estimated, and no ideal demanding a special mode of action, than the fact that we make a mistake in adding figures shows that there are no figures to be added, or a right way of adding them. In both instances what we want is control by the objective requirements of the case. The saint, like the thinker and the artist, has often said this in so many words. I feel most free, said St. Paul, precisely when I am most a slave.

We have now dealt, as best we can in a restricted space, with the three commonest objections to determinism. They all seem to admit of answers. To the objection that we always feel free, we answer that it is natural to feel so, even if we are determined, since our faces are set toward results and not toward causes, and the causes of present action always elude us. To the objection that science has gone indeterminist, we answer that that is only one interpretation of recent discoveries, and not the most plausible one, and that, even if it were true, it would not carry with it indeterminism for human choice. To the objection that determinism would reduce us to the level of mechanical puppets, we answer that though we are puppets in part we live, as Aristotle said, on various levels. And so far as causality in reflection, art, and moral choice involves control by immanent ideal, mechanism has passed over into that rational determinism that is the best kind of freedom.

FATE*

Richard Taylor

We are all, at certain moments of pain, threat, or bereavement, apt to entertain the idea of fatalism, the thought that what is happening at a particular moment is unavoidable, that we are powerless to prevent it. Sometimes we find ourselves in circumstances not of our own making, in which our very being and destinies are so thoroughly anchored that the thought of fatalism can be quite overwhelming, and sometimes consoling. One feels that whatever then happens, however good or ill, will be what those circumstances yield, and we are helpless. Soldiers, it is said, are sometimes possessed by such thoughts. Perhaps everyone would feel more inclined to them if they paused once in a while to think of how little they ever had to do with bringing themselves to wherever they have arrived in life, how much of their fortunes and destinies were decided for them by sheer circumstance, and how the entire course of their lives is often set, once and for all, by the most trivial incidents, which they did not produce and could not even have foreseen. If we are free to work out our destinies at all, which is doubtful, we have a freedom that is at best exercised within exceedingly narrow paths. All the important things—when we are born, or what parents, into what culture, whether we are loved or rejected, whether we are male or female, our temperament, our intelligence or stupidity, indeed, everything that makes for the bulk of our happiness and misery—all these are decided for us by the most casual and indifferent circumstances, by sheer coincidences, chance encounters, and seemingly insignificant fortuities. One can see this in retrospect if he searches, but few search. The fate that has given us our very being has given us also our pride and conceit, and has thereby formed us so that, being human, we congratulate ourselves

*METAPHYSICS, 4/E by Taylor, R., © 1992. Reprinted by permission of Pearson Education, Inc., Upper Saddle River, NJ.

on our blessings, which we call our achievements; blame the world for our blunders, which we call our misfortunes; and scarcely give a thought to that impersonal fate that arbitrarily dispenses both.

FATALISM AND DETERMINISM

Determinism . . . is the theory that all events are rendered unavoidable by their caus-es. The attempt is sometimes made to distinguish this from fatalism by saying that, according to the fatalist, certain events are going to happen no matter what, or in other words, regardless of causes. But this is enormously contrived. It would be hard to find in the whole history of thought a single fatalist, on that conception of it.

Fatalism is the belief that whatever happens is unavoidable. That is the clearest expression of the doctrine, and it provides the basis of the attitude of calm accept-ance that the fatalist is thought, quite correctly, to embody. One who endorses the claim of universal causation, then, and the theory of the causal determination of all human behavior, is a kind of fatalist—or at least he should be, if he is consistent. For that theory . . . once it is clearly spelled out and not hedged about with unresolved "ifs," does entail that whatever happens is rendered inevitable by the causal condi-tions preceding it, and is therefore unavoidable. One can indeed think of verbal for-mulas for distinguishing the two theories, but if we think of a fatalist as one who has a certain attitude, we find it to be the attitude that a thoroughgoing determinist should, in consistency, assume. That some philosophical determinists are not fatal-ists does not so much illustrate a great difference between fatalism and determinism but rather the humiliation to one's pride that a fatalist position can deliver, and the comfort that can sometimes be found in evasion.

FATALISM WITH RESPECT TO THE FUTURE AND THE PAST

A fatalist, then, is someone who believes that whatever happens is and always was unavoidable. He thinks it is not up to him what will happen a thousand years hence, next year, tomorrow, or the very next moment. Of course he does not pretend always to know what is going to happen. Hence, he might try sometimes to read signs and portents, as meteorologists and astrologers do, or to contemplate the effects upon him of the various things that might, for all he knows, be fated to occur. But he does not suppose that whatever happens could ever have really been avoidable.

A fatalist thus thinks of the future in the way we all think of the past, for every-one is a fatalist as he looks back on things. To a large extent we know what has hap-pened—some of it we can even remember—whereas the future is still obscure to us, and we are therefore tempted to imbue it, in our imagination, with all sorts of "possibilities." The fatalist resists this temptation, knowing that mere ignorance can hardly give rise to any genuine possibility in things. He thinks of both past and fu-ture "under the aspect of eternity," the way God is supposed to view them. We all think of the past this way, as something settled and fixed, to be taken for what it is. We are never in the least tempted to try to modify it. It is not in the least up to us what happened last year, yesterday, or even a moment ago, any more than are the motions of the heavens or the political developments in Tibet. If we are not fatalists, then we might think that past things once were up to us, to bring about or prevent, as long as they were still future—but this expresses our attitude toward the future, not the past.

Such is surely our conception of the whole past, whether near or remote. But the consistent fatalist thinks of the future in the same way. We say of past things that they are no longer within our power. The fatalist says they never were.

THE SOURCES OF FATALISM

A fatalistic way of thinking most often arises from theological ideas, or from what are generally thought to be certain presuppositions of science and logic. Thus, if God is really all-knowing and all-powerful, it is not hard to suppose that He has arranged for everything to happen just as it is going to happen, that He already knows every detail of the whole future course of the world, and there is nothing left for you and me to do except watch things unfold, in the here or the hereafter. But without bringing God into the picture, it is not hard to suppose . . . that everything that happens is wholly determined by what went before it, and hence that whatever happens at any future time is the only thing that can then happen, given what precedes it. Or even disregarding that, it seems natural to suppose that there is a body of truth concerning what the future holds, just as there is such truth concerning what is contained in the past, whether or not it is known to any person or even to God, and hence, that everything asserted in that body of truth will assuredly happen, in the fullness of time, precisely as it is described therein.

No one needs to be convinced that fatalism is the only proper way to view the past. That it is also the proper way to view the future is less obvious, due in part, perhaps, to our vastly greater ignorance of what the future holds. The consequences of holding such fatalistic views are obviously momentous. To say nothing of the consolation of fatalism, which enables a person to view all things as they arise with the same undisturbed mind with which he contemplates even the most revolting of history's horrors, the fatalist teaching also relieves one of all tendency toward both blame and approbation of others and of both guilt and conceit in himself. It promises that a perfect understanding is possible and removes the temptation to view things in terms of human wickedness and moral responsibility. This thought alone, once firmly grasped, yields a sublime acceptance of all that life and nature offer, whether to oneself or one's fellows; and although it thereby reduces one's pride, it simultaneously enhances the feelings, opens the heart, and expands the understanding.

DIVINE OMNISCIENCE

Suppose for the moment, just for the purpose of this discussion, that God exists and is omniscient. To say that God is omniscient means that He knows everything that is true. He cannot, of course, know that which is false. Concerning any falsehood, an omniscient being can know that it is false; but then it is a truth that is known, namely, the truth that the thing in question is a falsehood. So if it is false that the moon is a cube, then God can, like you or me, know that this is false; but He cannot know the falsehood itself, that the moon is a cube.

Thus, if God is omniscient He knows, as you probably do, the date of your birth. He also knows, as you may not, the hour of your birth. Furthermore, God knows, as you assuredly do not, the date of your conception—for there is such a truth, and we are supposing that God knows every truth. Moreover, He knows, as you surely do not, the date of your death, and the circumstances thereof—whether at that moment, known already to Him, you die as the result of an accident, a fatal malady, suicide, murder, whatever. And, still assuming God exists and knows everything, He knows whether any ant walked across my desk last night, and if so, what ant it was, where it came from, how long it was on the desk, how it came to be there, and so on, to every truth about this insect that there is. Similarly, of course, He knows when some ant will again appear on my desk, if ever. He knows the number of hairs on my head, notes the fall of every sparrow, knows why it fell, and why it was going to fall. These are simply a few of the consequences of the omniscience that we are for the moment assuming. A more precise way of expressing all this is to say that God knows, concerning any statement whatever that anyone could formulate, that it is true, in case it is, and otherwise, that it is false. And let us suppose that God, at some time or other, or perhaps from time to time, vouchsafes some of his knowledge to people, or perhaps to certain chosen persons. Thus prophets arise, proclaiming the coming of certain events, and things do then happen as they have foretold. Of course it is not surprising that they should, on the supposition we are making; namely, that the foreknowledge of these things comes from God, who is omniscient.

THE STORY OF OSMO

Now, then, let us make one further supposition, which will get us squarely into the philosophical issue these ideas are intended to introduce. Let us suppose that God has revealed a particular set of facts to a chosen scribe who, believing (correctly) that they came from God, wrote them all down. The facts in question then turned out to be all the more or less significant episodes in the life of some perfectly ordinary man named Osmo. Osmo was entirely unknown to the scribe, and in fact to just about everyone, but there was no doubt concerning whom all these facts were about, for the very first thing received by the scribe from God, was: "He of whom I speak is called Osmo." When the revelations reached a fairly voluminous bulk and appeared to be completed, the scribe arranged them in chronological order and assembled them into a book. He at first gave it the title The Life of Osmo, as Given by God, but thinking that people would take this to be some sort of joke, he dropped the reference to God.

The book was published but attracted no attention whatsoever, because it appeared to be nothing more than a record of the dull life of a very plain man named Osmo. The scribe wondered, in fact, why God had chosen to convey such a mass of seemingly pointless trivia.

The book eventually found its way into various libraries, where it gathered dust until one day a high school teacher in Indiana, who rejoiced under the name of Osmo, saw a copy on the shelf. The title caught his eye. Curiously picking it up and blowing the dust off, he was thunderstruck by the opening sentence: "Osmo is born in Mercy

Hospital in Auburn, Indiana, on June 6, 1965, of Finnish parentage, and after nearly losing his life from an attack of pneumonia at the age of five, he is enrolled in the St. James school there." Osmo turned pale. The book nearly fell from his hands. He thumbed back in excitement to discover who had written it. Nothing was given of its authorship nor, for that matter, of its publisher. His questions of the librarian produced no further information, he being as ignorant as Osmo of how the book came to be there.

So Osmo, with the book pressed tightly under his arm, dashed across the street for some coffee, thinking to compose himself and then examine this book with care. Meanwhile he glanced at a few more of its opening remarks, at the things said there about his difficulties with his younger sister, how he was slow in learning to read, of the summer on Mackinac Island, and so on. His emotions now somewhat quieted, Osmo began a close reading. He notice that everything was expressed in the present tense, the way newspaper headlines are written. For example, the text read, "Osmo is born in Mercy Hospital," instead of saying he was born there, and it recorded that he quarrels with his sister, is a slow student, is fitted with dental braces at age eight, and so on, all in the journalistic present tense. But the text itself made quite clear approximately when all these various things happened, for everything was in chronological order, and in any case each year of its subject's life constituted a separate chapter and was so titled—"Osmo's Seventh Year," "Osmo's Eighth Year," and so on through the book.

Osmo became absolutely engrossed, to the extent that he forgot his original astonishment, bordering on panic, and for a while even lost his curiosity concerning authorship. He sat drinking coffee and reliving his childhood, much of which he had all but forgotten until the memories were revived by the book now before him. He had almost forgotten about the kitten, for example, and had entirely forgotten its name, until he read, in the chapter called "Osmo's Seventh Year," this observation: "Sobbing, Osmo takes Fluffy, now quite dead, to the garden, and buries her next to the rose bush." Ah yes! And then there was Louise, who sat next to him in the eighth grade—it was all right there. And how he got caught smoking one day. And how he felt when his father died. On and on. Osmo became so absorbed that he quite forgot the business of the day, until it occurred to him to turn to Chapter 26, to see what might be said there, he having just recently turned twenty-six. He had no sooner done so than his panic returned, for lo! what the book said was true! That it rains on his birthday for example, that his wife fails to give him the binoculars he had hinted he would like, that he receives a raise in salary shortly thereafter, and so on. Now how in God's name, Osmo pondered, could anyone know that apparently before it had happened? For these were quite recent events, and the book had dust on it. Quickly moving on, Osmo came to this: "Sitting and reading in the coffee shop across from the library, Osmo, perspiring copiously, entirely forgets, until it is too late, that he was supposed to collect his wife at the hairdresser's at four." Oh my god! He had forgotten all about that. Yanking out his watch, Osmo discovered that it was nearly five o'clock—too late. She would be on her way home by now, and in a very sour mood.

Osmo's anguish at this discovery was nothing, though, compared with what the rest of the day held for him. He poured more coffee, and it now occurred to him to check the number of chapters in this amazing book: only twenty-nine! But surely, he thought, that doesn't mean anything. How anyone could have gotten all this stuff down so far was puzzling enough, to be sure, but no one on God's earth could possibly know in advance how long this or that person is going to live. (Only God could know that sort of thing, Osmo reflected.) So he read along; though not without considerable uneasiness and even depression, for the remaining three chapters were on the whole discouraging. He thought he had gotten that ulcer under control, for example. And he didn't see any reason to suppose his job was going to turn out that badly, or that he was really going to break a leg skiing; after all, he could just give up skiing. But then the book ended on a terribly dismal note. It said: "And Osmo, having taken Northwest flight 569 from O'Hare, perishes when the aircraft crashes on the runway at Fort Wayne, with considerable loss of life, a tragedy rendered the more calamitous by the fact that Osmo had neglected to renew his life insurance before the expiration of the grace period." And that was all. That was the end of the book.

So that's why it had only twenty-nine chapters. Some idiot thought he was going to get killed in a plane crash. But, Osmo thought, he just wouldn't get on that plane. And this would also remind him to keep his insurance in force.

(About three years later our hero, having boarded a flight for St. Paul, went berserk when the pilot announced they were going to land at Fort Wayne instead. According to one of the flight attendants, he tried to hijack the aircraft and divert it to another airfield. The Civil Aeronautics Board cited the resulting disruptions as contributing to the crash that followed as the plane tried to land.)

FOUR QUESTIONS

Osmo's extraordinary circumstances led him to embrace the doctrine of fatalism. Not quite completely, perhaps, for there he was, right up to the end, trying vainly to buck his fate—trying, in effect, to make a fool of God, though he did not know this, because he had no idea of the book's source. Still, he had the overwhelming evidence of his whole past life to make him think that everything was going to work out exactly as described in the book. It always had. It was, in fact, precisely this conviction that terrified him so.

But now let us ask these questions, in order to make Osmo's experiences more relevant to our own. First, why did he become, or nearly become, a fatalist? Second, just what did his fatalism amount to? Third, was his belief justified in terms of the evidence he had? And finally, is that belief justified in terms of the evidence we have—or in other words, should we be fatalists too?

This last, of course, is the important metaphysical question, but we have to approach it through the others.

Why did Osmo become a fatalist? Osmo became a fatalist because there existed a set of true statements about the details of his life, both past and future, and he came to know what some of these statements were and to believe them, including many concerning his future. That is the whole of it.

No theological ideas entered into his conviction, nor any presuppositions about causal determinism, the coercion of his actions by causes, or anything of this sort. The foundations of Osmo's fatalism were entirely in logic and epistemology, having to do only with truth and knowledge. Ideas about God did not enter in, for he never suspected that God was the ultimate source of those statements. And at no point did he think God was making him do what he did. All he was concerned about was that someone seemed somehow to know what he had done and was going to do.

What, then, did Osmo believe? He did not, it should be noted, believe that certain things were going to happen to him no matter what. That does not express a logically coherent belief. He did not think he was in danger of perishing in an airplane crash even in case he did not get into any airplane, for example, or that he was going to break his leg skiing, whether he went skiing or not. No one believes what he considers to be plainly impossible. If anyone believes that a given event is going to happen, he does not doubt that those things necessary for its occurrence are going to happen too. The expression "no matter what," by means of which some philosophers have sought an easy and even childish refutation of fatalism, is accordingly highly inappropriate in any description of the fatalist conviction.

Osmo's fatalism was simply the realization that the things described in the book were unavoidable.

Of course we are all fatalists in this sense about some things, and the metaphysical question is whether this familiar attitude should not be extended to everything. We know the sun will rise tomorrow, for example, and there is nothing we can do about it. Each of us knows he is sooner or later going to die, too, and there is nothing to be done about that either. We normally do not know just when, of course, but it is mercifully so! For otherwise we would sit simply checking off the days as they passed, with growing despair, like a man condemned to the gallows and knowing the hour set for his execution. The tides ebb and flow, and heavens revolve, the seasons follow in order, generations arise and pass, and no one speaks of taking preventive measures. With respect to those things each of us recognizes as beyond his control, we are of necessity fatalists.

The question of fatalism is simply: Of all the things that happen in the world, which, if any, are avoidable? And the philosophical fatalist replies: None of them. They never were. Some of them only seemed so.

Was Osmo's fatalism justified? Of course it was. When he could sit right there and read a true description of those parts of his life that had not yet been lived, it would be idle to suggest to him that his future might, nonetheless, contain alternative possibilities. The only doubts Osmo had were whether those statements could really be true. But here he had the proof of his own experience, as one by one they were tested. Whenever he tried to prevent what was set forth, he of course failed. Such failure, over and over, of even the most herculean efforts, with never a single success, must surely suggest, sooner or later, that he was destined to fail. Even to the end, when Osmo tried so desperately to save himself from the destruction described in the book, his effort was totally in vain—as he should have realized it was going to be had he really known that what was said there was true. No power in heaven or earth can render false a statement that is true. It has never been done, and never will be.

Is the doctrine of fatalism, then, true? This amounts to asking whether our circumstances are significantly different from Osmo's. Of course we cannot read our own biographies the way he could. Only people who become famous ever have their lives recorded, and even so, it is always in retrospect. This is unfortunate. It is too bad that someone with sufficient knowledge—God, for example—cannot set down the lives of great men in advance, so that their achievements can be appreciated better by their contemporaries, and indeed, by their predecessors—their parents, for instance. But mortals do not have the requisite knowledge, and if there are any gods who do, they seem to keep it to themselves.

None of this matters, as far as our own fatalism is concerned. For the important thing to note is that, of the two considerations that explain Osmo's fatalism, only one of them was philosophically relevant, and that one applies to us no less than to him. The two considerations were: (1) there existed a set of true statements about his life, both past and future, and (2) he came to know what those statements were and to believe them. Now the second of these two considerations explains why, as a matter of psychological fact, Osmo became fatalistic, but it has nothing to do with the validity of that point of view. Its validity is assured by (1) alone. It was not the fact that the statements happened to be written down that rendered the things they described unavoidable; that had nothing to do with it at all. Nor was it the fact that, because they had been written, Osmo could read them. His reading them and coming to believe them likewise had nothing to do with the inevitability of what they described. This was ensured simply by there being such a set of statements, whether written or not, whether read by anyone or not, and whether or not known to be true. All that is required is that they should be true.

Each of us has but one possible past, described by that totality of statements about us in the past tense, each of which happens to be true. No one ever thinks of rearranging things there; it is simply accepted as given. But so also, each of us has but one possible future, described by that totality of statements about oneself in the future tense, each of which happens to be true. The sum of these constitutes one's biography. Part of it has been lived. The main outlines of it can still be seen, in retrospect, though most of its details are obscure. The other part has not been lived, though it most assuredly is going to be, in exact accordance with that set of statements just referred to. Some of its outlines can already be seen, in prospect, but it is on the whole more obscure than the part belonging to the past. We have at best only premonitory glimpses of it. It is no doubt for this reason that not all of this part, the part that awaits us, is perceived as given, and people do sometimes speak absurdly of altering it—as though what the future holds, as identified by any true statement in the future tense, might after all not hold.

Osmo's biography was all expressed in the present tense because all that mattered was that the things referred to were real events; it did not matter to what part of time they belonged. His past consisted of those things that preceded his reading of the book, and he simply accepted it as given. He was not tempted to revise what he said there, for he was sure it was true. But it took the book to make him realize that his future was also something given. It was equally pointless for him to try to revise what was said there, for it, too, was true. As the past contains what has happened, the future contains what will happen, and neither contains, in addition to these things, various other things that did not and will not happen.

Of course we know relatively little of what the future contains. Some things we know. We know the sun will go on rising and setting, for example, that taxes will be levied and wars will rage, that people will continue to be callous and greedy, and that people will be murdered and robbed. It is only the details that remain to be discovered. But the same is true of the past; it is only a matter of degree. When I meet a total stranger, I do not know, and will probably never know, what his past has been, beyond certain obvious things—that he had a mother, and things of this sort. I know nothing of the particulars of the vast realm of fact that is unique to his past. And the same for his future, with only this difference—that all people are strangers to me as far as their futures are concerned, and here I am even a stranger to myself.

Yet there is one thing I know concerning any stranger's past and the past of everything under the sun; namely, that whatever it might hold, there is nothing anyone can do about it now. What has happened cannot be undone. The mere fact that it has happened guarantees this.

And so it is, by the same token, of the future of everything under the sun. Whatever the future might hold, there is nothing anyone can do about it now. What will happen cannot be altered. The mere fact that it is going to happen guarantees this.

THE LAW OF EXCLUDED MIDDLE

The presupposition of fatalism is therefore nothing but the commonest presupposition of all logic and inquiry; namely, that there is such a thing as truth, and that this has nothing at all to do with the passage of time. Nothing becomes true or ceases to be true; whatever is truth at all simply is true.

It comes to the same thing, and is perhaps more precise, to say that every meaningful statement, whether about oneself or anything else, is either true or else it is false; that is, its denial is true. There is no middle ground. The principle is thus appropriately called the law of excluded middle. It has nothing to do with what tense a statement happens to express, nor with the question whether anyone, man or god, happens to know whether it is true or false.

Thus no one knows whether there was an ant on my desk last night, and no one ever will. But we do know that either this statement is true or else its denial is true— there is no third alternative. If we say it might be true, we mean only that we do not happen to know. Similarly, no one knows whether or not there is going to be an ant there tonight, but we do know that either it will or else it will not be there.

In a similar way we can distinguish two mutually exclusive but exhaustive classes of statements about any person; namely, the class of all those that are true, and the class of all that are false. There are no others in addition to these. Included in each are statements never asserted or even considered by anyone but such that, if anyone were to formulate one of them, it would either be a true statement or else a false one.

Consider, then, that class of statements about some particular person—you, let us suppose—each of which happens to be true. Their totality constitutes your biography. One combination of such statements describes the time, place, and circumstances of your birth. Another combination describes the time, place, and circumstances of your death. Others describe in detail the rises and falls of your fortunes, your achievements and failures, your joys and sorrows—absolutely everything that is true of you.

Some of these things you have already experienced, others await you. But the entire biography is there. It is not written, and probably never will be; but it is nevertheless there, all of it. If, like Osmo, you had some way of discovering those statements in advance, then like him you could hardly help becoming a fatalist. But foreknowledge of the truth would not create any truth, nor invest your philosophy with truth, nor add anything to the philosophical foundations of fatalism that would then be so apparent to you. It would only serve to make it apparent.

OBJECTIONS

This thought, and the sense of its force, have tormented and frightened people from the beginning, and thinkers whose pride sometimes exceeds their acumen and their reverence for truth have attempted every means imaginable to demolish it. There are few articles of faith upon which virtually everyone can agree, but one of them is certainly the belief in their cherished free will. Any argument in opposition to the doctrine of fate, however feeble, is immediately and uncritically embraced, as though the refutation of fatalism required only the denial of it, supported by reasons that would hardly do credit to a child. It will be worthwhile, therefore, to look briefly at some of the arguments most commonly heard.

1. One can neither foresee the future nor prove that there is any god, or even if there is, that he could know in advance the free actions of men.

   The reply to this is that it is irrelevant. The thesis of fatalism rests on no theory of divination and on no theology. These ideas were introduced only illustratively.

2. True statements are not the causes of anything. Statements only entail; they do not cause, and hence threaten no man's freedom.

   But this, too, is irrelevant, for the claim here denied is not one that has been made.

3. The whole argument just conflates fact and necessity into one and the same thing, treating as unavoidable that which is merely true. The fact that a given thing is going to happen implies only that it is going to happen, not that is has to. Someone might still be able to prevent it—though of course no one will. For example, President Kennedy was murdered. This means it was true that he was going to be murdered. But it does not mean his death at that time and place was unavoidable. Someone could have rendered that statement false; though of course no one did.

   That is probably the commonest "refutation" of fatalism ever offered. But how strong is the claim that something can be done, when in fact it never has been done in the whole history of the universe, in spite, sometimes, of the most strenuous efforts? No one has ever rendered false a statement that was true, however hard some have tried. When an attempt, perhaps a heroic attempt, is made to avoid a given calamity, and the thing in question happens anyway, at just the moment and in just the way it was going to happen, we have reason to doubt that it could have been avoided. And in fact great effort was made to save President Kennedy, for example, from the destruction toward which he was heading on that fatal day, a whole legion of bodyguards having no other mission. And it failed. True, we can say if more strenuous precautions had been taken, the event would not have happened. But to this we must add true, they were not taken, and hence true, they were not going to be taken—and we have on our hands again a true statement of the kind that no one has ever had the slightest degree of success in rendering false.

4. The fatalist argument just rests on a "confusion of modalities." The fact that something is true entails only that its denial is false, not that its denial is impossible. All that is impossible is that both should be true, or both false. Thus, if the president is going to be murdered, it is certainly false that he is not—but not impossible. What is impossible is that he will be both murdered and spared.

Here again we have only a distracting irrelevancy, similar to the point just made. The fatalist argument has nothing to do with impossibility in those senses familiar to logic. It has to do with unavoidability. It is, in other words, concerned with human abilities. The fact that a statement is true does not, to be sure, entail that it is necessary, nor do all false statements express impossibilities. Nonetheless, no one is able to avoid what is truly described, however contingently, in any statement, nor to bring about what is thus falsely described. Nor can anyone convert the one to the other, making suddenly true that which was false, or vice versa. It has never been done, and it never will be. It would be a conceit indeed for someone now to suggest that he, alone among men, might be able to accomplish this feat. This inability goes far beyond the obvious impossibility of making something both true and false at once. No metaphysics turns on that simple point.

5. Perhaps it would be best, then, to discard the presupposition underlying the whole fatalist philosophy; namely, the idea that statements are true in advance of the things they describe. The future is the realm of possibilities, concerning any of which we should neither say it is true that it will happen, nor that it is false.

But, in reply, this desperate move is nothing but arbitrary fiction, resorted to for no other reason than to be rid of the detested doctrine of fatalism. What is at issue here is the very law of excluded middle, which, it is suggested, we shall be allowed to affirm only up to that point at which it threatens something dear. We shall permit it to hold for one part of time, but suddenly retract it in speaking of another, even though the future is continuously being converted to the past through sheer temporal passage.

Most surely, if the statement, made now, that President Kennedy has been murdered, is a true one, then the prediction, made before the event, that he was going to be murdered, was true too. The two statements have exactly the same content, and are in fact one and the same statement, except for the variation of tense. The fact that this statement is more easily known in retrospect than in prospect casts no doubt on its truth but only illustrates a familiar fact of epistemology. A prediction to be sure, must await fulfillment, but it does not thereupon for the first time acquire its truth. Indeed, had it not been true from the start, it could not have been fulfilled, nor its author congratulated for having it right. Fulfillment is nothing but the occurrence of what is correctly predicted.

The law of excluded middle is not like a blank check into which we can write whatever values we please, according to our preferences. We can no more make ourselves metaphysically free and masters of our destinies by adding qualifications to this law than a poor person can make himself rich just by adding figures to his bankbook. That law pronounces every meaningful statement true, or, if not true, then false. It leaves no handy peg between these two on which one may hang his beloved freedom of will for safekeeping, nor does it say anything whatever about time.

Every single philosophical argument against the teaching of fatalism rests upon the assumption that we are free to pursue and realize various alternative future possibilities—the very thing, of course, that is at issue. When some of these possibilities have become realized and moved on into the past, the supposed alternative possibilities usually appear to have been less real than they had seemed; but this somehow does not destroy the fond notion that they were there. Metaphysics and logic are weak indeed in the face of an opinion nourished by invincible pride, and most people would sooner lose their very souls than be divested of that dignity that they imagine rests upon their freedom of will.

INVINCIBLE FATE

We shall say, therefore, of whatever happens that it was going to be that way. And this is a comfort, both in fortune and in adversity. We shall say of him who turns out bad and mean that he was going to; of him who turns out happy and blessed that he was going to; neither praising nor berating fortune, crying over what has been, lamenting what was going to be, or passing moral judgments.

Shall we, then, sit idly by, passively observing the changing scene without participation, never testing our strength and our goodness, having no hand in what happens, or in making things come out as they should? This is a question for which each will find his own answer. Some people do little or nothing with their lives and might as well never have lived, they make such a waste of it. Others do much, and the lives of a few even shine like the stars. But we knew this before we ever began talking about fate. In time we will all know of which sort we were destined to be.

DARWINISM AND DETERMINISM*

Michael Ruse

Charles Darwin's great work *On the Origin of Species* was published in 1859. Only now, however, are we starting to appreciate and explore the full implications of Darwin's message: that all organisms including ourselves are the product of a long, slow natural process of evolution brought on primarily by the mechanism of natural selection. It is true, indeed, that Darwin himself appreciated the significance of his work.

*Michael Ruse, "Darwinism and Determinism," *Zygon* 22 (1987): 419–442. Reprinted with the kind permission of the author and the journal.

Particularly in his later publication *Descent of Man* (1871) Darwin showed how he thought his theory impinges upon the most distinctive facets of our natures—including our claim to be moral beings. Yet for many reasons—the incompleteness of the theory, outside hostility, and especially in this century the growth of the social sciences—few felt ready or able to respond to the full challenge and opportunity shown by the *Origin*.

Hence, even as the twentieth century draws to an end, most people are quite indifferent to their evolutionary origins. Although in the intellectual community there are few if any who take literally the story of Genesis, the general presumption is that humans are distinct and unique, as if we were in fact the favored creation of a good god some 6,000 years ago rather than modified monkeys. Homo sapiens is thought to be beyond biology in all important respects.

Fortunately, this prenineteenth-century attitude is crumbling beneath its own inadequacy. A growing number of scholars from both the sciences and the humanities are starting to realize that a biological approach to Homo sapiens need not be threatening and negative. It can be positively liberating. I am among that number, and in various publications written both separately and jointly with Edward O. Wilson I have tried to state the case for evolution by example. In particular, in light of the most recent developments of evolutionary theory (especially the application of the theory to social behavior, so-called sociobiology), we have tried to confirm and extend Darwin's own thesis about the key to human moral behavior lying ultimately in the mechanism of natural selection. We pride ourselves that this case can now be made with some conviction. (See Ruse 1984; 1986a; 1986b; Ruse & Wilson 1985; 1986. See also Wilson 1975; 1978. We think—and certainly hope—that the reader will see some evolution in the claims made in these various writings.)

However, these are still early days. On the one hand, one expects and receives vigorous criticism from those who still hold dearly to human uniqueness. On the other hand, however successful the central case may be, there remain many implications to be explored and elaborated. In this discussion I intend to bring together these two points, looking at a subject that must sooner or later be discussed by anyone who presumes to write on morality. I refer to the problem of free will and determinism. This is a matter which is of central concern to anyone who thinks about *right* and *wrong* and questions of moral responsibility.

Perhaps not surprisingly, those who criticize sociobiology generally and its application to morality in particular have been loud in their accusations of illicit "deterministic" thinking (e.g., Lewontin et al. 1984; Kitcher 1985). My aim, however, is positive rather than negative; so rather than attempting a line-by-line response I shall reply implicitly. I believe that a biological approach to morality throws very significant light on our precritical intuitive thinking about freedom and determinism, greatly carrying forward our understanding in this area. At the same time I can link my insights with important conclusions established by thinkers from earlier times.

HUMAN EVOLUTION

Let me begin with the essential scientific background. Many more organisms are born than can possibly survive and, more importantly, reproduce. This sets up a "struggle" for resources. The winners in the struggle (by definition the *fitter*) tend to have features not possessed by the losers. Given enough time and enough generations, this ongoing differential reproduction—christened by Darwin, in analogy with the work of the breeders, "natural selection"—leads to full-blown change or evolution. What must be noted is that the thus-produced organisms do not simply exist in any old fashion. They function in ways directed to the end of successful survival and reproduction. They are organized showing frequently intricate "adaptations" (Ayala & Valentine 1979; Ruse 1982).

Obviously, selection demands a constant supply of new organic variations—raw material—or the evolutionary process would soon grind to a halt. Also it is assumed that there is some kind of stability in the reproduction mechanism; otherwise, a variation conferring fitness (i.e., making its possessor better suited for the struggle) might simply vanish from sight. Fortunately, these and other requirements are known to be true. As a complement within the evolutionary picture to Darwinian selection, they are explained fully in the theory of heredity (genetics) developed in the past century. One of the triumphs of the life sciences in the past three decades has been the introduction of molecular theories and techniques into our understanding of the ways in which variations are produced and transmitted. It is now known that the unit of heredity, the gene, is a complex macromolecule, DNA. Of importance to evolutionism is the fact that genetically based variations appear randomly—not in the sense of being uncaused (in as much is known of these causes), but in the sense of not appearing to be dictated by needs. There is no direction or teleology of this kind in the story of evolution (Ayala 1985).

Everything we know of our own biological past fits in the above sketch. Indeed, although there are still many gaps, we now know enough that we have passed beyond simply making Homo sapiens consistent with the tale of evolution through selection. We have become aware of strong support for the overall story (Isaac 1983; Jerison 1982). The ancestors of the great apes appeared approximately ten million years ago with the future gorilla line diverging a short time later. Our line split from that of the chimpanzees a mere six million years ago (Pilbeam 1984). This fact can be inferred from the incredible genetic, similarities between us and our hairy cousins. To place matters in perspective we should note that evolution started over three and one-half billion years ago; thus we have been at one with the chimpanzees for very much more than 99 percent of life's history. If we had not done the classification ourselves, we would be in the same genus as the great apes (Ayala & Valentine 1979).

Two major events occurred since our own line, the hominids, broke away to evolve separately. First, we rose up on our back legs and walked. Second, from about four million years ago, our brains grew three to four times in size, from that of chimpanzees (they were not chimpanzee brains!) to the present capacity of about 1400cc. With the growth of brain size came a corresponding growth of intellectual ability which can be inferred from the use and type of tools. Why there was a strong selective pressure for such a thinking capacity is still in part an open question. For the Darwinian this capacity could never have "just happened." It could not be an inevitable growth upwards; there had to be some good reason. Thanks to detailed work of paleoanthropologists and others firm answers are starting to develop. It seems fairly clear that cooperation was a significant factor in human prehistory as our ancestors roamed the plains of Africa hunting, gathering, and scavaging especially on the carcasses of large mammals. Large mammals represent a valuable source of protein; thus, the intelligence required to pinpoint and utilize them properly would be of great adaptive value in life's struggles. However, large brains have costs, for instance in increasing the hazards of childbirth and in requiring much parental attention to offspring, but apparently for our ancestors the costs were worth it (Lovejoy 1981).

Our fully developed linguistic ability is probably a recent phenomenon depending for its full capacity upon certain necessary changes in the structure of our throats and mouths (Lieberman 1984). The appearance of Homo sapiens is usually dated from around 500,000 years ago; but full speech as we know it may have come only with the demise of the Neanderthals, a human subspecies, and the rise of modern humans, Homo sapiens, some 30,000 years ago. Be this as it may, it is from about the latter date that we can trace the explosive growth of a fully developed culture—an explosive growth which leads to modern humans living in today's societies.

EPIGENETIC RULES

Have we evidence suggesting that biology remains important to us as the twentieth century draws to a close? Is there reason to think that we humans reflect our evolutionary past? Do we work through and because of various adaptations which proved their worth in the struggle for existence even though modern civilization may have softened or at least altered life's traditional demands? At one level we are obviously still biological beings. We eat, drink, sleep, defecate, copulate according to nature's needs. Moreover, in a world where so many go to bed hungry it is surely presumptuous to imply that the struggle has entirely lost its grip in this respect. Yet, what of those things which we tend to think of as specifically human? What of those things we think separate us from the animals? At the ultimate limit what of our thinking—about the world and about ourselves?

The truth seems to be that the human mind (which we take to be an entirely natural reflection of the material brain) is not a *tabula rasa*. It is not some kind of all-purpose computer which exists and is able to guide us through life—any life which we might happen to find ourselves living. On the contrary, the mind is constrained or governed by various innate dispositions which are idiosyncratically human. These have been put into place by natural selection because those proto-humans who thought in such ways were fitter than those proto-humans who did not (Lumsden & Wilson 1981; 1983; 1985).

The innate dispositions, known technically as epigenetic rules, are at two levels. The primary dispositions process the raw information absorbed from the external world. For example, we see colors according to certain (human) universally shared categories. Likewise, we discriminate tastes in various biologically fixed ways. The adaptive virtues of this latter disposition hardly need stressing. The human who instinctively recognizes and prefers sweet things to sour or rotten things is at a clear advantage to the human whose palate is indifferent to tastes.

At the secondary level the epigenetic rules generally serve as guides to action, and they help us to organize our thoughts and desires, and to make sense of the information from without. The rules probably play a key role when we think mathematically. There are no Platonic forms of number that exist in some supersensible world and await our rational intuition. Rather, innately, we think in terms of symbol and quantity because such a way of thought proves its adaptive worth. The secondary rules also are most important socially. For example, virtually all societies have brother-sister incest barriers of some sort (van den Berghe 1983). That there are such obstacles to close mating needs no defense from a Darwinian for there is massive evidence that severe inbreeding leads to horrendously deleterious biological effects. It is in our biological interests that we do not breed with those with whom we have the greatest opportunity—and natural selection has seen to it that we positively do not want to.

Not all of the epigenetic rules play as vital a role now as when they were first formed although mathematical ability—not to mention incest avoidance—still have their uses. The point is that humans in their perceiving, thinking, and acting still have their roots firmly in the soil of their evolutionary past. Natural selection formed us and left its mark.

EVOLUTIONARY ETHICS

Ethics, the study of morality, is about right and wrong, good and bad. It is about caring for people and why you should or ought to care for people. It is about harming other people and why this is unacceptable behavior. It is about saints and sinners.

There is a long history of attempts to put ethics on a sound evolutionary basis. At least there is a long history of failed attempts to put ethics on a sound evolutionary basis. Unfortunately, the reasons for these failures are obvious in the eyes of most biologists (i.e., those concerned with evolution) and of most philosophers (i.e., those concerned with ethics). On the one hand, evolution seems to preach a doctrine of selfishness, the very antithesis of proper moral behavior. Evolution says that unless you are prepared to go out and grind the other fellow into the ground, he will grind you into the ground. "Nice guys finish last," and for that reason evolution has seen to it that we are not nice. On the other hand, even if you could show that morality was a human adaptation, it would tell you nothing of the value of morality. We want to be good, perhaps. Yet why should we be good other than for the sake of expediency—which seems a very bad reason indeed.

Things *have* moved on. The science of evolution has developed and can now be seen in a new light (in important respects the rediscovered light of the *Descent of Man*). The moral philosophy likewise has been recast and now attempts something which is at once more modest and more ambitious (although again in important respects it must be seen in the rediscovered light of earlier writings). Morality can now be viewed as a natural outgrowth of the evolutionary process; once this is recognized the answers to important questions about its nature and status fall readily into place (Ruse 1986a).

The empirical case for the evolution of morality—a capacity within humans for genuine sentiments of right and wrong—begins with today's understanding of the exact nature of natural selection. Contrary to the belief of many post-Darwin evolutionists (although not Darwin himself), natural selection can never promote adaptations which are of benefit to the group at the expense of the individual. Any cooperation or working together must rebound ultimately to the benefit of the individuals involved rather than residing at some higher level of payoff, whether to the population, the species, or an even larger unit.

Coupled with this theoretical realization about the functioning of selection has come the empirical discovery of the wide extent that animals actually cooperate and work together in the wild (Wilson 1975; Maynard Smith 1978). To use the term that evolutionists have appropriated, "altruism" is a pervasive biological phenomenon. Note that the term *altruism* as used here is a metaphor. Thus used, it simply means cooperation, perhaps at cost to oneself, there are no implications of intention, of wanting to do good, or even of consciousness.[1]

Today's evolutionists have been able to build a number of highly plausible models which explain and predict "altruism" entirely from an individual selectionist perspective. One model, "kin selection," explains cooperation in terms of the biological benefits that accrue to an individual whenever close relatives reproduce (Hamilton 1964). Another model, "reciprocal altruism," emphasizes the need of each of us for help at various times and the consequently favorable cost-benefits of being prepared to offer help in return (Trivers 1971).

These and other models are a triumph of modern evolutionary studies as they have been confirmed repeatedly while shedding new light on all kinds of puzzling phenomena. Yet, what relevance is all of this to humans and to their being literally altruistic—persons subject to and recognizing right and wrong? The place to begin is with the fact that we humans are almost uniquely in need of "altruism." Although its origin undoubtedly lay in a cause-and-effect feedback process, the truth is that the modern human on one's own would be practically helpless. We have neither weapons of attack nor means of defense. We are not particularly mobile nor particularly agile. We are neither too large to threaten nor too small to be overlooked. Thus, we need each other to survive and reproduce, and others need us.

How have we satisfied this need for "altruism"? The social insects, for example the ants, are highly "altruistic." They are in effect programed to work together harmoniously. They are unthinking cooperators. Yet, this is not our way and it is not difficult to see why this is not our way. Blind "altruism" is an excellent policy as long as nothing goes wrong. However, let there be the slightest disruption, for example a change in environment, and an organism can slip straight into maladaptive behaviour and die. To the queen ant the loss of a few hundred offspring is an acceptable cost. To the human being who necessarily puts so much effort into the raising of even one child, the price of programed cooperation is simply too high.

Another way in which human "altruism" might have been achieved lies at the other extreme—an extreme often favored by writers of science fiction. We might have evolved into supercalculating machines able and willing always to work out our own biological interests before making any move. In such a case we would indeed be truly selfish, for every action would be weighed entirely from the perspective of self-gain. However, we have clearly not taken this option—at least not as a general strategy. Reasons are fairly obvious. Apart from the technical details of producing such a brain capable of making such powerful calculations, a being thus endowed would probably be far too slow for real life. Better a "quick and dirty" solution than one which is perfect but which takes week's to arrive.

To be "altruistic" humans had to move somewhere between the two extremes; here it is time to recall the importance of the (secondary) epigenetic rules, those innate dispositions which inform our thinking and guide our actions. Simply, our thesis is that among the epigenetic rules are those which incline us to cooperation with our fellow humans. It is the rules which make us "altruistic." Yet what form do the rules have? How do they make themselves known to us? My claim is that the rules make us help each other by making us think we *ought* to help each other! In other words, to achieve "altruism" (in the biological sense) our biology makes us altruistic (in the moral sense).

However, is this genuine altruism—true morality? Are we not rather scheming to achieve our own ends even though putting on a facade of niceness? My response is that although we humans are undoubtedly hypocrites (some of us most of the time and most of us some of the time), we are also genuinely moral. In order for us to break out of our naturally selfish mode natural selection has imbued us with thoughts of right and wrong, good and bad. Stating the matter cynically we work better when we do things because we think it is right to do such things than when we do things because we consciously see them to be in our evolutionary interests. Although I have dealt with these questions in detail elsewhere let it be emphasized that I am not trying to slide over David Hume's law—the irreducibility of "ought" and "is"—by pretending that there are no real differences between "ought" and "is" statements. It is crucial to my thinking that there are differences. That which gets us to break out of our selfish cocoon is the "oughtness" or morality (see Ruse 1986a; 1986b).

So much for the empirical case. Turning now to the sorts of questions which interest philosophers and related students of human behavior, what does the evolutionary account tell us of the nature of morality? Perhaps even more importantly, what does the account tell us of the status of morality? Even if we grant that we now know how the moral capacity came into being, why should anyone take morality seriously? Why should we think it to be true?

As far as the actual nature of morality is concerned the scenario I have just sketched focuses upon beings whose moral content would be remarkably similar to those being discussed in recent years by moral philosophers. Morality, as I see it, involves a balance of interests of which we may be (and probably are) quite blind. Humans cooperate because there is more benefit for them if they do than if they do not. This is the ultimate reason, not the proximate reason. Consider the ideas of today's leading moral theorist, John Rawls (1971). He argues that we ought to be just, and to be just we ought to be fair. How do we get fairness? What is its content? Rawls invites us to think ourselves into the "original position," "behind the veil of ignorance." We all want to get as much out of life and society for ourselves as we possibly can, but we are to suppose that we do not know what role or status in society we actually will have. If we knew we were to be female, beautiful, and intelligent, we would maximally reward beautiful, intelligent females. Yet, what if we be male, ugly, and stupid?

In order to avoid the bad consequences Rawls thinks society ought to be balanced, handing out goods and making demands according to our needs and abilities. It seems to me that this is very much in line with the thinking patterns of beings whose evolution I have just sketched. Speaking anthropomorphically (i.e., using the metaphor of design that all Darwinians use when they are thinking about adaptations), we are all in this life together. How can we get the most out of it given that others likewise have such aims, and how must we protect against being one of nature's unfortunates else we simply be exploited? The answer seems to be in being animals with Rawlsian sentiments, that is, in being animals which think that one ought to be just where this cashes out in terms of fairness. Where Wilson and I go beyond Rawls is in showing that evolution actually simulates the original position, whereas Rawls is left lamely saying that it is "hypothetical" thus leaving the origins of morality in limbo.

Somewhat more controversially I argue that our empirical claims have implications about the status of morality. Traditional evolutionary ethics attempts to justify morality simply on the grounds that it—or the human capacity for morality—evolved, is clearly wrong. Value finds no foundation of this kind within Darwinian theory. Perhaps humans have certain aggressive tendencies because of their biology. This is no justification of warfare. As Tomas Henry Huxley (1894), Darwin's great supporter, pointed out, at this level morality consists in opposing nature rather than in quietly acquiescing in its demands.

Against the traditionalist I argue that evolution *explains* (not justifies) morality in the sense of showing where it came from. Furthermore, once such an explanation is given, one sees that the traditional call for justification is mistaken. There can be no ultimate support for morality in the sense of reasoned absolute foundations. (My position is close to that of the late John Mackie 1977; 1978; 1980. One moral philosopher who has explicitly linked evolution and ethics in the way I suggest is Jeffrie Murphy 1982.)

I am not saying that morality does not exist; nor am I preaching subjectivity and relativism. Morality is part of the makeup of ourselves and of our fellow humans. If there were not a shared morality that is binding, then some of us would be suckers and soon selected out of existence. Yet I do say that the moral capacity is no more than an adaptation like hands and teeth and penises and vaginas. I recognize that the human tendency is to think that morality is more than a mere adaptation—that it is an insight into objective reality; but I recognize also that we are practically bound to think this, otherwise we would not be altruists, and hence not "altruists." However, as all Darwinians know, our surface emotions are very poor guides to what is truly the case.

I shall say no more about my views now, except to note that my position on morality—known technically as *moral skepticism*—has a distinguished philosophical heritage. In particular, although no evolutionist, the great eighteenth-century Scottish philosopher David Hume (1978) argued for a very similar perspective: "vice and virtue . . . may be compar'd to sounds, colours, heat and cold, which . . . are not qualities in objects, but perceptions in the mind" (Hume 1978, 469). Hence: "Morality, therefore, is more properly felt than judg'd of" (Hume 1978, 470). Keeping this historical point in mind we can now go on to explore some of the consequences of our claims about humans and their morality.[2]

THREE KINDS OF DETERMINISM

It was Aristotle who most clearly stated that morality presupposes and demands some sort of freedom—some sort of ability and opportunity to put one's will into play. The prisoner locked away in his cell can hardly be held responsible for the riot going on outside. Likewise the man thrown overboard to lighten the raft may merit our pity but if he went kicking and screaming he hardly merits our moral approbation as did

Captain Oats when he left the tent on Robert Scott's ill-fated return from the South Pole. (We who threw the unfortunate overboard, however, are another matter.)

As Aristotle also realized matters are somewhat (a great deal!) more complex than this. The person in chains is unambiguously excused from moral responsibility. However, what about the person in the grip of some strong emotion? Do we want to excuse him/her from moral responsibility, and if so why, and if not why not? We certainly seem to think that not everyone is responsible for his/her actions. The idiot, for instance. Yet, what about the drunkard or the schizophrenic?

To state the matter mildly you might think that my biological approach to human nature exacerbates the problems of human freedom. Critics certainly think so and have argued the point loudly and at length! If everything about us is a function of the forces of evolution—the units of heredity (the genes) as gathered by natural selection—and if we are programed to survive and reproduce, then what hope is there of freedom? We are machines determined by our biology to go through life doing what we do with no more moral standing than any other machine (taken in its own right), namely none (Kitcher 1985).

Furthermore, matters are not helped much by popular accounts of human sociobiology, which are frequently illustrated by pictures of people with clockwork keys in their backs or (a favorite) suspended like marionettes from genes overhead (often graphically put in the form of a DNA molecule). At the very least we are like the poor fools in an Italian tragic opera buffeted by the forces of fate beyond our sight and control. We can take no credit and deserve no blame for our acts, which is perhaps just as well for, as has just been seen, our central thesis is that morality is an illusion.

I will say no more about this final charge. The very essence of my case is that morality is not an illusion; it exists and is genuine. What is illusory is the objective referent that people think morality has; however, that is entirely another matter. Here I want to concentrate on the charge that my approach in important, vital respects circumscribes human freedom, thus making genuine moral choice impossible. Indeed, in the eyes of some critics, I am opening the way for the acquiescence in, if not positive endorsement of, all kinds of vile social attitudes and policies.

Understanding the opposite to freedom being in some general sense "determinism," my reply is that my position is not in some peculiar or offensive way deterministic. Further, I argue that charges are generally based on confusions or worse. When these confusions are sorted out, I have much of importance to say on the whole question of freedom and determinism. Emphatically, what is not the case is that my approach denies the possibility of genuine moral thought and behavior.

I want to distinguish three main senses of determinism. I shall discuss each one in turn. Once various ideas have been separated, matters will become much clearer.

Causal determinism.   First, there is the whole question of *causation*: its bearing on the free will question in general and on my biological perspective in particular. The general argument is straightforward and well known. The world around us seems not to be one of randomness and chaos with things happening in haphazard manner. Rather, events are ordered, subject to regularities which hold "anywhere and anywhen" (Smart 1963). These regularities expressed by scientists as laws of nature apparently represent necessary connections obtaining between the world's object or events, so-called causes and effects. Given the causes, then the effects must happen. Humans seem to fall within the causal nexus. Everything we do and think is a cause of future events and, more significantly, effect of past events. This being true, we are obviously determined in our thoughts and actions. Hence, we have no genuine freedom and morality is a facade.

At this particular level the charge is that my Darwinian approach simply drives yet one more nail into the coffin of causal determinism within which lies the corpse of free will. I argue that humans are products of their biology, and that this biology still shows its effects in what we think and do. We accept that which we call morality because natural selection makes us do so, and because we accept that which we call morality we are led to behave "altruistically." Bob Geldorf cares for the unfortunate of Africa because his ancestors had that which enabled them to out-reproduce other would-be humans. This is not genuine morality—just the endless waves of struggle and reproduction, success and failure.

In reply to the charge of endorsing causal determinism I plead guilty! In a sense the thesis that the world is bound by cause and effect is not a proposition of science. It is rather a metaphysical presupposition of the possibility of doing science. Unless you think the world is regular, you can hardly attempt to explain the world in terms of those regularities. Yet, the thesis is not unreasonable. As science succeeds, it justifies the presumption. There is a circle here, not of the vicious variety but of the feedback type. The more you learn of actual causes and effects, the more it is reasonable to assume apparent anomalies will someday likewise fall beneath cause and effect. (I will here ignore all points about quantum mechanics and statistical regularities. Essentially, they leave my argument untouched.)

Everything upon which I have drawn and towards which I argue supposes and supports the thesis that Homo sapiens lies absolutely and entirely within the causal network. I presume that it does and the presumption pays confirming dividends. The science on which I base my case says this: humans evolved according to the usual causal laws of biology. The science/philosophy which I extract says this: the deepest aspects of the human personality are natural in origin and working. We apprehend goodness causally. We are good casually. We fail to be good causally. If I am correct in what I argued in the earlier sections of this discussion, causal determinism triumphs again.

However, what I would argue is that none of this is in any sense a true threat to freedom and morality! On the contrary, the genuinely free will does not exclude causal determinism, it demands it! Consider for a moment an unambiguously good act: Mother Teresa tending a dying man, and doing so (as we suppose she does) simply because it is right. What is going on here? Why does she wipe his fevered brow? Because she thinks it will comfort him and because (thanks to her beliefs) she wants to do it. Yet why does she want to comfort him? Ultimately she does because of factors in her past such as the moral training of her parents and her church. Whether this training is uniquely enough is, of course, where disputes come in. The point is that her past does play a role and the more you understand Mother Teresa the more it looks like a determining role.

All of this is starting to look very much like a causal situation, and it looks a lot more like one when you consider the alternative. Mother Teresa wipes the dying man's face but this action is the effect of nothing. Physically it just happened like the roll of the dice coming up six. (This roll is not uncaused but it gives the idea of an uncaused event.) You might perhaps say that although she wiped the face because of her beliefs, this provided "reasons" rather than "causes" of her actions. Yet unless you allow that in some sense reasons (or beliefs) can act as causes, you are left with the mysterious behavior of Mother Teresa—at the physical level, at least. More than this, you are left with acts for which she deserves no moral credit. Suppose your hand moves, uncaused, and pushes the bank robber's gun out of the way. Why should you get credit? Credit is merit only when behavior follows from past decisions, acts, beliefs, and so forth.

The result of all this is that morality positively presupposes a causal nexus, within which we all lie. Hence, in endorsing a causally deterministic view of humanity I am certainly not *per se* eliminating the possibility of freedom and morality. (This is not yet saying that my particular view leaves room for morality.) I might add as I bring this subdiscussion to a close that I know I am hardly being original in arguing that freedom and morality presuppose a causal perspective. Technically, my position is known as soft-determinism or compatibilism. Its most persuasive exponent was Hume in his *Treatise of Human Nature*. Given that my general approach to morality is Humean in spirit, it comes as no surprise to me that we should still be following in his intellectual footsteps.

Biological determinism.   The second sense of determinism is more distinctively *biological* in nature and may be thought to pose a special threat to a position like mine. To lay out this charge we start with the claim that biology, specifically evolution through natural selection, led to human nature. Not only did it lead to the human universals such as linguistic ability; it also led to human differences, for example, those between black and white, male and female, bright and stupid. Furthermore, the implication if not the explicit claim is that these features are fixed absolutely. Blacks like rhythm and crime, whites do not. Males like fighting and sex, females do not. The brights like poetry, the stupid like pushpin. This is the way nature made us, and this is the way it has to be.

Clearly says the critic we have determinism here, and a most offensive kind it is, too. All sorts of prejudices—male, Anglo-Saxon, Protestant prejudices—are being dressed up as science and forced down the listener's throats. Moreover, quite apart from the unpleasant moral implications of such a view—blacks, women, and the less gifted are being labelled innately inferior—the very possibility of genuine morality itself is being thrown out of the window. Rape, for instance, is being condoned as part of male nature and thus excusable on account of its unavoidability. Conversely, blacks are regarded as less than full moral beings because of their biological propensity to violence. We lock them up not because they merit punishment but because they are wild animals that need to be caged.

In order to counter fears like these just expressed, we must untangle two separate threads running through the critique. On the one hand, there is the claim that biology determines human nature including differences between natures. On the other hand, since biological determination in itself hardly threatens morality, there has to be the claim that aspects of human nature are such as to make genuine free choice impossible (as if we are all clockwork toys). Alternatively, there has to be the claim that aspects of certain human natures, presumably biologically determined human natures, are such as to make genuine free choice impossible for these people (as if they alone are clockwork toys). Claims of this second kind I will leave for now because they fall within the domain of the third kind of determinism I will discuss. Here I will concentrate on the first claim—the heart of the charge of biological determinism—although take note that even if it be true, genuine morality may still be possible. Despite having a strong sexual drive, you can still be a moral being. This holds true whether the drive be a function of your genes or of an excess of *Playboys* in your youth.

What about the charge of biological determinism? Are humans what they are as a function of their genes? Do we have our physical, behavioral, and mental features willy nilly? The answer, as any biologist knows or should know, is yes—and no (Bateson 1983). On the one side, we are what we are because of our biology. We are bipedal, we have large brains, we are rational because of our particular genetic constitution as put in place by natural selection. You cannot make a silk purse out of a sow's ear. You cannot make a human being out of a sow's genes. There is no reason to think that the human mind innately (i.e., from a biological point of view) is a blank sheet waiting to be written on anew in each generation. We have a natural tendency or disposition to be moral just as we have a natural tendency to walk on two legs. In this sense our morality is determined for us.

Yet, on the other side, we are what we are because of our biology *in conjunction with the environment.* Asparagus is green; if you grow it in the dark, it is white. Dogs are friendly; if you beat and starve them, they are vicious. Scotsmen are as tall as Englishmen; if you feed them simply on oats they are runts. As well-known, long-term study has shown how in this century, thanks to improved nutrition, the height and physique of the Scott has improved dramatically (Dobzhansky 1962).

Applying this second point to human thoughts, behaviors, and intentions, we expect to find—indeed we do find—that humans can be altered by their environments including especially their cultures. I refer here to education, social customs, and much more—not forgetting basic nutrition (even in America, for instance, much mental retardation still results from protein starvation). I see no reason to deny the obvious, namely that in their beliefs and behaviors humans are particularly malleable. (I speak now of the effects on development. Adults can be most stubborn.) The Jesuits did not boast for nothing that they could hold and form a person for ever as long as they had him (her?) until his seventh year. I doubt that humans are indefinitely malleable, but I strongly endorse the claim that social change is best effected by education rather than by drastic eugenic programs. Could you "educate" someone to be totally immoral or amoral? This strikes me as an empirical question, not to be answered simply by armchair reflection. I suspect, however, that it might not be as easy as you think; if certain thoughts and behaviors are highly adaptive, biology will make them fairly resistant to outside influences.

Whether or not I am right in what I claim, there is nothing particularly worrisome from a moral standpoint in my position. What of the more troublesome issues about biologically determined differences between people? It cannot be denied that evolutionary theory leads us to expect intraspecific biological variation and that this would extend to human thought patterns and behaviors. Moreover, the evidence from more direct (especially molecularly based) studies of Homo sapiens strongly confirms the existence of widespread biological variation within the species, and, in some cases it is certainly known that this variation affects behavior. How much of a general effect this variation has on the various roles that people play in societies (pre and postindustrial) is a highly controversial question. I am reluctant to get too far sidetracked specially since I (with Wilson) have discussed the matter in some detail elsewhere (Ruse & Wilson 1986). It is, however, plausible and strongly backed by a range of studies that many of the various factors (e.g., intelligence) which are loosely related to human success within their groups have a biological component in their causal background (Scarr & Carter-Saltzman 1982).

Perhaps even more controversial than claims, about variation in abilities between members of Homo sapiens taken as a whole are claims about variations between groups such as Europeans and black Africans. It is known from direct studies that most genetic variation spreads across the human species; it is not confined to the gaps between groups (Lewontin 1972). Moreover, it is worth remembering that Darwinians expect systematic variation to be associated with direct adaptive advantage at some point, past or present. It is plausible to link skin color variation to sunlight variation. It is quite another matter to argue plausibly for broad, biologically linked, behavioral variations. They may exist but their expression may be far more subtle than anyone expects. Consider the often noted differences between Western and Eastern drinking practices with Westerners tending to drink far more in less inhibited ways. This may be linked not to oriental genes for abstinence but to the differential ways in which various peoples can synthesize ethyl alcohol. Putting the matter bluntly, the Chinese and Japanese are far more prone to hangovers, although where the adaptive value lies in such matters remains obscure (see Ruse & Wilson 1986).

The dangers of simplistic conclusions about the significance of biological factors in questions of the sort just discussed was underlined by two recent separate reports in the British Press (see *The Times*, 19 & 21 June 1986). According to a ministerial statement in Parliament, on the average blacks (people of African descent) are over *ten* times more likely to go to prison than whites. I would argue that before one starts spinning hypotheses about black innate tendencies to violence, one ought to consider both the appalling social conditions within which many blacks live (and the grotesquely high unemployment) and the attitudes of the overwhelmingly white British police, judiciary, and juries. The virtues of such hesitation was confirmed by the release later in the week of a government-sponsored report detailing how the ratio of black children living in London who are unable to understand over 50 percent of what their teachers say on a daily basis is 79 percent. These children speak and only understand an idiosyncratic mixture of English and Creole.

The terrors of biological determinism have been much exaggerated. This applies even at the one point where there surely are some biologically based attitudinal and behavioral differences between humans, namely those between the sexes (Hinde 1984). Here there really is theory backing empirical findings, or there is much within modern Darwinian thought to suggest that creatures like ourselves will have sexually dimorphic reproductive strategies and that the differences will go beyond the purely physical. Yet, do not conclude that now, at last, we are facing pure biological determinism. The rapid changes between the sexes in Western society in the past two decades speaks most eloquently against this conclusion. At most, to use somewhat notorious words, "the twig is bent a little" (Wilson 1978). No one is arguing that all is fixed at conception. Most particularly, no one is decrying the virtues of equality of opportunity.

Control determinism.   I move now to our third and final sense of determinism, namely that centering on *control*. A great deal of the worrying about freedom and determinism in the context of morality centers on the question, who is in charge? In particular, is it I who am running my life, or my emotions? Let us grant the Humean point that true freedom lies not in some beyond-causation nirvana but in an absence of constraint. The prisoner is not a responsible moral agent, not because he is causally bound but because he is physically bound. The question now centers on the problem of life's straight jackets, particularly those of a psychological or internal nature.

The point at issue is that we all recognize the existence of internal constraints, which sometimes can be so powerful and overwhelming that the individual is not truly free. There is such a great compulsion that the person's actions are determined, and no moral fault (or praise) can be ascribed. We do not blame him or her, or punish him or her. This is something that can be properly done only to a free agent.

Now the worry is that our biological approach pushes the psychological constraint problem to the limit. Thanks to evolution we are so bound by our emotions and feelings that we are truly free in nothing we do. We are automata or marionettes controlled by strings which lead, first to our genes, and then through them to the forces of natural selection working on our would-be ancestors. We are, in fact, little more than large, white ants.

The philosopher Daniel Dennett has stated the point well. He quotes the following passage from P. Wooldridge:

> When the time comes for egg laying, the wasp Sphex builds a burrow for the purpose and seeks out a cricket which she stings in such a way as to paralyze but not kill it. She drags the cricket into the burrow, lays her eggs alongside, closes the burrow, then flies away, never to return. In due course, the eggs hatch and the wasp grubs feed off the paralyzed cricket, which has not decayed, having been kept in the wasp equivalent of deep freeze. To the human mind, such an elaborately organized and seemingly purposeful routine conveys a convincing flavour of logic and thoughtfulness—until more details are examined. For example, the Wasp's routine is to bring the paralyzed cricket to the burrow, leave it on the threshold, go inside to see that all is well, emerge, and then drag the cricket in. If the cricket is moved a few inches away while the wasp is inside making her preliminary inspection, the wasp, on emerging from the burrow, will bring the cricket back to the threshold, but not inside, and will then repeat the preparatory procedure of entering the burrow to see that everything is all right. If again the cricket is removed a few inches while the wasp is inside, once again she will move the cricket up to the threshold and re-enter the burrow for a final check. The wasp never thinks of pulling the cricket straight in. On one occasion this procedure was repeated forty times, always with the same result (Wooldridge 1963, 82; quoted in Dennett 1984, 11).

Then, he characterizes this aspect of the free will problem as the problem of "sphex-ishness." "The sphex is unmasked; she is not a free agent, but rather at the mercy brute physical causation, driven, inexorably into her states and activities by features of the environment outside her control" (Dennett 1984, 11). How do we know that we humans, thanks to our evolutionary background, are not sphex-like, going through the motions with no real control? (The term *sphexishness* is due to Dennett's friend and sometime collaborator Douglas Hofstadter [1982].)

As soon as matters are stated this bluntly, you should at once be starting to feel ill at ease. Remembering back to the discussion about the evolution of morality, *the whole point was that humans are not ant-or-wasp-like.* We are not determined by our genes to do things without thought like machines. Morality opens up a flexibility in humans which enables us to respond according to the situation. It is in this capacity to respond that I believe you can locate all of the freedom it is possible or necessary to have.

In order to make my case, let me elaborate in light of recent philosophical writings on the matter of freedom and determinism (e.g., Frankfurt 1970; Watson 1975; Neeley 1974; and Slote 1980). Freedom according to my conception lies in our being able to control our emotions. We rule them rather than having them rule us. What does this mean exactly? It means (using ideas which return to Plato's *Republic*) that we have the ability to bring our emotions into line with and to the service of other "higher" aims or wishes that we have. Clarifying further, let me distinguish between first-order desires and second-order desires. Taking an example (Plato's), a first-order desire might be to assuage thirst and a second-order desire might be to go on living. The free person is he or she who can use the first-order desire in the service of the second-order desire. This means that one can actually act on the basis of the second-order desire even though there may be other first-order desires or external factors going against it. Knowing that a pond is poisoned, the free person is one who can deny his or her thirst. The uncontrolled person is one who cannot deny the thirst. The nonperson or wanton is one who without second order desires lets his or her first-order desires rule the day.

As thus characterized, there is no question of the ant being free. Even if it has first-order desires (doubtful), it has no second-order desires to guide it. The ant does not say: "Should I help my sister now?" Humans to the contrary are free. Our moral aspirations make up our second-order desires, and our freedom lies in bringing first-order feelings and emotions to the ends of morality, so we actually do that which is moral. True freedom lies in the fact that there may well be other first-order desires pushing me away from morality. I see a child lying sick, possibly with a contagious infection. I should help, yet I am afraid. Nevertheless, I am sufficiently in control of myself—using other emotions like pity, self-pride, and more—freely to aid the child. The person who is not free is the one whose supreme second-order desire is to help but who is "paralyzed" by fear. (Plato's example in the *Republic* was of Leontius, son of Aglaion, who wanted not to gaze on the executed prisoners but whose base nature proved too much for him. He was "out of control.")

Freedom, therefore, does not lie in choice over our emotions or our goals in life. It may well be that these are thrust upon us. Indeed I accept that there is more than a hint of biological determinism about the fact that we are moral beings at all. The place where freedom enters—making it possible for us to be moral beings—lies in our ability to use our first-order feelings to achieve ends specified in our second-order desires. That is where control and responsibility come into our lives, and everything in the evolutionary account of morality affirms that humans, in this vital respect, are free, moral beings.

The analogy which springs to mind, distinguishing us from the ants, is that focusing on various types of missile. Ants are like missiles with fixed paths. If the goal is stationary, they work perfectly. We are like missiles with guidance systems. We are more difficult to produce but if the goal moves we can respond accordingly. This holds true even though our end remains unchanged (Ruse 1986b).

Note how this analogy brings out the fact that our abilities to use first-order desires to achieve second-order ends are intended to be normal, causally governed mechanisms, as are the guidance mechanisms of missiles. It is worth quoting Dennett on this point:

> Contrary to the familiar vision, *determinism does not in itself "erode control"*. The Viking spacecraft is as deterministic a device as any clock, but this does not prevent it from being able to control itself. Fancier deterministic devices cannot only control themselves; they can evade the attempts of other self-controllers to control them. If we are also deterministic devices, we need not on that account fear that we cannot be in control of ourselves and our destinies.
>
> Moreover, *the past does not control us*. It no more controls us than the people at NASA can control the space ships that have wandered out of reach in space. It is not that there are no causal links between the Earth and those craft. There are; reflected sunlight from the Earth still reaches them, for instance. But causal links are not enough for control. There must also be feedback to inform the controller. There are no feedback signals from the present to the past for the past to exploit. Moreover there is nothing in the past to foresee and plan for our particular acts, even if it is true that Mother Nature—gambling on our general needs and predicaments—did, in effect, design us to fend quite well for ourselves. Far from it being the case that we are completely under the control of our ancestors or our evolutionary past, it is rather the case that that heritage has tended to set us up as *self*-controllers—lucky us (Dennett 1984, 72).

IMPLICATIONS

Let me make some comments on my position while elaborating and showing its strength.

First, note how readily I can account for the fact that people get out of control. It is all a question of emotions and of whether they can be brought into line. At times of extreme stress, for example, someone may "go over the edge" and lose control of an otherwise governable emotion. Notice also how our basic intuitions are sensitive to various nuances. We may not find the man who kills in a drunken rage guilty of murder. His drink put him out of control. Yet, we might find him guilty of manslaughter and punish him accordingly; he was in control of the situation when he became drunk and he should have known better.

Could it be that some people have more control and that because of evolution this is reflected in a systematic way in Homo sapiens? One suggestion might center on male and female sexual desires. Certainly most societies assume that males are less in control of their emotions than females, and judge them accordingly. "Even the nicest boys are after only one thing. It's not their fault. It's part of their nature, and it's up to you to stop them"! Again, this fits in with what we know of male and female biology. Females simply have to have more control because they get pregnant. Do not misunderstand me. This is not an argument for exonerating the rapist from moral responsibility. Clearly, modern contraceptive technology has lifted some of the reasons for self-restraint although social diseases seem to have brought back reasons for control by both sexes.

One point which has been hovering for some time now should be stressed. I see no inherent reason why first-order emotions brought on by a fairly significant biological component should be less under control than emotions with a more significant environmental causal component. By definition they will not be so amenable to environmental manipulation, but that is another thing. Biological determinism does not imply control determinism. In fact it is too easy to think of cases where the environment brings on emotions quite out of control. Think of the adult systematically starved as a child who is now a compulsive eater.

Second, let us ask about whether morality is our only second-order desire or set of desires. Some argue that it is (Wolf 1980). On biological grounds I doubt this unique status of morality. It seems clear to me that we have other second-order desires, particularly that centering on self-preservation and reproduction, considered in some broad sense. These can conflict with morality and in serving them one freely does that which is wrong. Such a person is and can be knowingly immoral. The immoral person is one who denies moral goals. The amoral person has no such goals at all.

A variant of the morality-as-unique-goal argument allows that there are other goals but claims that they will always harmonize with morality. Plato, for instance, seems to allow the logically distinct goal of personal satisfaction, but he then argues in the *Republic* that only the truly good person is the truly happy person. Hence wrongdoing is always ultimately a function of ignorance. I doubt that this is always true. Personal well-being and morality may both have their biological functions, but like bipedalism and large-brainness they may (as at childbirth) clash. Doing good may bring peace of mind, but doing wrong may have its compensating pleasures. This is not to say that I think you need not always do good. You should, but because it is good, not because of other payoffs.

Third, there is the question of ignorance. It is clear that knowledge, particularly self-knowledge, is a factor entering into our thinking about freedom and responsibility. Consider homosexuality (Ruse 1987). In days of yore even having homosexual thoughts and desires was thought to be sinful. Today thanks to the advent of psychiatry it is recognized that no responsibility lies at the feet of the person, male or female, with homosexual inclinations. We now see that these are things over which we have no control. The person with homosexual inclinations no more chooses to have these inclinations than the person with heterosexual inclinations.

There is still debate about whether the inclinations are so strong that no guilt should be felt at subsequent acts. Among other things this shows that even with improved knowledge we sometimes find that our first-order desires or inclinations are so strong that we cannot achieve second-order goals. Fortunately, this is not necessarily the end of the matter. Recognizing the first-order desires and their force may be the first move towards bringing them under control. This was the hope of Baruch Spinoza and is certainly the program of Sigmund Freud and his followers. "The truth shall set you free." (It has not gone unnoticed that Spinoza and Freud draw on the same Jewish tradition [MacIntyre 1967].) I hasten to add that I do not intend to suggest that homosexual acts ought to be prescribed, or that they are morally wrong. Nor, indeed, was this the suggestion of Freud.

Fourth and finally, let us ask about our second order desires and goals. Might not these themselves be subject to control, perhaps beneath third-order principles? As noted, we do not (in the normal course of life) choose our second-order principles; these are thrust upon us (by biology and training and so forth). Indeed, I think this is a strength of the biology-acknowledging position over rival accounts of the origin and nature of morality such as social contract theories. Right is right, and not because we set it up and choose to follow it. However, having said this much, remember that nothing is fixed absolutely by biology or culture—or, if fixed for us, then not for our children. Could it be that we might want to bend our second-order desires to third-order ends, perhaps even wanting to manipulate the second-order through artificial interferences in the normal course of life?

This raises a question about the second-order desires. What is there beyond morality and personal existence? Thus posed, the question probably only becomes meaningful (and then it becomes important) if one distinguishes not so much between morality and something higher but between levels of morality (and personal existence) itself. Thanks to biology we have immediate moral urges—helping individuals and so forth—but thanks to our intellects we see that in the long run such immediate urges may be self-refuting. We want to let all persons have the freedom to determine the number of members in their family, but because of technology the effects will be disastrous—morally and to personal survival. This suggests the need for a second level of control and freedom, between immediate moral urges and more reflective long-term plans. Whether this need can be satisfied is a moot question, but in line with what we have just said about freedom and ignorance, our biological approach is at least a small step towards a fuller understanding.[3]

CONCLUSION

It will take a long time to work out the full implications of an evolutionary approach to humanity. I trust I have shown that the effort is worth it. New light is thrown on old problems; the best of previous thought is cherished and elaborated (which is what we, as evolutionists, would expect); and the critics can be answered in a constructive manner. Supposed faults turn out to be significant strengths. What more can one ask of any position?

NOTES

1. When I use the term *altruism* in the metaphorical biological sense, I will use quotation marks: "altruism." This will contrast with the term in the literal moral sense which will be used without quotes: altruism.

2. The "skepticism" in "moral skepticism" refers to doubts about ultimate foundations. No one doubts that there is genuine morality or altruism. The whole point is that there is.

3. Of course in a sense we *do* already interfere with second-order principles. Jehovah's Witnesses, for instance give their children special training (indoctrination) to make them believe that blood transfusions are immoral. However, this is basically a question of getting the principles right—in one's own opinion. However what if one thinks the principle is a good one yet will lead ultimately to disaster? Here it seems one appeals to a higher level of desire or goal.

CHAPTER 2
Freedom

In this chapter we will examine a variety of interpretations of the idea that human beings have free will. When we speak of being free we may be referring to one of several different senses of the concept. Sometimes when we talk about freedom, what we have in mind is the political freedom of being able to express our own thoughts without fear of punishment by the state, or the freedom to determine the government and laws that will rule over us. Other times we associate the idea of freedom with the ability to act without the obstacle of being physically restrained. (One can hardly be described as free to play the violin when one's hands are tied.) Alternatively, there is the conception of freedom as the ability to act in accordance with one's own desires together with an ability to choose which desires to act on. This is a more metaphysical understanding of what it is to be free, and this conception of free action is the subject of the following discussions.

Our first selection is C. A. Campbell's "Has the Self Free Will?" Campbell relies primarily on an examination of our experience of choosing freely in order to clarify the concept of free will. We all have the idea, he claims, that free will is a precondition of moral responsibility, and so, he argues, it is within the framework of moral responsibility that we should examine the concept of free will. What we need to do in order to state accurately what this free will amounts to is to explore our own moral experiences. This requires us to examine carefully what it is like to make moral decisions, and what kinds of assumptions we rely on when we assign moral praise and blame to others.

When we evaluate someone else's actions, we frequently make "allowances" for poor choices when the agent's decision is largely influenced by factors such as heredity and environment. To the extent that such elements influence an agent's choices, we think of the agent as only a part-author of his or her action. For example, an action that demonstrates a hatred of older men might be largely the result of years of abuse that a son has endured at the hands of his father. Under such circumstances, we take the agent to be only partially responsible for that act. This suggests two things to Campbell. First, that sole authorship is a necessary precondition of moral responsibility, and hence of freedom. Second, it suggests that agents are praised or blamed to the extent that they exert what Campbell calls "moral effort." The person who has suffered years of abuse by his father needs to try harder than most people to behave cordially toward strong paternal figures because of the way his behavior has been conditioned in the past.

For Campbell, however, the sole authorship of one's actions through the exercise of moral effort, though necessary for freedom and responsibility, is not sufficient. Often we think that an agent is free only if the agent could have acted otherwise. For example, I can be said to have been free and responsible when I lied and said that I thought the meal was delicious only if I could have told the truth and said it was awful. Campbell considers a variety of competing accounts of what it means to say that an agent could have acted otherwise and arrives at the conclusion that a proper analysis of this idea centers on the agent's ability to have *chosen otherwise*. That is, we are free when we are the sole authors of our decisions to exercise moral effort and when we could have decided equally well not to make a moral effort. When we struggle with the choice between doing the right thing and doing what we desire most (when what we desire most is not the right thing), we have an awareness of the ability to choose either alternative.

Campbell recognizes that this account of free will is, in a sense, very limited. If he is correct, then we are free only when we make moral decisions. Although we speak of making choices all the time in our daily behavior, unless that behavior has moral importance and requires the exercise of moral effort, Campbell asserts that it does not make sense to speak of such choices as free. On Campbell's analysis then, we have and exercise free will only in a quite narrow set of circumstances.

John Stuart Mill, best known for his work on the moral theory of utilitarianism, uses Sir William Hamilton's discussion of the freedom–determinism debate as a springboard for his own insights on the topic. Hamilton believed that free will and determinism (what he called "necessity") both involve absurdities. That is, both views require the acceptance of concepts we cannot possibly understand. The problem with the idea of free will is that it requires what Hamilton called an "absolute commencement." This is an uncaused cause in the human agent. If the will is genuinely free, then there must be such causes, but something seems wrong with this idea, because for any action we perform there are reasons why we performed it, and reasons for having those reasons, and so on. The idea of necessity, on the other hand, requires that we accept the idea of an infinite regress of causally connected events. Each event has a causal antecedent in a backward sequence that never comes to an end. Nevertheless, one of these theories must be true, in Hamilton's view, so we must accept whichever one has the most positive evidence in its favor. According to Hamilton, the doctrine of free will is more plausible because we have evidence for it in our consciousness.

Mill evaluates Hamilton's position and offers reasons to disagree both with his claim that the doctrine of necessity is incomprehensible and with his claim that consciousness really does give us convincing evidence in support of free will.

First, Mill points out that we do not find it completely absurd to identify causes to explain ordinary physical events in the world. When we invoke the idea of causation we need not, as Hamilton assumes, commit ourselves to an infinite regress of causal antecedents because any cause may be traced back to what Mill calls a "universal cause" (a first cause), or simply to a point that is unknowable by the human mind because of its complexity and remoteness. Furthermore, Mill argues that our experience of causal relations shows only that certain kinds of events are constantly conjoined, or happen together. We have always seen that, under normal conditions, a billiard ball moves when struck by a moving cue ball. Following the Scottish empiricist, David Hume, Mill points out that we do not have any experience of a necessary connection between causes and effects. All we experience are certain kinds of events happening together with regularity, and this does not warrant the conclusion that causes necessitate their effects. For all we know, the next time the cue ball strikes the eight ball, both of them will stop dead in their tracks. Thus, if we rely on our experience of such matters we ought not to associate the idea of necessity with causation in the first place.

Second, Mill asks what Hamilton's conscious awareness of freedom amounts to. In Mill's view, it boils down to the feeling that one could have chosen otherwise. All this means, according to Mill, is that we could have chosen the other option *if we had preferred it*, and our preferences could have been different only if the conditions under which our choice was made were different. For example, when I order a drink at the bar I might think to myself that I could have chosen beer rather than wine, but this is so only if I preferred beer, and the reason I didn't prefer beer is that I had too much of it the previous night. It is, in Mill's view, impossible to act contrary to one's strongest volition. To suggest otherwise is to say we could have performed another action even if we didn't prefer it to the alternatives. Since the consciousness of free action boils down to acting in accordance with one's strongest preferences, and what preferences are strongest is determined by antecedent conditions, the so-called consciousness of free action does not really give us any meaningful understanding of free will.

If free will is not directly apparent in our consciousness might it not still be implied by our consciousness of moral responsibility? In Mill's view, our sense of responsibility is almost entirely constituted by feeling deserving of punishment. When we believe we have done something wrong and feel responsible for it, we immediately feel that we should be punished in some way. Indeed, the very idea of taking responsibility for one's actions involves a readiness to accept whatever punishment others deem appropriate. However, for Mill this sense of responsibility is dependent upon an expectation that we will be punished. This is something we have been taught in our moral education. If we knew we would not be punished, Mill claims, we would not feel deserving of punishment and hence, would not feel responsible for our action. Thus, it is not the case that there is any necessary connection between being free and feeling responsible. In Mill's view, then, Hamilton has failed to provide us with any convincing reasons to think we possess free will.

The next selection, "Being and Doing: Freedom" by Jean-Paul Sartre, represents a very different approach from the others. Sartre was an extremely important thinker in post-World War II Europe and one of the most influential representatives of the philosophical movement known as existentialism. Existentialism, in broad terms, is concerned with the human condition: our nature as conscious free beings, with the heavy burden of responsibility this gives us. According to Sartre, human beings do not possess an essence, or fixed nature, but create themselves by making choices. Sartre believed that we are *completely* free and are responsible for *everything*.

For Sartre, the concept of an action is one that has been misunderstood by those embroiled in the traditional freedom–determinism debate. What most philosophers have failed to recognize is that actions are *intentional*. For Sartre this means that actions involve a projection of oneself into the future or realm of possibilities. The motives of actions, being directed to the future in this way, must therefore be understood in relation to a system of ideal, nonexistent objects. If a worker is to think that his life is intolerable and is to choose to do something about it, then he must regard his life as lacking something and must conceive of a better existence as a possibility. It is only in relation to this lack and this nonexistent state of affairs (the better life) that the worker can be said to act. Since the act of choosing is an act of creating the self, and since choosing must be understood in terms of unreal possibilities, Sartre often speaks of freedom both as "making oneself" and as "nothingness."

For Sartre, all of our choices make us who we are. Our freedom, then, is not limited only to the realm of moral decision making, but is all-encompassing. This is why Sartre says that we are responsible for everything. Often this responsibility extends well beyond what most of us would expect. A soldier who is drafted into military service might think of himself as an unwilling participant in a war. As such he may say to himself that he is the victim of circumstances beyond his control. In Sartre's view, however, the soldier can't help but be free because desertion, no matter what the penalty, remains an option. Even in circumstances where there appear to be no favorable options, Sartre would say we are still free because we can choose suicide. The only respect in which we are not free, according to Sartre, is in our freedom. Our freedom was thrust upon us when we were created and, being the very condition of our existence, is something from which we can never escape.

The next reading, "On the Absolute Freedom of Will," by Bernard Berofsky, provides a critical discussion of theories like Sartre's that claim the will is free in an absolute sense. Berofsky examines a variety of examples of compulsion in an attempt to distinguish freedom of will from freedom of action that, in his view, are thrust uncomfortably together by the views he criticizes.

Berofsky's starting point is to explore some of the implications of having free will in the absolute sense. According to Berofsky, if we accept the idea that the will is absolutely free, then we are forced between the following two choices: either we are never unfree to act since one does not act when one is compelled, or we can distinguish between having perfectly free will and a restricted freedom of action. Berofsky rejects the first option in favor of the second alternative. The alternative requires that we accept the distinction between performing an action (un)freely and being (un)free to perform an action. I go to a party unfreely if I am physically carried there by my friends but am unfree to leave the party if they lock me in a room.

Berofsky also considers whether knowledge can restrict the will. If so, then the view that the will is absolutely free is implausible. Some have argued that if I know I cannot do something (A), then I cannot even try to do A, which makes the will unfree with respect to A. This requires more than the belief that I can't do A, because my belief could turn out to be false, from which it follows that I can try to do A. Berofsky claims that if I was deluded and believed that I could fly, but eventually came to know through therapy that I couldn't, then my freedom with respect to flying is diminished in the sense that I will no longer try to do that. In either case, of course, I couldn't actually fly, so what is diminished is not the realm of possible actions, but possible acts of will. Berofsky's conclusion is that since willing is itself an act that can be limited, it is implausible to maintain, as Sartre and others have, that the will is absolutely free.

In the final selection from Henry Margenau, "Quantum Mechanics, Free Will, and Determinism," we see a gesture at how quantum mechanics can be employed in a partial explanation of human freedom. The kind of freedom Margenau is concerned with is what he calls "elemental" freedom as opposed to "practical" freedom. Practical freedom is freedom from internal or external constraints such as compulsion, coercion, habituation, or addiction. Elemental freedom is a more metaphysical variety that exists even in the absence of practical freedom. It is the kind of freedom that we *feel* is real and that seems to be in conflict with causal determinism.

When we act, Margenau claims, there are many complicated processes involved. There is a mental or psychological act of choosing or deciding, there is the resulting behavior, and in between and underlying both of these occurrences are a multitude of physical events and processes. Intentional actions involve events studied by psychology, biology, physics, and other disciplines. What is the relationship between the events studied by these different disciplines? Margenau considers three possibilities: (1) psychology can be reduced to physics; (2) psychology depends on but cannot be reduced to physics; (3) psychology cannot be reduced to physics, and its laws or principles are in direct conflict with physical laws. He claims that (2) is most plausible, in which case we can expect to find some sort of dependency relation between the concepts of psychology and the more basic physical sciences, even though we might never be able to reduce psychology to those other sciences.

Given the likelihood that what happens psychologically when we make choices depends on physical (or more specifically, neurochemical) processes, what does quantum mechanics have to say about the role of chance in this process? According to Margenau, quantum indeterminacy is a genuine feature of the world. There are physical events that are uncaused. This is not just a matter of such events *seeming* to be uncaused. It is not merely because we are ignorant of, or unable to discover the hidden causes of quantum events. Rather, Margenau argues that there are no such causes to discover. According to Margenau, this kind of indeterminacy frequently does creep into macroevents. That is, quantum indeterminacies are not always restricted to the domain of subatomic particles, but can play a role in the behavior of matter on a somewhat larger scale. This consideration allows us to introduce the idea of chance into what happens in our brains when we make choices. This kind of chance, Margenau claims, does not fully explain elemental freedom, but is a requirement for it. Chance, then, at the very least revives the concept of freedom that was genuinely threatened by Laplacean determinism.

HAS THE SELF FREE WILL?*

C. A. Campbell

... It is something of a truism that in philosophic enquiry the exact formulation of a problem often takes one a long way on the road to its solution. In the case of the Free Will problem I think there is a rather special need of careful formulation. For there are many sorts of human freedom; and it can easily happen that one wastes a great deal of

*From *On Selfhood And Godhood* (London: George Allen & Unwin, Ltd.; and New Jersey: Humanities Press, Inc., 1957), 158–179. Reprinted by permission of HarperCollins Publishers Ltd. © C. A. Campbell, 1957.

labour in proving or disproving a freedom which has almost nothing to do with the freedom which is at issue in the traditional problem of Free Will. The abortiveness of so much of the argument for and against Free Will in contemporary philosophical literature seems to me due in the main to insufficient pains being taken over the preliminary definition of the problem. There is, indeed, one outstanding exception, Professor Broad's brilliant inaugural lecture entitled, 'Determinism, Indeterminism, and Libertarianism',[1] in which forty-three pages are devoted to setting out the problem, as against seven to its solution! I confess that the solution does not seem to myself to follow upon the formulation quite as easily as all that:[2] but Professor Broad's eminent example fortifies me in my decision to give here what may seem at first sight a disproportionate amount of time to the business of determining the essential characteristics of the kind of freedom with which the traditional problem is concerned.

Fortunately we can at least make a beginning with a certain amount of confidence. It is not seriously disputable that the kind of freedom in question is the freedom which is commonly recognised to be in some sense a precondition of moral responsibility. Clearly, it is on account of this integral connection with moral responsibility that such exceptional importance has always been felt to attach to the Free Will problem. But in what precise sense is free will a precondition of moral responsibility, and thus a postulate of the moral life in general? This is an exceedingly troublesome question; but until we have satisfied ourselves about the answer to it, we are not in a position to state, let alone decide, the question whether 'Free Will' in its traditional, ethical, significance is a reality.

Our first business, then, is to ask, exactly what kind of freedom is it which is required for moral responsibility? And as to method of procedure in this inquiry, there seems to me to be no real choice. I know of only one method that carries with it any hope of success; viz. the critical comparison of those acts for which, on due reflection, we deem it proper to attribute moral praise or blame to the agents, with those acts for which, on due reflection, we deem such judgments to be improper. The ultimate touchstone, as I see it, can only be our moral consciousness as it manifests itself in our more critical and considered moral judgments. The 'linguistic' approach by way of the analysis of moral *sentences* seems to me, despite its present popularity, to be an almost infallible method for reaching wrong results in the moral field; but I must reserve what I have to say about this.

The first point to note is that the freedom at issue (as indeed the very name 'Free *Will* Problem' indicates) pertains primarily not to overt acts but to inner acts. The nature of things has decreed that, save in the case of one's self, it is only overt acts which one can directly observe. But a very little reflection serves to show that in our moral judgments upon others their overt acts are regarded as significant only in so far as they are the expression of inner acts. We do not consider the acts of a robot to be morally responsible acts; nor do we consider the acts of a man to be so save in so far as they are distinguishable from those of a robot by reflecting an inner life of choice. Similarly, from the other side, if we are satisfied (as we may on occasion be, at least in the case of ourselves) that a person has definitely elected to follow a course which he believes to be wrong, but has been prevented by external circumstances from translating his inner choice into an overt act, we still regard him as morally blameworthy. Moral freedom, then, pertains to *inner* acts.

The next point seems at first sight equally obvious and uncontroversial; but, as we shall see, it has awkward implications if we are in real earnest with it (as almost nobody is). It is the simple point that the act must be one of which the person judged can be regarded as the *sole* author. It seems plain enough that if there are any *other* determinants of the act, external to the self, to that extent the act is not an act which the *self* determines, and to that extent not an act for which the self can be held morally responsible. The self is only part-author of the act, and his moral responsibility can logically extend only to those elements within the act (assuming for the moment that these can be isolated) of which he is the *sole* author.

The awkward implications of this apparent truism will be readily appreciated. For, if we are mindful of the influences exerted by heredity and environment, we may well feel some doubt whether there is any act of will at all of which one can truly say that the self is sole author, sole determinant. No man has a voice is determining the raw material of impulses and capacities that constitute his hereditary endowment, and no man has more than a very partial control of the material and social environment in which he is destined to live his life. Yet it would be manifestly absurd to deny that these two factors do constantly and profoundly affect the nature of a man's choices. That this is so we all of us recognise in our moral judgments when we 'make allowances', as we say, for a bad heredity or a vicious environment, and acknowledge in the victim of them a diminished moral responsibility for evil courses. Evidently we do *try*, in our moral judgments, however crudely, to praise or blame a man only in respect of that of which we can regard him as *wholly* the author. And evidently we do recognise that, for a man to be the author of an act in the full sense required for moral responsibility, it is not enough merely that he 'wills' or 'chooses' the act: since even the most unfortunate victim of heredity or environment does, as a rule, 'will' what he does. It is significant, however, that the ordinary man, though well enough aware of the influence upon choices of heredity and environment, does not feel obliged thereby to give up his assumption that moral predicates *are* somehow applicable. Plainly he still believes that there is *something* for which a man is morally responsible, something of which we can fairly say that he is the sole author. *What is this something*? To that question common-sense is not ready with an explicit answer—though an answer is, I think, implicit in the line which its moral judgments take. I shall do what I can to give an explicit answer later in this lecture. Meantime it must suffice to observe that, if we are to be true to the deliverances of our moral consciousness, it is very difficult to deny that *sole* authorship is a necessary condition of the morally responsible act.

Thirdly we come to a point over which much recent controversy has raged. We may approach it by raising the following question. Granted an act of which the agent is sole author, does this 'sole authorship' suffice to make the act a morally free act? We may be inclined to think that it does, until we contemplate the possibility that an act of which the agent is sole author might conceivably occur as a necessary expression of the agent's nature; the way in which, e.g. some philosophers have supposed the Divine act of creation to occur. This consideration excites a legitimate doubt; for it is far from easy to see how a person can be regarded as a proper subject for moral praise or blame in respect of an act which he *cannot help* performing—even if it be his own 'nature' which necessitates it. Must we not recognise it as a condition of the morally free act that the agent 'could have acted otherwise' than he in fact did? It is true, indeed, that we sometimes praise or blame a man for an act about which we are prepared to say, in the light of our knowledge of his established character, that he 'could no other'. But I think that a little reflection shows that in such cases we are not praising or blaming the man strictly for what he does *now* (or at any rate we ought not to be), but rather for those past acts of his which have generated the firm habit of mind from which his *present* act follows 'necessarily'. In other words, our praise and blame, so far as justified, are really retrospective, being directed not to the agent *qua* performing *this* act, but to the agent *qua* performing those past acts which have built up his present character, and in respect to which we presume that he *could* have acted otherwise, that there really *were* open possibilities before him. These cases, therefore, seem to me to constitute no valid exception to what I must take to be the rule, viz. that a man can be morally praised or blamed for an act only if he could have acted otherwise.

Now philosophers today are fairly well agreed that it is a postulate of the morally responsible act that the agent 'could have acted otherwise' in *some* sense of that phrase. But sharp differences of opinion have arisen over the way in which the phrase ought to be interpreted. There is a strong disposition to water down its apparent meaning by insisting that it is not (as a postulate of moral responsibility) to be understood as a straightforward categorical proposition, but rather as a disguised hypothetical proposition. All that we really require to be assured of, in order to justify our holding X morally responsible for an act, is, we are told, that X could have acted otherwise *if* he had *chosen* otherwise (Moore, Stevenson); or perhaps that X could have acted otherwise *if* he had had a different character, or *if* he had been placed in different circumstances.

I think it is easy to understand, and even, in a measure, to sympathise with, the motives which induce philosophers to offer these counter-interpretations. It is not just the fact that 'X could have acted otherwise', as a bald categorical statement, is incompatible with the universal sway of causal law—though this is, to some philosophers, a serious stone of stumbling. The more widespread objection is that it at least looks as though it were incompatible with that causal continuity of an agent's character with his conduct which is implied when we believe (surely with justice) that we can often tell the sort of thing a man will do from our knowledge of the sort of man he is.

We shall have to make our accounts with that particular difficulty later. At this stage I wish merely to show that neither of the hypothetical propositions suggested—and I think the same could be shown for *any* hypothetical alternative—is an acceptable substitute for the categorical proposition 'X could have acted otherwise' as the presupposition of moral responsibility.

Let us look first at the earlier suggestion—'X could have acted otherwise *if* he had chosen otherwise'. Now clearly there are a great many acts with regard to which we are entirely satisfied that the agent is thus situated. We are often perfectly sure that—for this is all it amounts to—if X had chosen otherwise, the circumstances presented no external obstacle to the translation of that choice into action. For example, we often have no doubt at all that X, who in point of fact told a lie, could have told the truth *if* he had so chosen. But does our confidence on this score allay all legitimate doubts about whether X is really blameworthy? Does it entail that X is free in the sense required for moral responsibility? Surely not. The obvious question immediately arises: 'But *could* X have *chosen* otherwise than he did?' It is doubt about the true answer to *that* question which leads most people to doubt the reality of moral responsibility. Yet on this crucial question the hypothetical proposition which is offered as a sufficient statement of the condition justifying the ascription of moral responsibility gives us no information whatsoever.

Indeed this hypothetical substitute for the categorical 'X could have acted otherwise' seems to me to lack all plausibility unless one contrives to forget why it is, after all, that we ever come to feel fundamental doubts about man's moral responsibility. Such doubts are born, surely, when one becomes aware of certain reputable world-views in religion or philosophy, or of certain reputable scientific beliefs, which in their several ways imply that man's actions are necessitated, and thus could not be otherwise than they in fact are. But clearly a doubt so based is not even touched by the recognition that a man could very often act otherwise *if* he so chose. That proposition is entirely compatible with the necessitarian theories which generate our doubt: indeed it is this very compatibility that has recommended it to some philosophers, who are reluctant to give up either moral responsibility or Determinism. The proposition which we *must* be able to affirm if moral praise or blame of X is to be justified is the categorical proposition that X could have acted otherwise because—not if—he could have chosen otherwise; or, since it is essentially the inner side of the act that matters, the proposition simply that X could have chosen otherwise.

For the second of the alternative formulae suggested we cannot spare more than a few moments. But its inability to meet the demands it is required to meet is almost transparent. 'X could have acted otherwise', as a statement of a precondition of X's moral responsibility, really means (we are told) 'X could have acted otherwise *if* he were differently constituted, or *if* he had been placed in different circumstances'. It seems a sufficient reply to this to point out that the person whose moral responsibility is at issue is X; a specific individual, in a specific set of circumstances. It is totally irrelevant to X's moral responsibility that we should be able to say that some person differently constituted from X, or X in a different set of circumstances, could have done something different from what X did.

Let me, then, briefly sum up the answer at which we have arrived to our question about the kind of freedom required to justify moral responsibility. It is that a man can be said to exercise free will in a morally significant sense only in so far as his chosen act is one of which he is the sole cause or author, and only if—in the straightforward, categorical sense of the phrase—he 'could have chosen otherwise'.

I confess that this answer is in some ways a disconcerting one; disconcerting, because most of us, however objective we are in the actual conduct of our thinking, would *like* to be able to believe that moral responsibility is real: whereas the freedom required for moral responsibility, on the analysis we have given, is certainly far more difficult to establish than the freedom required on the analyses we found ourselves obliged to reject. If, e.g. moral freedom entails only that I could have acted otherwise *if* I had chosen otherwise, there is no real 'problem' about it at all. I am 'free' in the normal case where there is no external obstacle to prevent my translating the alternative choice into action, and not free in other cases. Still less is there a problem if all that moral freedom entails is that I could have acted otherwise *if* I had been a differently constituted person, or been in different circumstances. Clearly I am *always* free in *this* sense of freedom. But, as I have argued, these so-called 'freedoms' fail to give us the pre-conditions of moral responsibility, and hence leave the freedom of the traditional free-will problem, the freedom that people are really concerned about, precisely where it was.

Another interpretation of freedom which I am bound to reject on the same general ground, i.e. that it is just not the kind of freedom that is relevant to moral responsibility, is the old idealist view which identifies the *free* will with the *rational* will; the rational will in its turn being identified with the will which wills the moral law in whole-hearted, single-minded obedience to it. This view is still worth at least a passing mention, if only because it has recently been resurrected in an interesting work by Professor A.E. Teale.[3] Moreover, I cannot but feel a certain nostalgic tenderness for a view in which I myself was (so to speak) philosophically cradled. The almost apostolic fervour with which my revered nursing-mother, the late Sir Henry Jones, was wont to impart it to his charges, and, hardly less, his ill-concealed scorn for ignoble natures (like my own) which still hankered after a free will in the old 'vulgar' sense, are vividly recalled for me in Professor Teale's stirring pages.

The true interpretation of free will, according to Professor Teale, the interpretation to which Kant, despite occasional back-slidings, adhered in his better moments, is that 'the will is free in the degree that it is informed and disciplined by the moral principle'.[4]

Now this is a perfectly intelligible sense of the word 'free'—or at any rate it can be made so with a little explanatory comment which Professor Teale well supplies but for which there is here no space. But clearly it is a very different sort of freedom from that which is at issue in the traditional problem of free will. This idealist 'freedom' sponsored by Teale belongs, on his own showing, only to the self in respect of its *good* willing. The freedom with which the traditional problem is concerned, inasmuch as it is the freedom presupposed by moral responsibility, must belong to the self in respect of its *bad*, no less than its *good*, willing. It is, in fact, the freedom to decide between genuinely open alternatives of good and bad willing.

Professor Teale, of course, is not unaware that the freedom he favours differs from freedom as traditionally understood. He recognises the traditional concept under its Kantian title of 'elective' freedom. But he leaves the reader in no kind of doubt about his disbelief in both the reality and the value of this elective freedom to do, or forbear from doing, one's duty.

The question of the reality of elective freedom I shall be dealing with shortly; and it will occupy us to the end of the lecture. At the moment I am concerned only with its value, and with the rival view that all that matters for the moral life is the 'rational' freedom which a man has in the degree that his will is 'informed and disciplined by the moral principle'. I confess that to myself the verdict on the rival view seems plain and inescapable. No amount of verbal ingenuity or argumentative convolutions can obscure the fact that it is in flat contradiction to the implications of moral responsibility. The point at issue is really perfectly straightforward. If, as this idealist theory maintains, my acting in defiance of what I deem to be my duty is not a 'free' act in *any* sense, let alone in the sense that 'I could have acted otherwise', then I cannot be morally blameworthy, and that is all there is to it. Nor, for that matter, is the idealist entitled to say that I am morally praiseworthy if I act dutifully; for although that act *is* a 'free' act in the idealist sense, it is on his own avowal not free in the sense that 'I could have acted otherwise'.

It seems to me idle, therefore, to pretend that if one has to give up freedom in the traditional elective sense one is not giving up anything important. What we are giving up is, quite simply, the reality of the moral life. I recognise that to a certain type of religious nature (as well as, by an odd meeting of extremes, to a certain type of secular nature) that does not appear to matter so very much; but, for myself, I still think it sufficiently important to make it well worthwhile enquiring seriously into the possibility that the elective freedom upon which it rests may be real after all.

That brings me to the second, and more constructive, part of this lecture. From now on I shall be considering whether it is reasonable to believe that man does in fact possess a free will of the kind specified in the first part of the lecture. If so, just how and where within the complex fabric of the volitional life are we to locate it?— for although free will must presumably belong (if anywhere) to the volitional side of human experience, it is pretty clear from the way in which we have been forced to define it that it does not pertain simply to volition as such; not even to all volitions that are commonly dignified with the name of 'choices'. It has been, I think, one of the more serious impediments to profitable discussion of the Free Will problem that Libertarians and Determinists alike have so often failed to appreciate the comparatively narrow area within which the free will that is necessary to 'save' morality is required to operate. It goes without saying that this failure has been gravely prejudicial to the case for Libertarianism. I attach a good deal of importance, therefore, to the problem of locating free will correctly within the volitional orbit. Its solution forestalls and annuls, I believe, some of the more tiresome clichés of Determinist criticism.

We saw earlier that Common Sense's practice of 'making allowances' in its moral judgments for the influence of heredity and environment indicates Common Sense's conviction, both that a just moral judgment must discount determinants of choice over which the agent has no control, and also (since it still accepts moral judgments as legitimate) that *something* of moral relevance survives which can be regarded as genuinely self-originated. We are now to try to discover what this 'something' is. And I think we may still usefully take Common Sense as our guide. Suppose one asks the ordinary intelligent citizen *why* he deems it proper to make allowances for X, whose heredity and/or environment are unfortunate. He will tend to reply, I think, in some such terms as these: that X has more and stronger temptations to deviate from what is right than Y or Z, who are normally circumstanced, so that he must put forth a *stronger moral effort* if he is to achieve the same level of external conduct. The intended implication seems to be that X is just as morally praiseworthy as Y or Z *if* he exerts an equivalent moral effort, even though he may not thereby achieve an equal success in conforming his will to the 'concrete demands' of duty. And this implies, again, Common Sense's belief that *in moral effort* we have something for which a man is responsible *without qualification*, something that is *not* affected by heredity and environment but depends *solely* upon the self itself.

Now in my opinion Common Sense has here, in principle, hit upon the one and only defensible answer. Here, and here alone, so far as I can see, in the act of deciding whether to put forth or withhold the moral effort required to resist temptation and rise to duty, is to be found an act which is free in the sense required for moral responsibility; an act of which the self is sole author, and of which it is true to say that 'it could be' (or, after the event, 'could have been') 'otherwise'. Such is the thesis which we shall now try to establish.

The species of argument appropriate to the establishment of a thesis of this sort should fall, I think, into two phases. First, there should be a consideration of the evidence of the moral agent's own inner experience. What *is* the act of moral decision, and what does it imply, from the standpoint of the actual participant? Since there is no way of knowing the act of moral decision—or for that matter any other form of activity—except by actual participation in it, the evidence of the subject, or agent, is on an issue of this kind of palmary importance. It can hardly, however, be taken as in itself conclusive. For even if that evidence should be overwhelmingly to the effect that moral decision does have the characteristics required by moral freedom, the question is bound to be raised—and in view of considerations from other quarters pointing in a contrary direction is *rightly* raised—Can we *trust* the evidence of inner experience? That brings us to what will be the second phase of the argument. We shall have to go on to show, if we are to make good our case, that the extraneous considerations so often supposed to be fatal to the belief in moral freedom are in fact innocuous to it.

In the light of what was said in the last lecture ["Self-Activity and Its Modes"] about the self's experience of moral decision as a *creative* activity, we may perhaps be absolved from developing the first phase of the argument at any great length. The appeal is throughout to one's own experience in the actual taking of the moral decision in the situation of moral temptation. 'Is it possible', we must ask, 'for anyone so circumstanced to disbelieve that he could be deciding otherwise?' The answer is surely not in doubt. When we decide to exert moral effort to resist a temptation, we feel quite certain that we *could* withhold the effort; just as, if we decide to withhold the effort and yield to our desires, we feel quite certain that we *could* exert it—otherwise we should not blame ourselves afterwards for having succumbed. It may be, indeed, that this conviction is mere self-delusion. But that is not at the moment our concern. It is enough at present to establish that the act of deciding to exert or to withhold moral effort, as we know it from the inside in actual moral living, belongs to the category of acts which 'could have been otherwise'.

Mutatis mutandis, the same reply is forthcoming if we ask, 'Is it possible for the moral agent in the taking of his decision to disbelieve that he is the *sole* author of that decision?' Clearly he cannot disbelieve that it is *he* who takes the decision. That, however, is not in itself sufficient to enable him, on reflection, to regard himself as *solely* responsible for the act. For his 'character' as so far formed might conceivably be a factor in determining it, and no one can suppose that the constitution of his 'character' is uninfluenced by circumstances of heredity and environment with which *he* has nothing to do. But as we pointed out in the last lecture, the very essence of the moral decision as it is experienced is that it is a decision whether or not to *combat* our strongest desire, and our strongest desire is the expression in the situation of our character as so far formed. Now clearly our character cannot be a factor in determining the decision whether or not to *oppose* our character. I think we are entitled to say, therefore, that the act of moral decision is one in which the self is for itself not merely 'author' but 'sole author'.

We may pass on, then, to the second phase of our constructive argument; and this will demand more elaborate treatment. Even if a moral agent *qua* making a moral decision in the situation of 'temptation' cannot help believing that he has free will in the sense at issue—a moral freedom between real alternatives, between genuinely open possibilities—are there, nevertheless, objections to a freedom of this kind so cogent that we are bound to distrust the evidence of 'inner experience'?

I begin by drawing attention to a simple point whose significance tends, I think, to be underestimated. If the phenomenological analysis we have offered is substantially correct, no one while functioning as a moral agent can help believing that he enjoys free will. Theoretically he may be completely convinced by Determinist arguments, but when actually confronted with a personal situation of conflict between duty and desire he is quite certain that it lies with him here and now whether or not he will rise to duty. It follows that if Determinists could produce convincing theoretical arguments against a free will of this kind, the awkward predicament would ensue that man has to deny as a theoretical being what he has to assert as a practical being. Now I think the Determinist ought to be a good deal more worried about this than he usually is. He seems to imagine that a strong case on general theoretical grounds is enough to prove that the 'practical' belief in free will, even if inescapable for us as practical beings, is mere illusion. But in fact it proves nothing of the sort. There is no reason whatever why a belief that we find ourselves obliged to hold *qua* practical beings should be required to give way before a belief which we find ourselves obliged to hold *qua* theoretical beings; or, for that matter, *vice versa*. All that the theoretical arguments of Determinism can prove, unless they are reinforced by a refutation of the phenomenological analysis that supports Libertarianism, is that there is a radical conflict between the theoretical and the practical sides of man's nature, an antinomy at the very heart of the self. And this is a state of affairs with which no one can easily rest satisfied. I think therefore that the Determinist ought to concern himself a great deal more than he does with phenomenological analysis, in order to show, if he can, that the assurance of free will is not really an inexpugnable element in man's practical consciousness. There is just as much obligation upon him, convinced though he may be of the soundness of his theoretical arguments, to expose the errors of the Libertarian's phenomenological analysis, as there is upon us, convinced though we may be of the soundness of the Libertarian's phenomenological analysis, to expose the errors of the Determinist's theoretical arguments.

However, we must at once begin the discharge of our own obligation. The rest of this lecture will be devoted to trying to show that the arguments which seem to carry the most weight with Determinists are, to say the least of it, very far from compulsive.

Fortunately, a good many of the arguments which at an earlier time in the history of philosophy would have been strongly urged against us make almost no appeal to the bulk of philosophers today, and we may here pass them by. That applies to any criticism of 'open possibilities' based on a metaphysical theory about the nature of the universe as a whole. Nobody today *has* a metaphysical theory about the nature of the universe as a whole! It applies also, with almost equal force, to criticisms based upon the universality of causal law as a supposed postulate of science. There have always been, in my opinion, sound philosophic reasons for doubting the validity, as distinct from the convenience, of the causal postulate in its universal form, but at the present time, when scientists themselves are deeply divided about the need for postulating causality even within their own special field, we shall do better to concentrate our attention upon criticisms which are more confidently advanced. I propose to ignore also, on different grounds, the type of criticism of free will that is sometimes advanced from the side of religion, based upon religious postulates of Divine Omnipotence and Omniscience. So far as I can see, a postulate of human freedom is every bit as necessary to meet certain religious demands (e.g. to make sense of the 'conviction of sin'), as postulates of Divine Omniscience and Omnipotence are to meet certain other religious demands. If so, then it can hardly be argued that religious experience as such tells more strongly against than for the position we are defending; and we may be satisfied, in the present context, to leave the matter there. It will be more profitable to discuss certain arguments which contemporary philosophers do think important, and which recur with a somewhat monotonous regularity in the literature of anti-Libertarianism.

These arguments can, I think, be reduced in principle to no more than two: first, the argument from predictability; second, the argument from the alleged meaninglessness of an act supposed to be the self's act and yet not an expression of the self's character. Contemporary criticism of free will seems to me to consist almost exclusively of variations on these two themes. I shall deal with each in turn.

On the first we touched in passing at an earlier stage. Surely it is beyond question (the critic urges) that when we know a person intimately we can foretell with a high degree of accuracy how he will respond to at least a large number of practical situations. One feels safe in predicting that one's dog-loving friend will not use his boot to repel the little mongrel that comes yapping at his heels; or again that one's wife will not pass with incurious eyes (or indeed pass at all) the new hat shop in the city. So to behave would not be (as we say) 'in character'. But, so the criticism runs, you with your doctrine of 'genuinely open possibilities', of a free will by which the self can diverge from its own character, remove all rational basis from such prediction. You require us to make the absurd supposition that the success of countless predictions of the sort in the past has been mere matter of chance. If you *really* believed in your theory, you would not be surprised if tomorrow your friend with the notorious horror of strong drink should suddenly exhibit a passion for whisky and soda, or if your friend whose taste for reading has hitherto been satisfied with the sporting columns of the newspapers should be discovered on a fine Saturday afternoon poring over the works of Hegel. But of course you *would* be surprised. Social life would be sheer chaos if there were not well-grounded social expectations; and social life is not sheer chaos. Your theory is hopelessly wrecked upon obvious facts.

Now whether or not this criticism holds good against some versions of Libertarian theory I need not here discuss. It is sufficient if I can make it clear that against the version advanced in this lecture, according to which free will is localised in a relatively narrow field of operation, the criticism has no relevance whatsoever.

Let us remind ourselves briefly of the setting within which, on our view, free will functions. There is X, the course which we believe we ought to follow, and Y, the course towards which we feel our desire is strongest. The freedom which we ascribe to the agent is the freedom to put forth or refrain from putting forth the moral effort required to resist the pressure of desire and do what he thinks he ought to do.

But then there is surely an immense range of practical situations—covering by far the greater part of life—in which there is no question of a conflict within the self between what he most desires to do and what he thinks he ought to do? Indeed such conflict is a comparatively rare phenomenon for the majority of men. Yet over that whole vast range there is nothing whatever in our version of Libertarianism to prevent our agreeing that character determines conduct. In the absence, real or supposed, of any 'moral' issue, what a man chooses will be simply that course which, after such reflection as seems called for, he deems most likely to bring him what he most strongly desires; and that is the same as to say the course to which his present character inclines him.

Over by far the greater area of human choices, then, our theory offers no more barrier to successful prediction on the basis of character than any other theory. For where there is no clash of strongest desire with duty, the free will we are defending has no business. There is just nothing for it to do.

But what about the situations—rare enough though they may be—in which there is this clash and in which free will does therefore operate? Does our theory entail that there, at any rate, as the critic seems to suppose, 'anything may happen'?

Not by any manner of means. In the first place, and by the very nature of the case, the range of the agent's possible choices is bounded by what he thinks he ought to do on the one hand, and what he most strongly desires on the other. The freedom claimed for him is a freedom of decision to make or withhold the effort required to do what he thinks he ought to do. There is no question of a freedom to act in some 'wild' fashion, out of all relation to his characteristic beliefs and desires. This so-called 'freedom of caprice', so often charged against the Libertarian, is, to put it bluntly, a sheer figment of the critic's imagination, with no *habitat* in serious Libertarian theory. Even in situations where free will does come into play it is perfectly possible, on a view like ours, given the appropriate knowledge of a man's character, to predict within certain limits how he will respond.

But 'probable' prediction in such situations can, I think, go further than this. It is obvious that where desire and duty are at odds, the felt 'gap' (as it were) between the two may vary enormously in breadth in different cases. The moderate drinker and the chronic tippler may each want another glass, and each deem it his duty to abstain, but the felt gap between desire and duty in the case of the former is trivial beside the great gulf which is felt to separate them in the case of the latter. Hence it will take a far harder moral effort for the tippler than for the moderate drinker to achieve the same external result of abstention. So much is matter of common agreement. And we are entitled, I think, to take it into account in prediction, on the simple principle that the harder the moral effort required to resist desire the less likely it is to occur. Thus in the example taken, most people would predict that the tippler will very probably succumb to his desires, whereas there is a reasonable likelihood that the moderate drinker will make the comparatively slight effort needed to resist them. So long as the prediction does not pretend to more than a measure of probability, there is nothing in our theory which would disallow it.

I claim, therefore, that the view of free will I have been putting forward is consistent with predictability of conduct on the basis of character over a very wide field indeed. And I make the further claim that that field will cover all the situations in life concerning which there is any empirical evidence that successful prediction is possible.

Let us pass on to consider the second main line of criticism. This is, I think, much the more illuminating of the two, if only because it compels the Libertarian to make explicit certain concepts which are indispensable to him, but which, being desperately hard to state clearly, are apt not to be stated at all. The critic's fundamental point might be stated somewhat as follows:

'Free will as you describe it is completely unintelligible. On your own showing no *reason* can be given, because there just is no reason, why a man decides to exert rather than to withhold moral effort, or *vice versa*. But such an act—or more properly, such an "occurrence"—it is nonsense to speak of as an act of a *self*. If there is nothing in the self's character to which it is, even in principle, in any way traceable, the self has nothing to do with it. Your so-called "freedom", therefore, so far from supporting the self's moral responsibility, destroys it as surely as the crudest Determinism could do'.

If we are to discuss this criticism usefully, it is important, I think, to begin by getting clear about two different senses of the word 'intelligible'.

If, in the first place, we mean by an 'intelligible' act one whose occurrence is in principle capable of being inferred, since it follows necessarily from something (though we may not know in fact from what), then it is certainly true that the Libertarian's free will is unintelligible. But that is only saying, is it not, that the Libertarian's 'free' act is not an act which follows necessarily from something! This can hardly rank as a *criticism* of Libertarianism. It is just a description of it. That there can be nothing unintelligible in *this* sense is precisely what the Determinist has got to *prove*.

Yet it is surprising how often the critic of Libertarianism involves himself in this circular mode of argument. Repeatedly it is urged against the Libertarian, with a great air of triumph, that on his view he can't say *why* I now decide to rise to duty, or now decide to follow my strongest desire in defiance of duty. Of course he can't. If he could he wouldn't *be* a Libertarian. To 'account for' a 'free' act is a contradiction in terms. A free will is *ex hypothesi* the sort of thing of which the request for an *explanation* is absurd. The assumption that an explanation must be in principle possible for the act of moral decision deserves to rank as a classic example of the ancient fallacy of 'begging the question'.

But the critic usually has in mind another sense of the word 'unintelligible'. He is apt to take it for granted that an act which is unintelligible in the *above* sense (as the morally free act of the Libertarian undoubtedly is) is unintelligible in the *further* sense that we can attach no meaning to it. And this is an altogether more serious matter. If it could really be shown that the Libertarian's 'free will' were unintelligible in this sense of being meaningless, that, for myself at any rate, would be the end of the affair. Libertarianism would have been conclusively refuted.

But it seems to me manifest that this can *not* be shown. The critic has allowed himself, I submit, to become the victim of a widely accepted but fundamentally vicious assumption. He has assumed that whatever is meaningful must exhibit its meaningfulness to those who view it from the standpoint of external observation. Now if one chooses thus to limit one's self to the role of external observer, it is, I think, perfectly true that one can attach no meaning to an act which is the act of something we call a self and yet follows from nothing in that self's character. But then *why should we* so limit ourselves, when what is under consideration is a subjective activity? For the apprehension of subjective acts there is *another* standpoint available, that of *inner experience*, of the practical consciousness in its actual functioning. If our free will should turn out to be something to which we can attach a meaning from *this* standpoint, no more is required. And no more ought to be expected. For I must repeat that only from the inner standpoint of living experience *could* anything of the nature of 'activity' be directly grasped. Observation from without is in the nature of the case impotent to apprehend the active *qua* active. We can from without observe sequences of states. If into these we read activity (as we sometimes do), this can only be on the basis of what we discern in ourselves from the inner standpoint. It follows that if anyone insists upon taking his criterion of the meaningful simply from the standpoint of external observation, he is really deciding in advance of the evidence that the notion of activity, and *a fortiori* the notion of a free will, is 'meaningless'. He looks for the free act through a medium which is in the nature of the case incapable of revealing it, and then, because inevitably he doesn't find it, he declares that it doesn't exist!

But if, as we surely ought in this context, we adopt the inner standpoint, then (I am suggesting) things appear in a totally different light. From the inner standpoint, it seems to me plain, there is no difficulty whatever in attaching meaning to an act which is the self's act and which nevertheless does not follow from the self's character. So much I claim has been established by the phenomenological analysis, in this and the previous lecture, of the act of moral decision in face of moral temptation. It is thrown into particularly clear relief where the moral decision is to make the moral effort required to rise to duty. For the very function of moral effort, as it appears to the agent engaged in the act, is to enable the self to act against the line of least resistance, against the line to which his character as so far formed most strongly inclines him. But if the self is thus conscious here of *combating* his formed character, he surely cannot possibly suppose that the act, although his own act, *issues from* his formed character? I submit, therefore, that the self knows very well indeed—from the inner standpoint—what is meant by an act which is the self's act and which nevertheless does not follow from the self's *character*.

What this implies—and it seems to me to be an implication of cardinal importance for any theory of the self that aims at being more than superficial—is that the nature of the self is for itself something more than just its character as so far formed. The 'nature' of the self and what we commonly call the 'character' of the self are by no means the same thing, and it is utterly vital that they should not be confused. The 'nature' of the self comprehends, but is not without remainder reducible to, its 'character'; it must, if we are to be true to the testimony of our experience of it, be taken as including *also* the authentic creative power of fashioning and re-fashioning 'character'.

The misguided, and as a rule quite uncritical, belittlement, of the evidence offered by inner experience has, I am convinced, been responsible for more bad argument by the opponents of Free Will than has any other single factor. How often, for example, do we find the Determinist critic saying, in effect, '*Either* the act follows necessarily upon precedent states, *or* it is a mere matter of chance and accordingly of no moral significance'. The disjunction is invalid for it does not exhaust the possible alternatives. It seems to the critic to do so only because he *will* limit himself to the standpoint which is proper, and indeed alone possible, in dealing with the physical world, the standpoint of the external observer. If only he would allow himself to assume the standpoint which is not merely proper for, but necessary to, the apprehension of subjective activity, the inner standpoint of the practical consciousness in its actual functioning, he would find himself obliged to recognise the falsity of his disjunction. Reflection upon the act of moral decision as apprehended from the inner standpoint would force him to recognise a *third* possibility, as remote from chance as from necessity, that, namely, of *creative activity*, in which (as I have ventured to express it) nothing determines the act save the agent's doing of it.

There we must leave the matter. But as this lecture has been, I know, somewhat densely packed, it may be helpful if I conclude by reminding you, in bald summary, of the main things I have been trying to say. Let me set them out in so many successive theses.

1. The freedom which is at issue in the traditional Free Will problem is the freedom which is presupposed in moral responsibility.
2. Critical reflection upon carefully considered attributions of moral responsibility reveals that the only freedom that will do is a freedom which pertains to inner acts of choice, and that these acts must be acts (*a*) of which the self is *sole* author, and (*b*) which the self could have performed otherwise.
3. From phenomenological analysis of the situation of moral temptation we find that the self as engaged in this situation is inescapably convinced that it possesses a freedom of precisely the specified kind, located in the decision to exert or withhold the moral effort needed to rise to duty where the pressure of its desiring nature is felt to urge it in a contrary direction.
4. Passing to the question of the *reality* of this moral freedom which the moral agent believes himself to possess, we argued:
5. Of the two types of Determinist criticism which seem to have most influence today, that based on the predictability of much human behaviour fails to touch a Libertarianism which confines the area of free will as above indicated. Libertarianism so understood is compatible with all the predictability that the empirical facts warrant. And:
6. The second main type of criticism, which alleges the 'meaninglessness' of an act which is the self's act and which is yet not determined by the self's character, is based on a failure to appreciate that the standpoint of inner experience is not only legitimate but indispensable where what is at issue is the reality and nature of a subjective activity. The creative act of moral decision is inevitably meaningless to the mere external observer; but from the inner standpoint it is as real, and as significant, as anything in human experience.

NOTES

1. Reprinted in Ethics and the History of Philosophy, Selected Essays.
2. I have explained the grounds for my dissent from Broad's final conclusion on pp. 27 ft. of *In Defence of Free Will* (Jackson Son & Co., 1938).
3. Kantian Ethics.
4. op. cit., p. 261.

THE FREEDOM OF THE WILL*

John Stuart Mill

Sir William Hamilton's view of the controversy is peculiar, but harmonizes with his Philosophy of the Conditioned, which seems indeed to have been principally suggested to him by the supposed requirements of this question. He is of opinion that Free-will and Necessity are both inconceivable. Free-will, because it supposes volitions to originate without cause: because it affirms an absolute commencement, which, as we are aware, our author deems it impossible for the human mind to conceive. On the other hand, the mind is equally unable to conceive an infinite regress; a chain of causation going back to all eternity. Both the one and the other theory thus involve difficulties insurmountable by the human faculties. But, as Sir W. Hamilton has so often told us, the inconceivability of a thing by us, is no proof that it is objectively impossible by the laws of the universe; on the contrary, it often happens that both sides of an alternative are alike incomprehensible to us, while from their nature we are certain that the one or the other must be true. Such an alternative, according to Sir W. Hamilton, exists between the conflicting doctrines of Free-will and Necessity. By the law of Excluded Middle, one or other of them must be true; and inconceivability, as common to both, not operating more against one than against the other, does not operate against either. The balance, therefore, must turn in favor of the side for which there is positive evidence in favor of Free-will we have the distinct testimony of consciousness; perhaps directly, though of this he speaks with some appearance of doubt;[1] but at all events, indirectly, freedom being implied in the consciousness of moral responsibility. As there is no corresponding evidence in favor of the other theory, the Free-will doctrine must prevail. "How[2] the will can

*From John Stuart Mill, "The Freedom of the Will," in *An Examination of Sir William Hamilton's Philosophy*, vol. II. (New York: Holt, Rinehart and Winston, 1874), 272–290.

possibly be free must remain to us, under the present limitation of our faculties, wholly incomprehensible. We cannot conceive absolute commencement; we cannot, therefore, conceive a free volition. But as little can we conceive the alternative on which liberty is denied, on which necessity is affirmed. And in favor of our moral nature, the fact that we are free is given us in the consciousness of an uncompromising law of Duty in the consciousness of our moral accountability; and this fact of liberty cannot be redargued on the ground that it is incomprehensible, for the doctrine of the Conditioned proves, against the necessitarian, that something may, nay, must, be true, of which the mind is wholly unable to construe to itself the possibility, whilst it shows that the objection of incomprehensibility applies no less to the doctrine of fatalism than to the doctrine of moral freedom."

The inconceivability of the Free-will doctrine is maintained by our author, not only on the general ground just stated, of our incapacity to conceive an absolute commencement, but on the further and special ground, that the will is determined by motives. In rewriting the preceding passage for the Appendix to his "Discussions," he made the following addition to it:[3] "A determination by motives cannot, to our understanding, escape from necessitation. Nay, were we even to admit as true, what we cannot think as possible, still the doctrine of a motiveless volition would be only casualism; and the free acts of an indifferent, are, morally and rationally, as worthless as the preordered passions of a determined will.[4] *How*, therefore, I repeat, moral liberty is possible in man or God, we are utterly unable speculatively to understand. But . . . the scheme of freedom is not more inconceivable than the scheme of necessity. For whilst fatalism is a recoil from the more obtrusive inconceivability of an *absolute* commencement, on the fact of which commencement the doctrine of liberty proceeds, the fatalist is shown to overlook the equal, but less obtrusive, inconceivability of an *infinite* non-commencement, on the assertion of which non-commencement his own doctrine of necessity must ultimately rest." It rests on no such thing, if he believes in a First Cause, which a Necessitarian may. What is more, even if he does not believe in a First Cause, he makes no "assertion of non-commencement"; he only declines to make an assertion of commencement; a distinction of which Sir W. Hamilton, of all men, ought to recognize the importance. But to resume the quotation: "As equally unthinkable, the two counter, the two one-sided, schemes are thus theoretically balanced. But, practically, our consciousness of the moral law, which, without a moral liberty in man, would be a mendacious imperative, gives a decisive preponderance to the doctrine of freedom over the doctrine of fate. We are free in act, if we are accountable for our actions."

Sir W. Hamilton is of opinion that both sides are alike unsuccessful in repelling each other's attacks. The arguments against both are, he thinks, to the human faculties, irrefutable. "The champions[5] of the opposite doctrines arc at once resistless in assault and impotent in defense. Each is hewn down, and appears to die under the home thrusts of his adversary; but each again recovers life from the very death of his antagonist, and, to borrow a simile, both are like the heroes in Valhalla, ready in a moment to amuse themselves anew in the same bloodless and interminable conflict. The doctrine of Moral Liberty cannot be made conceivable, for we can only conceive the determined and the relative. As already stated, all that can be done is to show, 1. That, for the *fact* of Liberty, we have immediately or mediately, the evidence of Consciousness; and 2. That there are among the phænomena of mind, many facts which we *must* admit as actual, but of whose possibility we are wholly unable to form any notion. I may merely observe that the fact of *Motion* can be shown to be impossible, on grounds not less strong than those on which it is attempted to disprove the fact of Liberty. These "grounds no less strong" are the mere paralogisms which we examined in a recent chapter, and with regard to which our author showed so surprising a deficiency in the acuteness and subtlety to be expected from the general quality of his mind.

Conformably to these views, Sir W. Hamilton, in his footnotes on Reid, promptly puts an extinguisher on several of that philosopher's arguments against the doctrine of so-called Necessity. When Reid affirms that Motives are not causes—that they may influence to action, but do not act, Sir W. Hamilton observes,[6] "If Motives influence to action, they must co-operate in producing a certain effect upon the agent; and the determination to act, and to act in a certain manner, is that effect. They are thus, on Reid's own view, in this relation, *causes*, and *efficient* causes. It is of no consequence in the argument whether motives be said to determine a man to act, or to influence (that is, to determine) him to determine himself to act."[7] This is one of the neatest specimens in our author's writings of a fallacy cut clean through by a single stroke.

Again, when Reid says that acts are often done without any motive, or when there is no motive for preferring the means used, rather than others by which the same end might have been attained, Sir W. Hamilton asks,[8] "Can we conceive any act of which there was not a sufficient cause or concourse of causes why the man performed it and no other? If not, call this cause, or these concauses, the *motive*, and there is no longer a dispute."

Reid asks, "Is there no such thing as willfulness, caprice, or obstinacy among mankind?" Sir W. Hamilton, *e contra*:[9] "But are not these all tendencies, and fatal tendencies, to act or not to act? By contradistinguishing such tendencies from motives strictly so called, or rational impulses, we do not advance a single step towards rendering liberty comprehensible."

According to Reid, the determination is made by the man, and not by the motive. "But," asks Sir W. Hamilton,[10] "was the *man* determined by no motive to that determination? Was his specific volition to this or to that without a cause? On the supposition that the sum of influences motives, dispositions, and tendencies) to volition A, is equal to 12, and the sum of influences to counter-volition B equal to 8— can we conceive that the determination of volition A should not be necessary?—We can only conceive the volition B to be determined by supposing that the man *creates* (calls from non-existence into existence) a certain supplement of influences. But this creation as actual, or in itself, is inconceivable, and even to conceive the possibility of this inconceivable act, we must suppose some cause by which the man is determined to exert it. We thus, in *thought*, never escape determination and necessity. It will be observed that I do not consider this inability to the *notion*, any disproof of the *fact* of Free-will." Nor is it: but if, as our author so strongly inculcates, "every[11] effort to bring the fact of liberty within the compass of our conceptions only results in the substitution in its place of some more or less disguised form of necessity," it is a strong indication that some form of necessity is the opinion naturally suggested by our collective experience of life.[12]

Sir W. Hamilton having thus, as is often the case (and it is one of the best things he does), saved his opponents the trouble of answering his friends, his doctrine is left resting exclusively on the supports which he has himself provided for it. In examining them, let us place ourselves, in the first instance, completely at his point of view, and concede to him the coequal inconceivability of the conflicting hypotheses, an uncaused commencement, and an infinite regress. But this choice of inconceivabilities is not offered to us in the case of volitions only. We are held, as he not only admits but contends, to the same alternative in all cases of causation whatsoever. But we find our way out of the difficulty, in other cases, in quite a different manner. In the case of every other kind of fact, we do not elect the hypothesis that the event took place without a cause: we accept the other supposition, that of a regress, not indeed to infinity, but either generally into the region of the Unknowable, or back to a Universal Cause, regarding which, as we are only concerned with it in relation to what it preceded, and not as itself preceded by anything, we can afford to make a plain avowal of our ignorance.

Now, what is the reason, which, in the case of all things within the range of our knowledge except volitions, makes us choose this side of the alternative? Why do we, without scruple, register all of them as depending on causes, by which (to use our author's language) they are determined necessarily, though, in believing this, we, according to Sir W. Hamilton, believe as utter an inconceivability as if we supposed them to take place without a cause? Apparently it is because the causation hypothesis, inconceivable as he may think it, possesses the advantage of having experience on its side. And how, or by what evidence, does experience testify to it? Not by disclosing any *nexus* between the cause and the effect, any Sufficient Reason in the cause itself why the effect should follow it. No philosopher now makes this supposition, and Sir W. Hamilton positively disclaims it. What experience makes known, is the fact of an invariable sequence between every event and some special combination of antecedent conditions, in such sort that wherever and whenever that union of antecedents exists, the event does not fail to occur. Any *must* in the case, any necessity, other than the unconditional universality of the fact, we know nothing of. Still, this it posteriori "does," though not confirmed by an it priori "must," decides our choice between the two inconceivables, and leads us to the belief that every event within the phænomenal universe, except human volitions, is determined to take place by a cause. Now, the so-called Necessitarians demand the application of the same rule of judgment to our volitions. They maintain that there is the same evidence for it. They affirm, as a truth of experience, that volitions do, in point of fact, follow determinate moral antecedents with the same uniformity, and (when we have sufficient knowledge of the circumstances) with the same certainty, as physical effects follow their physical causes. These moral antecedents are desires, aversions, habits, and dispositions, combined with outward circumstances suited to call those internal incentives into action. All these again are effects of causes, those of them which are mental being consequences of education, and of other moral and physical influences. This is what Necessitarians affirm: and they court every possible mode in which its truth can be verified. They test it by each person's observation of his own volitions. They test it by each person's observation of the voluntary actions of those with whom he comes into contact; and by the power which every one has of foreseeing actions with a degree of exactness proportioned to his previous experience and knowledge of the agents, and with a certainty often quite equal to that with which we predict the commonest physical events. They test it further, by the statistical results of the observation of human beings acting in numbers sufficient to eliminate the influences which operate only on a few, and which on a large scale neutralize one another, leaving the total result about the same as if the volitions of the whole mass had been affected by such only of the determining causes as were common to them all. In cases of this description the results are as uniform, and may be as accurately foretold, as in any physical inquiries in which the effect depends upon a multiplicity of causes. The cases in which volitions seem too uncertain to admit of being confidently predicted, are those in which our knowledge of the influences antecedently in operation is so incomplete, that with equally imperfect data there would be the same uncertainty in the predictions of the astronomer and the chemist. On these grounds it is contended, that our choice between the conflicting inconceivables should be the same in the case of volitions as of all other phænomena; we must reject equally in both cases the hypothesis of spontaneousness, and consider them all as caused. A volition is a moral effect, which follows the corresponding moral causes as certainly and invariably as physical effects follow their physical causes. Whether it *must* do so, I acknowledge myself to be entirely ignorant, be the phænomenon moral or physical; and I condemn, accordingly, the word Necessity as applied to either case. All I know is, that it always *does*.

This argument from experience Sir W. Hamilton passes unnoticed, but urges, on the opposite side of the question, the argument from Consciousness. We are conscious, he affirms, either of our freedom, or at all events (it is odd that, on this theory, there should be any doubt) of something which implies freedom. If this is true, our internal consciousness tells us one thing, and the whole outward experience of the human race tells another. This is surely a very unfortunate predicament we are in, and a sore trial to the puzzled metaphysician. Philosophy is far from having so easy a business before her as our author thinks: the arbiter Consciousness is by no means invoked to turn the scale between two equally balanced difficulties; on the contrary, she has to sit in judgment between herself and a complete Induction from experience. Consciousness, it will probably be said, is the best evidence; and so it would be, if we were always certain what is Consciousness. But while there are so many varying testimonies respecting this; when Sir W. Hamilton can himself say,[13] "many philosophers have attempted to establish, on the principles of common sense, propositions which are not original data of consciousness, while the original data of consciousness from which these propositions were derived, and to which they owed all their necessity and truth, these same philosophers were (strange to say) not disposed to admit"; when M. Cousin and nearly all Germany find the Infinite and the Absolute in Consciousness, Sir W. Hamilton thinking them utterly repugnant to it; when philosophers, for many generations, fancied that they had Abstract Ideas—that they could conceive a triangle which was neither equilateral, isosceles, nor scalene,[14] which Sir W. Hamilton and all other people now consider to be simply absurd; with all these conflicting opinions respecting the things to which Consciousness testifies, what is the perplexed inquirer to think? Does all philosophy end, as in our author's opinion Hume believed it to do, in a persistent contradiction between one of our mental faculties and another? We shall find there is a solution, which relieves the human mind from this embarrassment: namely, that the question to which experience says yes, and that to which consciousness says no, are different questions.

Let us cross-examine the alleged testimony of consciousness. And, first, it is left in some uncertainty by Sir W. Hamilton whether Consciousness makes only one deliverance on the subject, or two; whether we are conscious only of moral responsibility, in which free-will is implied, or are directly conscious of free-will. In his Lectures, Sir W. Hamilton speaks only of the first. In the notes on Reid, which were written subsequently, he seems to affirm both, but the latter of the two in a doubtful and hesitating manner: so difficult, in reality, does he find it to ascertain with certainty what it is that Consciousness certifies. But as there are many who maintain, with a confidence far greater than his, that we are directly conscious of free-will,[15] it is necessary to examine that question.

To be conscious of free-will, must mean, to be conscious, be-fore I have decided, that I am able to decide either way. Exception may be taken *in limine* to the use of the word consciousness in such an application. Consciousness tells me what I do or feel. But what I am *able* to do, is not a subject of consciousness. Consciousness is not prophetic; we are conscious of what is, not of what will or can be. We never know that we are able to do a thing, except from having done it, or something equal and similar to it. We should not know that we were capable of action at all, if we had never acted. Having acted, we know, as far as that experience reaches, how we are able to act; and this knowledge, when it has become familiar, is often confounded with, and called by the name of, consciousness. But it does not derive any increase of authority from being misnamed; its truth is not supreme over, but depends on, experience. If our so-called consciousness of what we are able to do is not borne out by experience, it is a delusion. It has no title to credence but as an interpretation of experience, and if it is a false interpretation, it must give way.

But this conviction, whether termed consciousness or only belief, that our will is free—what is it? Of what are we convinced? I am told, that whether I decide to do or to abstain, I feel that I could have decided the other way. I ask my consciousness what I do feel, and I find, indeed, that I feel (or am convinced) that I could have chosen the other course *if I had preferred it*; but not that I could have chosen one course while I preferred the other. When I say preferred, I of course include with the thing itself, all that accompanies it. I know that I can, because I know that I often do, elect to do one thing, when I should have preferred another in itself, apart from its consequences, or from a moral law which it violates. And this preference for a thing in itself, abstractedly from its accompaniments, is often loosely described as preference for the thing. It is this unprecise mode of speech which makes it not seem absurd to say that I act in opposition to my preference; that I do one thing when I would rather do another; that my conscience prevails over my desires—as if conscience were not itself a desire—the desire to do right. Take any alternative: say, to murder or not to murder. I am told, that if I elect to murder, I am conscious that I could have elected to abstain: but am I conscious that I could have abstained if my aversion to the crime, and my dread of its consequences, had been weaker than the temptation? If I elect to abstain: in what sense am I conscious that I could have elected to commit the crime? Only if I had desired to commit it with a desire stronger than my horror of murder; not with one less strong. When we think of ourselves hypothetically as having acted otherwise than we did, we always suppose a difference in the antecedents: we picture ourselves as having known something that we did not know, or not known something that we did know; which is a difference in the external motives; or as having desired something, or disliked something, more or less than we did; which is a difference in the internal motives.

I therefore dispute altogether that we are conscious of being able to act in opposition to the strongest present desire or aversion. The difference between a bad and a good man is not that the latter acts in opposition to his strongest desires; it is that his desire to do right, and his aversion to doing wrong, are strong enough to overcome, and in the case of perfect virtue, to silence, any other desire or aversion which may conflict with them. It is because this state of mind is possible to human nature, that human beings are capable of moral government: and moral education consists in subjecting them to the discipline which has most tendency to bring them into this state. The object of moral education is to educate the will: but the will can only be educated through the desires and aversions; by eradicating or weakening such of them as are likeliest to lead to evil; exalting to the highest pitch the desire of right conduct and the aversion to wrong; cultivating all other desires and aversions of which the ordinary operation is auxiliary to right, while discountenancing so immoderate an indulgence of them, as might render them too powerful to be overcome by the moral sentiment, when they chance to be in opposition to it. The other requisites are, a clear intellectual standard of right and wrong, that moral desire and aversion may act in the proper places, and such general mental habits as shall prevent moral considerations from being forgotten or overlooked, in cases to which they are rightly applicable.

Rejecting, then, the figment of a direct consciousness of the freedom of the will, in other words, our ability to will in opposition to our strongest preference; it remains to consider whether, as affirmed by Sir W. Hamilton, a freedom of this kind is implied in what is called our consciousness of moral responsibility. There must be something very plausible in this opinion, since it is shared even by Necessitarians. Many of these—in particular Mr. Owen and his followers—from a recognition of the fact that volitions are effects of causes, have been led to deny human responsibility. I do not mean that they denied moral distinctions. Few persons have had a stronger sense of right and wrong, or been more devoted to the things they deemed right. What they denied was the rightfulness of inflicting punishment. A man's actions, they said, are the result of his character, and he is not the author of his own character. It is made *for* him, not *by* him. There is no justice in punishing him for what he cannot help. We should try to convince or persuade him that he had better act in a different manner; and should educate all, especially the young, in the habits and dispositions which lead to well-doing: though how this is to be effected without any use whatever of punishment as a means of education, is a question they have failed to resolve. The confusion of ideas, which makes the subjection of human volitions to the law of Causation seem inconsistent with accountability, must thus be very natural to the human mind; but this may be said of a thousand errors, and even of some merely verbal fallacies. In the present case there is more than a verbal fallacy, but verbal fallacies also contribute their part.

What is meant by moral responsibility? Responsibility means punishment. When we are said to have the feeling of being morally responsible for our actions, the idea of being punished for them is uppermost in the speaker's mind. But the feeling of liability to punishment is of two kinds. It may mean, expectation that if we act in a certain manner, punishment will actually be inflicted upon us, by our fellow-creatures or by a Supreme Power. Or it may only mean, being conscious that we shall deserve that infliction.

The first of these cannot, in any correct meaning of the term, be designated as a consciousness. If we believe that we shall be punished for doing wrong, it is because the belief has been taught to us by our parents and tutors, or by our religion, or is generally held by those who surround us, or because we have ourselves come to the conclusion by reasoning, or from the experience of life. This is not Consciousness. And, by whatever name it is called, its evidence is not dependent on any theory of the spontaneousness of volition. The punishment of guilt in another world is believed with undoubting conviction by Turkish fatalists, and by professed Christians who are not only Necessitarians, but believe that the majority of mankind were divinely predestined from all eternity to sin and to be punished for sinning. It is not, therefore, the belief that we shall be *made* accountable, which can be deemed to require or presuppose the free-will hypothesis; it is the belief that we ought so to be; that we are justly accountable; that guilt deserves punishment. It is here that the main issue is joined between the two opinions.

In discussing it, there is no need to postulate any theory respecting the nature or criterion of moral distinctions. It matters not, for this purpose, whether the right and wrong of actions depends on the consequences they tend to produce, or on an inherent quality of the actions themselves. It is indifferent whether we are utilitarians or anti-utilitarians; whether our ethics rest on intuition or on experience. It is sufficient if we believe that there is a difference between right and wrong, and a natural reason for preferring the former; that people in general, unless when they expect personal benefit from a wrong, naturally and usually prefer what they think to be right: whether because we are all dependent for what makes existence tolerable, upon the right conduct of other people, while their wrong conduct is a standing menace to our security, or for some more mystical and transcendental reason. Whatever be the cause, we are entitled to assume the fact; and its consequence is, that whoever cultivates a disposition to wrong, places his mind out of sympathy with the rest of his fellow-creatures, and if they are aware of his disposition, becomes a natural object of their active dislike. He not only forfeits the pleasure of their good will, and the benefit of their good offices, except when compassion for the human being is stronger than distaste towards the wrongdoer; but he also renders himself liable to whatever they may think it necessary to do in order to protect themselves against him; which may probably include punishment, as such, and will certainly involve much that is equivalent in its operation on himself. In this way he is certain to be made accountable, at least to his fellow-creatures, through the normal action of their natural sentiments. And it is well worth consideration, whether the practical expectation of being thus called to account, has not a great deal to do with the internal feeling of being accountable; a feeling, assuredly, which is seldom found existing in any strength in the absence of that practical expectation. It is not usually found that Oriental despots, who cannot be called to account by anybody, have much consciousness of being morally accountable. And (what is still more significant) in societies in which caste or class distinctions are really strong—a state so strange to us now, that we seldom realize it in its full force—it is a matter of daily experience that persons may show the strongest sense of moral accountability as regards their equals, who can make them accountable, and not the smallest vestige of a similar feeling towards their inferiors who cannot.

Another fact which it is of importance to keep in view, is, that the highest and strongest sense of the worth of goodness, and the odiousness of its opposite, is perfectly compatible with even the most exaggerated form of Fatalism. Suppose that there were two peculiar breeds of human beings,—one of them so constituted from the beginning, that however educated or treated, nothing could prevent them from always feeling and acting so as to be a blessing to all whom they approached; another, of such original perversity of nature that neither education nor punishment could inspire them with a feeling of duty, or prevent them from being active in evil doing. Neither of these races of human beings would have free-will; yet the former would be honored as demigods, while the latter would be regarded and treated as noxious beasts; not punished perhaps, since punishment would have no effect on them, and it might be thought wrong to indulge the mere instinct of vengeance: but kept carefully at a distance, and killed like other dangerous creatures when there was no other convenient way of being rid of them. We thus see that even under the utmost possible exaggeration of the doctrine of Necessity, the distinction between moral good and evil in conduct would not only subsist, but would stand out in a more marked manner than now, when the good and the wicked, however unlike, are still regarded as of one common nature. . .

NOTES

1. Foot-notes to Reid. pp. 599. 602. 624.

2. Lectures, ii. 412. 413.

3. Appendix to Discussions, pp. 624, 625.

4. To the same effect in another passage: "That, though inconceivable, a motiveless volition would, if conceived, be conceived as morally worthless, only shows our impotence more clearly." (Appendix to Discussions, pp. 614, 615.) And in a footnote to Reid (p. 602). "Is the person an *original undetermined* cause of the determination of his will? If he be not, then he is not a *free agent*, and the scheme of Necessity is admitted. If he be, in the first place, it is impossible to *conceive* the possibility of this; and, in the second, if the fact, though inconceivable, be allowed, it is impossible to see how a cause, undetermined by any motive, can be a rational, moral, and accountable cause."

5. Foot-note on Reid, p. 602.

6. Foot-note on Reid, p. 608.

7. To the same effect see Discussions, Appendix on Causality, p. 614.

8. Foot-note on Reid, p. 609.

9. Foot-note to Reid, p. 610.

10. *Ibid.* p. 611.

11. Lectures, i. 34.

12. So difficult is it to escape from this fact, that Sir W. Hamilton himself says (Lectures, i. 188), "Voluntary conation is a faculty which can only be determined to energy through a pain or pleasure—through an estimate of the relative worth of objects." If I am determined to prefer innocence to the satisfaction of a particular desire, through an estimate of the relative worth of innocence and of the gratification, can this estimate, while unchanged, leave me at liberty to choose the gratification in preference to innocence?

13. Dissertations on Reid, p. 749.

14. "Does it not require," says Locke (Essay on the Human Understanding, Book iv. chap. 7, sect. 9), "some pains and skill to form the general idea of a triangle (which yet is none of the most abstract, comprehensive, and difficult)? for it must be neither oblique nor rectangle, neither equilateral, equicrural, nor scalene; but all and none of these at once. In effect, it is something imperfect, that cannot exist; an idea wherein some parts of several different and inconsistent ideas are put together." Yet this union of contradictory elements such a philosopher as Locke was able to fancy that he conceived. I scarcely know a more striking example of the tendency of the human mind to believe that things can exist separately because they can be separately named; a tendency strong enough, in this case, to make a mind like Locke's believe itself to be conscious of that which by the laws of mind cannot be a subject of consciousness to any one.

15. Mr. Mansel, among others, makes the assertion in the broadest form it is capable of, saying. "In every act of volition, I am fully conscious that I can at this moment act in either of two ways, and that, all the antecedent phenomena being precisely the same, I may determine one way to-day and another way to-morrow." (Prolegomena Logica, p. 152.) Yes, though the antecedent phænomena remain the same; but not if my judgment of the antecedent phænomena remains the same. If my conduct changes, either the external inducements or my estimate of them must have changed.

Mr. Mansel (as I have already observed) goes so far as to maintain that our immediate intuition of Power is given us by the ego producing its own volitions, not by its volitions producing bodily movements (pp. 139, 140, and 151).

BEING AND DOING: FREEDOM*

Jean-Paul Sartre

FREEDOM: THE FIRST CONDITION OF ACTION

It is strange that philosophers have been able to argue endlessly about determinism and free-will, to cite examples in favor of one or the other thesis without ever attempting first to make explicit the structures contained in the very idea of *action*. The concept of an act contains, in fact, numerous subordinate notions which we

---

*From Jean-Paul Sartre. "Being and Doing: Freedom," in *Being and Nothingness*, trans. H. E. Barnes. (New York: Citadel Press, 1956), 433–438; 439–445; 450–451; 553–556. Reprinted with permission of Philosophical Library, New York.)

shall have to organize and arrange in a hierarchy: to act is to modify the *shape* of the world; it is to arrange means in view of an end; it is to produce an organized instrumental complex such that by a series of concatenations and connections the modification effected on one of the links causes modifications throughout the whole series and finally produces an anticipated result. But this is not what is important for us here. We should observe first that an action is on principle *intentional*. The careless smoker who has through negligence caused the explosion of a powder magazine has not *acted*. On the other hand the worker who is charged with dynamiting a quarry and who obeys the given orders has acted when he has produced the expected explosion; he knew what he was doing or, if you prefer, he intentionally realized a conscious project.

This does not mean, of course, that one must foresee all the consequences of his act. The emperor Constantine when he established himself at Byzantium, did not foresee that he would create a center of Greek culture and language, the appearance of which would ultimately provoke a schism in the Christian Church and which would contribute to weakening the Roman Empire. Yet he performed an act just in so far as he realized his project of creating a new residence for emperors in the Orient. Equating the result with the intention is here sufficient for us to be able to speak of action. But if this is the case, we establish that the action necessarily implies as its condition the recognition of a "desideratum"; that is, of an objective lack or again of a *négatité*. The intention of providing a rival for Rome can come to Constantine only through the apprehension of an objective lack: Rome lacks a counterweight; to this still profoundly pagan city ought to be opposed a Christian city which at the moment *is missing*. Creating Constantinople is understood as an act only if first the conception of a new city has preceded the action itself or at least if this conception serves as an organizing theme for all later steps. But this conception cannot be the pure representation of the city as *possible*. It apprehends the city in its essential characteristic, which is to be a *desirable* and not yet realized possible.

This means that from the moment of the first conception of the act, consciousness has been able to withdraw itself from the full world of which it is consciousness and to leave the level of being in order frankly to approach that of non-being. Consciousness in so far as it is considered exclusively in its being, is perpetually referred from being to being and can not find in being any motive for revealing non-being. The imperial system with Rome as its capital functions positively and in a certain real way which can be easily discovered. Will someone say that the taxes are collected badly, that Rome is not secure from invasions, that it does not have the geographical location which is suitable for the capital of a Mediterranean empire which is threatened by barbarians, that its corrupt morals make the spread of the Christian religion difficult? How can anyone fail to see that all these considerations are *negative*; that is, that they aim at what is not, not at what is. To say that sixty per cent of the anticipated taxes have been collected can pass, if need be for a positive appreciation of the situation *such as it* is. To say that they are *badly* collected is to consider the situation across a situation which is posited as an absolute end but which precisely *is not*. To say that the corrupt morals at Rome hinder the spread of Christianity is not to consider this diffusion for what it is; that is, for a propagation at a rate which the reports of the clergy can enable us to determine. It is to posit the diffusion in itself as insufficient; that is, as suffering from a secret nothingness. But it appears as such only if it is surpassed toward a limiting-situation posited a *priori* as a value (for example, toward a certain rate of religious conversions, toward a certain mass morality). This limiting-situation can not be conceived in terms of the simple consideration of the real state of things; for the most beautiful girl in the world can offer only what she *has*, and in the same way the most miserable situation can by itself be designated only as it *is* without any reference to an ideal nothingness.

In so far as man is immersed in the historical situation, he does not even succeed in conceiving of the failures and lacks in a political organization or determined economy; this is not, as is stupidly said, because he "is accustomed to it," but because he apprehends it in its plenitude of being and because he can not even imagine that he can exist in it otherwise. For it is necessary here to reverse common opinion and on the basis of what it is not, to acknowledge the harshness of a situation or the sufferings which it imposes, both of which are motives for conceiving of another state of affairs in which things would be better for everybody. It is on the day that we can conceive of a different state of affairs that a new light falls on our troubles and our suffering and that we *decide* that these are unbearable. A worker in 1830 is capable of revolting if his salary is lowered, for he easily conceives of a situation in which his wretched standard of living would be not as low as the one which is about to be imposed on him. But he does not represent his sufferings to himself as unbearable; he adapts himself to them not through resignation but because he lacks the education and reflection necessary for him to conceive of a social state in which these sufferings would not exist. Consequently *he* does not act. Masters of Lyon following a riot, the workers at Croix-Rousse do not know what to do with their victory; they return home bewildered, and the regular army has no trouble in overcoming them. Their misfortunes do not appear to them "habitual" but rather *natural*; they *are*, that is all, and they constitute the worker's condition. They are not detached; they are not seen in the clear light of day, and consequently they are integrated by the worker with his being. He suffers without considering his suffering and without conferring value upon it. To suffer and to *be* are one and the same for him. His suffering is the pure affective tenor of his non-positional consciousness, but he does not contemplate it. Therefore this suffering can not be in itself a *motive*[1] for his acts. Quite the contrary, it is after he has formed the project of changing the situation that it will appear intolerable to him. This means that he will have had to give himself room, to withdraw in relation to it, and will have to have effected a double nihilation: on the one hand, he must posit an ideal state of affairs as a pure *present* nothingness; on the other hand, he must posit the actual situation as nothingness in relation to this state of affairs. He will have to conceive of a happiness attached to his class as a pure possible—that is, presently as a certain nothingness—and on the other hand, he will return to the present situation in order to illuminate it in the light of this nothingness and in order to nihilate it in turn by declaring: "I *am not* happy."

Two important consequences result. (1) No factual state whatever it may be (the political and economic structure of society, the psychological "state," *etc.*) is capable by itself of motivating any act whatsoever. For an act is a projection of the for-itself toward what is not, and what is can in no way determine by itself what is not. (2) No factual state can determine consciousness to apprehend it as a *négatité* or as a lack. Better yet no factual state can determine consciousness to define it and to circumscribe it since, as we have seen, Spinoza's statement, "Omnis determinatio est negation," remains profoundly true. Now every action has for its express condition not only the discovery of a state of affairs as "lacking in *i.e.*, as a *négatité*—but also, and before all else, the constitution of the state of things under consideration into an isolated system. There is a factual state—satisfying or not—only by means of the nihilating power of the for-itself. But this power of nihilation can not be limited to realizing a simple *withdrawal* in relation to the world. In fact in so far as consciousness is invested" by being, in so far as it simply suffers what is, it must be included in being. It is the organized form—worker-finding-his-suffering-natural—which must be surmounted and denied in order for it to be able to form the object of a revealing contemplation. This means evidently that it is by a pure wrenching away from himself and the world that the worker can posit his suffering as unbearable suffering and consequently can *make of it the motive* for his revolutionary action. This implies for consciousness the permanent possibility of effecting a rupture with its own past, of wrenching itself away from its past so as to be able to consider it in the light of a non-being and so as to be able to confer on it the meaning which *it has* in terms of the project of a meaning which it *does not have*. Under no circumstances can the past in any way by itself produce *an act*; that is, the positing of an end which turns back upon itself so as to illuminate it. This is what Hegel caught sight of when he wrote that "the mind is the negative," although he seems not to have remembered this when he came to presenting his own theory of action and of freedom. In fact as soon as one attributes to consciousness this negative power with respect to the world and itself, as soon as the nihilation forms an integral part of the *positing* of an end, we must recognize that the indispensable and fundamental condition of all action is the freedom of the acting being.

Thus at the outset we can see what is lacking in those tedious discussions between determinists and the proponents of free will. The latter are concerned to find cases of decision for which there exists no prior cause, or deliberations concerning two opposed acts which are equally possible and possess causes (and motives) of exactly the same weight. To which the determinists may easily reply that there is no action without a *cause* and that the most insignificant gesture (raising the right hand rather than the left hand, *etc.*) refers to causes and motives which confer its meaning upon it. Indeed the case could not be otherwise since every action must be *intentional*; each action must, in fact, have an end, and the end in turn is referred to a cause. Such indeed is the unity of the three temporal ekstases; the end or temporalization of my future implies a cause (or motive); that is, it points toward my past, and the present is the upsurge of the act. To speak of an act without a cause is to speak of an act which would lack the intentional structure of every act; and the proponents of free will by searching for it on the level of the act which is in the process of being performed can only end up by rendering the act absurd. But the determinists in turn are weighing the scale by stopping their investigation with the mere designation of the cause and motive. The essential question in fact lies beyond the complex organization "cause-intention-act-end"; indeed we ought to ask how a cause (or motive) can be constituted as such.

Now we have just seen that if there is no act without a cause, this is not in the sense that we can say that there is no phenomenon without a cause. In order to be a *cause*, the *cause* must be *experienced* as such. Of course this does not mean that it is to be thematically conceived and made explicit as in the case of deliberation. But at the very least it means that the for-itself must confer on it its value as cause or motive. And, as we have seen, this constitution of the cause as such can not refer to another real and positive existence; that is, to a prior cause. For otherwise the very nature of the act as engaged intentionally in non-being would disappear. The motive is understood only by the end; that is, by the non-existent. It is therefore in itself a *négatité*. If I accept a niggardly salary it is doubtless because of fear; and fear is a motive. But it is *fear of dying from starvation*; that is, this fear has meaning only outside itself in an end ideally posited, which is the preservation of a life which I apprehend as "in danger." And this fear is understood in turn only in relation to the *value which I* implicitly give to this life; that is, it is referred to that hierarchal system of ideal objects which are values. Thus the motive makes itself understood as what it is by means of the ensemble of beings which "are not," by ideal existences, and by the future. Just as the future turns back upon the present and the past in order to elucidate them, so it is the ensemble of my projects which turns back in order to confer upon the *motive* its structure as a motive. It is only because I escape the in-itself by nihilating myself toward my possibilities that this in-itself can take on value as cause or motive. Causes and motives have meaning only inside a projected ensemble which is precisely an ensemble of non-existents. And this ensemble is ultimately myself as transcendence; it is Me in so far as I have to be myself outside of myself.

If we recall the principle which we established earlier—namely that it is the apprehension of a revolution as possible which gives to the workman's suffering its value as a motive—we must thereby conclude that it is by fleeing a situation toward our possibility of changing it that we organize this situation into complexes of causes and motives. The nihilation by which we achieve a withdrawal in relation to the situation is the same as the ekstasis by which we project ourselves toward a modification of this situation. The result is that it is in fact impossible to find an act without a motive but that this does not mean that we must conclude that the motive causes the act; the motive is an integral part of the act. For as the resolute project toward a change is not distinct from the act, the motive, the act, and the end are all constituted in a single upsurge. Each of these three structures claims the two others as its meaning. But the organized totality of the three is no longer explained by any particular structure, and its upsurge as the pure temporalizing nihilation of the in-itself is one with freedom. It is the act which decides its ends and its motives, and the act is the expression of freedom.

In our attempt to reach to the heart of freedom we may be helped by the few observations which we have made on the subject in the course of this work and which we must summarize here . . . we established the fact that if negation comes into the world through human-reality, the latter must be a being who can realize a nihilating rupture with the world and with himself, and we established that the permanent possibility of this rupture is the same as freedom. But on the other hand, we stated that this permanent possibility of nihilating what I am in the form of "having-been" implies for man a particular type of existence. We were able then to determine by means of analyses like that of bad faith that human reality is its own nothingness. For the for-itself, to be is to nihilate the in-itself which it is. Under these conditions freedom can be nothing other than this nihilation. It is through this that the for-itself escapes its being as its essence; it is through this that the for-itself is always something other than what can be said of it. For in the final analysis the for-itself is the one which escapes this very denomination, the one which is already beyond the name which is given to it, beyond the property which is recognized in it. To say that the for-itself has to be what it is, to say that it is what it is not while not being what it is, to say that in it existence precedes and conditions essence or inversely according to Hegel, that for it "Wesen ist was gewesen ist"—all this is to say one and the same thing: to be aware that man is free. Indeed by the sole fact that I am conscious of the causes which inspire my action, these causes are already transcendent objects for my consciousness; they are outside. In vain shall I seek to catch hold of them; I escape them by my very existence. I am condemned to exist forever beyond my essence, beyond the causes and motives of my act. I am condemned to be free. This means that no limits to my freedom can be found except freedom itself or, if you prefer, that we are not free to cease being free. To the extent that the for-itself wishes to hide its own nothingness from itself and to incorporate the in itself as its true mode of being, it is trying also to hide its freedom from itself.

The ultimate meaning of determinism is to establish within us an unbroken continuity of existence in itself. The motive conceived as a psychic fact—i.e., as a full and given reality—is, in the deterministic view, articulated without any break with the decision and the act, both of which are equally conceived as psychic givens. The in-itself has got hold of all these "data"; the motive provokes the act as the physical cause its effect; everything is real, everything is full. Thus the refusal of freedom can be conceived only as an attempt to apprehend oneself as being-in-itself; it amounts to the same thing. Human reality may be defined as a being such that in its being its freedom is at stake because human reality perpetually tries to refuse to recognize its freedom. Psychologically in each one of us this amounts to trying to take the causes and motives as *things*. We try to confer permanence upon them. We attempt to hide from ourselves that their nature and their weight depend each moment on the meaning which I give to them; we take them for constants. This amounts to considering the meaning which I gave to them just now or yesterday--which is irremediable because it is past—and extrapolating from it a character fixed still in the present. I attempt to persuade myself that the cause *is* as it was. Thus it would pass whole and untouched from my past consciousness to my present consciousness. It would inhabit my consciousness. This amounts to trying to give an essence to the for-itself. In the same way people will posit ends as transcendences, which is not an error. But instead of seeing that the transcendences there posited are maintained in their being by my own transcendence, people will assume that I encounter them upon my surging up in the world; they come from God, from nature, from "my" nature, from society. These ends ready made and pre-human will therefore define the meaning of my act even before I conceive it, just as causes as pure psychic givens will produce it without my even being aware of them.

Cause, act, and end constitute a *continuum*, a *plenum*. These abortive attempts to stifle freedom under the weight of being (they collapse with the sudden upsurge of anguish before freedom) show sufficiently that freedom in its foundation coincides with the nothingness which is at the heart of man. Human-reality is free because it *is not enough*. It is free because it is perpetually wrenched away from itself and because it has been separated by a nothingness from what it is and from what it will be. It is free, finally, because its present being is itself a nothingness in the form of the "reflection-reflecting." Man is free because he is not himself but presence to himself. The being which is what it is can not be free. Freedom is precisely the nothingness which *is made-to-be* at the heart of man and which forces human-reality *to make itself* instead of to be. As we have seen, for human reality, to be is to *choose oneself*; nothing comes to it either from the outside or from within which it can *receive or accept*. Without any help whatsoever, it is entirely abandoned to the intolerable necessity of making itself be—down to the slightest detail. Thus freedom is not a being; it is *the being* of man—i.e., his nothingness of being. If we start by conceiving of man as a plenum, it is absurd to try to find in him afterwards moments or psychic regions in which he would be free. As well look for emptiness in a container which one has filled beforehand up to the brim! Man can not be sometimes slave and sometimes free; he is wholly and forever free or he is not free at all.

These observations can lead us, if we know how to use them, to new discoveries. They will enable us first to bring to light the relations between freedom and what we call the "will." There is a fairly common tendency to seek to identify free acts with voluntary acts and to restrict the deterministic explanation to the world of the passions. In short the point of view of Descartes. The Cartesian will is free, but there are "passions of the soul." Again Descartes will attempt a physiological interpretation of these passions. Later there will be an attempt to instate a purely psychological determinism. Intellectualistic analyses such as Proust, for example, attempts with respect to jealousy or snobbery can serve as illustrations for this concept of the passional "mechanism." In this case it would be necessary to conceive of man as simultaneously free and determined, and the essential problem would be that of the relations between this unconditioned freedom and the determined processes of the psychic life: how will it master the passions, how will it utilize them for its own benefit? A wisdom which comes from ancient times—the wisdom of the Stoics—will teach us to come to terms with these passions so as to master them; in short it will counsel us how to conduct ourselves with regard to affectivity as man does with respect to nature in general when he obeys it in order better to control it. Human reality therefore appears as a free power besieged by an ensemble of determined processes. One will distinguish wholly free acts, determined processes over which the free will has power, and processes which on principle escape the human-will.

It is clear that we shall not be able to accept such a conception. But let us try better to understand the reasons for our refusal. There is one objection which is obvious and which we shall not waste time in developing; this is that such a trenchant duality is inconceivable at the heart of the psychic unity. How in fact could we conceive of a being which could be *one* and which nevertheless on the one hand would be constituted as a series of facts determined by one another—hence existents in exteriority—and which on the other hand would be constituted as a spontaneity determining itself to be and revealing only itself? *A priori* this spontaneity would be capable of no action on a determinism already *constituted*. On what could it act? On the object itself (the present psychic fact)? But how could it modify an in-itself which by definition is and can be only what it is? On the actual law of the process? This is self-contradictory. On the antecedents of the process? But it amounts to the same thing whether we act on the present psychic fact in order to modify it in itself or act upon it in order to modify its consequences. And in each case we encounter the same impossibility which we pointed out earlier. Moreover, what instrument would this spontaneity have at its disposal? If the hand can clasp, it is because it can be clasped. Spontaneity, since by definition it is *beyond reach* can not in turn *reach*; it can produce only itself. And if it could dispose of a special instrument, it would then be necessary to conceive of this as of an intermediary nature between free will and determined passions—which is not admissible. For different reasons the passions could get no hold upon the will. Indeed it is impossible for a determined process to act upon a spontaneity, exactly as it is impossible for objects to act upon consciousness. Thus any synthesis of two types of existents is impossible; they are not homogeneous; they will remain each one in its incommunicable solitude. The only bond which a nihilating spontaneity could maintain with mechanical processes would be the fact that it *produces itself by an internal negation directed toward these existents.* But then the spontaneity will exist precisely only in so far as it denies concerning itself that it is these passions. Henceforth the ensemble of the determined πάθος will of necessity be apprehended by spontaneity as a pure transcendent; that is, as what is necessarily *outside,* as what *is not* it.[2] This internal negation would therefore have for its effect only the dissolution of the πάθος in the world, and the πάθος would exist as some sort of object in the midst of the world for a free spontaneity which would be simultaneously will and consciousness. This discussion shows that two solutions and only two are possible: either man is wholly determined (which is inadmissible, especially because a determined consciousness—i.e., a consciousness externally motivated—becomes itself pure exteriority and ceases to be consciousness) or else man is wholly free.

But this is not all: the will, far from being the unique or at least the privileged manifestation of freedom, actually—like every event of the for-itself—must presuppose the foundation of an original freedom in order to be able to constitute itself as will. The will in fact is posited as a reflective decision in relation to certain ends. But it does not create these ends. It is rather a mode of being in relation to them: it decrees that the pursuit of these ends will be reflective and deliberative. Passion can posit the same ends. For example, if I am threatened, I can run away at top speed because of my fear of dying. This passional fact nevertheless posits implicitly as a supreme end the value of life. Another person in the same situation will, on the contrary, understand that he must remain at his post even if resistance at first appears more dangerous than flight; he "will stand firm." But his goal, although better understood and explicitly posited, remains the same as in the case of the emotional reaction. It is simply that the methods of attaining it are more clearly conceived; certain of them are rejected as dubious or inefficacious, others are more solidly organized. The difference here depends on the choice of means and on the degree of reflection and of making explicit, not on the end. Yet the one who flees is said to be "passionate," and we reserve the term "voluntary" for the man who resists. Therefore the question is of a difference of subjective attitude in relation to a transcendent end. But if we wish to avoid the error which we denounced earlier and not consider these transcendent ends as prehuman and as an *a priori* limit to our transcendence, then we are indeed compelled to recognize that they are the temporalizing projection of our freedom. Human reality can not receive its ends, as we have seen, either from outside or from a so-called inner "nature." It chooses them and by this very choice confers upon them a transcendent existence as the external limit of its projects. From this point of view—and if it is understood that the existence of the *Dasein* precedes and commands its essence—human reality in and through its very upsurge decides to define its own being by its ends. It is therefore the positing of my ultimate ends which characterizes my being and which is identical with the sudden thrust of the freedom which is mine. And this thrust is an *existence*; it has nothing to do with an essence or with a property of a being which would be engendered conjointly with an idea.

Thus since freedom is identical with my existence, it is the foundation of ends which I shall attempt to attain either by the will or by passionate efforts. Therefore it can not be limited to voluntary acts. Volitions, on the contrary, like passions are certain subjective attitudes by which we attempt to attain the ends posited by original freedom. By original freedom, of course, we should not understand a freedom which would be *prior* to the voluntary or passionate act but rather a foundation which is strictly contemporary with the will or the passion and which these *manifest*, each in its own way. Neither should we oppose freedom to the will or to passion as the "profound self" of Bergson is opposed to the superficial self; the for-itself is wholly self-ness and can not have a "profound self," unless by this we mean certain transcendent structures of the psyche. Freedom is nothing but the *existence* of our will or of our passions in so far as this existence is the nihilation of facticity; that is, the existence of a being which is its being in the mode of having to be it. We shall return to this point. In any case let us remember that the will is determined within the compass of motives and ends already posited by the for-itself in a transcendent projection of itself toward its possibles. If this were not so, how could we understand deliberation, which is an evaluation of means in relation to already existing ends?

If these ends are already posited, then what remains to be decided at each moment is the way in which I shall conduct myself with respect to them; in other words, the attitude which I shall assume. Shall I act by volition or by passion? Who can decide except me? In fact, if we admit that circumstances decide for me (for example, I can act by volition when faced with a minor danger but if the peril increases, I shall fall into passion), we thereby suppress all freedom. It would indeed be absurd to declare that the will is autonomous when it appears but that external circumstances strictly determine the moment of its appearance. But, on the other hand, how can it be maintained that a will which does not yet exist can suddenly decide to shatter the chain of the passions and suddenly stand forth on the fragments of these chains? Such a conception would lead us to consider the will as a *power* which sometimes would manifest itself to consciousness and at other times would remain hidden, but which would in any case possess the permanence and the existence "in-itself" of a property. This is precisely what is inadmissible. It is, however, certain that common opinion conceives of the moral life as a struggle between a will-thing and passion-substances. There is here a sort of psychological Manichaeism which is absolutely insupportable.

Actually it is not enough to will; it is necessary to will to will. Take, for example, a given situation: I can react to it emotionally. We have shown elsewhere that emotion is not a physiological tempest;[3] it is a reply adapted to the situation; it is a type of conduct, the meaning and form of which are the object of an intention of consciousness which aims at attaining a particular end by particular means. In fear, fainting and cataplexie[4] aim at suppressing the danger by suppressing the consciousness of the danger. There is an *intention* of losing consciousness in order to do away with the formidable world in which consciousness is engaged and which comes into being through consciousness. Therefore we have to do with magical behavior provoking the symbolic satisfactions of our desires and revealing by the same stroke a magical stratum of the world. In contrast to this conduct voluntary and rational conduct will consider the situation scientifically, will reject the magical, and will apply itself to realizing determined series and instrumental complexes which will enable us to resolve the problems. It will organize a system of means by taking its stand on instrumental determinism. Suddenly it will reveal a technical world; that is, a world in which each instrumental-complex refers to another larger complex and so on. But what will make me decide to choose the magical aspect or the technical aspect of the world? It can not be the world itself, for this in order to be manifested waits to be discovered. Therefore it is necessary that the for-itself in its project must choose being the one by whom the world is revealed as magical or rational; that is, the for-itself must as a free project of itself give to itself magical or rational existence. It is responsible for either one, for the for-itself can *be* only if it has chosen itself. Therefore the for-itself appears as the free foundation of its emotions as of its volitions. My fear *is* free and manifests my freedom; I have put all my freedom into my fear, and I have chosen myself as fearful in this or that circumstance. Under other circumstances I shall exist as deliberate and courageous, and I shall have put all my freedom into my courage. In relation to freedom there is no privileged psychic phenomenon. All my "modes of being" manifest freedom equally since they are all ways of being my own nothingness.

Yet if the motive is transcendent, if it is only the irremediable being which we have to be in the mode of the "was," if like all our past it is separated from us by a breadth of nothingness, then it can act only if it is *recovered*; in itself it is without force. It is therefore by the very thrust of the engaged consciousness that a value and a weight will be conferred on motives and on prior causes. What they have been does not depend on consciousness, but consciousness has the duty of maintaining them in their existence in the past. I have willed this or that: here is what remains irremediable and which even constitutes my essence, since my essence is what I have been. But the meaning held for me by this desire, this fear, these objective considerations of the world when presently I project myself toward my futures—this must be decided by me alone. I determine them precisely and only by the very act by which I project myself toward my ends. The recovery of former motives—or the rejection or new appreciation of them—is not distinct from the project by which I assign new ends to myself and by which in the light of these ends I apprehend myself as discovering a supporting cause in the world. Past motives, past causes, present motives and causes, future ends, all are organized in an indissoluble unity by the very upsurge of a freedom which is beyond causes, motives, and ends.

The result is that a voluntary deliberation is always a deception. How can I evaluate causes and motives on which I myself confer their value before all deliberation and by the very choice which I make of myself? The illusion here stems from the fact that we endeavor to take causes and motives for entirely transcendent things which I balance in my hands like weights and which possess a weight as a permanent property. Yet on the other hand we try to view them as contents of consciousness, and this is self-contradictory. Actually causes and motives have only the weight which my project—i.e., the free production of the end and of the known act to be realized—confers upon them. When I deliberate, the chips are down.[5] And if I am brought to the point of deliberating, this is simply because it is a part of my original project to realize motives by means of *deliberation* rather than by some other form of discovery (by passion, for example, or simply by action, which reveals to me the organized ensemble of causes and of ends as my language informs me of my thought). There is therefore a choice of deliberation as a procedure which will make known to me what I project and consequently what I am. And *the choice* of deliberation is organized with the ensemble motives-causes and end by free spontaneity. When the will intervenes, the decision is taken, and it has no other value than that of making the announcement.

The essential consequence of our earlier remarks is that man being condemned to be free carries the weight of the whole world on his shoulders; he is responsible for the world and for himself as a way of being. We are taking the word "responsibility" in its ordinary sense as "consciousness (of) being the incontestable author of an event or of an object." In this sense the responsibility of the for-itself is overwhelming since he[6] is the one by whom it happens that there is a world; since he is also the one who makes himself be, then whatever may be the situation in which he finds himself, the for-itself must wholly assume this situation with its peculiar coefficient of adversity, even though it be insupportable. He must assume the situation with the proud consciousness of being the author of it, for the very worst disadvantages or the worst threats which can endanger my person have meaning only in and through my project; and it is on the ground of the engagement which I am that they appear. It is therefore senseless to think of complaining since nothing foreign has decided what we feel, what we live, or what we are.

Furthermore this absolute responsibility is not resignation; it is simply the logical requirement of the consequences of our freedom. What happens to me happens through me, and I can neither affect myself with it nor revolt against it nor resign myself to it. Moreover everything which happens to me is *mine*. By this we must understand first of all that I am always equal to what happens to me *qua* man, for what happens to a man through other men and through himself can be only human. The most terrible situations of war, the worst tortures do not create a non-human state of things; there is no non-human situation. It is only through fear, flight, and recourse to magical types of conduct that I shall decide on the non-human, but this decision is human, and I shall carry the entire responsibility for it. But in addition the situation is *mine* because it is the image of my free choice of myself, and everything which it presents to me is *mine* in that this represents me and symbolizes me. Is it not I who decide the coefficient of adversity in things and even their unpredictability by deciding myself?

Thus there are no *accidents* in a life; a community event which suddenly bursts forth and involves me in it does not come from the outside. If I am mobilized in a war, this war is *my* war; it is in my image and I deserve it. I deserve it first because I could always get out of it by suicide or by desertion; these ultimate possibles are those which must always be present for us when there is a question of envisaging a situation. For lack of getting out of it, I have *chosen* it. This can be due to inertia, to cowardice in the face of public opinion, or because I prefer certain other values to the value of the refusal to join in the war (the good opinion of my relatives, the honor of my family, etc.). Anyway you look at it, it is a matter of a choice. This choice will be repeated later on again and again without a break until the end of the war. Therefore we must agree with the statement by J. Romains, "In war there are no innocent victims."[7] If therefore I have preferred war to death or to dishonor, everything takes place as if I bore the entire responsibility for this war. Of course others have declared it, and one might be tempted perhaps to consider me as a simple accomplice. But this notion of complicity has only a juridical sense, and it does not hold here. For it depended on me that for me and by me this war should not exist, and I have decided that it does exist. There was no compulsion here, for the compulsion could have got no hold on a freedom. I did not have any excuse; for as we have said repeatedly in this book, the peculiar character of human-reality is that it is without excuse. Therefore it remains for me only to lay claim to this war.

But in addition the war is *mine* because by the sole fact that it arises in a situation which I cause to be and that I can discover it there only by engaging myself for or against it, I can no longer distinguish at present the choice which I make of myself from the choice which I make of the war. To live this war is to choose myself through it and to choose it through my choice of myself. There can be no question of considering it as "four years of vacation" or as a "reprieve," as a "recess," the essential part of my responsibilities being elsewhere in my married, family, or professional life. In this war which I have chosen I choose myself from day to day, and I make it mine by making myself. If it is going to be four empty years, then it is I who bear the responsibility for this.

Finally, as we pointed out earlier, each person is an absolute choice of self from the standpoint of a world of knowledge and of techniques which this choice both assumes and illumines; each person is an absolute upsurge at an absolute date and is perfectly unthinkable at another date. It is therefore a waste of time to ask what I should have been if this war had not broken out, for I have chosen myself as one of the possible meanings of the epoch which imperceptibly led to war. I am not distinct from this same epoch; I could not be transported to another epoch without contradiction. Thus *I am* this war which restricts and limits and makes comprehensible the period which preceded it. In this sense we may define more precisely the responsibility of the for-itself if to the earlier quoted statement, "There are no innocent victims," we add the words, "We have the war we deserve." Thus, totally free, undistinguishable from the period for which I have chosen to be the meaning, as profoundly responsible for the war as if I had myself declared it, unable to live without integrating it in *my* situation, engaging myself in it wholly and stamping it with my seal, I must be without remorse or regrets as I am without excuse; for from the instant of my upsurge into being, I carry the weight of the world by myself alone without anything or any person being able to lighten it.

Yet this responsibility is of a very particular type. Someone will say, "I did not ask to be born." This is a naive way of throwing greater emphasis on our facticity. I am responsible for everything, in fact, except for my very responsibility, for I am not the foundation of my being. Therefore everything takes place as if I were compelled to be responsible. I am *abandoned* in the world, not in the sense that I might remain abandoned and passive in a hostile universe like a board floating on the water, but rather in the sense that I find myself suddenly alone and without help, engaged in a world for which I bear the whole responsibility without being able, whatever I do, to tear myself away from this responsibility for an instant. For I am responsible for my very desire of fleeing responsibilities. To make myself passive in the world, to refuse to act upon things and upon others is still to choose myself, and suicide is one mode among others of being-in-the-world. Yet I find an absolute responsibility for the fact that my facticity (here the fact of my birth) is directly inapprehensible and even inconceivable, for this fact of my birth never appears as a brute fact but always across a projective reconstruction of my for-itself. I am ashamed of being born or I am astonished at it or I rejoice over it, or in attempting to get rid of my life I affirm that I live and I assume this life as bad. Thus in a certain sense I *choose* being born. This choice itself is integrally affected with facticity since I am not able not to choose, but this facticity in turn will appear only in so far as I surpass it toward my ends. Thus facticity is everywhere but inapprehensible; I never encounter anything except my responsibility. That is why I can not ask, "*Why* was I born?" or curse the day of my birth or declare that I did not ask to be born, for these various attitudes toward my birth—i.e., toward the *fact* that I realize a presence in the world—are absolutely nothing else but ways of assuming this birth in full responsibility and of making it *mine*. Here again I encounter only myself and my projects so that finally my abandonment—i.e., my facticity—consists simply in the fact that I am condemned to be wholly responsible for myself. I am the being which is in such a way that in its being its being is in question. And this "is" of my being *is* as present and inapprehensible.

Under these conditions since every event in the world can be revealed to me only as an *opportunity* (an opportunity made use of, lacked, neglected, *etc.*), or better yet since everything which happens to us can be considered as a *chance* (*i.e.*, can appear to us only as a way of realizing this being which is in question in our being) and since others as transcendences-transcended are themselves only *opportunities* and *chances*, the responsibility of the for-itself extends to the entire world as a peopled-world. It is precisely thus that the for-itself apprehends itself in anguish; that is, as a being which is neither the foundation of its own being nor of the Other's being nor of the in-itselfs which form the world, but a being which is compelled to decide the meaning of being—within it and everywhere outside of it. The one who realizes in anguish his condition as *being* thrown into a responsibility which extends to his very abandonment has no longer either remorse or regret or excuse; he is no longer anything but a freedom which perfectly reveals itself and whose being resides in this very revelation. But as we pointed out at the beginning of this work, most of the time we flee anguish in bad faith.

NOTES

1. In this and following sections Sartre makes a sharp distinction between motif and mobile. The English word "motive" expresses sufficiently adequately the French mobile, which refers to an inner subjective fact or attitude. For motif there is no true equivalent. Since it refers to an external fact or situation, I am translating it by "cause." The reader must remember, however, that this carries with it no idea of determinism. Sartre emphatically denies the existence of any cause in the usual deterministic sense. Tr.

2. I.e., is not spontaneity. Tr.

3. Esquisse d'une théorie phénoménologique des emotions, Hermann, 1939. In English, The Emotions: Outline of a Theory. Tr. by Bernard Frechtman. Philosophical Library, 1948.

4. A word invented by Preyer to refer to a sudden inhibiting numbness produced by any shock. Tr.

5. Les jeux sont faits. Sartre has written a novel by this title. Tr.

6. I am shifting to the personal pronoun here since Sartre is describing the for-itself in concrete personal terms rather than as a metaphysical entity. Strictly speaking, of course, this is his position throughout, and the French "il" is indifferently "he" or "it." Tr.

7. J. Romains: *Les hommes de bonne volonté*; "Prelude a Verdun."

ON THE ABSOLUTE FREEDOM
OF THE WILL*

Bernard Berofsky

Among the efforts to defend the reality of freedom of will is a radical one: an unfree will, some philosophers contend, is a conceptual impossibility. If we choose or will at all, and surely we sometimes do, then we choose freely. This stance or some associated doctrine has been defended by Aristotle, Descartes, Bradley, Sartre, Ginet,[1] and, most recently, Albritton.

ARISTOTLE:	"Choice seems to be voluntary. . . . The object of choice being one of the things in our own power which is desired after deliberation, choice will be deliberate desire of things in our own power."[2]
DESCARTES:	The will is "by its nature free in such a way that it can never be constrained."[3]
DESCARTES AGAIN:	"Even though the will may be incomparably greater in God than in myself, either because of the knowledge and power which are joined with it and which make it surer and more efficacious, or because of its object, since it

*Bernard Berofsky "On the Absolute Freedom of the Will," AMERICAN PHILOSOPHICAL QUARTERLY, vol. 29, No. 3 (July 1992), pp. 279–289. Reprinted with the kind permission of the journal.

extends to infinitely more things, nevertheless it does not appear any greater when I consider it formally and precisely by itself. For it consists only in the fact that we can [make a choice; we can] do a given thing or not do it. . . . Or more properly, our free will consists in the fact that . . . we behave in such a way that we do not feel that any external force has constrained us in our decision."[4]

BRADLEY: "If by 'will' we mean 'choice', 'Volition', the conscious realizing of myself in the object of one desire (in the widest sense), Which has been separated from and put before the mind, as a possibility not yet real—then the will can not be forced . . . There is no Saying, 'If I could have willed, I would have willed otherwise'."

"But if will be used . . . in a lower sense, then . . . the will . . . often is forced . . . because, by the application of compulsion, the psychical conditions of volition can be suppressed, so that it becomes impossible for me to decide myself for this and not for that."[5]

Thus, according to Bradley, compulsion can only bring about the suppression of volition. Conditions can be created under which we cannot will at all. But when we will, there is no forcing, no compulsion.

The theme is repeated in Albritton. "Of course, chains and the like can in a certain sense undermine apparent choices. But it isn't the *freedom* of those choices that chains can abolish, it's the *choices*, in an objective sense."[6]

SARTRE: "When we say a man who's out of work is free, we don't mean that he can do whatever he wants and change himself into a rich and tranquil bourgeois on the spot. *He is free because he can always choose to accept his lot with resignation or to rebel against it.*"[7]; "We shall not say that a prisoner is always free to go out of prison, which would be absurd, . . . but that he is always free to try to escape."[8]

The last sentence of the quotation from the *Meditations* suggests that the doctrine Descartes is advocating is a more conventional one, to wit, the compatibility of free will and determinism, and that interpretation is borne out in the next paragraph of the *Meditations*. He there observes that freedom is not undermined by causation when the cause is the agent's understanding of the good and the true. The position would not then rule out an unfree will by conceptual fiat; for my will would be unfree when it is determined by an imperfect understanding. This is precisely what happens when I err and sin.

Yet Descartes rather says that, in such a case, I have misused my "free will." My will apparently remains free even when I sin. This conclusion is grounded in the fact that I am not bound by an admittedly imperfect understanding which can "lead to" error and sin. I need not be victimized by my finitude because I also possess the capacity "firmly to adhere to the resolution never to pass judgment upon things whose truth is not clearly known to me."[9] Thus, error resulting from ignorance has a concurring cause, to wit, the failure to exercise this capacity. Since we all have this capacity, we are free to avoid error and are culpable for failing to do so. The capacity to limit the exercise of will enables the will to remain free during those lapses brought on by avoidable intellectual recklessness.

Thus, Descartes is not guilty of a failure to distinguish will from freewill. One can imagine a class of agents who, like us, have both the capacity to choose and a natural propensity to act from limited information; but, unlike us, lack the capacity to control this propensity. These creatures have wills which are unfree—they affirm and act at the drop of a hat. (They are unlikely to survive as a species very long.)

Had Descartes simply identified will with free will, he would have erred. For the bare capacity to choose is not freedom of will since the latter is *not* just the freedom to choose, that is, to make *some* choices. It matters what we can choose. Otherwise, there would be no difference in freedom between God and a person who can only choose the color of her socks. (Imagine as well, if you must, that she wants to be able to choose a great deal more. But every time she enters a decision making situation other than one involving the color of her socks, she undergoes narcolepsy.) The point is important as a response to the claim that one does not lose the power to *choose* when one's will is ostensibly limited. Freedom is affected (diminished, enhanced) by the *range* of choices available to agents in spite of disagreements about the characterization of this range. (For example, some do and some do not think it important to liberty that people be free to choose the things they *want*. Independently of *this* controversy, then, if Superman and Lois both want to fly, it is agreed that Superman has more freedom.) Not all agents who can choose are equally free.

The same mistake occurs in the following dilemma argument: either one can choose or one cannot choose. If one can choose, one is free; if one cannot choose, there is no subject (choice) about which one can predicate unfreedom. So either way, where there is will, there is free will.

If "choose" is short for "choose a specific action which is in the circumstances the relevant one," the second conditional is false—there is an unfree subject or choice, to wit, the one forced upon the agent. If "choose" means rather "exercise some choice or other," then the first conditional is false since, if one cannot choose some specific action which is, in the context, the relevant one, one is not *free to do that* and that is the important sort of unfreedom. So the argument fails even though it is quite true that a being that cannot choose at all may not be unfree (in the way a lizard or a stone, neither of which *can* be free, is also not unfree).

Albritton advances a similar argument. Sometimes I'm forced to do things which do not implicate my will at all. I find myself where you brought me. "If I'm forcibly carried to your rotten garden party, I'm there against my will . . . But . . . I'm not there of my will at all."[10] I did not choose freely to be at the party because I did not choose simpliciter to be at your party. But when factors prevent me from making a certain choice, is Albritton suggesting that there is no unfreedom for the absence of choice implies the absence of unfree choice? That would be misleading. For even though we retain the power of choice, the range of things upon which we can exercise choice matters a great deal. Consider the analogy with action. I retain the power to act (to do *something*) even when bound and gagged.

This limitation on freedom is important even if we come to decide that the actions which are performed when we are unfree to do certain important things are performed *freely*. We must highlight the importance of the distinction between X-ing (un)freely and being (un)free to X. Hume's prisoner in chains is not free *to* leave his cell even though, preferring bondage to liberty, he remains freely.

Aristotle and Bradley are clearly working with this second conception of freedom, freedom as a qualifier of actions. They need not be taken as denying the obvious truth that we are often not free to do many things. When Bradley links freedom and the will, he is not challenging either the view that we are not free to *do* many things or even the view that we are not free to *will* many things. He is rather denying of a specific, performed act of will that it can be unfree. And it is compatible with this position that one person's will may extend beyond that of another. For each person, when he wills, he wills freely; but one can will far more (and perhaps about far more important matters) than the other.

Inevitably, will is contrasted with action. The latter, of course, can be compelled. "And a human being of intact free will might have almost *no* freedom of action, indeed no freedom of physical action at all."[11] On a wide construal of actions, Aristotle and Bradley agree. For Aristotle, a person is compelled when the moving principle is totally outside him. And Bradley tells us that compulsion is "the production, in the body or mind of an animate being, of a result which is not related as a consequence to its will."[12]

But the issue is more complex because one might argue that actions proper are never compelled for Aristotle and Bradley. If the person makes no contribution to what he does, it is, as Aristotle says, as "if he were to be carried somewhere by a wind, or by men who had him in their power."[13] In such instances, the body is forced to move and no action occurs at all. Since these sorts of cases are the only ones in which compulsion obtains, actions are not the sorts of things which are compelled. Bradley's view is similar. "Whenever I *can* not collect myself, so as by conscious volition to decide one way or the other, there I did not do the act; there was force put upon me; whether proceeding simply from my nature, or, in addition, from a will outside me . . . But where we collect ourselves and volition does take place, I think I we must say that, given knowledge, there is always imputation."[14] In case of insanity, violent pain or emotion, great weakness, or extreme terror, we may be compelled; but, Bradley tells us, there we do not act. Whereas when I knowingly decide to give the robber all my money in order to save my life, I am acting, but not under compulsion. And since the will itself cannot be compelled, as we saw above, compulsion applies to beings with wills only when their wills are inoperative.

Both Aristotle and Bradley introduce qualifications and emendations; but my concern is not an historically accurate account of their views. I have used them to expose an ambiguity in the position under consideration. If we deny that the will can be bound, should we say the same of action and conclude therefrom that the liberty of the human agent is limitless, or should we, with Albritton, distinguish perfect freedom of will with greatly restricted freedom of action?

If we remind ourselves of the distinction between *freedom to act* and *acting freely*, we must agree with Albritton that our power or freedom *to* act is greatly limited. Now Aristotle says that the presence of choice, although not necessary for voluntariness, is sufficient. Even actions which appear "mixed," i.e., ones which are chosen by the agent, but in response to a threat, are more like voluntary ones because they are chosen. Why? Aristotle notes that we only choose those things which are in our power to do. Once we realize that we cannot achieve an objective, we stop deliberating about it and it is no longer a possible object of choice.

But those who believe that we sometimes lack free will do not deny that a coerced will chooses only what is in the power of the agent to effect. They rather affirm the inability to choose what the will *fails* to choose. So we cease deliberating about an option when we believe we are *not free* to realize it.

Bradley would observe, though, that this sort of unfreedom is, again, the inability *to* choose. So, although Albritton may be right that we are not free to *do* anything—although we are free to *will* anything—Bradley would insist that an agent who is not free to act otherwise nonetheless chooses and acts freely when he knowingly and deliberately selects from alternatives placed before it (even if he is looking down the barrel of a gun). It remains to be seen whether we wish to uphold Bradley's view that a robbery victim who is not so terrorized as to be rendered temporarily will-less is, therefore, not compelled or coerced.

Albritton defends his position against the argument that knowledge can restrict the will. The argument: if I know I cannot do A, I cannot try to do A. So I lack freedom of will with respect to A. Moreover, the knowledge can be acquired from another human being, thereby giving that person control over my willing. He can, that is, incapacitate my will by teaching me that I cannot do A.

Albritton responds with a dilemma argument: either I can try to do what I know is not possible, in which case I do not lack freedom of will; or the purported lack of freedom here is grounded in an impossibility whose conceptual nature makes it irrelevant. In either case my freedom of will is unrestricted.

Consider the conceptual impossibility horn. If I cannot try to do what I know is impossible, then, according to Albritton, this means that we are disposed not to count anything I do as fulfilling the description "trying to." Let us first assume that the relevant component of knowledge in this context is belief. Then, however *I* would describe what I am doing, I am not trying to do A unless I believe that I can do A. But, Albritton observes, logical limits on the will are not the intended sort of limits. Why? Albritton's answer: since logical limits determine what is to count as willing, nothing or no one can truly control another's will for all that will happen is that the person will not will at all rather than be induced to will unfreely.

Albritton's response is misleading. If I can induce beliefs in another, I can control his will by determining what he wills. I can induce him to will otherwise just as I can induce someone to act otherwise when I restrict his freedom of action. The fact that, in preventing the prisoner from leaving the room, I am not preventing him from thinking ill of me, does not mean that I do not limit his freedom of action. He is free to think ill of me, but not free to leave the room. If I want to leap over tall buildings and am caused to believe I am not Superman by my psychiatrist, he will render me unable to *try* to do this because of the conceptual link between believing and trying. There is no difference from the following situation: Coca Cola removes Classic Coke from the market and destroys it, rendering me unfree to drink Classic Coke and this is so because of the conceptual link between the existence of Classic Coke and my drinking it. Someone can use the conceptual connection between believing and trying to limit a person's ability to try *to do that which the person is induced to believe he cannot do* and this is a real limit on freedom even if the general capacity to try or will remains intact.

I would be prepared to concede to this point of view that we *can* try to do the impossible, even when it is unbelievably bizarre: eat Chicago, say, to use one of Albritton's examples. But if *I* cannot try to eat Chicago because I am firmly convinced I cannot under present circumstances do it, my will is limited in the prosaic manner my freedom of action is limited in so many ways. Why can't I bemoan my current state as I imagine my self being transformed slowly into a being with such extraordinary capacities? (Science fiction accounts do not strain our imagination that much.)

Is there something special about *knowledge* in contrast with *belief*? If I only believe I cannot do something, I can also concede that I might be wrong and that concession might be enough to create the possibility of trying. Whereas if the inability to try rests on knowledge, then I am in a state from which it follows that I do not try at all. This conceptual fact does not limit my perfect freedom of will. If knowledge that A is impossible logically precludes trying to do A, then it does not constrain the will the way gravity constrains the direction of my fall or a robber constrains my decision concerning the dispensation of my cash. The force of gravity is a real constraint on the path of my fall; but knowledge "forces" me to refrain from making an effort in the same sense my wealth "forces" me not to be poor.

Surely, however, this is small comfort to one for whom the freedom to try or choose A is important. If she moves from ignorance to knowledge, her freedom is reduced no matter how the situation is described. Believing that I am Superman, I have the power to try to leap over tall buildings in a single bound. I lose this power under successful psychiatric treatment when I come to know that I lack the capacity for success. If what was said above about belief is correct, my will's freedom has been impaired. How can my freedom be enhanced or these limitations removed simply in virtue of the fact that my belief is firmly held and adequately grounded, that is, adds up to knowledge? Clearly, it cannot. The mistake here is familiar. Since, let us suppose, it follows from the knowledge that I cannot do A that I will not try to do A, then, observes Albritton, the trying will not take place and one cannot speak of an unfree will. Again, however, the point is that we will try to do something other than A. So our will need not be generally incapacitated, only relative to A. And this is the exact sort of unfreedom we have in the arena of action.

It is evident to all that our freedom of will is far greater than our freedom of action. Often, I am free to decide to do A and then discover I cannot do A. It is also evident that many ordinary laments of the form "I cannot decide to do A" are not literally true in that obstacles inducing me to draw this conclusion are too weak literally to bind my will. Alternatively, we often say quite properly that we must (decide to) do A because of a commitment or a promise or a role, etc., when we are free to reject that commitment, etc. It, of course, follows from these thoughts neither that I have perfect freedom to will all nor that all willing is free willing.

In order to reach the required conclusion that obstacles *never* bind the will, we need a stronger argument. If we were to locate it in the gap between surmountable obstacles and absolute barriers, we would be able to defend the absolute freedom of the will only by defining freedom in terms of the bare possibility of doing otherwise.

We would then, in consistency, have to define freedom of action similarly and we would find ourselves with an extremely narrow definition of freedom. It would also be intolerably vague—which crack addicts are free to desist or who is not free to assassinate the President or stay awake for 96 hours? (There may be *some* possible, remote way of effecting these difficult outcomes.) Moreover, as noted by many, the definition is not only remote from ordinary usage; it is also useless for the roles we would like a conception of freedom to play. For example, we cannot hold an agent morally responsible for falling asleep after 88 hours when he exerted Herculean efforts to remain awake just because there was one more strategy available to him involving the ingestion of a fatal drug which would initially have kept him awake for 8 hours before killing him. As Greenspan says, "Calling someone free . . . amounts to a claim about the reasonableness of making certain practical *demands* on that person."[15]

If we then choose a conception of freedom of action along these value-laden lines, we shall have to apply it to freedom of will, and it will be an easy matter to show that we are often unfree even to will certain things. For barriers may be placed in the path of the agent which render even his willing to do some action unreasonable. Imagine simply that his life is threatened if he even tries to do something.

The case against this defense of the absolute freedom of will is not undermined by the bona fide point that we often excuse ourselves too readily in many contexts by pleading inability or lack of freedom. Often, when we say we cannot, in a very important sense, we can. And the classification of certain conditions as compulsions or obsessions is compatible with the agent's being able (in one important sense) to resist the act the agent is "compelled" to perform. There are morally extreme circumstances in which it would not be inappropriate to demand that a person refrain from doing something which, had it been done in different circumstances, would have been excused on grounds of compulsion or the inability to do otherwise.

The point I would stress is the parallel between action and will. Although it is a truism that we have greater freedom to will than to act, the intended contrast between an absolute freedom of will versus a relative freedom of action is lacking. The limits on the will are as real and as constraining as those on action. To be sure, there are many clearly physical limitations on specific actions; whereas physical limitations on the will, e.g., through drugs and surgery, are more general in character. But it is surely only a matter of time before we will be able to influence the will in very specific ways through physical means the way we are now able to influence the will through psychological means.

And if certain psychological devices, e.g., threats and brainwashing, limit freedom of action, they ought to count sometimes as limiting freedom of will. Indeed, often, I am not free to act *because* I am not free to choose to act. I cannot bring myself to do many things because I cannot make up my mind to do those things.

If I cannot bring myself to call my sister when the phones are working, my dialing capacities are not impaired, I know the number, and I am not mute, the reason may well be that I cannot bring myself to *decide* to do so. "Decide" here is serious; what I reflect upon when I imagine myself deciding is the readiness to initiate steps to perform the act, a prospect I find so appalling that the contemplation of it renders me powerless. To decide to do *A* is to insure that, if the decision is not revoked and *A* is not done, the reason will lie outside the will of the agent.

Obviously, we do have perfect freedom of will if we do not take will seriously as a real executive faculty. It is easy to utter the words "I will" or "I decide"; it is easy to imagine doing pretty much anything; it is easy for many addicts to fool themselves into believing they have decided to quit. But it is often very hard to decide for a decision is a commitment. And if it is often very hard to exercise our volition, how can one fail at least sometimes to be free to do it?

Yes, one can challenge the above, as earlier indicated, by noting that there is a perfectly good sense in which I *can* call my sister, I would if I learned that her life is in danger (or, better, that my life is in danger if I fail to call her). But that is not the present situation; in that situation (suppose), it is unfair to ask me to do it for the psychological costs are severe and the benefits quite limited. And we earlier listed the disadvantages of a shift to a different account of freedom according to which freedom requires the barest possibility of performing the act.

We turn to the more difficult task, that of addressing Bradley's argument that the will must be free because it is "the conscious realizing of myself in the object of one desire (in the widest sense), which has been rated from and put before the mind, as a possibility not yet real." If I collect myself and knowingly will one way or the other, I am not forced either "from my nature, or, in addition, from a will outside me."

Compulsion can "lead to" but not "cause" the will.[16] For willing is the expression of the self. If we bracket the question of the responsibility of the self for its desires, there is no doubt that it is my desire which is implicated when a bribe or threat is proffered or a temptation placed in my path.

If we look closely at the *Notes*, it is not clear that a consistent doctrine emerges. For example, in response to this idea that compulsion only leads to, but does not cause the will, Bradley recants a bit: "This is not satisfactory. An act may be technically, and formally, a volition in the proper sense; and yet, if it is the result of an abnormal state into which a person has been forced, or again led by a false pretence or ignorantly (e.g., hypnotism), the volition is *not* (as such) imputable, and the other person *has* used what *may be called* 'force'."[17]

Bradley's position has exerted a strong influence on recent discussions of coercion as philosophers have conceded to his position that it is very difficult to provide a convincing analysis. The central stumbling block, as Bradley saw, is that so-called coercion of the will occurs when the agent is doing what he overall most prefers to do. I prefer the pair {lose money, retain life} over the pair {retain money, lose life}; so in giving all my money to the robber, I am doing what I most want to do. And coercion cannot be constituted by the fact that the situation is one I would prefer not to be in for that is often true of people we do not regard as deciding under coercion. I am neither coerced, compelled, nor absolved of responsibility when I choose dessert after a large meal, even though I would prefer not to have the option.

Nor can coercion be based on the fact that I have nothing to gain in the robbery situation—in the temptation case, I at least get to dessert—for we often freely choose "the lesser of two evils," hoping to *preserve*, not *enlarge*, as much as possible of our share of life's bounty. For example, suppose, for tax purposes only, I must give money to charity *A* or charity *B*. I am not a charitable man, that is, I prefer giving to neither over giving to *A* or giving to *B*. But I prefer giving to either over an IRS audit. So no outcome will improve my lot. Nonetheless, I am neither forced to choose charity *A* over charity *B* (or vice-versa) nor, given that I have some confidence in my ability to sweet talk the agent, am I forced to choose an audit over giving to either. And if it is said that, through a charitable donation I am reprieved from an IRS audit, one may similarly say that I gain freedom from death (a little better) by giving the robber my money.

It is worth observing that coercion is but one way of curtailing a person's liberty. My liberty is restricted by physical barriers and the absence of certain abilities, e.g., to speak Hungarian. But for advocates of the doctrine under examination, coercion is not a way of restricting the will. To maintain this position against the common assumption that there are clear cases of coercion of will, they must uphold the primacy of theory over intuition, assuming, of course, that the right sort of theory is in the offing. This is what Frankfurt did when he endorsed a version of the hierarchical theory of freedom and applied it to the robbery case. He concluded that, contrary to common sense, the "victim" of a robbery acts freely because he suffers no internal dissonance; he overall prefers to do what he does and moreover prefers to act on that preference.

Bradley's account of freedom as self-determination belongs in the same general group of theories as does the hierarchical theory and is to be contrasted with accounts in terms of power. He does not deny that an apparently coerced agent lacks the freedom *to will and to do* many things. (And Frankfurt says similarly that the wills of both willing and unwilling addicts are unfree if they are powerless to change them.) Relative to the bona fide limits imposed by the past and by the features of the situation one happens to be in, the particular decision is made by the agent (we may suppose) in full awareness of all relevant features and in terms of the agent's own nature, that is, his or her desires, aspirations, and character. That he may lack the power to do otherwise does not undermine the freedom (of self-expression) he does possess.

The objection I wish to focus upon here is not directed to this position as such, but rather to the implicit contrast its advocates make between action and will. If the will is perfectly free in the above sense, even when the agent is a robbery victim, then how can the agent ever fail to *act* freely? Sometimes our bodies are made to move by outside forces and then we are not acting at all. But if we are acting, then by parity of reasoning, we will be acting freely. For the action will also be done in light of the agent's full awareness of all relevant features and in terms of the agent's own nature, that is, his or her desires, aspirations, and character.

If a typical robbery victim fails to be a clear case of unfreedom of will, what about the hierarchical theorist's case, an unwilling addict? Even though the urge which drives her is, in a sense, hers, the conflict within her requires that we choose between the irresistible urge and the rejection of that urge by the reflective component of the self in order to determine the true or deepest self. Since the agent would do otherwise if she could, Frankfurt opts for the second-order rejection of the first-order addictive drive as constitutive of the self. Since that component loses the battle, the agent does not act of her own free will and this is a misfortune over and above her will's not being free to change. (Let us assume that her will is indeed implicated, that is, she does choose to pursue her addiction and is not so overwhelmed by it that she is like an automaton, pulled to and fro without conscious concurrence.)

The dissonance between second- and first-order will counts as unfreedom of will for Frankfurt only because the self is identified with the higher-order will. My will is unfree because *I* reject it. Bradley's view is similar. For both the will is free when it can express the self.

In contemplating the shortcomings of this doctrine,[18] we must not forget an elementary psychological observation that the intellect is often a tool of the passions and that reasoning on behalf of some desire may well be a rationalization designed to disguise an agent's true motivation. If powerful motives lead me unconsciously to endorse an end as good, why should we think of the real me as defined by that process of reasoning which is a distorted expression of elements of my psyche far more central to my being? These elements, say, certain unconscious first-order desires, may dominate other facets of my existence and may produce profound disturbances if brought to consciousness or if efforts are made to eliminate them. Am I really to be identified with some first-order desire I endorse in order to continue some deception which will conceal these elements? Also, a negative judgment of critical reflection may take place from the perspective of a personal ideal which is embedded in a shallow level of the self. Just because a judgment is higher-level in virtue of its *object*, i.e., a desire, does not imply that the judgment takes place on a *deeper* level than the desire which is its object. The failure to satisfy the first-order level desire may have far more profound personal repercussions than the failure to satisfy the higher-order judgment directed against that desire. The failure to achieve what I deeply want (level 1) may contribute more to personal disintegration than the failure to honor reservations about that desire.

The direction of this line of thought accords with that of Bradley since it accentuates the difficulty of rejecting the first-order will as not expressive of the self. Yet that would certainly take us too far in the opposite direction. Surely we sometimes rightly refuse to identify with a strong desire which has the upper hand, yet is antithetical to our nature and everything we otherwise stand for. If we too readily identify ourselves with our reflections, we also have the right sometimes to condemn an obstinate hangover from a period of our life we have taken serious steps to put behind us. Many instances of weakness of will are backsliding, cases of succumbing to temptation when the strength of an impulse does not always recede in step with the depth of commitment to change past. I accept a cigarette after months of abstinence in spite of my active and unequivocal commitment to quit smoking. In such cases, our wills are unfree because we knowingly decide to act contrary to the self on one plausible construal of that idea.

If we were radically simpler creatures, Bradley's doctrine would win the day. For there would be no point in denying freedom when the will knowingly expresses the overall economy of the psyche. To put it crudely, we would be what we most want to will if we suppose our cat chooses freely or unfreely one food over another, no argument can establish that its choice is unfree—its psyche is too simple.

But we want our concept of freedom to serve a variety of purposes and, for each we are obliged to countenance the possibility of unfreedom. If an agent succumbs to temptation, the strength of the temptation may absolve him from blame and we may conclude that it is unreasonable to hold him liable for the decision. He knows that what he did was wrong and he would not have made that decision had the temptation been weaker: There is a big difference between *degree of strength* and *degree of dominance in the self*. Morality can be very important to a person even if he has not been able to rid himself of immoral tendencies which remain powerful. An obscene phone caller may acknowledge the depravity of his behavior; but if this really is a vestige of an immoral past, no longer connected to other elements of his personality, then his refusal to identify with it may not be dismissed just because the urge is overwhelming. To count the *will* as unfree, we must, to be sure, suppose that he *decides* to make the calls. And so he does even if he is responding to powerful internal pressures. It is surely unreasonable to insist that a decision be constituted by a calm, conflict-free, (internal) utterance of words equivalent to "I hereby decide to . . . " Very few decisions are like that. The obscene phone caller performs this act deliberately and knowingly, albeit it with reservations deep enough to permit the conclusion that he willed unfreely.

Not only does Sartre hold the view we are challenging here; it is a cornerstone of his philosophy. That he distinguishes freedom of choice from freedom of action is first of all crucial to understanding the puzzling pronouncements he often makes regarding our absolute freedom. It is clear, as Detmer has shown, that Sartre does not deny bona fide limits on human freedom; he just thinks these are limits on freedom of action or the "freedom of obtaining," the sort of freedom that demands success of one's projects.[19] We are very often unfree to do many things. Absolute freedom applies only to freedom of *choice*, the freedom to formulate goals on the basis of our interpretations of the world and the freedom at least to set out to achieve these goals.

In order to understand why Sartre believes that freedom of choice is unlimited, we have to understand his views about consciousness and we are not free even to undertake that project in the space at our disposal. I shall, however, selectively attend to those facets of Sartre's discussion which bear on the issue before us in the belief that his view on this matter can be undermined without distorting or seriously misinterpreting his position.

Sartre adopts the incompatibilist position that the freedom of an act of choice would be secured if it can be shown that acts of consciousness, of which acts of choice are a subset, are not the sorts of things that can be determined. It is tempting to confuse consciousness with many things which can, in a sense, be determined. Consciousness is not its real objects—the tree is different from my consciousness of it—nor even its phenomenal objects—the pain is different from my consciousness of it. Consciousness is not the Cartesian ego nor is it any one act for any act can become the subject of a future act of consciousness.

Although one might agree with the above, there still remains the possibility of identifying consciousness with the history of acts of consciousness. In any case, the key fact bout consciousness for Sartre—embodied in the slogan that consciousness is nothing—the power of a nihilating withdrawal from reality. A conscious being has the ability to interpret any situation in any way and to formulate any project in response to that situation. The features of the situation do not uniquely determine the response; the same salary in similar circumstances can be perceived by one person as adequate, by another as inadequate. But inadequacy is not a feature of Being-in-Itself. It is introduced "freely" by the agent through conscious interpretation.

Sartre repeatedly emphasizes the tendency to deny one's freedom and the correlative need to identify this mistake either by fostering the individual's power of "purifying reflection," or, as he stresses in later years, by changing the external conditions which "present 'coefficients of adversity' of such magnitude as to render the lucid awareness of one's ontological freedom *highly unlikely*."[20]

These external conditions limit my power to recognize my freedom by comprehending meanings antecedent to my interpretation; I find myself in a world of meanings I did not create. In addition, I have the power to deceive myself in order to achieve certain ends.

It is not clear to me why these limitations are described as limitations on the recognition of one's freedom rather than limitations on freedom itself. To be sure, there are often excellent reasons to believe that a person's circumstances do not empirically determine her choice or her perception of her situation. A frustrated woman may wrongly believe that she has no choice but to remain in her unhappy marriage. She fails to acknowledge bona fide possibilities which would improve her lot and which she can at least try to institute.

Thus, if the issue were an empirical one, we would seek to discover whether this woman's appreciation of her situation is or is not determined. But in this assessment, it is ludicrous to consider only the current situation for it is quite obvious that different people respond differently to the same situation. We are surely entitled to consider as possibly causally relevant factors beyond situational ones, for example, her own background and genetic endowment, just as we take these into account when we seek the factors which determine a trait or overt act.

Now it is still true, as we observed earlier, that as a general truth about human beings. The range of possibilities open to our minds is vastly greater than those available to our bodies. It is a straightforward empirical truth that our freedom of choice surpasses our freedom of action. And for all we know, there may be no acts of choice that are really determined; there may be no psychological laws governing choice at all.

But Sartre's point is a priori. In some way the structure of consciousness itself determines its freedom from determination. Its nihilating nature renders it immune. But the logical point that any situation *can* be interpreted in different ways by consciousness does not imply that acts of consciousness are not *in fact* determined. *That it is logically possible for the unhappy woman to deny that she is trapped does not entail that her seeing herself as trapped is not empirically determined.*

So the belief that a case can be made on conceptual grounds that choice or volition is immune from the imposition of limits again fails.

Nobody denies that we occasionally act unfreely. Some of our acts are acts of will (choices, decisions) and there is no special reason to exclude them in this context: we sometimes choose unfreely.

NOTES

1. In "Can the Will Be Caused?" (*Philosophical Review*, vol. 71 [1962], pp. 49–55), Ginet claimed that freedom of will cannot be undermined by determinism because it is conceptually impossible for acts of will to be determined. I criticized his case in "Determinism and the Concept of a Person," (*The Journal of Philosophy*, vol. 61 [1964]). In a later paper ("Might We Have No Choice?" *Freedom and Determinism*,

ed. Keith Lehrer [New York: Random House, 1966], pp. 87–104), Ginet appeared to have changed his position for he says there that determinism is incompatible with the reality of choice. It turns out, though, that the claim he is really advancing is that physiological determinism is incompatible with *effective* choice. (He presupposes that genuine choice is effective choice.) So his thesis is very different from the one which concerns us, to wit, whether all choice is free choice.

2. Aristotle, *Nicomachean Ethics*, III, chs. 2,3 in *The Basic Works of Aristotle*, ed. Richard McKeon (New York: Random House, 1941), pp. 967–71.

3. Rene Descartes, *Passions of the Soul*, tr. Stephen Voss, Pt. I, Article XLI (Indianapolis: Hackett I 1989), p. 41.

4. Rene Descartes, *Meditations on First Philosophy*, tr. Laurence L. Lafleur (Indianapolis: Library of Liberal Arts, 1960), p. 55.

5. F. H. Bradley, "The Vulgar Notion of Responsibility in Connexion with the Theories of Free-Will and Necessity, Note A: Compulsion and Responsibility," *Ethical Studies*, 2nd ed. (Oxford: Clarendon Press, 1959).

6. Rogers Albritton, "Freedom of Will and Freedom of Action," *Proceedings and Addresses of the American Philosophical Association*, vol. 59 (1985), p. 246.

7. Jean-Paul Sartre, "A More Precise Characterization of Existentialism," tr. R. C. McCleary, *The Writings of Jean-Paul Sartre*, vol. 2: *Selected Prose*, eds. M. Contat & M. Rybalka (Evanston: Northwestern University Press, 1974), p. 159.

8. Jean-Paul Sartre, *Being and Nothingness*, tr. H. E. Barnes (New York: Philosophical Library, 1956), pp. 483–84.

9. *Meditations*, p. 59.

10. "Freedom of Will and Freedom of Action," p. 242.

11. *Ibid.*

12. "The Vulgar Notion of Responsibility in Connexion with the Theories of Free Will and Necessity."

13. "*Nicomachean Ethics*; p. 964.

14. "The Vulgar Notion of Responsibility in Connexion with the Theories of Free-Will and Necessity, Note A: Compulsion and Responsibility," pp. 4547.

15. Patricia Greenspan, "Unfreedom and Responsibility," *Responsibility, Character, and the Emotions*; cd. F. Schoeman (Cambridge: Cambridge University Press, 1987), p. 64.

16. "The Vulgar Notion of Responsibility in Connexion with the Theories of Free-Will and Necessity, Note A: Compulsion and Responsibility," p. 44.

17. *Ibid.*

18. Compare Bernard Berofsky, *Freedom from Necessity: The Metaphysical Basis of Responsibility* (London: Routledge & Kegan Paul, 1987), ch. 10.

19. David Detmer, *Freedom as a Value: A Critique of the Ethical Theory of Jean-Paul Sartre* (LaSalle, Ill.: Open Court, 1986).

20. *Ibid.*, p. 129.

QUANTUM MECHANICS, FREE WILL, AND DETERMINISM*

Henry Margenau

There are, I think, eternal questions, but no eternally valid answers. Philosophy shows itself to be alive when it raises, again and again, the deep concerns that plague man's reason; it dies when it presumes to have resolved them with finality. Determinism and freedom in their conjunction pose one of the eternal questions, and the partial answer I propose affords no stagnant resolution. It is intended to show compatibilities between disciplines that seemed discrepant, and by bringing recent scientific insights to bear upon the problem of freedom I hope to revive its fascination and perhaps to suggest ways in which progressively it can be solved, not in closed form to be sure, but along the vista of an infinite series of approximations.

A very limited aspect of the problem of freedom will enter our discussion. Modern usage has made this word so utterly meaningless that any useful treatment must be preceded by a statement of the sense we wish to convey and the nonsense we wish to avoid when the word's oracular sound appears. First a trivial point. There will never in the sequel be a reference to free will; we pass by the old psychological controversy based on a compartmentalization of human faculties. Man as an agent is free or bound; the question is whether his action is fully and under all circumstances conditioned by antecedent states. If not, the precise location of the elements of chance within the psychological complex will not form part of our inquiry: we shall not ask whether the causal hiatus occurs in the acting, or in the willing, or in the selection of alternatives, or in the reasoning that precedes the act. These, to be sure, are interesting questions; but I fear that the present state of psychology does not tolerate their formulation, let alone their solution. At any rate they lie beyond my competence.

A clear distinction must be made between at least two kinds of freedom. One of these I shall call, for want of a better word, elemental, the other practical. Practical freedom is overt freedom and resides in the absence of visible constraints or coercions. Usually these constraints are external or physical; they may result from application of force by others, from uncontrollable factors in a situation, or from personal inability to achieve a chosen goal. Or they may be internal, stemming from

*Henry Margenau, "Quantum Mechanics, Free Will, and Determinism," *The Journal of Philosophy*, LXIV, 21 (November 9, 1967): 714–725. Reprinted with kind permission of the journal and the estate of Profesor Margenau.

habituation, addiction, incompetence, and so on. These constraints which inhibit practical freedom are objectively discernible, and their absence can likewise be certified. Elemental, or, in a certain sense, metaphysical freedom, may or may not be present even when practical freedom is at hand. Indeed if Kant is right, it is entirely indifferent to the presence or absence of coercion. This is what led him to claim that only the will is free and, therefore, the seat of moral responsibility and of moral qualities. Stripped of unnecessary impediments, elemental freedom involves the existence of genuine, causeless alternatives in any prevoluntary situation that is dominated by conscious deliberation relative to the performance of an act or the making of a decision. Only elemental freedom involves us in deep metaphysical problems; practical freedom (or freedoms!), although extremely important in ethics, jurisprudence, and politics, will not concern us here.

This places the largest part of the legal concept of freedom outside of our present purview. Although I do not share this view, it can perhaps be maintained that responsibility is based solely upon the presence of practical freedom. If that is true, this paper does not touch upon the problem of human responsibility.

Nor does it present a semantic analysis of the prevalent meanings of the words 'freedom' and 'determinism'. I doubt if problems can ever be solved, even progressively, by an inspection of the usages of words. They are often clarified, sometimes unmasked as pseudoproblems, nearly always proliferated, but never, by that method, carried up to the level of creative understanding. The reward of semantic analysis is a satisfied smile, not the excitement of discovery. Nothing is gained by seeing how the word 'freedom' is used in common parlance, except perhaps to note that it is not employed in a uniform sense at all. There are easy ways of making it, indeed of making all so-called eternal questions, seem silly; but it is the business of philosophy to phrase them in pregnant ways which are adequate to refined experience and by this token to preserve rather than destroy their meaning. Indeed, may not the philosopher be pardoned if he prides himself on having insights that transcend the marketplace, and therefore claims the right to cast them in a coin of language?

Persons unfamiliar with the literature pertaining to the problem of freedom may feel that reminders of the foregoing effusive kind are out of place in a disciplined discourse because they are an attack against windmills. This, unfortunately, is not the case. Nearly all the errors just criticized are made, for example, in a book by Stace[1]—to cite a notable instance—who, probably because of a basic confusion between elemental and practical freedom and a belief in the peculiar redemptive qualities of language, proceeds to argue that freedom cannot be established because it has not been properly defined. Man, he says, could not be certified as existing if he were defined as a five-legged animal. Redefine him and he will be there! Suggestions of this sort, if significant, should greatly appeal to scientists who, after a weary search, fail to discover their quarry: they ought to console themselves because they merely used an erroneous definition. Or should they have fixed up their definition to begin with and not have searched at all?

Let us turn now to a positive statement of the problem to be attacked—not solved. Like many philosophic challenges, this one springs from an evident incompatibility between a certain ubiquitous kind of protocol experiences and the conceptual formalism available for their explanation.[2] The uncoordinated P-fact in question is the clear and present awareness of freedom or feeling of choice that accompanies every conscious decision. It stands in contradiction to certain highly successful and widely accepted scientific theories which entail universal causation and, hence, a deterministic chain of events, even mental events—unless provision is made for an unpalatable dualism contrasting the mental and the material.

An acceptable resolution of the dilemma between the self-declarative protocol evidence of freedom and the constructed and powerfully documented thesis of determinism could involve one of the following tasks: one might show that customary theory can be extended without violating already approved and explained tests of it, and yet accommodate the subjective fact of freedom; or one might demonstrate that the customary rules of correspondence which link protocol facts with constructs are in need of revision, again without prejudice to what is already accepted; or a mixture of both procedures may be necessary. In the sequel we endeavor to show that a slightly mixed strategy of the latter kind is indicated, that in fact the extension of theory had already taken place without stimulus from the freedom quarter, and that a slight modification of the rules of correspondence between states of awareness and physical fact (verified constructs, verifacts) opens an avenue of attractive inquiry promising harmony between the inchoate components of the freedom paradox.

What is not permitted is to deny offhand the veridicality of the freedom awareness. That this is a cherished nostrum among many writers need here not be emphasized; it is the vogue among hard-boiled scientists, chiefly psychologists, and it feeds upon the claim that reality exhibits no namable counterpart to the intimate experience of choice. To this one can only answer that there is no preestablished concrete reality to which this particular protocol refers. For the scientist's reality, when philosophically analyzed, turns out to be the minimal set of posits (well-connected constructs) that render our experience, including the experience of freedom, coherent. Hence no appeal to it is possible until the problem of reality itself is solved. To deny the claim of felt freedom a hearing because it is an introspective phase of consciousness is to kill the spark of every incipient scientific venture. Subjective experiences of this very sort are both the first glimmer and the last instance of appeal in all acts of scientific validation.

Another attempt to eject this candidate from the halls of scientific respectability was once made by Professor Wood,[3] who wrote:

> . . . The belief that there are genuine alternatives of action and that the choice between them is indeterminate is usually stronger in prospect and in retrospect than at the time of actual decision. The alternatives exist in prospect as imaginatively envisaged possibilities of action and in retrospect as the memory of the state of affairs before the agent had, so to speak, "made up his mind." Especially in retrospect does the agent recall his earlier decision with remorse and repentance, dwelling sorrowfully upon rejected possibilities of action which now loom up as opportunities missed (390).

Were I to comment on this passage I would have to say that it is out of accord with my own recollections. The agony, the accentuated awareness of risk that accompanies a truly important decision appear to me more memorable than any prospect or recall; indeed it is that intensified peak of consciousness to which regret and remorse later attach themselves as secondary feelings. Even more realistically, repentance in most instances deplores the circumstance that we have failed without ourselves to create the protocol consciousness of choice at the proper time, not that we have forgotten it as unimportant. But even if Wood's argument were correct, the fact that one tends to forget a feeling or a fact does not make it irrelevant.

After these preliminaries, let us turn to an examination of the theories in terms of which a solution of the problem now posed will be sought. Although the main thesis of this article presupposes a clear understanding of classical determinism and of quantal indeterminacy, limitations of space forbid their thoroughgoing discussion.[4] Hence I merely state here the principal facts that enter as preambles into the later arguments concerning freedom.

1. The ordinary doctrine of determinism (Laplace's formula) does not afford an acceptable explanation even of the facts of classical physics. No "demon" can have contingent knowledge without a slight margin of uncertainty. For example, if he knew the positions of all the molecules in this room with the unlikely error of one-millionth of one per cent at the present time, this knowledge would be completely wiped out by interactions in one microsecond. Hence this dynamically detailed manner of description is essentially illusory.
2. Probability in science is not a subjective index of confidence in the outcome of an event: it is a regular and normal physical quantity, wholly on a par with other observables which serve as ultimate determinants of events in the physical universe. Their reduction to more elementary dynamic certainties is not always possible; an indeterminate world does not presuppose a cryptodeterminism.
3. The probabilities of quantum mechanics are of this irreducible kind.
4. The uncertainty principle does not involve merely lack of knowledge, is not a proscription of certain kinds of measurement. It affects being as well as knowledge and is an expression of the latency[5] of observables.

The numberless attempts made before radically stochastic theories like quantum mechanics were known cannot be reviewed here. Most widely accepted, perhaps, is a view set forth in the writings of Kant and Cassirer.[6] Their philosophy (i.e., transcendental idealism) regards causality as a category of human understanding, a necessary form in which all knowledge of events must be cast. For things in themselves, which lie beyond our comprehension, causality and all other basic modes of thought are irrelevant. From this point of view universal causality or determinism, whether of the classical or the quantum-mechanical sort, must not be regarded as a metaphysical constraint upon all forms of being. It must be distinguished from what Cassirer calls a "dinglichen Zwang." Freedom, too, is a transcendental principle, but one regulating our actions, and it therefore controls another realm. If both were factual, descriptive attributes of the world, they would indeed collide; only their transcendental nature keeps them out of conflict and makes them "complementary," to use a currently cherished term.

Now it seems to me that classical determinism and freedom do collide—in a factual sense if both are taken as ultimate metaphysical principles, and in the form of logical irreconcilables if they are transcendental modes of explanation that regulate our understanding. Let me illustrate the meaning of this claim by reference to a trivial example.

Suppose I am asked to raise my hand. I can do this mechanically without thought and without engaging my will. In that case, habit acquired during my student days will probably cause me to raise my right hand. One may look upon this action as a causal one, whose result is predictable in terms of conditions existing in my brain, of associations acquired of neural pathways previously established, and so on. But notice: I took care to say that I would probably raise my right hand, thereby implying something less than strict predictability.

But if I am told: raise whichever hand you wish, the sequence of events is different. I am somehow challenged to think and then to make a choice. To believe that, during the moment of reflection preceding the decision to raise my left hand, the configuration of the molecules in my body, the currents in my brain cells, or even the psychological variables composing my mental state have already predetermined that I must raise my left hand is clearly false, for it contradicts the most elementary, reliable, self-declarative awareness of choice which accompanies this act. Thus a serious contradiction arises if strict causality is a metaphysical fact.

Nor can the situation be saved by saying, with Kant and Cassirer, that causality is merely a transcendental principle in terms of which we are required to conceive things. For in that case we should require one principle of understanding to comprehend the sequence of events that compose the objective course leading to the raising of my left hand, and a different, incompatible one to explain my feeling of freedom. Reason does not tolerate two incoherent principles where a single one will do. I shall now show that the loosening of causality required by quantum mechanics enlarges the scope of that principle sufficiently to allow removal of these difficulties and to cover both determination and freedom.

What we hope to accomplish needs careful statement. It might seem to be a proof that quantum mechanics has solved the problem of freedom. This is a vastly different task from showing that quantum mechanics has removed an essential obstacle from the road toward its solution, while the problem remains unsolved in its major details. The following analysis is directed toward this latter, much more modest aim. As we approach it, many of the difficulties, whose resolution constitutes the difference between the first and second tasks, will helpfully move into view.

Let it be noted again that we are not raising moral questions at this point. The decision which hand to raise is totally without ethical relevance; it merely illustrates the contrast between instinctive-reflexive, almost mechanical behavior and an action that involves thought and will, thereby engaging to a small extent the quality of freedom. The question of motivation, so essential in ethics, hardly enters at all. Or if it does, if for some conscious reason—perhaps the desire to surprise my partner—I have chosen to lift my left arm when he expected the right one to be raised, that reason is far from the concerns of ethics. The distance from here to choices that can be said to be morally good or bad, that conform or do not conform to ethical principles, is very great. Yet somehow it can be traveled by vehicles already at our disposal. Most theories of ethics achieve their end, the explanation of moral behavior, once the possibility of freedom and motivation is established. These qualities, however, are present at least in embryonic form in the example we chose for discussion; hence we return to it. Its relative simplicity is an important advantage.

Precisely what happened to me as a conscious person during that crucial interval in which I "made up my mind" to raise my left hand? Of the enormous variety of physical and chemical processes that took place in my body I am not aware. I do know, however, that the physical condition before the arm raising and that after the act were connected by a continuous series of objective physical happenings. And the entire series could have been different because of my decision, because of a choice of physical possibilities that were open to me.

The mental processes during the crucial interval are likewise difficult to record in detail. Nevertheless the following is perfectly clear. I was aware of having a choice; there was a moment of reflection, perhaps a brief recall of past occasions; then came a glimmer of rudimentary satisfaction in doing the unexpected, next a decision, and finally the act. The choice was enacted within consciousness, and it evidently was permitted, but merely permitted, by the physical processes that took place.

One thing, then, is utterly apparent: freedom is not wholly a problem of physical science but one involving biology, physiology, and psychology as well. Upon realizing this one immediately confronts the standard question of reducibility: Are the laws of psychophysiology merely elaborate versions of those encountered in the physicochemical world, or do they differ radically? The first alternative, which assumes the possibility of reducing all behavior to physicochemical bases, need not be tied to the naive supposition that all the laws of basic sciences are now known, and it will not be construed in this narrow sense here. The second, which maintains a radical difference, takes two essential forms. First, one may interpret the difference as mere transcendence, secondly as outright violation of physicochemical laws.

To avoid circumlocutions, let us refer to the first alternative, that of reducibility, as I. The second will be labeled II, and we shall designate transcendence by IIa, violation by IIb. As already mentioned, acceptance of I does not commit us to the view that all basic laws of nature are already known.

The precise meaning of IIa involves a theory of levels of complexity among physical phenomena. It is most simply illustrated by recalling the relation between the mechanics of point masses and the statistical mechanics of gases which are here viewed as large assemblages of molecules, each in the form of a point mass. To describe the mechanical state of every individual molecule one needs to specify its position and its velocity, nothing more. The totality of molecules, the gas, however, exhibits measurable properties like pressure, temperature, and entropy which have no meaning whatever with respect to single molecules. In this sense they are radically different from the properties of point masses. Yet if the positions and velocities of all molecules were known, the aggregate observables, i.e., pressure temperature, and entropy, could be calculated. These latter characterize a level of complexity above the mechanics of mass points. Explanation is continuous from below; the concepts of the lower level have meaning on the upper, but not the reverse.

It is seen, therefore, that thesis IIa asserts no incompatibility between concepts and principles on two different levels. The physicochemical and the physicopsychological can probably be regarded similarly as two different levels of complexity, even though the differences are so great that the full connection is not at present in evidence. The view, however, seems reasonable. If it is accepted, and the gap can some day be filled, the higher-level concepts can be reached from below and thus be "reduced."

The bearing of alternative IIa upon the problem of freedom, which as we have seen in encountered in the upper realm, is now apparent. Freedom cannot appear in the domains of physiology and psychology if indeterminacy is not already lodged in physics. Strict causality among the molecules, applied upward as a principle of nature to explain the behavior of aggregates, cannot entail freedom because of the requirement of continuity from below. It is equally impossible to engender freedom in the realm of psychology when strict determinism rules physics, so long as hypothesis IIa is maintained.

For our present purpose, therefore, IIa can be identified with I: neither permits freedom unless strict determinism is abandoned in physics.

Only alternative IIb provides the possibility of freedom in the face of unrelieved classical causality as it is understood in pre-quantum physics. That view cannot be rejected out of hand; indeed it is still occasionally held. Since it is forced to assume the occurrence of violations of the normal order of nature, it is tantamount to a belief in miracles. As for myself, I refuse to regard freedom as a miracle so long as other avenues of explanation are open. This is the case if alternative I or IIa is adopted, provided physical indeterminacy is taken seriously.

I judge IIa to be the safest hypothesis, and propose to describe its consequences. This is a somewhat unpopular course; it forces us to part company with many distinguished moral philosophers who see the autonomy of ethics threatened when a relation of any sort is assumed to exist between that august discipline and science. For centuries, humanists have been impressed by the slogan that science deals with facts, ethics with values, and these two categories are so disparate that they must forever stand apart. If unanalyzed, this is a foolish and a dangerous dogma. Some feel that a view that finds a root of freedom in physical science desecrates and demeans the high estate of ethics, whose legitimate concerns should not seek refuge in the indeterminacies of natural events. Ethics, says Cassirer, should not be forced to build its nests in the gaps of physical causation; but he fails to tell where else it should build them, if at all.

Throughout this article one single physical law is continually called upon to do extremely heavy duty, namely Heisenberg's indeterminacy principle. It is unreasonable to suppose that this item of knowledge is absolute in its present understanding, forever immune to reformulation and refinement. Future discoveries will doubtless place it in a new light, but it is difficult to see how its essence, which is drawn upon in the present context, can ever be relinquished. No one, of course, can rule out this possibility. But it seems far more likely, and here is where I would place my bet, that further principles even more widely restrictive of Laplacian causality will enter science, in which case the position here taken will be reenforced.

Some of them are already on the horizon, vaguely visible but portentous. The theory of turbulence in hydrodynamics, meteorology, and several promising new approaches in the behavioral sciences seem radically and perhaps irreducibly stochastic.

I now turn to a few logical arguments which have been leveled against the possibility of freedom, quite apart from physical indeterminacy. J.J.C. Smart[7] has attempted to dispose of freedom as an inconsistent concept by employing a simple and seemingly cogent logical argument. He constructs two theses, which he assumes to be exhaustive of all possibilities and also mutually exclusive: (I) one is La Laplacian determinism as we have discussed it earlier; the other (2) is the view that "there are some events that even a superhuman calculator could not predict, however precise his knowledge of however wide a region of the universe at some previous time" (294). Freedom, he holds, violates both of them and is therefore ruled out.

Certainly the requirement of impeccable logic is to be imposed on every phase of scientific and philosophic reasoning; nevertheless logic, in spite of its merited vogue, is not the sole arbiter of truth. There are instances where the diffuseness of the meaning of terms makes its formal application impossible and its conclusions spurious in spite of all the reverence it commands. In the present instance, its use to settle the argument concerning freedom is as ineffectual as the application of arithmetic to clouds.

Smart's algorithm was challenged neatly by Errol Harris,[8] who rightly insists that the two alternatives above are not mutually exclusive. If freedom were identical with Smart's second alternative we would call it erratic behavior or caprice. What makes Harris's point important is, first of all, the looseness that afflicts the term 'event' ('state' or 'observation' or 'measurement' would be more acceptable) and, second, the fact that physical indeterminacy is precisely the kind of intermediate alternative that is coincident neither with proposition 1 nor with proposition 2.

One of the most serious confusions about freedom arises in connection with the uniqueness of history. The course of events in the universe is a single flow; there is no ambiguity about the happenings at any given time, aside from our knowledge of them, and if a superhuman intellect knew everything that happened up to a certain time t, he would perceive, in looking backward, not only clear determinism but a rigid, filled space-time structure of events. He could in fact, if he were a mathematician, write a formula—with a proper qualitative text defining the nature of all events—which would represent all history up to t. Where, then, can freedom enter in the presence of that timeless formula which, although it was unknown at times before t, nevertheless "existed" in a mathematical sense?

The answer involves recognition of the fact that retrodiction is not the same as prediction. Indeterminacy permits the former but not the latter. Only Laplacian determinism makes inferences along the time axis symmetric in both directions. In classical mechanics, full knowledge of the state of a physical system at time t allows in principle the calculation of its state at any time before or after t. Indeterminacy introduces a peculiar asymmetry into states with respect to their temporal implications: the past is certain, and the future is not. This causal irreversibility of time is, and must always be, asserted along with the affirmation of freedom. It is the agency which, in the phraseology of William James, "transforms an equivocal future into an inalterable and simple past."

Nor is this without consequences with respect to the nature of time. A recent controversy concerning emergence or becoming, and the sense in which time is a fourth dimension of space[9] is strongly affected by it. Relativity theory, which is thus far an outgrowth of classical mechanics and does not incorporate indeterminacy, speaks in Laplace's voice and precludes creativity and emergence of features not already foreshadowed in the presence. In the controversy to which reference has just been made, Capek is right in arguing for emergence, not for any philosophic reason but for the simple scientific fact that ordinary four-dimensional relativity, the basis for the claim of frozen passage, is not applicable to the atomic domain.

Having reviewed the most common objections met by those who affirm human freedom and having attempted to expose their weaknesses, let me now summarize and state my case.

Classical determinism made freedom intrinsically impossible, unless its application to psychophysical phenomena is arbitrarily interdicted.

Historic arguments designed to reconcile freedom with classical causality were able merely to establish a subjective illusion, a personal feeling of freedom.

Modern physics, through Heisenberg's principle of indeterminacy, has loosened Laplacian determinism sufficiently to allow uncaused atomic events, creating in certain specifiable situations the occurrence of genuine chance.

The consequences of such microcosmic indeterminacies, while usually insignificant in the molar world, do ingress into the macrocosm at least in several known instances. It is very likely that they play a role in delicate neurophysical and chemical processes.

Physics thus makes understandable the occurrence of chance, of true alternatives upon which the course of events can seize. Physics alone, in its present state, can account for unpredictable, erratic human behavior.

Human freedom involves more than chance: it joins chance with deliberate choice. But it needs the chance. In so far, and so long, as science can say nothing about this latter active, decisive, creative element it has not fully solved the problem of freedom.

But it has lifted it out of the wastebasket of illusions and paradoxes and re-established it as a challenging problem to be further resolved.

And now an afterthought. Suppose physical science, perhaps with the aid of sister disciplines like psychology, philosophy, and even theology, had solved the problem of choice supervening upon chance to explain freedom, would this fuller understanding not restore determinism? If we can explain how the agency effecting choice selects from the alternatives presented by physics a particular one, will the inclusion of that agency into the scheme of things not leave us where we started, i.e., with an amplified Laplacian formula?

The answer cannot be foreseen. It may be affirmative, but I strongly doubt it. For if that agency were one which looked into the future rather than into the past, were drawn by purposes rather than impelled by drives, partook of the liveliness of the incalculable human spirit-freedom in a unique sense would survive. At any rate causal closure of any conceivable sort, inasmuch as it must accommodate probabilistic science, will have a scope far larger than any branch of knowledge now known as science or philosophy.

NOTES

1. W. T. Stace, *Religion and the Modern Mind* (Philadelphia: Lippincott, 1952).

2. For epistemological details, see the author's *Nature of Physical Reality* (New York: McGraw-Hill, 1950).

3. Ledger Wood, *Philosophy*, XVI, 64 (October 1941): 386–397.

4. A longer version of this article which includes a relevant account of these items and fuller arguments will be published as the 1966 Wimmer Lecture, St. Vincent College, Latrobe, Pa.

5. See Margenau, op. cit.

6. E. Cassirer. *Determinism and Indeterminism in Modern Physics* (New Haven, Conn.: Yale, 1956).

7. "Free Will, Praise and Blame," *Mind*, LXX, 279 (July 1961): 291–306.

8. *Foundations of Metaphysics in Science* (New York: Humanities, 1965).

9. Donald C. Williams, "The Myth of Frozen Passage," *Journal of Philosophy*, XL VIII, 15 (July 19, 1951): 457–472; and Milic Capek, "The Myth of Frozen Passage: The Status of Becoming in the Physical World," in R. S. Cohen and M. W. Wartofsky, eds., *Boston Studies in the Philosophy of Science*, II (New York: Humanities, 1966) pp. 441–463, with comment by Williams.

CHAPTER 3
Responsibility

In chapter 3 we examine the concept of moral responsibility and its relationship to the freedom–determinism debate. Here the central issue is to specify the conditions under which an action is performed that are required in order to hold someone morally accountable for what they do.

The first selection, *Nicomachean Ethics,* from the ancient Greek philosopher Aristotle has two aims. The first aim is to answer the question, "How do we become good people?" The second aim is to explain when we can hold other people responsible for the actions they perform, or in other words, to provide an account of when people can be praised or blamed for what they do.

To be a good person, for Aristotle, is to become morally virtuous. Unfortunately, moral virtue is not something that can be taught. It is not a matter of learning certain moral principles and then acting in accordance with them. Instead, becoming virtuous is a matter of acquiring a virtuous disposition. A disposition is a tendency to do something or to act in a particular way. When we say that Jones is disposed to anger, we mean that he often behaves angrily. To have a virtuous disposition, then, is a matter of having the tendency to act virtuously. What does it mean to act virtuously, and if one can't be taught to be virtuous, how can one learn to be virtuous?

Virtuous actions, according to Aristotle, share a common feature: they all lie between the extremes of excess and deficiency. For instance, courage is a virtue. It is something we all recognize as good, but a deficiency or lack of courage is bad, for it is to act cowardly. Too much courage, on the other hand, is also a bad thing, for it leads to foolhardiness. To be virtuous is a matter of following what Aristotle calls "the mean," the middle ground between excess and deficiency. To have a virtuous disposition is therefore to have the tendency to follow the mean, to refrain from acts of excess or deficiency.

The manner in which one acquires a virtuous disposition is through habituation. One must, through practice, develop the habit to act virtuously. This will lead to having a virtuous character. This cannot be achieved by learning and obeying a rule along the lines *follow the mean*. To follow a rule is to be guided by something external to oneself. That is quite different from performing the actions one does simply because that's the kind of person one is. The idea of being virtuous is that one's acts flow naturally from one's character, not from the intellectual decision to adhere to a moral rule.

For Aristotle, people are deserving of praise or blame to the extent that they performed their actions voluntarily. In his view, an act is voluntary if it is free from compulsion and ignorance. An act is compelled if it is the result of ignorance and/or compulsion.

An act is compelled if it is caused by external constraints. For instance, if I place a gun in your hand and physically force you to aim it at someone and pull the trigger, I have compelled you to shoot the victim, though you fired the shot. In such a case Aristotle would say that your action was compelled and that you cannot be blamed or held morally responsible for the shooting. An act is performed out of ignorance if the agent (the person who acts) is not in possession of certain facts about the action in question. For instance, suppose you are ill and I come to visit. You ask me to give you your medicine. Unknown to me someone has replaced your pills with cyanide capsules. By giving you the pills, I poison you. Since I was ignorant of the fact that the pills contained poison, I am not morally responsible for poisoning you. Note that this is ignorance of the facts about the action I performed and not ignorance of the law, or of right and wrong. Ignorance of the law, Aristotle claims, is no excuse for doing wrong. In those cases where we are compelled to act because of something else we did voluntarily, we are morally responsible. If I perform an act of vandalism while drunk, although the immediate act (breaking the store window) is involuntary, my getting drunk in the first place was voluntary. Since the second act occurred because of the first, and the first was voluntary, I am responsible for the second.

In "What Means this Freedom?" John Hospers provides a view of human motivation and responsibility that contrasts with Aristotle's. Of central importance in Hospers's discussion is the role of *unconscious* motivation. Drawing on Freudian psychoanalytic theory, Hospers takes it as a given that human beings act, in part if not in whole, on the basis of unconscious fears, desires, and other feelings that are the result of early childhood experiences. Hospers shares with Aristotle the idea that our actions flow from our character; but while Aristotle believed that we form our own character through the habituation of action, Hospers thinks the kind of character we have is totally beyond our control. For Hospers our character is the result of our childhood, and what happens to us during childhood is up to our parents and to circumstances we are powerless to change.

In light of the tremendous influence that unconscious motivation can have on our behavior, Hospers explores a number of possible accounts of voluntary action. He agrees with Aristotle that actions that are compelled or coerced by outside forces are involuntary, but what of acts that are compelled by *inner* forces, such as unconscious motivations? Since actions that are compelled by unconscious motivations are the result of influences beyond our control, Hospers claims that we should not be held responsible for such acts. It doesn't matter if these actions are premeditated or can be defended with reasons. We might have all kinds of perfectly rational conscious reasons about which we thought long and hard when we chose our actions. If our actions really have their origins in unconscious motivations, then none of those conscious reasons matter. Only in the absence of unconscious motivation can we truly be said to act voluntarily.

This has the obvious implication that many more of our actions are involuntary than we probably like to think. What does Hospers say about moral responsibility, about reward and punishment? In his view, when we act involuntarily we do not deserve moral praise or blame. This does not mean that criminals whose crimes are the result of neuroses should not be imprisoned. On the contrary, Hospers claims that such criminals should be put in jail, but not because they are responsible and deserve punishment; instead, it is simply for the benefit and protection of society that they should be jailed. Hence, the practice of reward and punishment, in Hospers's view, should continue as usual since it serves the interests of society. The moral superiority with which we regard the criminal elements of society, however, is something that cannot be defended, for the moral attitude presumes that the criminal is the master of his or her own fate. If the criminal's acts are the result of unconscious motivations, the criminal is not a master of anything, but is a slave to events that occurred during childhood. Thus, we ought not to regard criminals with moral outrage.

In "Liberty and Necessity," David Hume argues for a form of compatibilism, which views freedom and moral responsibility as compatible with determinism. Instead of speaking of determinism, Hume refers to "necessity," and instead of "freedom," he uses the word "liberty."

Hume's view of causal necessity is a little different from the idea of causal determinism that is associated with the scientific view of the world. The necessity that we ascribe to nature is, in Hume's view, really a reflection of our own psychological expectation of certain events. The world seems to us to be an ordered place. Everywhere around us, we see regularities in the behavior of objects. Stones always fall to the ground after they are thrown into the air; night always follows day; fragile objects always break when dropped onto a hard surface. Hume describes these regularities by saying that certain events are constantly conjoined in our experience. Since we've always observed night being followed by day, we come to expect day when it is night. This habit of association is the origin of the idea of causal necessity. Because night and day are constantly conjoined in our experience, and because we come to expect day when it is night, our habit of associating the two finds expression in the belief that day *must* follow night.

These kinds of regularities are not limited to mindless matter, but exist in human behavior as well. Hume points out that there are definite patterns of behavior, that certain actions always follow certain motives. Indeed, Hume suggests that we depend on these regularities and assume their existence when we interact with one another. If we never had any idea what a person was going to do next, we would be unable to form lasting relationships or engage in activities such as commerce.

Despite the fact that there is as much necessity in human action as there is in ordinary events, human beings still possess liberty or freedom. In Hume's view, liberty is the power of acting or not acting in accordance with the will. We are able to act in accordance with our wills so long as we are not in chains. Our actions need not be uncaused in order to be free. They need only to be caused in the appropriate way (by an act of will) and under specific circumstances (they are not impeded by outside forces).

Moral responsibility, reward, and punishment are also compatible with necessity, according to Hume. In fact, the idea of responsibility presupposes such necessity.

This is reflected in our practice of punishing people more severely for premeditated acts than for hasty ones. The premeditated crime is more fully caused by the agent's bad character than the hasty action, and so deserves a harsher punishment. Hume adopts a view that is similar to Hospers's in the sense that reward and punishment are justified to the extent that they contribute positively to the nexus of causes and effects in the world. But while Hospers thought that punishment serves only to protect the innocent from criminal elements, Hume sees it as serving a more constructive purpose. Reward and punishment, in Hume's view, can serve to aid in the production of good actions and prevent evil ones. Punishment, then, works not only by removing the potential of the criminal to do society harm, but deters future criminal acts.

It is quite natural to say, as Mill did, that one is morally responsible for one's actions only if one could have done otherwise; that is, if one could have acted differently. Indeed, the apparent tension between determinism and responsibility would seem to lie squarely on this very idea. Since one's behavior is determined (by causal antecedents or childhood trauma), one could not have acted otherwise and should not be morally accountable, for all actions are, in a way, coerced. Harry Frankfurt, in his "Alternate Possibilities and Moral Responsibility," questions this idea and argues that it should be rejected.

Frankfurt describes the idea that one could have acted otherwise as the "principle of alternate possibilities." When one could have acted otherwise, the idea is that there were a number of possible options from which the agent could choose. These are the *alternate possibilities*. How is it that we can hold someone morally responsible even when they could not have done otherwise?

Frankfurt develops several examples in which outside forces conspire to ensure that if an agent decides not to perform a certain act, *A*, these forces will become active and coerce the agent to perform *A* anyway. So suppose I am deliberating about whether or not to kill my wife. Imagine that a mad neuroscientist can control my mind and will produce in me the decision to commit the murder if I am about to decide not to do it. Let's say that I then decide, all on my own, to go ahead with the crime. Am I responsible? Your first reaction is probably that I am. Notice, however, that I could not have done otherwise. One way or another I was going to kill my wife.

The lesson to be learned from examples like this is that in cases where our behavior is determined our lack of responsibility is not owed to the fact that we could not have acted differently. Those who have adopted incompatibilism because they accept the principle of alternative possibilities are mistaken. Frankfurt's conclusion is that if an action is performed *because* it is determined, then we are not responsible for the action. However, if those determining factors only serve to constrain the number of possible courses of action without actually *causing* the action in question, the act is a responsible one. Responsibility and determinism might be incompatible, but if there is an incompatibility it is not because determinism entails that agents could not have done otherwise, it is because their actions were causally determined.

NICOMACHEAN ETHICS, BOOK III*

Aristotle

ACTIONS VOLUNTARY AND INVOLUNTARY

Virtue or excellence is, as we have seen, concerned with emotions and actions. When these are voluntary we receive praise and blame; when involuntary, we are pardoned and sometimes even pitied. Therefore, it is, I dare say, indispensable for a student of virtue to differentiate between voluntary and involuntary actions, and useful also for lawgivers, to help them in meting out honors and punishments.[1]

It is of course generally recognized that actions done under constraint or due to ignorance are involuntary. An act is done under constraint when the initiative or source of motion comes from without. It is the kind of act in which the agent or the person acted upon contributes nothing. For example, a wind might carry a person somewhere (he did not want to go), or men may do so who have him in their power. But a problem arises in regard to actions that are done through fear of a greater evil or for some noble purpose, for instance, if a tyrant were to use a man's parents or children as hostages in ordering him to commit a base deed, making their survival or death depend on his compliance or refusal. Are actions of this kind voluntary or involuntary? A similar problem also arises when a cargo is jettisoned in a storm. Considering the action itself, nobody would voluntarily throw away property; but when it is a matter of saving one's own life and that of his fellow passengers, any sensible man would do so. Actions of this kind are, then, of a mixed nature, although they come closer to being voluntary than to being involuntary actions. For they are desirable at the moment of action; and the end for which an action is performed depends on the time at which it is done. Thus the terms "voluntary" and "involuntary" are to be used with reference to the moment of action. In the cases just mentioned, the agent acts voluntarily, because the initiative in moving the parts of the body which act as instruments rests with the agent himself; and where the source of motion is within oneself, it is in one's power to act or not to act. Such actions, then, are voluntary, although in themselves they are perhaps involuntary, since nobody would choose to do any one of them for its own sake.

---

*Excerpted from *Aristotle: Nicomachean Ethics*, translated by Martin Ostwald (New Jersey: Prentice Hall, 1962) pp. 52–63, 64–68. Reprinted with the permission of the publisher.

(That actions of this kind are considered as voluntary is also shown by the fact that) sometimes people are even praised for doing them, for example, if they endure shameful or painful treatment in return for great and noble objectives. If the opposite is the case, reproach is heaped upon them, for only a worthless man would endure utter disgrace for no good or reasonable purpose. There are some instances in which such actions elicit forgiveness rather than praise, for example, when a man acts improperly under a strain greater than human nature can bear and which no one could endure. Yet there are perhaps also acts which no man can possibly be compelled to do, but rather than do them he should accept the most terrible sufferings and death. Thus, the circumstances that compel Alcmaeon in Euripides' play to kill his own mother are patently absurd.[2] In making a choice, it is sometimes hard to decide what advantages and disadvantages should be weighed against one another, and what losses we should endure to gain what we want; but it is even harder to abide by a decision once it is made. For as a rule, what we look forward to is painful and what we are forced to do is base. It is because of this difficulty that praise or blame depends on whether or not a man successfully resists compulsion.

What kind of actions can we say, then, are done under constraint? To state the matter without qualification, are all actions done under constraint of which the cause is external and to which the agent contributes nothing? On the other hand, actions which are in themselves involuntary, yet chosen under given circumstances in return for certain benefits and performed on the initiative of the agent—although such actions are involuntary considered in themselves, they are nonetheless voluntary under the circumstances, and because benefits are expected in return. In fact, they have a greater resemblance to voluntary actions. For actions belong among particulars, and the particular act is here performed voluntarily. But it is not easy to lay down rules how, in making a choice, two alternatives are to be balanced against one another; there are many differences in the case of particulars.

(There is a conceivable objection to this definition of "voluntary.") Suppose someone were to assert that pleasant and noble acts are performed under constraint because the pleasant and the noble are external to us and have a compelling power. But on this view, all actions would be done under constraint: for every man is motivated by what is pleasant and noble in everything he does. Furthermore, it is painful to act under constraint and involuntarily, but the performance of pleasant and noble acts brings pleasure. Finally, it is absurd to blame external circumstances rather than oneself for falling an easy prey to such attractions, and to hold oneself responsible for noble deeds, while pleasure is held responsible for one's base deeds.

It appears, thus, that an act done under constraint is one in which the initiative or source of motion comes from without, and to which the person compelled contributes nothing.

Turning now to acts due to ignorance, we may say that all of them are non-voluntary, but they are involuntary only when they bring sorrow and regret in their train: a man who has acted due to ignorance and feels no compunction whatsoever for what he has done was not a voluntary agent, since he did not know what he was doing, nor yet was he involuntary, inasmuch as he feels no sorrow. There are, therefore, two distinct types of acts due to ignorance: a man who regrets what he has done is considered an involuntary agent, and a man who does not may be called a non-voluntary agent; for as the two cases are different, it is better to give each its own name.

There also seems to be a difference between actions *due to* ignorance and acting *in* ignorance. A man's action is not considered to be due to ignorance when he is drunk or angry, but due to intoxication and anger, although he does not know what he is doing and is in fact acting in ignorance.

Now every wicked man is in a state of ignorance as to what he ought to do and what he should refrain from doing, and it is due to this kind of error that men become unjust and, in general, immoral. But an act can hardly be called involuntary if the agent is ignorant of what is beneficial. Ignorance in moral choice does not make an act involuntary—it makes it wicked; nor does ignorance of the universal, for that invites reproach; rather, it is ignorance of the particulars[3] which constitute the circumstances and the issues involved in the action.

It is on these that pity and pardon depend, for a person who acts in ignorance of a particular circumstance acts involuntarily.

It might, therefore, not be a bad idea to distinguish and enumerate these circumstances. They are: ignorance of (1) who the agent is, (2) what he is doing, (3) what thing or person is affected, and sometimes also (4) the means he is using, e.g., some tool, (5) the result intended by his action, e.g., saving a life, and (6) the manner in which he acts, e.g., gently or violently.

Now no one except a madman would be ignorant of all these factors, nor can he obviously be ignorant of (1) the agent; for how could a man not know his own identity? But a person might be ignorant of (2) what he is doing. For example, he might plead that something slipped out of his mouth, or that he did not know that he was divulging a secret, as Aeschylus said when he was accused of divulging the Mysteries;[4] or again, as a man might do who discharges a catapult, he might allege that it went off accidentally while he only wanted to show it. Moreover, (3) someone might, like Merope, mistake a son for an enemy;[5] or (4) he might mistake a pointed spear for a foil, or a heavy stone for a pumice stone. Again, (5) someone might, in trying to save a man by giving him something to drink, in fact kill him; or, (6) as in sparring, a man might intend merely to touch, and actually strike a blow.

As ignorance is possible with regard to all these factors which constitute an action, a man who acts in ignorance of any one of them is considered as acting involuntarily, especially if he is ignorant of the most important factors. The most important factors are the thing or person affected by the action and the result. An action upon this kind of ignorance is called involuntary, provided that it brings also sorrow and regret in its train.

Since an action is involuntary when it is performed under constraint or through ignorance, a voluntary action would seem to be one in which the initiative lies with the agent who knows the particular circumstances in which the action is performed.

(This implies that acts due to passion and appetite are voluntary.) For it is perhaps wrong to call involuntary those acts which are due to passion and appetite. For on that assumption we would, in the first place, deny that animals or even children are capable of acting voluntarily. In the second place, do we perform none of the actions that are motivated by appetite and passion voluntarily? Or do we perform noble acts voluntarily and base acts involuntarily? The latter alternative is ridiculous, since the cause in both cases is one and the same. But it is no doubt also absurd to call those things which we ought to desire "involuntary." For in some cases we should be angry and there are some things for which we should have an appetite, as for example, health and learning. Moreover, we think of involuntary actions as painful, while actions that satisfy our appetite are pleasant. And finally, what difference is there, as far as involuntariness is concerned, between a wrong committed after calculation and a wrong committed in a fit of passion? Both are to be avoided; but the irrational emotions are considered no less a part of human beings than reasoning is, and hence, the actions of a man which spring from passion and appetite (are equally a part of him). It would be absurd, then, to count them as involuntary.

CHOICE

After this definition of voluntary and involuntary actions, our next task is to discuss choice. For choice seems to be very closely related to virtue and to be a more reliable criterion for judging character than actions are.

Choice clearly seems to be something voluntary, but it is not the same as voluntariness; voluntariness is a wider term. For even children and animals have a share in the voluntary, but not in choice. Also, we can describe an act done on the spur of the moment as a voluntary act, but not the result of choice.

It seems to be a mistake to identify choice, as some people do,[6] with appetite, passion, wish, or some form of opinion. For choice is not shared by irrational creatures, whereas appetite and passion are. Moreover, the acts of a morally weak person are accompanied by appetite, but not by choice, while a morally strong person acts from choice, but not from appetite. Also, appetite can be opposed to choice, but not appetite to appetite. Again, appetite deals with what is pleasant and painful, while choice deals neither with the pleasant nor with the painful. The resemblance between choice and passion is even slighter. For an act due to passion hardly seems to be based on choice.

Choice is not even the same as wish, although the two seem to be close to one another. For choice does not have the impossible as its object, and if anyone were to assert that he was *choosing* the impossible, he would be considered a fool. But wish can be for the impossible, e.g., immortality.[7] Wish has as its objects also those things which cannot possibly be attained through our own agency. We might, for instance, wish for the victory of a particular actor or a particular athlete. But no one chooses such things, for we choose only what we believe might be attained through our own agency. Furthermore, wish is directed at the end rather than the means, but choice at the means which are conducive to a given end. For example, we *wish* to be healthy and *choose* the things that will give us health. Similarly, we say that we *wish* to be happy and describe this as our wish, but it would not be fitting to say that we *choose* to be happy. In general, choice seems to be concerned with the things that lie within our power.

Again, choice cannot be identified with opinion. For opinion may refer to any matter, the eternal and the impossible no less than things within our power. Also, opinions are characterized by their truth or falsity, not by their moral goodness or badness, as choices are.

Now, perhaps no one identifies choice with opinion in general; but it would not even be correct to identify it with some particular opinion. For our character is determined by our choosing good or evil, not by the opinions we hold. We choose to take or avoid a good or an evil, but we hold opinions as to what a thing is, whom it will benefit, or how: but (the decision) to take or avoid is by no means an opinion.

Also, a choice is praised for being directed to the proper object or for being correctly made, but opinions are praised for being true. Moreover, we make a choice of things which we definitely know to be good, whereas we form opinions about what we do not quite know. Nor does it seem that the same people make the best choices and also hold the best opinions: some hold rather good opinions, but because of a moral depravity they do not make the right choice. Whether opinion precedes or follows choice is immaterial; for we are not concerned with this problem, but only whether choice is to be identified with some form of opinion.

Since choice, then, is none of the things mentioned, what is it or what kind of thing? As we have said, it clearly seems to be something voluntary, but not everything voluntary is the object of choice. Could it be the result of preceding deliberation? (This is probably correct,) for choice involves reason and thought. The very name "choice"[8] seems to suggest that it is something "chosen before" other things.

DELIBERATION

(To turn to deliberation:) do people deliberate about everything? And is everything an object of deliberation? Or are there some things about which one cannot deliberate? Perhaps we ought to say that an object of deliberation is what a sensible man would deliberate about, but not a fool or madman. Now, nobody deliberates about the eternal, such as the order of the universe or the incommensurability of the diagonal and the side of the square. Nor, on the other hand, do we deliberate about things that are in motion if they always occur in the same way, whether by sheer necessity, by nature, or by some other cause: for example, we do not deliberate about solstices and sunrises. Neither do we deliberate about irregular occurrences, such as drought or rain, nor about chance events, such as the discovery of a treasure. We do not even deliberate about anything and everything that concerns man: no Spartan deliberates about what form of government would be best for the Scythians. For none of these things can happen through our agency.

But what we do deliberate about are things that are in our power and can be realized in action; in fact, these are the only things that remain to be considered. For in addition to nature, necessity, and chance, we regard as causal principles intelligence and anything done through human agency. But of course different groups of people deliberate only about what is attainable by their own actions. Also, there can be no deliberation in any science that is exact and self-contained, such as writing the letters of the alphabet: we have no differences of opinion as to how they are to be written.[9] Rather, we deliberate about matters which are done through our own agency, though not always in the same manner, e.g., about questions of medicine or of acquiring wealth. We deliberate more about navigation than about physical training, because navigation is less exact as a discipline. The same principle can also be applied to the other branches of knowledge. But we deliberate more about the arts than about the sciences, since we have more differences of opinion about them. Deliberation, then, operates in matters that hold good as a general rule, but whose outcome is unpredictable, and in cases in which an indeterminate element is involved. When great issues are at stake, we distrust our own abilities as insufficient to decide the matter and call in others to join us in our deliberations.

We deliberate not about ends but about the means to attain ends: no physician deliberates whether he should cure, no orator whether he should be convincing, no statesman whether he should establish law and order, nor does any expert deliberate about the end of his profession. We take the end for granted, and then consider in what manner and by what means it can be realized. If it becomes apparent that there is more than one means by which it can be attained, we look for the easiest and best; if it can be realized by one means only, we consider in what manner it can be realized by that means, and how that means can be achieved in its turn. We continue that process until we come to the first link in the chain of causation, which is the last step in order of discovery. For when a man deliberates, he seems to be seeking something and to be analyzing his problem in the manner described, as he would a geometrical figure: the last step in the analysis is at once the first in constructing the figure.[10] (By the way, it seems that not all investigation is deliberation—mathematical investigation is not—though every deliberation is an investigation.) Moreover, if in the process of investigation we encounter an insurmountable obstacle, for example, if we need money and none can be procured, we abandon our investigation; but if it turns out to be possible, we begin to act. By "possible" I mean those things which can be realized through our own agency: for even what our friends do for us is, in a way, done through our own agency, since the initiative is our own. Sometimes the object of our investigation is to find the instruments we need and sometimes to discover how to use them. The same is true of other matters, too: sometimes we have to find what the means are, and sometimes how they are to be used or through whom they can be acquired. To sum up our conclusions: (1) man is the source of his actions; (2) deliberation is concerned with things attainable by human action; and (3) actions aim at ends other than themselves. For we cannot deliberate about ends but about the means by which ends can be attained. Nor can we deliberate about particular facts, e.g., whether this is a loaf of bread or whether this loaf of bread has been properly baked: such facts are the object of sense perception. And if we continue deliberating each point in turn, we shall have to go on to infinity.

The object of deliberation and the object of choice are identical, except that the object of choice has already been determined, since it has been decided upon on the basis of deliberation. For every man stops inquiring how he is to act when he has traced the initiative of action back to himself and to the dominant part of himself: it is this part that exercises choice. This may be illustrated by the ancient political systems represented in Homer, where the kings would make a choice and then proclaim it to the people.

Since, then, the object of choice is something within our power which we desire as a result of deliberation, we may define choice as a deliberate desire for things that are within our power: we arrive at a decision on the basis of deliberation, and then let the deliberation guide our desire. So much for an outline of choice, its objects, and the fact that it is concerned with means rather than ends. . .

MAN AS RESPONSIBLE AGENT

Now, since the end is the object of wish, and since the means to the end are the objects of deliberation and choice, it follows that actions concerned with means are based on choice and are voluntary actions. And the activities in which the virtues find their expression deal with means. Consequently, virtue or excellence depends on ourselves, and so does vice. For where it is in our power to act, it is also in our power not to act, and where we can say "no," we can also say "yes." Therefore, if we have the power to act where it is noble to act, we also have the power not to act where not to act is base; and conversely, if we have the power not to act where inaction is noble, we also have the power to act where action is base. But if we have the power to act nobly or basely, and likewise the power not to act, and if such action or inaction constitutes our being good and evil, we must conclude that it depends on us whether we are decent or worthless individuals. The saying, "No one is voluntarily wicked nor involuntarily happy," seems to be partly false and partly true. That no one is involuntarily happy is true, but wickedness is voluntary. If we do not accept that, we must contradict the conclusions at which we have just arrived, and must deny that man is the source and begetter of his actions as a father is of his children. But if our conclusions are accepted, and if we cannot trace back our actions to starting points other than those within ourselves, then all actions in which the initiative lies in ourselves are in our power and are voluntary actions.

These conclusions are corroborated by the judgment of private individuals and by the practice of lawgivers. They chastise and punish evildoers, except those who have acted under constraint or due to some ignorance for which they are not responsible, but honor those who act nobly; their intention seems to be to encourage the latter and to deter the former. Yet nobody encourages us to perform what is not within our power and what is not voluntary: there would be no point in trying to stop by persuasion a man from feeling hot, in pain, or hungry, and so forth, because we will go on feeling these conditions no less for that.

Even ignorance is in itself no protection against punishment if a person is thought to be responsible for his ignorance. For example, the penalty is twice as high if the offender acted in a state of drunkenness, because the initiative is his own: he had the power not to get drunk, and drunkenness was responsible for his ignorance. Moreover, punishment is inflicted for offenses committed in ignorance of such provisions of the law as the offender ought to have known or might easily have known. It is also inflicted in other cases in which ignorance seems to be due to negligence: it was in the offender's power not to be ignorant, it is argued, and he could have made sure had he wanted to.

But, it might be objected, carelessness may be part of a man's character. We counter, however, by asserting that a man is himself responsible for becoming careless, because he lives in a loose and carefree manner; he is likewise responsible for being unjust or self-indulgent, if he keeps on doing mischief or spending his time in drinking and the like. For a given kind of activity produces a corresponding character. This is shown by the way in which people train themselves for any kind of contest or performance: they keep on practicing for it. Thus, only a man who is utterly insensitive can be ignorant of the fact that moral characteristics are formed by actively engaging in particular actions.

Moreover, it is unreasonable to maintain that a man who acts unjustly or self-indulgently does not wish to be unjust or self-indulgent. If a man is not ignorant of what he is doing when he performs acts which will make him unjust, he will of course become unjust voluntarily; nor again, can wishing any more make him stop being unjust and become just than it can make a sick man healthy. Let us assume the case of a man who becomes ill voluntarily through living a dissolute life and dis-obeying doctors' orders. In the beginning, before he let his health slip away, he could have avoided becoming ill: but once you have thrown a stone and let it go, you can no longer recall it, even though the power to throw it was yours, for the initiative was within you. Similarly, since an unjust or a self-indulgent man initially had the possibility not to become unjust or self-indulgent, he has acquired these traits voluntarily; but once he has acquired them it is no longer possible for him not to be what he is.

There are some cases in which not only the vices of the soul, but also those of the body are voluntary and are accordingly criticized. Nobody blames a man for being ugly by nature; but we do blame those who become ugly through lack of exer-cise and through taking no care of their person. The same applies to infirmities and physical handicaps: every one would pity rather than reproach a man who was blind by nature or whose blindness is due to disease or accident, but all would blame him if it were caused by drunkenness or some other form of self-indulgence. In other words, those bodily vices which depend on ourselves are blamed and those which do not are not blamed. This being so, we may conclude that other kinds of vice for which we are blamed also depend upon ourselves.

But someone might argue as follows: "All men seek what appears good to them, but they have no control over how things appear to them; the end appears different to different men." If, we reply, the individual is somehow responsible for his own charac-teristics, he is similarly responsible for what appears to him (to be good). But if he is not so responsible, no one is responsible for his own wrongdoing, but everyone does wrong through ignorance of the proper end, since he believes that his actions will bring him the greatest good. However, the aim we take for the end is not determined by the choice of the individual himself, but by a natural gift of vision, as it were, which en-ables him to make correct judgments and to choose what is truly good: to be well en-dowed by nature means to have this natural gift. For to be well and properly provided by nature with the greatest and noblest of gifts, a gift which can be got or learned from no one else, but which is one's possession in the form in which nature has given it: that is the meaning of being well endowed by nature in the full and true sense of the word.

But if this theory is true, how will virtue be any more voluntary than vice? The end has been determined for, and appears to, a good man and a bad man alike by na-ture or something of that sort; and both will use the end thus determined as the stan-dard for any actions they may undertake. Thus, whether the end that appears (to be good) to a particular person, whatever it may be, is not simply given to him by nature but is to some extent due to himself; or whether, though the end is given by nature, virtue is voluntary in the sense that a man of high moral standards performs the ac-tions that lead up to the end voluntarily: in either case vice, too, is bound to be no less voluntary than virtue. For, like the good man, the bad man has the requisite ability to perform actions through his own agency, even if not to formulate his own ends. If, then, our assertion is correct, viz., that the virtues are voluntary because we share in some way the responsibility for our own characteristics and because the ends we set up for ourselves are determined by the kind of persons we are, it follows that the vices, too, are voluntary; for the same is true of them.

To sum up: we have described the virtues in general and have given an outline of the genus to which they belong, i.e., that they are means and that they are charac-teristics. We have stated that they spontaneously tend to produce the same kind of actions as those to which they owe their existence; that they are in our power and voluntary; and that they follow the dictates of right reason. However, our actions and our characteristics are not voluntary in the same sense: we are in control of our actions from beginning to end, insofar as we know the particular circumstances surrounding them. But we control only the beginning of our characteristics: the particular steps in their development are imperceptible, just as they are in the spread of a disease; yet since the power to behave or not to behave in a given way was ours in the first place, our characteristics are voluntary.

NOTES

1. There is no clear equivalent in English to express *hekousion* and its opposite *akousion*, which form the theme of this chapter. An agent is described as *hekōn* when he has consented to perform the action which he is performing. This consent may range from mere passive acquiescence to intentional and deliberate conduct. The neuter *hekousion* is used to denote an action so performed. Conversely, an *akōn* is a man who has not given his consent to acting the way he does, regardless of whether he acts unconsciously, inadvertently, or even against his own will, and an *akousion* is an action performed by such a man.

2. Euripides' play has not come down to us. According to the myth, Alcmaeon killed his mother, Eriphyle, to avenge the death of his father, Amphiaraus. Amphiaraus, foreknowing through his gift of prophecy that he would be doomed if he joined the expedition of the Seven against Thebes, refused to join it until compelled to do so by his wife, who had been bribed by the gift of a necklace to make him join. An ancient commentator on this passage tells us that Alcmaeon's motive for killing his mother in Euripides' play was to escape the curse of his father.

3. A few remarks ought to be made about the practical syllogism involved in this passage. Reasoning on matters of conduct involves two premises, one major and one minor. The major premise is always universal, e.g., "to remove by stealth another person's property is stealing," and the minor premise particular, e.g., "this horse is another person's property," so that the conclusion would be: "To remove this horse by stealth is stealing." What Aristotle says here is that ignorance of the major premise produces an immoral act, while ignorance of the minor premise produces an involuntary act which may be pitied or pardoned. Thus it is a moral defect for a man not to know that to remove by stealth another person's property is stealing. In an involuntary act, on the other hand, the agent does know the universal premise, but is ignorant of the particular, i.e., that this horse is the property of another. . .

4. The details of this story are preserved only in some late, but ancient, authors: Clement of Alexandria, *Stromateis* II. 14. 60, and Aelian, *Variae Historiae* V. 19. The Mysteries were a secret form of religious worship whose doctrines and rites were revealed only to the initiated; Aeschylus was accused before the Areopagus of having divulged some of the secrets of the Eleusinian Mysteries. These particular Mysteries, celebrated at Eleusis in Attica, were administered for the Athenian state by certain Eleusinian families, and honored Demeter, goddess of corn and patroness of agriculture, and her daughter Persephone. Aeschylus pleaded that he had not known the matter was secret and was acquitted.

5. In a lost play of Euripides, Merope was about to slay her son Cresphontes, believing him to be an enemy. Cf. *Poetics* 1454a5.

6. We do not know whom Aristotle had in mind.

7. This statement must not be regarded as a rejection on Aristotle's part of a doctrine of immortality. What he is asserting here is merely a reflection of the common Greek distinction between "mortal" men and "immortal" gods: it is impossible to choose to live forever, but it is possible to wish it. To a certain extent Aristotle does believe in the possibility of human immortality, see X. 7, 1177b26 ff. and *De Anima* 111.5, 430a22–25.

8. *Proairesis*, literally 'fore-chioice' or 'preference.'

9. Aristotle's meaning here is elucidated by the corresponding passage in the *Eudemiun Ethics* 11. 10, 1226a33–b2, where the difference between a physician and a writer is taken as the example. In his deliberations, a physician is liable to two kinds of mistakes: (1) he may adopt the wrong kind of treatment or (2) he may give the right treatment to the wrong particular case. In writing, on the other hand, only the second kind of mistake is possible: the writer always knows how the letters should be written, but he may place a correctly drawn letter where it does not belong.

10. Aristotle is thinking of the steps followed in constructing a geometrical figure. We first assume the completed figure as constructed and then proceed by analysis to see, one by one, what the various steps are by which it was constructed. These steps reveal the constituent parts of the completed figure, i.e., the means by which the end—here the figure—is attained. We thus begin our analysis with the completed figure, but begin our construction with the last part analyzed.

WHAT MEANS THIS FREEDOM?*

John Hospers

I am in agreement to a very large extent with the conclusions of Professor Edwards' paper, and am happy in these days of "soft determinism" to hear the other view so forcefully and fearlessly stated. As a preparation for developing my own views on the subject, I want to mention a factor that I think is of enormous importance and relevance: namely, unconscious motivation. There are many actions—not those of an

*From John Hospers, "What Means this Freedom?" in *Determinism and Freedom in the Age of Modern Science*, ed. Sidney Hook. (New York: Collier Books, 1961), 124–142. Reprinted with the kind permission of the estate of Sidney Hook.

insane person (however the term insane be defined), nor of a person ignorant of the effects of his action, nor ignorant of some relevant fact about the situation, nor in any obvious way mentally deranged—for which human beings in general and the courts in particular are inclined to hold the doer responsible, and for which, I would say, he should not be held responsible. The deed may be planned, it may be carried out in cold calculation, it may spring from the agent's character and be continuous with the rest of his behavior, and it may be perfectly true that he could have done differently *if* he had wanted to; nonetheless his behavior was brought about by unconscious conflicts developed in infancy, over which he had no control and of which (without training in psychiatry) he does not even have knowledge. He may even *think* he knows why he acted as he did, he may *think* he has conscious control over his actions, he may even *think* he is fully responsible for them; but he is not. Psychiatric casebooks provide hundreds of examples. The law and common sense, though puzzled sometimes by such cases, are gradually becoming aware that they exist; but at this early stage countless tragic blunders still occur because neither the law nor the public in general is aware of the genesis of criminal actions. The mother blames her daughter for choosing the wrong men as candidates for husbands; but though the daughter thinks she is choosing freely and spends a considerable amount of time "deciding" among them, the identification with her sick father, resulting from Oedipal fantasies in early childhood, prevents her from caring for any but sick men, twenty or thirty years older than herself. Blaming her is beside the point; she cannot help it, and she cannot change it. Countless criminal acts are thought out in great detail; yet the participants are (without their own knowledge) acting out fantasies, fears, and defenses from early childhood, over whose coming and going they have no conscious control.

Now, I am not saying that none of these persons should be in jails or asylums. Often society must be protected against them. Nor am I saying that people should cease the practices of blaming and praising, punishing and rewarding; in general these devices are justified by the results—although very often they have practically no effect; the deeds are done from inner compulsion, which is not lessened when the threat of punishment is great. I am only saying that frequently persons we think responsible are not properly to be called so; we mistakenly think them responsible because we assume they are like those in whom no unconscious drive (toward this type of behavior) is present, and that their behavior can be changed by reasoning, exhorting, or threatening.

I

I have said that these persons are not responsible. But what is the criterion for responsibility? Under precisely what conditions is a person to be held morally responsible for an action? Disregarding here those conditions that have to do with a person's *ignorance* of the situation or the effects of his action, let us concentrate on those having to do with his "inner state." There are several criteria that might be suggested:

1. The first idea that comes to mind is that responsibility is determined by the presence or absence of *premeditation*—the opposite of "premeditated" being, presumably, "unthinking" or "impulsive." But this will not do—both because some

acts are not premeditated but responsible, and because some are premeditated and not responsible.

Many acts we call responsible can be as unthinking or impulsive as you please. If you rush across the street to help the victim of an automobile collision, you are (at least so we would ordinarily say) acting responsibly, but you did not do so out of premeditation; you saw the accident, you didn't think, you rushed to the scene without hesitation. It was like a reflex action. But you acted responsibly: unlike the knee jerk, the act was the result of past training and past thought about situations of this kind; that is why you ran to help instead of ignoring the incident or running away. When something done originally from conviction or training becomes habitual, it becomes *like* a reflex action. As Aristotle said, virtue should become second nature through habit: a virtuous act should be performed *as if* by instinct; this, far from detracting from its moral worth, testifies to one's mastery of the desired type of behavior; one does not have to make a moral effort each time it is repeated.

There are also premeditated acts for which, I would say, the person is not responsible. Premeditation, especially when it is so exaggerated as to issue in no action at all, can be the result of neurotic disturbance or what we sometimes call an emotional "block," which the person inherits from long-past situations. In Hamlet's revenge on his uncle (I use this example because it is familiar to all of us), there was no lack, but rather a surfeit, of premeditation, his actions were so exquisitely premeditated as to make Freud and Dr. Ernest Jones look more closely to find out what lay behind them. The very premeditation camouflaged unconscious motives of which Hamlet himself was not aware. I think this is an important point, since it seems that the courts often assume that premeditation is a criterion of responsibility. If failure to kill his uncle had been considered a crime, every court in the land would have convicted Hamlet. Again: a woman's decision to stay with her husband in spite of endless "mental cruelty" is, if she is the victim of an unconscious masochistic "will to punishment," one for which she is not responsible; she is the victim and not the agent, no matter how profound her conviction that she is the agent; she is caught in a masochistic web (of complicated genesis) dating back to babyhood, perhaps a repetition of a comparable situation involving her own parents, a repetition-compulsion that, as Freud said, goes "beyond the pleasure principle." Again: a criminal whose crime was carefully planned step by step is usually considered responsible, but as we shall see in later examples, the overwhelming impulse toward it, stemming from an unusually humiliating ego defeat in early childhood, was as compulsive as any can be.

2. Shall we say, then, that a person is not responsible for his act unless he can *defend it with reasons*? I am afraid that this criterion is no better than the previous one. First, intellectuals are usually better at giving reasons than nonintellectuals, and according to this criterion would be more responsible than persons acting from moral conviction not implemented by reasoning; yet it is very doubtful whether we should want to say that the latter are the more responsible. Second, the giving of reasons itself may be suspect. The reasons may be rationalizations camouflaging unconscious motives of which the agent knows nothing. Hamlet gave many reasons for not doing what he felt it was his duty to do: the time was not right, his uncle's soul might go to heaven, etc. His various "reasons" contradicted one

another, and if an overpowering compulsion had not been present, the highly intellectual Hamlet would not have been taken in for a moment by these rationalizations. The real reason, the Oedipal conflict that made his uncle's crime the accomplishment of his own deepest desire, binding their fates into one and paralyzing him into inaction, was unconscious and of course unknown to him. One's intelligence and reasoning power do not enable one to escape from unconsciously motivated behavior; it only gives one greater facility in rationalizing that behavior; one's intelligence is simply used in the interests of the neurosis—it is pressed into service to justify with reasons what one does quite independently of the reasons.

If these two criteria are inadequate, let us seek others.

3. Shall we say that a person is responsible for his action unless it is the *result of unconscious forces* of which he knows nothing? Many psychoanalysts would probably accept this criterion. If it is not largely reflected in the language of responsibility as ordinarily used, this may be due to ignorance of fact most people do not know that there are such things as unconscious motives and unconscious conflicts causing human beings to act. But it may be that if they did, perhaps they would refrain from holding persons responsible for certain actions.

I do not wish here to quarrel with this criterion of responsibility. I only want to point out the fact that if this criterion is employed a far greater number of actions will be excluded from the domain of responsibility than we might at first suppose. Whether we are neat or untidy, whether we are selfish or unselfish, whether we provoke scenes or avoid them, even whether we can exert our powers of will to change our behavior—all these may, and often do, have their source in our unconscious life.

4. Shall we say that a person is responsible for his act unless it is *compelled*? Here we are reminded of Aristotle's assertion (*Nicomachean Ethics*, Book III) that a person is responsible for his act except for reasons of either ignorance or compulsion. Ignorance is not part of our problem here (unless it is unconsciously induced ignorance of facts previously remembered and selectively forgotten—in which case the forgetting is again compulsive), but compulsion is. How will compulsion do as a criterion? The difficulty is to state just what it means. When we say an act is compelled in a psychological sense, our language is metaphorical—which is not to say that there is no point in it or that, properly interpreted, it is not true. Our actions are compelled in a literal sense if someone has us in chains or is controlling our bodily movements. When we say that the storm compelled us to jettison the cargo of the ship (Aristotle's example), we have a less literal sense of compulsion, for at least it is open to us to go down with the ship. When psychoanalysts say that a man was compelled by unconscious conflicts to wash his hands constantly, this is also not a literal use of "compel"; for nobody forced his hands under the tap. Still, it is a typical example of what psychologists call *compulsive* behavior: it has unconscious causes inaccessible to introspection, and moreover nothing can change it—it is as inevitable for him to do it as it would be if someone were forcing his hands under the tap. In this it is exactly like the action of a powerful external force; it is just as little within one's conscious control.

In its area of application this interpretation of responsibility comes to much the same as the previous one. And this area is very great indeed. For if we cannot be held responsible for the infantile situations (in which we were after all passive victims), then neither, it would seem, can we be held responsible for compulsive actions occurring in adulthood that are inevitable consequences of those infantile situations. And, psychiatrists and psychoanalysts tell us, actions fulfilling this description are characteristic of all people some of the time and some people most of the time. Their occurrence, once the infantile events have taken place, is inevitable, just as the explosion is inevitable once the fuse has been lighted; there is simply more "delayed action" in the psychological explosions than there is in the physical ones.

(I have not used the word "inevitable" here to mean "causally determined," for according to such a definition every event would be inevitable if one accepted the causal principle in some form or other; and probably nobody except certain philosophers uses "inevitable" in this sense. Rather, I use "inevitable" in its ordinary sense of "cannot be avoided." To the extent, therefore, that adult neurotic manifestations *can* be avoided, once the infantile patterns have become set, the assertion that they are inevitable is not true.)

5. There is still another criterion, which I prefer to the previous ones, by which a man's responsibility for an act can be measured: the degree to which that act can (or could have been) *changed by the use of reasons*. Suppose that the man who washes his hands constantly does so, he says, for hygienic reasons, believing that if he doesn't do so he will be poisoned by germs. We now convince him, on the best medical authority, that his belief is groundless. Now, the test of his responsibility is whether the changed belief will result in changed behavior. If it does not, as with the compulsive hand washer, he is not acting responsibly, but if it does, he is. It is not the *use* of reasons, but their *efficacy in changing behavior* that is being made the criterion of responsibility. And clearly in neurotic cases no such change occurs; in fact, this is often made the defining characteristic of neurotic behavior: it is unchangeable by any rational considerations.

II

I have suggested these criteria to distinguish actions for which we can call the agent responsible from those for which we cannot. Even persons with extensive knowledge of psychiatry do not, I think, use any one of these criteria to the exclusion of the others; a conjunction of two or more may be used at once. But however they may be combined or selected in actual application, I believe we can make the distinction along some such lines as we have suggested.

But is there not still another possible meaning of "responsibility" that we have not yet mentioned? Even after we have made all the above distinctions, there remains a question in our minds whether we are, in the final analysis, *responsible for any of our actions at all*. The issue may be put this way: How can anyone be responsible for his actions, since they grow out of his character, which is shaped and molded and made what it is by influence—some hereditary, but most of them stemming from early parental environment—that were not of his own making or choosing? This question, I believe, still troubles many people who would agree to all the distinctions we have just made but still have the feeling that "this isn't all." They have the uneasy suspicion that there is a more ultimate sense, a "deeper" sense, in which we are *not* responsible for our actions, since we are not responsible for the character out of which those actions spring. . .

Let us take as an example a criminal who, let us say, strangled several persons and is himself now condemned to die in the electric chair. Jury and public alike hold him fully responsible (at least they utter the words "he is responsible"), for the murders were planned down to the minutest detail, and the defendant tells the jury exactly how he planned them. But now we find out how it all came about; we learn of parents who rejected him from babyhood, of the childhood spent in one foster home after another, where it was always plain to him that he was not wanted; of the constantly frustrated early desire for affection, the hard shell of nonchalance and bitterness that he assumed to cover the painful and humiliating fact of being unwanted, and his subsequent attempts to heal these wounds to his shattered ego through defensive aggression.

> The criminal is the most passive person in this world, helpless as a baby in his motorically inexpressible fury. Not only does he try to wreak revenge on the mother of the earliest period of his babyhood; his criminality is based on the inner feeling of being incapable of making the mother even feel that the child seeks revenge on her. The situation is that of a dwarf trying to annoy a giant who superciliously refuses to see these attempts. . . . Because of his inner feeling of being a dwarf, the criminotic uses, so to speak, dynamite. Of that the giant must take cognizance. True, the "revenge" harms the avenger. He may be legally executed. However, the primary inner aim of forcing the giant to acknowledge the dwarf's fury is fulfilled.[1]

The poor victim is not conscious of the inner forces that exact from him this ghastly toll; he battles, he schemes, he revels in pseudo-aggression, he is miserable, but he does not know what works within him to produce these catastrophic acts of crime. His aggressive actions are the wriggling of a worm on a fisherman's hook. And if this is so, it seems difficult to say any longer, "He is responsible." Rather, we shall put him behind bars for the protection of society, but we shall no longer flatter our feeling of moral superiority by calling him personally responsible for what he did.

Let us suppose it were established that a man commits murder only if, sometime during the previous week, he has eaten a certain combination of foods—say, tuna fish salad at a meal also including peas, mushroom soup, and blueberry pie. What if we were to track down the factors common to all murders committed in this country during the last twenty years and found this factor present in all of them, and only in them? The example is of course empirically absurd; but may it not be that there is *some* combination of factors that regularly leads to homicide, factors such as are described in general terms in the above quotation? (Indeed the situation in the quotation is less fortunate than in our hypothetical example, for it is easy to avoid certain foods once we have been warned about them, but the situation of the infant is thrust on him; something has already happened to him once and for all, before he knows it has happened.) When such specific factors are discovered, won't they make it clear that it is foolish and pointless, as well as immoral, to hold human beings responsible for crimes? Or, if one prefers biological to psychological factors, suppose a neurologist is called in to testify at a murder trial and produces X-ray pictures of the brain of the criminal; anyone can see, he argues, that the *cella turcica* was already calcified at the age of nineteen; it should be a flexible bone, growing, enabling the gland to grow.[2] All the defendant's disorders might have resulted from this early calcification. Now, this particular explanation may be empirically false; but who can say that no such factors, far more complex, to be sure, exist?

When we know such things as these, we no longer feel so much tempted to say that the criminal is responsible for his crime; and we tend also (do we not?) to excuse him—not legally (we still confine him to prison) but morally; we no longer call him a monster or hold him personally responsible for what he did. Moreover, we do this in general, not merely in the case of crime: "You must excuse Grandmother for being irritable; she's really quite ill and is suffering some pain all the time." Or: "The dog always bites children after she's had a litter of pups; you can't blame her for it: she's not feeling well, and besides she naturally wants to defend them." Or: "She's nervous and jumpy, but do excuse her: she has a severe glandular disturbance."

Let us note that the more *thoroughly* and *in detail* we know the causal factors leading a person to behave as he does, the more we tend to exempt him from responsibility. When we know nothing of the man except what we see him do, we say he is an ungrateful cad who expects much of other people and does nothing in return, and we are usually indignant. When we learn that his parents were the same way and, having no guilt feelings about this mode of behavior themselves, brought him up to be greedy and avaricious, we see that we could hardly expect him to have developed moral feelings in this direction. When we learn, in addition, that he is not aware of being ungrateful or selfish, but unconsciously represses the memory of events unfavorable to himself, we feel that the situation is unfortunate but "not really his fault." When we know that this behavior of his, which makes others angry, occurs more constantly when he feels tense or insecure, and that he now feels tense and insecure, and that relief from pressure will diminish it, then we tend to "feel sorry for the poor guy" and say he's more to be pitied than censured. We no longer want to say that he is personally responsible; we might rather blame nature or his parents for having given him an unfortunate constitution or temperament.

In recent years a new form of punishment has been imposed on middle-aged and elderly parents. Their children, now in their twenties, thirties or even forties, present them with a modern grievance: "My analysis proves that *you* are responsible for my neurosis." Overawed by these authoritative statements, the poor tired parents fall easy victims to the newest variations on the scapegoat theory.

In my opinion, this senseless cruelty—which disinters educational sins which had been burned for decades, and uses them as the basis for accusations which the victims cannot answer—is unjustified. Yes "the truth loves to be centrally located" (Melville), and few parents—since they are human—have been perfect. But granting their mistakes, they acted as *their* neurotic difficulties forced them to act. To turn the tables and declare the children not guilty because of the *impersonal* nature of their own neuroses, while at the same time the parents are *personally* blamed, is worse than illogical; it is profoundly unjust.[3]

And so, it would now appear, neither of the parties is responsible: "they acted as their neurotic difficulties forced them to act." The patients are not responsible for their neurotic manifestations, but then neither are the parents responsible for theirs; and so, of course, for their parents in turn, and theirs before them. It is the twentieth-century version of the family curse, the curse on the House of Atreus.

"But," a critic complains, "it's immoral to exonerate people indiscriminately in this way. I might have thought it fit to excuse somebody because he was born on the other side of the tracks, if I didn't know so many bank presidents who were also born on the other side of the tracks." Now, I submit that the most immoral thing in this situation is the critic's caricature of the conditions of the excuse. Nobody is excused merely because he was born on the other side of the tracks. But if he was born on the other side of the tracks *and* was a highly narcissistic infant to begin with *and* was repudiated or neglected by his parents *and* . . . (here we list a finite number of conditions), and if this complex of factors is *regularly* followed by certain behavior traits in adulthood, and moreover *unavoidably* so—that is, they occur no matter what he or anyone else tries to do—then we excuse him morally and say he is not responsible for his deed. If he is not responsible for *A*, a series of events occurring in his babyhood, then neither is he responsible for *B*, a series of things he does in adulthood, provided that *B* inevitably—that is, unavoidably— follows upon the occurrence of *A*. And according to psychiatrists and psychoanalysts, this often happens.

But one may still object that so far we have talked only about neurotic behavior. Isn't nonneurotic or normal or not unconsciously motivated (or whatever you want to call it) behavior still within the area of responsibility? There are reasons for answering "No" even here, for the normal person no more than the neurotic one has caused his own character, which makes him what he is. Granted that neurotics are not responsible for their behavior (that part of it which we call neurotic) because it stems from undigested infantile conflicts that they had no part in bringing about, and that are external to them just as surely as if their behavior had been forced on them by a malevolent deity (which is indeed one theory on the subject); but the so-called normal person is equally the product of causes in which his volition took no part. And if, unlike the neurotic's, his behavior is changeable by rational considerations, and if he has the will power to overcome the effects of an unfortunate early environment, this again is no credit to him; he is just lucky. If energy is available to him in a form in which it can be mobilized for constructive purposes, this is no credit to him, for this too is part of his psychic legacy. Those of us who can discipline ourselves and develop habits of concentration of purpose tend to blame those who cannot, and call them lazy and weak-willed; but what we fail to see is that they literally *cannot* do what we expect; if their psyches were structured like ours, they could, but as they are burdened with a tyrannical superego (to use psychoanalytic jargon for the moment), and a weak defenseless ego whose energies are constantly consumed in fighting endless charges of the superego, they simply cannot do it, and it is irrational to expect it of them. We cannot with justification blame them for their inability, any more than we can congratulate ourselves for our ability. This lesson is hard to learn, for we constantly and naïvely assume that other people are constructed as we ourselves are.

For example: A child raised under slum conditions, whose parents are socially ambitious and envy families with money, but who nevertheless squander the little they have on drink, may simply be unable in later life to mobilize a drive sufficient to overcome these early conditions. Common sense would expect that he would develop the virtue of thrift; he would make quite sure that he would never again endure the grinding poverty he had experienced as a child. But in fact it is not so: the exact conditions are too complex to be specified in detail here, but when certain conditions are fulfilled (concerning the subject's early life), he will always thereafter be a spendthrift, and no rational considerations will be able to change this. He will listen to the rational considerations and see the force of these, but they will not be able to change him, even if he tries; he cannot change his wasteful habits any more than he can lift the Empire State Building with his bare hands. We moralize and plead with him to be thrifty, but we do not see how strong, how utterly overpowering, and how constantly with him, is the opposite drive, which is so easily manageable with us. But he is possessed by the all-consuming, all-encompassing urge to make the world see that he belongs, that he has arrived, that he is just as well off as anyone else, that the awful humiliations were not real, that they never actually occurred, for isn't he now able to spend and spend? The humiliation must be blotted out; and conspicuous, fleshy, expensive, and wasteful buying will do this; it shows the world what the world must know! True, it is only for the moment; true, it is in the end self-defeating, for wasteful consumption is the best way to bring poverty back again; but the person with an overpowering drive to mend a lesion to his narcissism cannot resist the avalanche of that drive with his puny rational consideration. A man with his back against the wall and a gun at his throat doesn't think of what may happen ten years hence. (Consciously, of course, he knows nothing of this drive; all that appears to consciousness is its shattering effects; he knows only that he must keep on spending— not why—and that he is unable to resist.) He hasn't in him the psychic capacity, the energy to stem the tide of a drive that at that moment is all-powerful. We, seated comfortably away from this flood, sit in judgment on him and blame him and exhort him and criticize him; but he, carried along by the flood, cannot do otherwise than he does. He may fight with all the strength of which he is capable, but it is not enough. And we, who are rational enough at least to exonerate a man in a situation of "overpowering impulse" when we recognize it to be one, do not even recognize this as an example of it; and so, in addition to being swept away in the flood that childhood conditions rendered inevitable, he must also endure our lectures, our criticisms, and our moral excoriation.

But, one will say, he could have overcome his spendthrift tendencies; some people do. Quite true: some people do. They are lucky. They have it in them to overcome early deficiencies by exerting great effort, and they are capable of exerting the effort. Some of us, luckier still, can overcome them with but little effort; and a few, the luckiest, haven't the deficiencies to overcome. It's all a matter of luck. The least lucky are those who can't overcome them, even with great effort, and those who haven't the ability to exert the effort.

But, one persists, it isn't a matter simply of luck; it *is* a matter of effort. Very well then, it's a matter of effort; without exerting the effort you may not overcome the deficiency. But whether or not you are the kind of person who has it in him to exert the effort is a matter of luck.

All this is well known to psychoanalysts. They can predict, from minimal cues that most of us don't notice, whether a person is going to turn out to be lucky or not. "The analyst," they say, "must be able to use the residue of the patient's unconscious guilt so as to remove the symptom or character trait that creates the guilt. The guilt must not only be present, but *available* for use, *mobilizable*. If it is used up (absorbed) in criminal activity, or in an excessive amount of self-damaging tendencies, then it cannot be used for therapeutic purposes, and the prognosis is negative." Not all philosophers will relish the analyst's way of putting the matter, but at least as a physician he can soon detect whether the patient is lucky or unlucky—and he knows that whichever it is, it *isn't the patient's fault*. The patient's conscious volition cannot remedy the deficiency. Even whether he will co-operate with the analyst is really out of the patient's hands: if he continually projects the denying-mother fantasy on the analyst and unconsciously identifies him always with the cruel, harsh forbidder of the nursery, thus frustrating any attempt at impersonal observation, the sessions are useless; yet if it happens that way, he can't help that either. That fatal projection is not under his control; whether it occurs or not depends on how his unconscious identifications have developed since his infancy. He can try, yes—but the ability to try enough for the therapy to have effect is also beyond his control; the capacity to try more than just so much is either there or it isn't—and either way "it's in the lap of the gods."

The position, then, is this: if we *can* overcome the effects of early environment, the ability to do so is itself a product of the early environment. We did not give ourselves this ability; and if we lack it we cannot be blamed for not having it. Sometimes, to be sure, moral exhortation brings out an ability that is there but not being used, and in this lies its *occasional* utility; but very often its use is pointless, because the ability is not there. The only thing that can overcome a desire, as Spinoza said, is a stronger contrary desire; and many times there simply is no wherewithal for producing a stronger contrary desire. Those of us who do have the wherewithal are lucky.

There is one possible practical advantage in remembering this. It may prevent us (unless we are compulsive blamers) from indulging in righteous indignation and committing the sin of spiritual pride, thanking God that we are not as this publican here. And it will protect from our useless moralizings those who are least equipped by nature for enduring them. As with responsibility, so with deserts. Someone commits a crime and is punished by the state; "he deserved it," we say self-righteously—as if we were moral and he immoral, when in fact we are lucky and he is unlucky—forgetting that there, but for the grace of God and a fortunate early environment, go we. Or, as Clarence Darrow said in his speech for the defense in the Loeb-Leopold case:

> I do not believe that people are in jail because they deserve to be . . . I know what causes the emotional life . . . I know it is practically left out of some. Without it they cannot act with the rest. They cannot feel the moral shocks which safeguard others. Is [this man] to blame that his machine is imperfect? Who is to blame? I do not know. I have never in my life been interested so much in fixing blame as I have in relieving people from blame. I am not wise enough to fix it.[4]

III

I want to make it quite clear that I have not been arguing for determinism. Though I find it difficult to give any sense to the term "indeterminism," because I do not know what it would be like to come across an uncaused event, let us grant indeterminists everything they want, at least in words—influences that suggest but do not constrain, a measure of acausality in an otherwise rigidly causal order, and so on—whatever these phrases may mean. With all this granted, exactly the same situation faces the indeterminist and the determinist; all we have been saying would still hold true. "Are our powers innate or acquired?"

> Suppose the powers are declared innate; then the villain may sensibly ask whether he is responsible for what he was born with. A negative reply is inevitable. Are they then acquired? Then the ability to acquire them—was *that* innate? or acquired? It is innate? Very well then. . . .[5]

The same fact remains—that we did not cause our characters, that the influences that made us what we are are influences over which we had no control and of whose very existence we had no knowledge at the time. This fact remains for "determinism" and "indeterminism" alike. And it is this fact to which I would appeal, not the specific tenets of traditional forms of "determinism," which seem to me, when analyzed, empirically empty.

"But," it may be asked, "isn't it your view that nothing ultimately *could* be other than it is? And isn't this deterministic? And isn't it deterministic if you say that human beings could never act otherwise than they do, and that their desires and temperaments could not, when you consider their antecedent conditions, be other than they are?"

I reply that all these charges rest on confusions.

1. To say that nothing *could* be other than it is, if taken literally, is nonsense; and if taken as a way of saying something else, misleading and confusing. If you say, "I can't do it," this invites the question, "No? Not even if you want to?" "Can" and "could" are power words, used in the context of human action; when applied to nature they are merely anthropomorphic. "Could" has no application to nature—unless, of course, it is uttered in a theological context: one might say that God *could* have made things different. But with regard to inanimate nature "could" has no meaning. Or perhaps it is intended to mean that the order of nature is in some sense *necessary*. But in that case the sense of "necessary" must be specified. I know what "necessary" means when we are talking about propositions, but not when we are talking about the sequence of events in nature.
2. What of the charge that we could never have acted otherwise than we did? This, I submit, is simply not true. Here the exponents of Hume-Mill-Schlick-Ayer "Soft determinism" are quite right. I could have gone to the opera today instead of coming here; that is, if certain conditions had been different, I should have gone. I could have done many other things instead of what I did, if some condition or other had been different, specifically if my desire had been different. I repeat that "could" is a power word, and "I could have done this" means approximately "I *should* have done this *if* I had wanted to." In this sense, all of us could often have done otherwise than we did. I would not want to say that I should have done differently even if *all* the conditions leading up to my action had been the same (this is generally not what we mean by "could" anyway); but to assert that I could have is empty, for if I *did* act different from the time before, we would automatically say that one or more of the conditions were different, whether we had independent

evidence for this or not, thus rendering the assertion immune to empirical refutation. (Once again, the vacuousness of "determinism.")

3. Well, then, could we ever have, not acted, but *desired* otherwise than we did desire? This gets us once again to the heart of the matter we were discussing in the previous section. Russell said, "We can do as we please but we can't please as we please." But I am persuaded that even this statement conceals a fatal mistake. Let us follow the same analysis through. "I could have done X" means "I should have done X if I had wanted to." "I could have wanted X" by the same analysis would mean "I should have wanted X if I had wanted to"—which seems to make no sense at all. (What does Russell want? To please as he doesn't please?)

What does this show? It shows, I think, that the only meaningful context of "can" and "could have" is that of *action*. "Could have acted differently" makes sense; "could have desired differently," as we have just seen, does not. Because a word or phrase makes good sense in one context, let us not assume that it does so in another.

I conclude, then, with the following suggestion: that we operate on two levels of moral discourse, which we shouldn't confuse; one (let's call it the upper level) is that of actions; the other (the lower, or deeper, level) is that of the springs of action. Most moral talk occurs on the upper level. It is on this level that the Hume-Mill-Schlick-Ayer analysis of freedom fully applies. As we have just seen, "can" and "could" acquire their meaning on this level; so, I suspect, does "freedom." So does the distinction between compulsive and noncompulsive behavior, and among the senses of "responsibility," discussed in the first section of this paper, according to which we are responsible for some things and not for others. All these distinctions are perfectly valid on this level (or in this dimension) of moral discourse; and it is, after all, the usual one—we are practical beings interested in changing the course of human behavior, so it is natural enough that 99 per cent of our moral talk occurs here.

But when we descend to what I have called the lower level of moral discourse, as we occasionally do in thoughtful moments when there is no immediate need for action, then we must admit that we are ultimately the kind of persons we are because of conditions occurring outside us, over which we had no control. But while this is true, we should beware of extending the moral terminology we used on the other level to this one also, "Could" and "can," as we have seen, no longer have meaning here. "Right" and "wrong," which apply only to actions, have no meaning here either. I suspect that the same is true of "responsibility," for now that we have recalled often forgotten facts about our being the product of outside forces, we must ask in all seriousness what would be added by saying that we are not *responsible* for our own characters and temperaments. What would it mean even? Has it a significant opposite? What would it be like to be responsible for one's own character? What possible situation is describable by this phrase? Instead of saying that it is *false* that we are responsible for our own characters, I should prefer to say that the utterance is meaningless—meaningless in the sense that it describes no possible situation, though it *seems* to because the word "responsible" is the same one we used on the upper level, where it marks a real distinction. If this is so, the result is that *moral* terms—at least the terms "could have" and "responsible"—simply drop out on the lower level. What remains, shorn now of moral terminology, is the point we tried to bring out in Part II: whether or not we have personality disturbances, whether or not we have the ability to overcome deficiencies of early environment, is like the answer to the question whether or not we shall be struck down by a dread disease: "it's all a matter of luck." It is important to keep this in mind, for people almost always forget it, with consequences in human intolerance and unnecessary suffering that are incalculable.

NOTES

1. Edmund Bergler, *The Basic Neurosis* (New York: Grune and Stratton, 1949), p. 305.

2. Meyer Levin, *Compulsion* (New York: Simon and Schuster, 1956), p. 403.

3. Edmund Bergler, *The Superego* (New York: Grune and Stratton, 1952), p. 320.

4. Levin, *op. cit.*, pp. 43940, 469.

5. W. I. Matson, "The Irrelevance of Free-will to Moral Responsibility," *Mind*, LXV (October 1956), p. 495.

LIBERTY AND NECESSITY

David Hume

PART I

It might reasonably be expected, in questions which have been canvassed and disputed with great eagerness since the first origin of science and philosophy, that the meaning of all the terms, at least, should have been agreed upon among the disputants, and our inquiries, in the course of two thousand years, been able to pass from words to the true and real subject of the controversy. For how easy may it seem to give exact definitions of the terms employed in reasoning, and make these definitions, not the mere sound of words, the object of future scrutiny and examination? But if we consider the matter more narrowly, we shall be apt to draw a quite opposite conclusion. From this circumstance alone, that a controversy has been long kept on foot and remains still undecided, we may presume that there is some ambiguity in the expression, and that the disputants affix different ideas to the terms employed in the controversy. For as the faculties of the mind are supposed to be naturally alike in every individual—otherwise nothing could be more fruitless than to reason or dispute together—it were impossible, if men affix the same ideas to their terms, that they could so long form different opinions of the same subject, especially when they communicate their views and each party turn themselves on all sides in search of arguments which may give them the victory over their antagonists. It is true, if men attempt the discussion of questions which lie entirely beyond the reach of human capacity, such as those concerning the origin of worlds or the economy of the intellectual system or region of spirits, they may long beat the air in their fruitless contests and never arrive at any determinate conclusion. But if the question regard any subject of common life and experience, nothing, one would think, could preserve the dispute so long undecided, but some ambiguous expressions which keep the antagonists still at a distance and hinder them from grappling with each other.

This has been the case in the long-disputed question concerning liberty and necessity, and to so remarkable a degree that, if I be not much mistaken, we shall find that all mankind, both learned and ignorant, have always been of the same opinion with regard to this subject, and that a few intelligible definitions would immediately have put an end to the whole controversy. I own that this dispute has been so much canvassed on all hands, and has led philosophers into such a labyrinth of obscure sophistry, that it is no wonder if a sensible reader indulge his ease so far as to turn a deaf ear to the proposal of such a question from which he can expect neither instruction nor entertainment. But the state of the argument here proposed may, perhaps, serve to renew his attention, as it has more novelty, promises at least some decision of the controversy, and will not much disturb his ease by any intricate or obscure reasoning.

I hope, therefore, to make it appear that all men have ever agreed in the doctrine both of necessity and of liberty, according to any reasonable sense which can be put on these terms, and that the whole controversy has hitherto turned merely upon words. We shall begin with examining the doctrine of necessity.

It is universally allowed that matter, in all its operations, is actuated by a necessary force, and that every natural effect is so precisely determined by the energy of its cause that no other effect, in such particular circumstances, could possibly have resulted from it. The degree and direction of every motion is, by the laws of nature, prescribed with such exactness that a living creature may as soon arise from the shock of two bodies, as motion, in any other degree or direction than what is actually produced by it. Would we, therefore, form a just and precise idea of necessity, we must consider whence that idea arises when we apply it to the operation of bodies.

It seems evident that, if all the scenes of nature were continually shifted in such a manner that no two events bore any resemblance to each other, but every object was entirely new, without any similitude to whatever had been seen before, we should never, in that case, have attained the least idea of necessity or of a connection among these objects. We might say, upon such a supposition, that one object or event has followed another, not that one was produced by the other. The relation of cause and effect must be utterly unknown to mankind. Inference and reasoning concerning the operations of nature would, from that moment, be at an end; and the memory and senses remain the only canals by which the knowledge of any real existence could possibly have access to the mind. Our idea, therefore, of necessity and causation arises entirely from the uniformity observable in the operations of nature, where similar objects are constantly conjoined together, and the mind is determined by custom to infer the one from the appearance of the other. These two circumstances form the whole of that necessity which we ascribe to matter. Beyond the constant conjunction of similar objects and the consequent inference from one to the other, we have no notion of any necessity of connection.

If it appear, therefore, that all mankind have ever allowed, without any doubt or hesitation, that these two circumstances take place in the voluntary actions of men and in the operations of mind, it must follow that all mankind have ever agreed in the doctrine of necessity, and that they have hitherto disputed merely for not understanding each other.

As to the first circumstance, the constant and regular conjunction of similar events, we may possibly satisfy ourselves by the following considerations. It is universally acknowledged that there is a great uniformity among the actions of men, in all nations and ages, and that human nature remains still the same in its principles and operations. The same motives always produce the same actions; the same events follow from the same causes. Ambition, avarice, self-love, vanity, friendship, generosity, public spirit—these passions, mixed in various degrees and distributed through society, have been, from the beginning of the world, and still are, the source of all the actions and enterprises which have ever been observed among mankind. Would you know the sentiments, inclinations, and course of life of the Greeks and Romans? Study well the temper and actions of the French and English: you cannot be much mistaken in transferring to the former most of the observations which you have made with regard to the latter. Mankind are so much the same, in all times and places, that history informs us of nothing new or strange in this particular. Its chief use is only to discover the constant and universal principles of human nature by showing men in all varieties of circumstances and situations, and furnishing us with materials from which we may form our observations and become acquainted with the regular springs of human action and behavior. These records of wars, intrigues, factions, and revolutions are so many collections of experiments by which the politician or moral philosopher fixes the principles of his science, in the same manner as the physician or natural philosopher becomes acquainted with the nature of plants, minerals, and other external objects, by the experiments which he forms concerning them. Nor are the earth, water, and other elements examined by Aristotle and Hippocrates more like to those which at present lie under our observation than the men described by Polybius and Tacitus are to those who now govern the world.

Should a traveler, returning from a far country, bring us an account of men wholly different from any with whom we were ever acquainted, men who were entirely divested of avarice, ambition, or revenge, who knew no pleasure but friendship, generosity, and public spirit, we should immediately, from these circumstances, detect the falsehood and prove him a liar with the same certainty as if he had stuffed his narration with stories of centaurs and dragons, miracles and prodigies. And if we would explode any forgery in history, we cannot make use of a more convincing argument than to prove that the actions ascribed to any person are directly contrary to the course of nature, and that no human motives, in such circumstances, could ever induce him to such a conduct. The veracity of Quintus Curtius is as much to be suspected when he describes the supernatural courage of Alexander by which he was hurried on singly to attack multitudes, as when he describes his supernatural force and activity by which he was able to resist them. So readily and universally do we acknowledge a uniformity in human motives and actions as well as in the operations of body.

Hence, likewise, the benefit of that experience acquired by long life and a variety of business and company, in order to instruct us in the principles of human nature and regulate our future conduct as well as speculation. By means of this guide we mount up to the knowledge of men's inclinations and motives from their actions, expressions, and even gestures, and again descend to the interpretation of their actions from our knowledge of their motives and inclinations. The general observations, treasured up by a course of experience, give us the clue of human nature and teach us to unravel all its intricacies. Pretexts and appearances no longer deceive us. Public declarations pass for the specious coloring of a cause. And though virtue and honor be allowed their proper weight and authority, that perfect disinterestedness, so often pretended to, is never expected in multitudes and parties, seldom in their leaders, and scarcely even in individuals of any rank or station. But were there no uniformity in human actions, and were every experiment which we could form of this kind irregular and anomalous, it were impossible to collect any general observations concerning mankind, and no experience, however accurately digested by reflection, would ever serve to any purpose. Why is the aged husbandman more skillful in his calling than the young beginner, but because there is a certain uniformity in the operation of the sun, rain, and earth toward the production of vegetables, and experience teaches the old practitioner the rules by which this operation is governed and directed?

We must not, however, expect that this uniformity of human actions should be carried to such a length as that all men, in the same circumstances, will always act precisely in the same manner, without making any allowance for the diversity of characters, prejudices, and opinions. Such a uniformity, in every particular, is found in no part of nature. On the contrary, from observing the variety of conduct in different men we are enabled to form a greater variety of maxims which still suppose a degree of uniformity and regularity.

Are the manners of men different in different ages and countries? We learn thence the great force of custom and education, which mold the human mind from its infancy and form it into a fixed and established character. Is the behavior and conduct of the one sex very unlike that of the other? It is thence we become acquainted with the different characters which nature has impressed upon the sexes, and which she preserves with constancy and regularity. Are the actions of the same person much diversified in the different periods of his life from infancy to old age? This affords room for many general observations concerning the gradual change of our sentiments and inclinations, and the different maxims which prevail in the different ages of human creatures. Even the characters which are peculiar to each individual have a uniformity in their influence, otherwise our acquaintance with the persons, and our observations of their conduct, could never teach us their dispositions or serve to direct our behavior with regard to them.

I grant it possible to find actions which seem to have no regular connection with any known motives and are exceptions to all the measures of conduct which have ever been established for the government of men. But if we could willingly know what judgment should be formed of such irregular and extraordinary actions, we may consider the sentiments commonly entertained with regard to those irregular events which appear in the course of nature and the operations of eternal objects. All causes are not conjoined to their usual effects with like uniformity. An artificer who handles only dead matter may be disappointed of his aim, as well as the politician who directs the conduct of sensible and intelligent agents.

The vulgar, who take things according to their first appearance, attribute the uncertainty of events to such an uncertainty in the causes as makes the latter often fail of their usual influence, though they meet with no impediment in their operation. But philosophers, observing that almost in every part of nature there is contained a vast variety of springs and principles which are hid by reason of their minuteness or remoteness, find that it is at least possible the contrariety of events may not proceed from any contingency in the cause but from the secret operation of contrary causes. This possibility is converted into certainty by further observation, when they remark that, upon an exact scrutiny, a contrariety of effects always betrays a contrariety of causes and proceeds from their mutual opposition. A peasant can give no better reason for the stopping of any clock or watch than to say that it does not commonly go right. But an artist easily perceives that the same force in the spring or pendulum has always the same influence on the wheels, but fails of its usual effect perhaps by reason of a grain of dust which puts a stop to the whole movement. From the observation of several parallel instances philosophers form a maxim that the connection between all causes and effects is equally necessary, and that its seeming uncertainty in some instances proceeds from the secret opposition of contrary causes.

Thus, for instance, in the human body, when the usual symptoms of health or sickness disappoint our expectation, when medicines operate not with their wonted powers, when irregular events follow from any particular cause, the philosopher and physician are not surprised at the matter, nor are ever tempted to deny, in general, the necessity and uniformity of those principles by which the animal economy is conducted. They know that a human body is a mighty complicated machine, that many secret powers lurk in it which are altogether beyond our comprehension, that to us it must often appear very uncertain in its operations, and that, therefore, the irregular events which outwardly discover themselves can be no proof that the laws of nature are not observed with the greatest regularity in its internal operations and government.

The philosopher, if he be consistent, must apply the same reasonings to the actions and volitions of intelligent agents. The most irregular and unexpected resolutions of men may frequently be accounted for by those who know every particular circumstance of their character and situation. A person of an obliging disposition gives a peevish answer; but he has the toothache, or has not dined. A stupid fellow discovers an uncommon alacrity in his carriage; but he has met with a sudden piece of good fortune. Or even when an action, as sometimes happens, cannot be particularly accounted for, either by the person himself or by others, we know, in general that the characters of men are to a certain degree inconstant and irregular. This is, in a manner, the constant character of human nature, though it be applicable, in a more particular manner, to some persons who have no fixed rule for their conduct, but proceed in a continual course of caprice and inconstancy. The internal principles and motives may operate in a uniform manner, notwithstanding these seeming irregularities—in the same manner as the winds, rains, clouds, and other variations of the weather are supposed to be governed by steady principles, though not easily discoverable by human sagacity and inquiry.

Thus it appears not only that the conjunction between motives and voluntary actions is as regular and uniform as that between the cause and effect in any part of nature, but also that this regular conjunction has been universally acknowledged among mankind and has never been the subject of dispute either in philosophy or common life. Now, as it is from past experience that we draw all inferences concerning the future, and as we conclude that objects will always be conjoined together which we find to have always been conjoined, it may seem superfluous to prove that this experienced uniformity in human actions is a source whence we draw inferences concerning them. But in order to throw the argument into a greater variety of lights, we shall also insist, though briefly, on this latter topic.

The mutual dependence of men is so great in all societies that scarce any human action is entirely complete in itself or is performed without some reference to the actions of others, which are requisite to make it answer fully the intention of the agent. The poorest artificer who labors alone expects at least the protection of the magistrate to insure him the enjoyment of the fruits of his labor. He also expects that when he carries his goods to market and offers them at a reasonable price, he shall find purchasers and shall be able, by the money he acquires, to engage others to supply him with those commodities which are requisite for his subsistence. In proportion as men extend their dealings and render their intercourse with others more complicated, they always comprehend in their schemes of life a greater variety of voluntary actions which they expect, from the proper motives, to co-operate with their own. In all these conclusions, they take their measures from past experience, in the same manner as in their reasonings concerning external objects, and firmly believe that men, as well as all the elements, are to continue in their operations the same that they have ever found them. A manufacturer reckons upon the labor of his servants for the execution of any work as much as upon the tools which he employs, and would be equally surprised were his expectations disappointed. In short, this experimental inference and reasoning concerning the actions of others enters so much into human life that no man, while awake, is ever a moment without employing it. Have we not reason, therefore, to affirm that all mankind have always agreed in the doctrine of necessity, according to the foregoing definition and explication of it?

Nor have philosophers ever entertained a different opinion from the people in this particular. For, not to mention that almost every action of their life supposes that opinion, there are even few of the speculative parts of learning to which it is not essential. What would become of history had we not a dependence on the veracity of the historian according to the experience which we have had of mankind? How could politics be a science if laws and forms of government had not a uniform influence upon society? Where would be the foundation of morals if particular characters had no certain or determinate power to produce particular sentiments, and if these sentiments had no constant operation on actions? And with what pretense could we employ our criticism upon any poet or polite author if we could not pronounce the conduct and sentiments of his actors either natural or unnatural to such characters and in such circumstances? It seems almost impossible, therefore, to engage either in science or action of any kind without acknowledging the doctrine of necessity, and this inference from motives to voluntary action, from characters to conduct.

And, indeed, when we consider how aptly natural and moral evidence link together and form only one chain of argument, we shall make no scruple to allow that they are of the same nature and derived from the same principles. A prisoner who has neither money nor interest discovers the impossibility of his escape as well when he considers the obstinacy of the jailer as the walls and bars with which he is surrounded, and in all attempts for his freedom chooses rather to work upon the stone and iron of the one than upon the inflexible nature of the other. The same prisoner, when conducted to the scaffold, foresees his death as certainly from the constancy and fidelity of his guards as from the operation of the ax or wheel. His mind runs along a certain train of ideas: the refusal of the soldiers to consent to his escape; the action of the executioner; the separation of the head and body; bleeding, convulsive motions, and death. Here is a connected chain of natural causes and voluntary actions, but the mind feels no difference between them in passing from one link to another, nor is less certain of the future event than if it were connected with the objects present to the memory or senses by a train of causes cemented together by what we are pleased to call a "physical" necessity. The same experienced union has the same effect on the mind, whether the united objects be motives, volition, and actions, or figure and motion. We may change the names of things, but their nature and their operation on the understanding never change.

Were a man whom I know to be honest and opulent, and with whom I lived in intimate friendship, to come into my house, where I am surrounded with my servants, I rest assured that he is not to stab me before he leaves it in order to rob me of my silver standish; and I no more suspect this event than the falling of the house itself, which is new and solidly built and founded.—But he may have been seized with a sudden and unknown frenzy.— So may a sudden earthquake arise, and shake and tumble my house about my ears. I shall, therefore, change the suppositions. I shall say that I know with certainty that he is not to put his hand into the fire and hold it there till it be consumed. And this event I think I can foretell with the same assurance as that, if he throw himself out of the window and meet with no obstruction, he will not remain a moment suspended in the air. No suspicion of an unknown frenzy can give the least possibility to the former event which is so contrary to all the known principles of human nature. A man who at noon leaves his purse full of gold on the pavement at Charing Cross may as well expect that it will fly away like a feather as that he will find it untouched an hour after. Above onehalf of human reasonings contain inferences of a similar nature, attended with more or less degrees of certainty, proportioned to our experience of the usual conduct of mankind in such particular situations.

I have frequently considered what could possibly be the reason why all mankind, though they have ever, without hesitation, acknowledged the doctrine of necessity in their whole practice and reasoning, have yet discovered such a reluctance to acknowledge it in words, and have rather shown a propensity, in all ages, to profess the contrary opinion. The matter, I think, may be accounted for after the following manner. If we examine the operations of body and the production of effects from their causes, we shall find that all our faculties can never carry us further in our knowledge of this relation than barely to observe that particular objects are constantly conjoined together, and that the mind is carried, by a customary transition, from the appearance of the one to the belief of the other. But though this conclusion concerning human ignorance be the result of the strictest scrutiny of this subject, men still entertain a strong propensity to believe that they penetrate further into the powers of nature and perceive something like a necessary connection between the cause and the effect. When, again, they turn their reflections toward the operations of their own minds and feel no such connection of the motive and the action, they are thence apt to suppose that there is a difference between the effects which result from material force and those which arise from thought and intelligence. But being once convinced that we know nothing further of causation of any kind than merely the constant conjunction of objects and the consequent inference of the mind from one to another, and finding that these two circumstances are universally allowed to have place in voluntary actions, we may be more easily led to own the same necessity common to all causes. And though this reasoning may contradict the systems of many philosophers in ascribing necessity to the determinations of the will, we shall find, upon reflection, that they dissent from it in words only, not in their real sentiments. Necessity, according to the sense in which it is here taken, has never yet been rejected, nor can ever, I think, be rejected by any philosopher. It may only, perhaps, be pretended that the mind can perceive in the operations of matter some further connection between the cause and effect, and a connection that has no place in the voluntary actions of intelligent beings. Now, whether it be so or not can only appear upon examination, and it is incumbent on these philosophers to make good their assertion by defining or describing that necessity and pointing it out to us in the operations of material causes.

It would seem, indeed, that men begin at the wrong end of this question concerning liberty and necessity when they enter upon it by examining the faculties of the soul, the influence of the understanding, and the operations of the will. Let them first discuss a more simple question, namely, the question of body and brute unintelligent matter, and try whether they can there form any idea of causation and necessity, except that of a constant conjunction of objects and subsequent inference of the mind from one to another. If these circumstances form, in reality, the whole of that necessity which we conceive in matter, and if these circumstances be also universally acknowledged to take place in the operations of the mind, the dispute is at an end; at least, must be owned to be thenceforth merely verbal. But as long as we will rashly suppose that we have some further idea of necessity and causation in the operations of external objects, at the same time that we can find nothing further in the voluntary actions of the mind, there is no possibility of bringing the question to any determinate issue while we proceed upon so erroneous a supposition. The only method of undeceiving us is to mount up higher, to examine the narrow extent of science when applied to material causes, and to convince ourselves that all we know of them is the constant conjunction and inference above mentioned. We may, perhaps, find that it is with difficulty we are induced to fix such narrow limits to human understanding, but we can afterwards find no difficulty when we come to apply this doctrine to the actions of the will. For as it is evident that these have a regular conjunction with motives and circumstances and character, and as we always draw inferences from one to the other, we must be obliged to acknowledge in words that necessity which we have already avowed in every deliberation of our lives and in every step of our conduct and behavior.[1]

But to proceed in this reconciling project with regard to the question of liberty and necessity—the most contentious question of metaphysics, the most contentious science—it will not require many words to prove that all mankind have ever agreed in the doctrine of liberty as well as in that of necessity, and that the whole dispute, in this respect also, has been hitherto merely verbal. For what is meant by liberty when applied to voluntary actions? We cannot surely mean that actions have so little connection with motives, inclinations, and circumstances that one does not follow with a certain degree of uniformity from the other, and that one affords no inference by which we can conclude the existence of the other. For these are plain and acknowledged matters of fact. By liberty, then, we can only mean a power of acting or not acting according to the determinations of the will; that is, if we choose to remain at rest, we may; if we choose to move, we also may. Now this hypothetical liberty is universally allowed to belong to everyone who is not a prisoner and in chains. Here then is no subject of dispute.

Whatever definition we may give of liberty, we should be careful to observe two requisite circumstances: first, that it be consistent with plain matter of fact; secondly, that it be consistent with itself. If we observe these circumstances and render our definition intelligible, I am persuaded that all mankind will be found of one opinion with regard to it.

It is universally allowed that nothing exists without a cause of its existence, and that chance, when strictly examined, is a mere negative word and means not any real power which has anywhere a being in nature. But it is pretended that some causes are necessary, some not necessary. Here then is the advantage of definitions. Let anyone define a cause without comprehending, as a part of the definition, a necessary connection with its effect, and let him show distinctly the origin of the idea expressed by the definition, and I shall readily give up the whole controversy. But if the foregoing explication of the matter be received, this must be absolutely impracticable. Had not objects a regular conjunction with each other, we should never have entertained any notion of cause and effect; and this regular conjunction produces that inference of the understanding which is the only connection that we can have any comprehension of. Whoever attempts a definition of cause exclusive of these circumstances will be obliged either to employ unintelligible terms or such as are synonymous to the term which he endeavors to define.[2] And if the definition above mentioned be admitted, liberty, when opposed to necessity, not to constraint, is the same thing with chance, which is universally allowed to have no existence.

PART II

There is no method of reasoning more common, and yet none more blamable, than in philosophical disputes to endeavor the refutation of any hypothesis by a pretense of its dangerous consequences to religion and morality. When any opinion leads to absurdity, it is certainly false; but it is not certain that an opinion is false because it is of dangerous consequence. Such topics, therefore, ought entirely to be forborne as serving nothing to the discovery of truth, but only to make the person of an antagonist odious. This I observe in general, without pretending to draw any advantage from it. I frankly submit to an examination of this kind, and shall venture to affirm that the doctrines both of necessity and liberty, as above explained, are not only consistent with morality, but are absolutely essential to its support.

Necessity may be defined two ways, conformably to the two definitions of cause of which it makes an essential part. It consists either in the constant conjunction of like objects or in the inference of the understanding from one object to another. Now necessity, in both these senses (which, indeed, are at bottom the same), has universally, though tacitly, in the schools, in the pulpit, and in common life been allowed to belong to the will of man, and no one has ever pretended to deny that we can draw inferences concerning human actions, and that those inferences are founded on the experienced union of like actions, with like motives, inclinations, and circumstances. The only particular in which anyone can differ is that either perhaps he will refuse to give the name of necessity to this property of human actions—but as long as the meaning is understood I hope the word can do no harm—or that he will maintain it possible to discover something further in the operations of matter. But this, it must be acknowledged, can be of no consequence to morality or religion, whatever it may be to natural philosophy or metaphysics. We may here be mistaken in asserting that there is no idea of any other necessity or connection in the actions of the body, but surely we ascribe nothing to the actions of the mind but what everyone does and must readily allow of. We change no circumstance in the received orthodox system with regard to the will, but only in that with regard to material objects and causes. Nothing, therefore, can be more innocent at least than this doctrine.

All laws being founded on rewards and punishments, it is supposed, as a fundamental principle, that these motives have a regular and uniform influence on the mind and both produce the good and prevent the evil actions. We may give to this influence what name we please; but as it is usually conjoined with the action, it must be esteemed a cause and be looked upon as an instance of that necessity which we would here establish.

The only proper object of hatred or vengeance is a person or creature endowed with thought and consciousness; and when any criminal or injurious actions excite that passion, it is only by their relation to the person, or connection with him. Actions are, by their very nature, temporary and perishing; and where they proceed not from some cause in the character and disposition of the person who performed them, they can neither redound to his honor if good, nor infamy if evil. The actions themselves may be blamable; they may be contrary to all the rules of morality and religion; but the person is not answerable for them and, as they proceeded from nothing in him that is durable and constant and leave nothing of that nature behind them, it is impossible he can, upon their account, become the object of punishment or vengeance. According to the principle, therefore, which denies necessity and, consequently, causes, a man is as pure and untainted, after having committed the most horrid crime, as at the first moment of his birth, nor is his character anywise concerned in his actions, since they are not derived from it; and the wickedness of the one can never be used as a proof of the depravity of the other.

Men are not blamed for such actions as they perform ignorantly and casually, whatever may be the consequences. Why? But because the principles of these actions are only momentary and terminate in them alone. Men are less blamed for such actions as they perform hastily and unpremeditately than for such as proceed from deliberation. For what reason? But because a hasty temper, though a constant cause or principle in the mind, operates only by intervals and infects not the whole character. Again, repentance wipes off every crime if attended with a reformation of life and manners. How is this to be accounted for? But by asserting that actions render a person criminal merely as they are proofs of criminal principles in the mind; and when, by an alteration of these principles, they cease to be just proofs, they likewise cease to be criminal. But, except upon the doctrine of necessity, they never were just proofs, and consequently never were criminal.

It will be equally easy to prove, and from the same arguments, that liberty, according to that definition above mentioned, in which all men agree, is also essential to morality, and that no human actions, where it is wanting, are susceptible of any moral qualities or can be the objects of approbation or dislike. For as actions are objects of our moral sentiment so far only as they are indications of the internal character, passions, and affections, it is impossible that they can give rise either to praise or blame where they proceed not from these principles, but are derived altogether from external violence.

I pretend not to have obtained or removed all objections to this theory with regard to necessity and liberty. I can foresee other objections derived from topics which have not here been treated of. It may be said, for instance, that if voluntary actions be subjected to the same laws of necessity with the operations of matter, there is a continued chain of necessary causes, preordained and predetermined, reaching from the Original Cause of all to every single volition of every human creature. No contingency anywhere in the universe, no indifference, no liberty. While we act, we are at the same time acted upon. The ultimate Author of all our volitions is the Creator of the world, who first bestowed motion on this immense machine and placed all beings in that particular position whence every subsequent event, by an inevitable necessity, must result. Human actions, therefore, either can have no moral turpitude at all, as proceeding from so good a cause, or if they have any turpitude, they must involve our Creator in the same guilt, while he is acknowledged to be their ultimate cause and Author. For as a man who fired a mine is answerable for all the consequences, whether the train he employed be long or short, so, wherever a continued chain of necessary causes is fixed, that Being, either finite or infinite, who produces the first is likewise the author of all the rest and must both bear the blame and acquire the praise which belong to them. Our clear and unalterable ideas of morality establish this rule upon unquestionable reasons when we examine the consequences of any human action; and these reasons must still have greater force when applied to the volitions and intentions of a Being infinitely wise and powerful. Ignorance or impotence may be pleaded for so limited a creature as man, but those imperfections have no place in our Creator. He foresaw, he ordained, he intended all those actions of men which we so rashly pronounce criminal. And we must, therefore, conclude either that they are not criminal or that the Deity, not man, is accountable for them. But as either of these positions is absurd and impious, it follows that the doctrine from which they are deduced cannot possibly be true, as being liable to all the same objections. An absurd consequence, if necessary, proves the original doctrine to be absurd in the same manner as criminal actions render criminal the original cause if the connection between them be necessary and inevitable.

This objection consists of two parts, which we shall examine separately:

First, that if human actions can be traced up, by a necessary chain, to the Deity, they can never be criminal, on account of the infinite perfection of that Being from whom they are derived, and who can intend nothing but what is altogether good and laudable. Or, secondly, if they be criminal, we must retract the attribute of perfection which we ascribe to the Deity and must acknowledge him to be the ultimate author of guilt and moral turpitude in all his creatures.

The answer to the first objection seems obvious and convincing. There are many philosophers who, after an exact scrutiny of the phenomena of nature, conclude that the WHOLE, considered as one system, is, in every period of its existence, ordered with perfect benevolence; and that the utmost possible happiness will, in the end, result to all created beings without any mixture of positive or absolute ill and misery. Every physical ill, say they, makes an essential part of this benevolent system, and could not possibly be removed, by even the Deity himself, considered as a wise agent, without giving entrance to greater ill or excluding greater good which will result from it. From this theory some philosophers, and the ancient Stoics among the rest, derived a topic of consolation under all afflictions, while they taught their pupils that those ills under which they labored were in reality goods to the universe, and that to an enlarged view which could comprehend the whole system of nature every event became an object of joy and exultation. But though this topic be specious and sublime, it was soon found in practice weak and ineffectual. You would surely more irritate than appease a man lying under the racking pains of the gout by preaching up to him the rectitude of those general laws which produced the malignant humors in his body and led them through the proper canals to the sinews and nerves, where they now excite such acute torments. These enlarged views may, for a moment, please the imagination of a speculative man who is placed in ease and security, but neither can they dwell with constancy on his mind, even though undisturbed by the emotions of pain or passion, much less can they maintain their ground when attacked by such powerful antagonists. The affections take a narrower and more natural survey of their object and, by an economy more suitable to the infirmity of human minds, regard alone the beings around us, and are actuated by such events as appear good or ill to the private system.

The case is the same with moral as with physical ill. It cannot reasonably be supposed that those remote considerations which are found of so little efficacy with regard to the one will have a more powerful influence with regard to the other. The mind of man is so formed by nature that, upon the appearance of certain characters, dispositions, and actions, it immediately feels the sentiment of approbation or blame; nor are there any emotions more essential to its frame and constitution. The characters which engage our approbation are chiefly such as contribute to the peace and security of human society, as the characters which excite blame are chiefly such as tend to public detriment and disturbance; whence it may reasonably be presumed that the moral sentiments arise, either mediately or immediately, from a reflection on these opposite interests. What though philosophical meditations establish a different opinion or conjecture that everything is right with regard to the whole, and that the qualities which disturb society are, in the main, as beneficial, and are as suitable to the primary intention of nature, as those which more directly promote its happiness and welfare? Are such remote and uncertain speculations able to counterbalance the sentiments which arise from the natural and immediate view of the objects? A man who is robbed of a considerable sum, does he find his vexation for the loss anywise diminished by these sublime reflections? Why, then, should his moral resentment against the crime be supposed incompatible with them? Or why should not the acknowledgment of a real distinction between vice and virtue be reconcilable to all speculative systems of philosophy, as well as that of a real distinction between personal beauty and deformity? Both these distinctions are founded in the natural sentiments of the human mind; and these sentiments are not to be controlled or altered by any philosophical theory or speculation whatsoever.

The second objection admits not of so easy and satisfactory an answer, nor is it possible to explain distinctly how the Deity can be the immediate cause of all the actions of men without being the author of sin and moral turpitude. These are mysteries which mere natural and unassisted reason is very unfit to handle; and whatever system she embraces, she must find herself involved in inextricable difficulties, and even contradictions, at every step which she takes with regard to such subjects. To reconcile the indifference and contingency of human actions with prescience or to defend absolute decrees, and yet free the Deity from being the author of sin, has been found hitherto to exceed all the power of philosophy. Happy, if she be thence sensible of her temerity, when she pries into these sublime mysteries, and, leaving a scene so full of obscurities and perplexities, return with suitable modesty to her true and proper province, the examination of common life, where she will find difficulties enough to employ her inquiries without launching into so boundless an ocean of doubt, uncertainty, and contradiction.

NOTES

1. The prevalence of the doctrine of liberty may be accounted for from another cause, viz., a false sensation, or seeming experience, which we have, or may have, of liberty or indifference in many of our actions. The necessity of any action, whether of matter or of mind, is not, properly speaking, a quality in the agent but in any thinking or intelligent being who may consider the action; and it consists chiefly in the determination of his thoughts to infer the existence of that action from some preceding objects; as liberty, when opposed to necessity, is nothing but the want of that determination, and a certain looseness or indifference which we feel in passing, or not passing, from the idea of one object to that of any succeeding one. Now we may observe that though, in *reflecting* on human actions, we seldom feel such a looseness or indifference, but are commonly able to infer them with considerable certainty from their motives, and from the disposition of the agent; yet it frequently happens that, in *performing* the actions themselves, we are sensible of something like it; and as all resembling objects are readily taken for each other, this has been employed as a demonstrative and even intuitive proof of human liberty. We feel that our actions are subject to our will on most occasions, and imagine we feel that the will itself is subject to nothing, because, when by a denial of it we are provoked to try, we feel that it moves easily every way, and produces an image of itself (or a "velleity," as it is called in the schools), even on that side on which it did not settle. This image, or faint motion, we persuade ourselves, could at that time have been completed into the thing itself, because, should that be denied, we find upon a second trial that at present it can. We consider not that the fantastical desire of showing liberty is here the motive of our actions. And it seems certain that however we may imagine we feel a liberty within ourselves, a spectator can commonly infer our actions from our motives and character; and even where he cannot, he concludes in general that he might, were he perfectly acquainted with every circumstance of our situation and temper, and the most secret springs of our complexion and disposition. Now this is the very essence of necessity, according to the foregoing doctrine.

2. Thus, if a cause be defined, *that which produces anything*, it is easy to observe that *producing* is synonymous to *causing*. In like manner, if a cause be defined, *that by which anything exists*, this is liable to the same objection. For what is meant by these words, "*by which*"? Had it been said that a cause is *that* after which *anything constantly exists*, we should have understood the terms. For this is, indeed, all we know of the matter. And this constancy forms the very essence of necessity, nor have we any other idea of it.

ALTERNATE POSSIBILITIES AND MORAL RESPONSIBILITY*

Harry Frankfurt

A dominant role in nearly all recent inquiries into the free-will problem has been played by a principle which I shall call "the principle of alternate possibilities." This principle states that a person is morally responsible for what he has done only if he could have done otherwise. Its exact meaning is a subject of controversy, particularly concerning whether someone who accepts it is thereby committed to believing that moral responsibility and determinism are incompatible. Practically no one, however, seems inclined to deny or even to question that the principle of alternate possibilities (construed in so some way or other) is true. It has generally seemed so overwhelmingly plausible that some philosophers have even characterized it as an a priori truth. People whose accounts of free will or of moral responsibility are radically at odds evidently find in it a firm and convenient common ground upon which they can profitably take their opposing stands.

But the principle of alternate possibilities is false. A person may well be morally responsible for what he has done even though he could not have done otherwise. The principle's plausibility is an illusion, which can be made to vanish by bringing the relevant moral phenomena into sharper focus.

I

In seeking illustrations of the principle of alternate possibilities, it is most natural to think of situations in which the same circumstances both bring it about that a person does something and make it impossible for him to avoid doing it. These include, for example, situations in which a person is coerced into doing something, or in which he is impelled to act by a hypnotic suggestion, or in which some inner compulsion drives him to do what he does. In situations of these kinds there are circumstances that make it impossible for the person to do otherwise, and these very circumstances also serve to bring it about that he does whatever it is that he does.

*Harry Frankfurt "Alternate Possibilities and Moral Responsibility," *The Journal of Philosophy*, LXVI, 23 (December 4, 1969): 829–839. Reprinted with the kind permission of the author and the journal.

However, there may be circumstances that constitute sufficient conditions for a certain action to be performed by someone and that therefore make it impossible for the person to do otherwise, but that do not actually impel the person to act or in any way produce his action. A person may do something in circumstances that leave him no alternative to doing it, without these circumstances actually moving him or leading him to do it—without them playing any role, indeed, in bringing it about that he does what he does.

An examination of situations characterized by circumstances of this sort casts doubt, I believe, on the relevance to questions of moral responsibility of the fact that a person who has done something could not have done otherwise. I propose to develop some examples of this kind in the context of a discussion of coercion and to suggest that our moral intuitions concerning these examples tend to disconfirm the principle of alternate possibilities. Then I will discuss the principle in more general terms, explain what I think is wrong with it, and describe briefly and without argument how it might appropriately be revised.

II

It is generally agreed that a person who has been coerced to do something did not do it freely and is not morally responsible for having done it. Now the doctrine that coercion and moral responsibility are mutually exclusive may appear to be no more than a somewhat particularized version of the principle of alternate possibilities. It is natural enough to say of a person who has been coerced to do something that he could not have done otherwise. And it may easily seem that being coerced deprives a person of freedom and of moral responsibility simply because it is a special case of being unable to do otherwise. The principle of alternate possibilities may in this way derive some credibility from its association with the very plausible proposition that moral responsibility is excluded by coercion.

It is not right, however, that it should do so. The fact that a person was coerced to act as he did may entail both that he could not have done otherwise and that he bears no moral responsibility for his action. But his lack of moral responsibility is not entailed by his having been unable to do otherwise. The doctrine that coercion excludes moral responsibility is not correctly understood, in other words, as a particularized version of the principle of alternate possibilities.

Let us suppose that someone is threatened convincingly with a penalty he finds unacceptable and that he then does what is required of him by the issuer of the threat. We can imagine details that would make it reasonable for us to think that the person was coerced to perform the action in question, that he could not have done otherwise, and that he bears no moral responsibility for having done what he did. But just what is it about situations of this kind that warrants the judgment that the threatened person is not morally responsible for his act?

This question may be approached by considering situations of the following kind. Jones decides for reasons of his own to do something, then someone threatens him with a very harsh penalty (so harsh that any reasonable person would submit to the threat) unless he does precisely that, and Jones does it. Will we hold Jones morally responsible for what he has done? I think this will depend on the roles we think were played, in leading him to act, by his original decision and by the threat.

One possibility is that Jones$_1$ is not reasonable man: he is, rather, a man who does what he has once decided to do no matter what happens next and no matter what the cost. In that case, the threat actually exerted no effective force up on him. He acted without any regard to it, very much as if he were not aware that it had been made. If this is indeed the way it was, the situation did not involve coercion at all. The threat did not lead Jones$_1$ to do what he did. Nor was it in fact sufficient to have prevented him from doing otherwise: if his earlier decision had been to do something else, the threat would not have deterred him in the slightest. It seems evident that in these circumstances the fact that Jones$_1$ was threatened in no way reduces the moral responsibility he would otherwise bear for his act. This example, however, is not a counterexample either to the doctrine that coercion excuses or to the principle of alternate possibilities. For we have supposed that Jones$_1$ is a man upon whom the threat had no coercive effect and, hence, that it did not actually deprive him of alternatives to doing what he did.

Another possibility is that Jones$_2$ was stampeded by the threat. Given that threat, he would have performed that action regardless of what decision he had already made. The threat upset him so profoundly, moreover, that he completely forgot his own earlier decision and did what was demanded of him entirely because he was terrified of the penalty with which he was threatened. In this case, it is not relevant to his having performed the action that he had already decided on his own to perform it. When the chips were down he thought of nothing but the threat, and fear alone led him to act. The fact that at an earlier time Jones$_2$ had decided for his own reasons to act in just that way may be relevant to an evaluation of his character, he may bear full moral responsibility for having made that decision. But he can hardly be said to be morally responsible for his action. For he performed the action simply as a result of the coercion to which he was subjected. His earlier decision played no role in bringing it about that he did what he did, and it would therefore be gratuitous to assign it a role in the moral evaluation of his action.

Now consider a third possibility. Jones$_3$ was neither stampeded by the threat nor indifferent to it. The threat impressed him, as it would impress any reasonable man, and he would have submitted to it wholeheartedly if he had not already made a decision that coincided with the one demanded of him. In fact, however, he performed the action in question on the basis of the decision he had made before the threat was issued. When he acted, he was not actually motivated by the threat but solely by the considerations that had originally commended the action to him. It was not the threat that led him to act, though it would have done so if he had not already provided himself with a sufficient motive for performing the action in question.

No doubt it will be very difficult for anyone to know, in a case like this one, exactly what happened. Did Jones$_3$ perform the action because of the threat, or were his reasons for acting simply those which had already persuaded him to do so? Or did he act on the basis of two motives, each of which was sufficient for his action? It is not impossible, however, that the situation should be clearer than situations of this kind usually are. And suppose it is apparent to us that Jones$_3$ acted on the basis of his own decision and not because of the threat. Then I think we would be justified in regarding his moral responsibility for what he did as unaffected by the threat even though, since he would in any case have submitted to the threat, he could not have avoided doing what he did. It would be entirely reasonable for us to make the same judgment concerning his moral responsibility that we would have made if we had not known of the threat. For the threat did not in fact influence his performance of the action. He did what he did just as if the threat had not been made at all.

III

The case of Jones₃ may appear at first glance to combine coercion and moral responsibility, and thus to provide a counterexample to the doctrine that coercion excuses. It is not really so certain that it does so, however, because it is unclear whether the example constitutes a genuine instance of coercion. Can we say of Jones₃ that he was coerced to do something, when he had already decided on his own to do it and when he did it entirely on the basis of that decision? Or would it be more correct to say that Jones₃ was not coerced to do what he did, even though he himself recognized that there was an irresistible force at work in virtue of which he had to do it? My own linguistic intuitions lead me toward the second alternative, but they are somewhat equivocal. Perhaps we can say either of these things, or perhaps we must add a qualifying explanation to whichever of them we say.

This murkiness, however, does not interfere with our drawing an important moral from an examination of the example. Suppose we decide to say that Jones₃ was not coerced. Our basis for saying this will clearly be that it is incorrect to regard a man as being coerced to do something unless he does it because of the coercive force exerted against him. The fact that an irresistible threat is made will not, then, entail that the person who receives it is coerced to do what he does. It will also be necessary that the threat is what actually accounts for his doing it. On the other hand, suppose we decide to say that Jones₃ was coerced. Then we will be bound to admit that being coerced does not exclude being morally responsible. And we will also surely be led to the view that coercion affects the judgment of a person's moral responsibility only when the person acts as he does because he is coerced to do so—i.e., when the fact that he is coerced is what accounts for his action.

Whichever we decide to say, then, we will recognize that the doctrine that coercion excludes moral responsibility is not a particularized version of the principle of alternate possibilities. Situations in which a person who does something cannot do otherwise because he is subject to coercive power are either not instances of coercion at all, or they are situations in which the person may still be morally responsible for what he does if it is not because of the coercion that he does it. When we excuse a person who has been coerced, we do not excuse him because he was unable to do otherwise. Even though a person is subject to a coercive force that precludes his performing any action but one, he may nonetheless bear full moral responsibility for performing that action.

IV

To the extent that the principle of alternate possibilities derives its plausibility from association with the doctrine that coercion excludes moral responsibility, a clear understanding of the latter diminishes the appeal of the former. Indeed the case of

Jones$_3$ may appear to do more than illuminate the relationship between the two doctrines. It may well seem to provide a decisive counterexample to the principle of alternate possibilities and thus to show that this principle is false. For the irresistibility of the threat to which Jones$_3$ is subjected might well be taken to mean that he cannot but perform the action he performs. And yet the threat, since Jones$_3$ performs the action without regard to it, does not reduce his moral responsibility for what he does.

The following objection will doubtless be raised against the suggestion that the case of Jones$_3$ is a counterexample to the principle of alternate possibilities. There is perhaps a sense in which Jones$_3$ cannot do otherwise than perform the action he performs, since he is a reasonable man and the threat he encounters is sufficient to move any reasonable man. But it is not this sense that is germane to the principle of alternate possibilities. His knowledge that he stands to suffer an intolerably harsh penalty does not mean that Jones$_3$, strictly speaking, cannot perform any action but the one he does perform. After all it is still open to him, and this is crucial, to defy the threat if he wishes to do so and to accept the penalty his action would bring down upon him. In the sense in which the principle of alternate possibilities employs the concept of "could have done otherwise," Jones$_3$'s inability to resist the threat does not mean that he cannot do otherwise than perform the action he performs. Hence the case of Jones$_3$ does not constitute an instance contrary to the principle.

I do not propose to consider in what sense the concept of "could have done otherwise" figures in the principle of alternate possibilities, nor will I attempt to measure the force of the objection I have just described.[1] For I believe that whatever force this objection may be thought to have can be deflected by altering the example in the following way.[2] Suppose someone—Black, let us say—wants Jones$_4$ to perform a certain action. Black is prepared to go to considerable lengths to get his way, but he prefers to avoid showing his hand unnecessarily. So he waits until Jones$_4$ is about to make up his mind what to do, and he does nothing unless it is clear to him (Black is an excellent judge of such things) that Jones$_4$ is going to decide to do something other than what he wants him to do. If it does become clear that Jones$_4$ is going to decide to do something else, Black takes effective steps to ensure that Jones$_4$ decides to do, and that he does do, what he wants him to do.[3] Whatever Jones$_4$'s initial preference and inclinations, then, Black will have his way.

What steps will Black take, if he believes he must take steps, in order to ensure that Jones$_4$ decides and acts as he wishes? Anyone with a theory concerning what "could have done otherwise" means may answer this question for himself by describing whatever measures he would regard as sufficient to guarantee that, in the relevant sense, Jones$_4$ cannot do otherwise. Let Black pronounce a terrible threat, and in this way both force Jones$_4$ to perform the desired action and prevent him from performing a forbidden one. Let Black give Jones$_4$ a potion, or put him under hypnosis, and in some such way as these generate in Jones$_4$ an irresistible inner compulsion to perform the act Black wants performed and to avoid others. Or let Black manipulate the minute processes of Jones$_4$'s brain and nervous system in some more direct way, so that causal forces running in and out of his synapses and along the poor man's nerves determine that he chooses to act and that he does act in the one way and not in any other. Given any conditions under which it will be maintained that Jones$_4$ cannot do otherwise, in other words, let Black bring it about that those conditions prevail. The structure of the example is flexible enough, I think, to find a way around any charge of irrelevance by accommodating the doctrine on which the charge is based.[4]

Now suppose that Black never has to show his hand because $Jones_4$ for reasons for his own, decides to perform and does perform the very action Black wants him to perform. In that case, it seem clear, $Jones_4$ will bear precisely the same moral responsibility for what he does as he would have borne if Black had not been ready to take steps to ensure that he do it. It would be quite unreasonable to excuse Jones, for his action, or to withhold the praise to which it would normally entitle him, on the basis of the fact that he could not have done otherwise. This fact played no role at all in leading him to act as he did. He would have acted the same even if it had not been a fact. Indeed, everything happened just as it would have happened without Black's presence in the situation and without his readiness to intrude into it.

In this example there are sufficient conditions for $Jones_4$'s performing the action in question. What action he performs is not up to him. Of course it is in a way up to him whether he acts on his own or as a result of Black's intervention. That depends upon what action he himself is inclined to perform. But whether he finally acts on his own or as a result of Black's intervention, he performs the same action. He has no alternative but to do what Black wants him to do. If he does it on his own, however, his moral responsibility for doing it is not affected by the fact that Black was lurking in the background with sinister intent, since this intent never comes into play.

V

The fact that a person could not have avoided doing something is a sufficient condition of his having done it. But, as some of my examples show, this fact may play no role whatever in the explanation of why he did it. It may not figure at all among the circumstances that actually brought it about that he did what he did, so that his action is to be accounted for on another basis entirely. Even though the person was unable to do otherwise, that is to say, it may not be the case that he acted as he did because he could not have done otherwise. Now if someone had no alternative to performing a certain action but did not perform it because he was unable to do otherwise, then he would have performed exactly the same action even if he could have done otherwise. The circumstances that made it impossible for him to do otherwise could have been subtracted from the situation without affecting what happened or why it happened in any way. Whatever it was that actually led the person to do what he did, or that made him do it, would have led him to do it or made him do it even if it had been possible for him to do something else instead.

Thus it would have made no difference, so far as concerns his action or how he came to perform it, if the circumstances that made it impossible for him to avoid performing it had not prevailed. The fact that he could not have done otherwise clearly provides no basis for supposing that he might have done otherwise if he had been able to do so. When a fact is in this way irrelevant to the problem of accounting for a person's action it seems quite gratuitous to assign it any weight in the assessment of his moral responsibility. Why should the fact be considered in reaching it moral judgment concerning the person when it does not help in any way to understand either what made him act as he did or what, in other circumstances, he might have done?

This then, is why the principle of alternate possibilities is mistaken. It asserts that a person bears no moral responsibility—that is, he is to be excused—for having performed an action if there were circumstances that made it impossible or him to avoid performing it. But there may be circumstances that make it impossible for a person to avoid performing some action without those circumstances in any way bringing it about that he performs that action. It would surely be no good for the person to refer to circumstances of this sort in an effort to absolve himself of moral responsibility for performing the action in question. For those circumstances, by hypothesis, actually had nothing to do with his having done what he did. He would have done precisely the same thing, and he would have been led or made in precisely the same way to do it, even if they had not prevailed.

We often do, to be sure, excuse people for what they have done when they tell us (and we believe them) that they could not have done otherwise. But this is because we assume that what they tell us serves to explain why they did what they did. We take it for granted that they are not being disingenuous, as a person would be who cited as an excuse the fact that he could not have avoided doing what he did but who knew full well that it was not at all because of this that he did it.

What I have said may suggest that the principle of alternate possibilities should be revised so as to assert that a person is not morally responsible for what he has done if he did it because he could not have done otherwise. It may be noted that this revision of the principle does not seriously affect the arguments of those who have relied on the original principle in their efforts to maintain that moral responsibility and determinism are incompatible. For if it was causally determined that a person perform a certain action, then it will be true that the person performed it because of those causal determinants. And if the fact that it was causally determined that a person perform a certain action means that the person could not have done otherwise, as philosophers who argue for the incompatibility thesis characteristically suppose, then the fact that it was causally determined that a person perform a certain action will mean that the person performed it because he could not have done otherwise. The revised principle of alternate possibilities will entail, on this assumption concerning the meaning of 'could have done otherwise', that a person is not morally responsible for what he has done if it was causally determined that he do it. I do not believe, however, that this revision of the principle is acceptable.

Suppose a person tells us that he did what he did because he was unable to do otherwise; or suppose he makes the similar statement that he did what he did because he had to do it. We do often accept statements like these (if we believe them) as valid excuses, and such statements may well seem at first glance to invoke the revised principle of alternate possibilities. But I think that when we accept such statements as valid excuses it is because we assume that we are being told more than the statements strictly and literally convey. We understand the person who offers the excuse to mean that he did what he did only because he was unable to do otherwise, or only because he had to do it. And we understand him to mean, more particularly, that when he did what he did it was not because that was what he really wanted to do. The principle of alternate possibilities should thus be replaced, in my opinion, by the following principle: a person is not morally responsible for what he has done if he did it only because he could not have done otherwise. This principle does not appear to conflict with the view that moral responsibility is compatible with determinism.

The following may all be true: there were circumstances that made it impossible for a person to avoid doing something; these circumstances actually played a role in bringing it about that he did it, so that it is correct to say that he did it because he could not have done otherwise; the person really wanted to do what he did; he did it because it was what he really wanted to do, so that it is not correct to say that he did what he did only because he could not have done otherwise. Under these conditions, the person may well be morally responsible for what he had done. On the other hand, he will not be morally responsible for what he has done if he did it only because he could not have done otherwise, even if what he did was something he really wanted to do.

NOTES

1. The two main concepts employed in the principle of alternate possibilities are "morally responsible" and "could have done otherwise." To discuss the principle without analyzing either of these concepts may well seem like an attempt at piracy. The reader should take notice that my Jolly Roger is now unfurled.

2. After thinking up the example that I am about to develop I learned that Robert Nozick, in lectures given several years ago, had formulated an example of the same general type and had proposed it as a counterexample to the principle of alternate possibilities.

3. The assumption that Black can predict what $Jones_4$ will decide to do does not beg the question of determinism. We can imagine that $Jones_4$ has often confronted the alternatives—A and B—that he now confronts, and that his face has invariably twitched when he was about to decide to do A and never when he was about to decide to do B. Knowing this, and observing the twitch, Black would have a basis for prediction. This does, to be sure, suppose that there is some sort of causal relation between $Jones_4$'s state at the time of the twitch and his subsequent states. But any plausible view of decision or of action will allow that reaching a decision and performing an action both involve earlier and later phases, with causal relations between them, and such that the earlier phases are not themselves part of the decision or of the action. The example does not require that these earlier phases be deterministically related to still earlier events.

4. The example is also flexible enough to allow for the elimination of Black altogether. Anyone who thinks that the effectiveness of the example is undermined by its reliance on a human manipulator, who imposes his will on $Jones_4$ can substitute for Black a machine programmed to do what Black does. If this is still not good enough, forget both Black and the machine and suppose that their role is played by natural forces involving no will or design at all.

CHAPTER 4

Reconciliations

In this last section, we will examine several attempts to reconcile freedom and determinism by showing that the problem, as it is traditionally understood, proceeds from some false assumptions. The first approach, by Richard Taylor, questions the assumption that all causal chains are infinite and proposes a form of "agent causation," according to which human agents initiate new causal chains. The remaining three approaches invoke different analyses of the explanations we provide for human action in terms of mental states (reasons, desires, beliefs, etc.) and their relation to the causal explanations of behavior that invoke causal laws.

Richard Taylor's "Freedom and Determinism," offers the following observation: neither determinism nor indeterminism is compatible with free will. However, the observation about indeterminism reveals that causal determinism is, oddly enough, necessary for us to make sense of free will. This suggests to Taylor that we might need to rethink the way the freedom-determinism debate is usually formulated.

Taylor begins with an examination of causal determinism and its incompatibility with the elements that make up freedom of choice. The kind of determinism Taylor considers is much like the physical determinism of Laplace, represented in the first section of this book. According to this view, every event is caused to exist and to have the properties it does because of events that happened in the past. This principle, which Taylor calls "the thesis of causal determinism," has the implication that we cannot really deliberate about our actions, nor is it ever up to us what we do; for our actions are the result of chains of causation that started long before we ever existed. It seems, then, that our sense of freedom of choice (that we deliberate, and that it is sometimes up to us what we do) is an illusion that is the result of our ignorance of the real causes of our actions.

According to Taylor, the attempt simply to deny the truth of determinism and assert the truth of indeterminism in its place will be no help if one's aim is to rescue our freedom and responsibility. If indeterminism is true, nothing is causally determined. This means that we must forever be ignorant of why all events, including our own actions, happen. In Taylor's view, without causal determinism we would become erratic jerking phantoms that behave without rhyme or reason. If I strike someone with a broom, and that action is not caused in accordance with any law or principle, then I must say that I do not know why I struck that person, for according to indeterminism there can be no explanation for my action. Not only is this an odd suggestion, but it also undercuts the very notion of freedom and responsibility that indeterminism was introduced to protect. If my actions are uncaused and I never know from one minute to the next what I might do, I can hardly be described as free and responsible. Indeed, unless my actions are causally determined to some extent, it is hard to regard my actions as mine at all. This raises the interesting notion that, although freedom and determinism seem to be incompatible, a certain level of causal determinism must be necessary for genuine freedom and responsibility.

154

In light of this, Taylor proposes a theory of action that attempts to bring these ideas together in a consistent manner. He calls this the "theory of agency." In this view, causal determinism remains true, except that some causal chains are not infinite. Occasionally, human beings, or "agents," can produce or initiate new causal chains. The concept of an agent is a difficult one to understand. Usually we say that a human being is made up of many parts and is subject to many events. Among these events are things such as desiring to go golfing or deciding to make a sandwich. Typically we say that it is these events that cause us to act, and the problem we have seen is that these events are themselves causally determined by events that preceded them. The theory of agency claims that our actions are not caused by events such as deciding to do such and such, or willing to do X; instead, it claims that human beings as a whole, as a kind of metaphysical substance, can cause new things to happen.

Such an approach seems to do justice to the stubborn commitment most of us feel to our sense of freedom, yet it also admits the truth of causal determinism, which is equally hard to deny. However, this view is not without its problems. The theory of agency introduces a new category of object into the world—an agent—and it is unclear in what way a human being is more than a collection of parts and processes. This approach also introduces a new kind of causation—agent causation—which functions differently from the way all other familiar causal relations work. To be truly compelling, the theory of agency will have to defend and explain these ideas in more detail than Taylor is prepared to offer.

The second approach we will consider is offered by Donald Davidson in his two articles, "Actions, Reasons, and Causes," and "Mental Events." Although the task of reconciling freedom with determinism lies principally in the second of these works, the first provides vital background for Davidson's understanding of the nature of the reasons for which we act and the role they play in our behavior.

In "Actions, Reasons, and Causes," Davidson examines how we explain the behavior of others and ourselves when we appeal to mental states such as beliefs, desires, and reasons. Playing a central role in such explanations are what Davidson calls "primary reasons." In his view, a primary reason usually has two elements. It consists of a "pro attitude" and a related belief. When an agent has a pro attitude toward a given action, this means that the agent sees something desirable about performing that action; he or she *wants* to do it. This is a general and familiar feature of our behavior. When I say that I went to the refrigerator because I was thirsty, this must be because I saw something desirable about going to the refrigerator. The related beliefs that make up the other part of a primary reason are a little more complicated. In general, what this means is that when I act, part of my reason for acting must be that I understand my action in a certain way, or regard my action as an act of a certain type. For instance, in the previous example I must regard my going to the refrigerator as an act of getting a drink. I must also believe (or suspect) that there is something in the refrigerator to drink, that drinking will relieve my thirst, and so on.

The related beliefs mentioned previously might seem obvious, but play a very important role in the way we understand our actions. Davidson writes about how we can "redescribe" our actions. To redescribe an action is to identify the action in a different way by using different words. We do this all the time not only when we talk about actions, but also when we talk about people and objects. I can be described as "the author of this textbook," "a philosophy professor at Wilfrid Laurier University," "the son of Janis and Colin," and in a multitude of other ways. Each description is true and each one tells you something different about me. We can do the same thing with our actions; which description we use can make a very important difference to how we understand and explain our actions. Imagine that I am very foolishly playing with a rifle, point it at a friend and pull the trigger, not knowing it is loaded. My action of aiming the rifle and pulling the trigger can be truly described as "shooting and killing my friend," or as "playing a practical joke." Only the second description captures the way I understood my action when I performed it. That is, when I explain why I did what I did, the fact that I *believed* I was playing a practical joke rather than committing homicide is of the utmost importance. This is the kind of consideration Davidson has in mind when he talks about the "related beliefs" that make up part of a primary reason.

In connection with the previous observations, Davidson points out that the identification of an agent's primary reason for acting tends to *justify* the action in question. That is, when one describes an action in a way that captures an agent's primary reason for performing it, the action appears rational in the light of the agent's beliefs and desires. Imagine that a man suddenly undresses in the middle of a supermarket and then wraps himself in aluminum foil. Such behavior would appear odd to say the least. But when we learn that he believes the CIA is after him, suspects that his clothes contain listening devices, and thinks aluminum foil will block the signal from the homing device he thinks is implanted in his body, his behavior is no longer as mysterious as it seemed at first. In fact, his behavior now demonstrates a certain degree of rationality and is justified in proportion to the rationality his action exhibits.

The final point Davidson defends in "Actions, Reasons, and Causes" is the claim that primary reasons are the causes of actions. In large part, Davidson is reacting to an opposing view that was popular at the time. The contrary view, associated with Wittgenstein, is that reasons are not causes of actions precisely because of the rationalizing or justificatory role they play in explanations. Wittgenstein and others claimed that primary reasons explain actions by rationalizing them, not by causing them. Davidson is happy to admit that action-explanations possess this rationalizing character, but argues that these explanations are causal as well. Without regarding the primary reason for an action as its cause, there is no way to account for the fact that one can have a reason for an action and yet fail to do it. Only if the primary reason has actual causal significance will we have an intentional action that can be rationalized, otherwise we would not explain anything by appealing to the primary reason, or the action would not have happened. Both elements need to be present for our explanations to work.

In "Mental Events," Davidson offers a means of reconciling the claim that human beings have free will with the claim that the thesis of causal determinism is true. The solution lies in his theory of mind, which he calls "anomalous monism." At the heart of Davidson's approach is the idea that mental events (beliefs, perceptions, desires, etc.) can enter into causal relationships, as when they cause us to act, but he denies there are any strict laws connecting reasons and actions. This means that the mental is anomalous or free even if the physical world and its causal laws are entirely deterministic.

The thesis of causal determinism is often characterized as the belief that everything that happens is determined by antecedent conditions and the laws of nature. Davidson accepts this account of the physical world as a genuine possibility, but asks us to pay closer attention to the relationship between causal laws and singular causal claims. A singular causal claim is simply a statement to the effect that one thing caused another, such as "*A* caused *B*." Philosophers who think that there are laws of nature that determine the way the world works will say that wherever there is a true singular causal claim, there is a law of nature. Hence, there must be a law connecting *A* and *B*. Davidson's insight is that the relevant law need not use the description of the events employed in the singular claim.

Remember Davidson saying in "Actions, Reasons, and Causes" that we can describe any event, including actions, in numerous ways? Well, this is also true of causal claims. When I say "*A* caused *B*," I am picking out two events and saying that the first caused the second. Notice, however, that when I do this I have to describe *A* and *B* in some way. For instance, if I say, "The hurricane caused a catastrophe," I am making a causal claim about two events. I have described the first event, the cause, as "the hurricane" and the second event, the effect (the collapse of a bridge), as "a catastrophe." These are not the only descriptions available. If the first event is reported on the news on Wednesday and the second is reported on the news on Thursday, then we might also say, truthfully, "The event reported on the news on Wednesday caused the event reported on the news on Thursday."

Whatever descriptions we use to identify a cause and its effect have no bearing on the truth of the singular causal claim in which those descriptions figure. The claim "The hurricane caused a catastrophe," is no truer than the claim "The event reported on the news on Wednesday caused the event reported on the news on Thursday." However, certain descriptions of events are more helpful for identifying the causal law that underlies any particular causal relation. Going back to the hurricane causing the catastrophe, we obviously will not find a law of nature connecting news reports. However, when we use the descriptions "hurricane" and "collapse of the bridge" we begin to see how the first caused the second, we gain some insight into the kind of vocabulary we would need to use to formulate what the underlying physical law might be. Of course, hurricanes are not connected by a natural law to the collapsing of bridges since each event can happen without the other. What we see is that there is a way to refine our descriptions of the cause and the effect that could, in principle, enable us to discover the law that was at work here.

We saw that Davidson thinks primary reasons are the causes of actions and that primary reasons usually consist of a pro attitude and a set of beliefs about the intended action. Thus, when I say, "I went to the refrigerator because I wanted a drink," I am identifying a causal relationship between two events where the cause is picked out under the description, "wanting a drink" and the effect is picked out under the description, "going to the refrigerator." According to Davidson, we should not look for a law connecting wanting a drink and going to the refrigerator just as we should not look for a law connecting news headlines. He thinks that mental events, such as having primary reasons, are identical to physical events and so have physical descriptions. The relevant law, then, will connect the reason and the action under different, more precise physical descriptions of those events. This has the effect of rendering the mental anomalous. That is, there can be no causal laws connecting mental states such as primary reasons to actions. Freedom and determinism are reconciled in the following sense: since the mental is anomalous (it is not bound by causal laws) our choices and decisions are free; to the extent that we are physical beings we are controlled by laws of nature.

Jaegwon Kim's article, "Self-Understanding and Rationalizing Explanations," is not an attempt to reconcile freedom and determinism as such, but does point to a way of doing this that will become clearer after the last selection from Melden. In his article, Kim adopts the assumption that Davidson is correct that the mental is anomalous, but he disagrees with Davidson's account of how primary reasons explain intentional actions. Kim, therefore, provides us with a critique of Davidson's approach and offers an alternative understanding of the nature of reason giving.

Davidson insists that reasons explain actions because they cause them. Kim thinks this is inadequate. His reason is this: since there are no laws connecting reasons and actions, reasons cause actions only because of their physical characteristics, in particular, because of those characteristics that figure in causal laws. This means that reasons do not cause actions because they are the reasons they are. They cause them because of the kind of physical events they are. The features of a primary reason that rationalize the action, then, are not the features that cause it. Thus, Davidson must be mistaken in insisting that reasons explain actions by causing them.

Think back to the example of the hurricane and the catastrophe. It is true of the hurricane that it was reported on the news. It would be very odd, however, to insist that it was in virtue of the fact that the hurricane was reported on the news that it caused the catastrophe. The hurricane would have caused the catastrophe regardless of whether or not it was reported on the news. Thus, only some features of the hurricane contribute to what it causes. Other features are irrelevant. Kim sees something similar happening in Davidson's account of reasons causing actions. The features of a reason that are relevant to what it causes are its physical features, not the fact that the reason involved certain beliefs and desires. Since our primary reasons are nevertheless central to how explanations of our actions function, Kim thinks that Davidson has made a mistake.

In light of the suggested shortcomings of Davidson's approach, Kim offers an alternative account of the nature of reason giving. He proposes that we should regard the connection between reasons and actions as normative rather than causal. This means we should treat reasons and actions as part of a general framework for decision making that is based on the concepts of rationality and coherence. Kim, then, places a great deal more emphasis on the rationalizing or justificatory role of reasons than Davidson does. In the six theses Kim provides, in broad outline, the principles of rationality that govern decision making and that determine the way our explanations of intentional action, work. In general, he emphasizes our need to regard ourselves as rational beings and suggests that, much of the time, doing so involves identifying primary reasons for our actions. When we identify primary reasons to explain our own behavior or the behavior of others, we are not identifying the causes of action; we are instead engaged in the broader task of situating behavior in a rational context, and achieving this explains our actions.

The final selection is the concluding chapter of A. I. Melden's book, *Free Action*. Although Melden's work historically precedes the papers by Davidson and Kim, their work can be seen to support Melden's conclusions. Like Kim, Melden thinks it is a mistake to regard the explanations of actions that make reference to mental states or traits of character as causal explanations. However, Melden's conclusions go well beyond claims about the nature of action-explanations. In his view, we should not even regard actions as causal episodes. Instead, we should understand actions as human events within a moral-rational framework, as the product of moral agents. This is not to deny that there are causal relationships in the world. However, to focus on causal relations is to study bodily movement rather than action. These are two entirely different categories of investigation.

FREEDOM AND DETERMINISM*

Richard Taylor

If I consider the world or any part of it at any particular moment, it seems certain that it is perfectly determinate in every detail. There is no vagueness, looseness, or ambiguity. There is, indeed, vagueness, and even error, in my conceptions of reality, but not in reality itself. A lilac bush, which surely has a certain exact number of blossoms, appears to me only to have many blossoms, and I do not know how many. Things seen in the distance appear of indefinite form, and often of a color and size that in fact they are not. Things near the border of my visual field seem to me vague and amorphous, and I can never even say exactly where that border itself is, it is so indefinite and vague. But all such indeterminateness resides solely in my conceptions and ideas; the world itself shares none of it. The sea, at any exact time and place, has exactly a certain salinity and temperature, and every grain of sand on its shore is exactly disposed with respect to all the others. The wind at any point in space has at any moment a certain direction and force, not more nor less. It matters not whether these properties and relations are known to anyone. A field of wheat at any moment contains just an exact number of ripening grains, each having reached just the ripeness it exhibits, each presenting a determinate color and shade, an exact shape and mass. A person, too, at any given point in his life, is perfectly determinate to the minutest cells of his body. My own brain, nerves—even my thoughts, intentions, and feelings—are at any moment just what they then specifically are. These thoughts might, to be sure, be vague and even false as representations, but as thoughts they are not, and even a false idea is no less an exact and determinate idea than a true one.

Nothing seems more obvious. But if I now ask *why* the world and all its larger or smaller parts are this moment just what they are, the answer comes to mind: because the world, the moment before, was precisely what it then was. Given exactly what went before, the world, it seems, could now be none other than it is. And what it was a moment before, in all its larger and minuter parts, was the consequence of what had

---

*From Richard Taylor, *Metaphysics*, 4th ed., Chapter 5 (New Jersey: Prentice Hall, 1992). Reprinted with the kind permission of the publisher.

gone just before then, and so on, back to the very beginning of the world, if it had a beginning, or through an infinite past time, in case it had not. In any case, the world as it now is, and every part of it, and every detail of every part, would seem to be the only world that now could be, given just what it has been.

DETERMINISM

Reflections such as this suggest that, in the case of everything that exists, there are antecedent conditions, known or unknown, which, because they are given, mean that things could not be other than they are. That is an exact statement of the metaphysical thesis of determinism. More loosely, it says that everything, including every cause, is the effect of some cause or causes; or that everything is not only determinate but causally determined. The statement, moreover, makes no allowance for time, for past, or for future. Hence, if true, it holds not only for all things that have existed but for all things that do or ever will exist.

Of course people rarely think of such a principle, and hardly one in a thousand will ever formulate it to himself in words. Yet all do seem to assume it in their daily affairs, so much so that some philosophers have declared it an *a priori* principle of the understanding, that is, something that is known independently of experience, while others have deemed it to be at least a part of the common sense of mankind. Thus, when I hear a noise I look up to see where it came from. I never suppose that it was just a noise that came from nowhere and had no cause. Everyone does the same—even animals, though they have never once thought about metaphysics or the principle of universal determinism. People believe, or at least act as though they believed, that things have causes, without exception. When a child or animal touches a hot stove for the first time, it hesitatingly believes that the pain then felt was caused by that stove, and so firm and immediate is that belief that hot stoves are avoided ever after. We all use our metaphysical principles, whether we think of them or not, or are even capable of thinking of them. If I have a bodily or other disorder—a rash, for instance, or a fever or a phobia—I consult a physician for a diagnosis and explanation in the hope that the cause of it might be found and removed or moderated. I am never tempted to suppose that such things just have no causes, arising from nowhere, else I would take no steps to remove the causes. The principle of determinism is here, as in everything else, simply assumed, without being thought about.

DETERMINISM AND HUMAN BEHAVIOR

I am a part of the world. So is each of the cells and minute parts of which I am composed. The principle of determinism, then, in case it is true, applies to me and to each of those minute parts, no less than to the sand, wheat, winds, and waters of which we have spoken. There is no particular difficulty in thinking so, as long as I consider only what are sometimes called the "purely physiological" changes of my body, like growth, the pulse, glandular secretions, and the like. But what of my thoughts and ideas? And what of my behavior that is supposed to be deliberate, purposeful, and perhaps morally significant? These are all changes of my own being, changes that I undergo, and if these are all but the consequences of the conditions under which they occur, and these conditions are the only ones that could have obtained, given the state of the world just before and when they arose, what now becomes of my responsibility for my behavior and of the control over my conduct that I fancy myself to possess? What am I but a helpless product of nature, destined by her to do whatever I do and to become whatever I become?

There is no moral blame nor merit in anyone who cannot help what he does. It matters not whether the explanation for his behavior is found within him or without, whether it is expressed in terms of ordinary physical causes or allegedly "mental" ones, or whether the causes be proximate or remote. I am not responsible for being a man rather than a woman, nor for having the temperament and desires characteristic of that sex. I was never asked whether these should be given to me. The kleptomaniac, similarly, steals from compulsion, the alcoholic drinks from compulsion, and sometimes even the hero dies from compulsive courage. Though these causes are within them, they compel no less for that, and their victims never chose to have them inflicted upon themselves. To say they are compulsions is to say only that they compel. But to say that they compel is only to say that they cause; for the cause of a thing being given, the effect cannot fail to follow. By the thesis of determinism, however, everything whatever is caused, and not one single thing could ever be other than exactly what it is. Perhaps one thinks that the kleptomaniac and the drunkard did not have to become what they are, that they could have done better at another time and thereby ended up better than they are now, or that the hero could have done worse and then ended up a coward. But this shows only an unwillingness to understand what made them become as they are. Having found that their behavior is caused from within them, we can hardly avoid asking what caused these inner springs of action, and then asking what were the causes of these causes, and so on through the infinite past. We shall not, certainly, with our small understanding and our fragmentary knowledge of the past ever know why the world should at just this time and place have produced just this thief, this drunkard, and this hero, but the vagueness and smattered nature of our knowledge should not tempt us to imagine a similar vagueness in nature herself. Everything in nature is and always has been determinate, with no loose edges at all, and she was forever destined to bring forth just what she has produced, however slight may be our understanding of the origins of these works. Ultimate responsibility for anything that exists, and hence for any person and his deeds, can thus rest only with the first cause of all things, if there is such a cause, or nowhere at all, in case there is not. Such, at least, seems to be the unavoidable implication of determinism.

DETERMINISM AND MORALS

Some philosophers, faced with all this, which seems quite clear to the ordinary understanding, have tried to cling to determinism while modifying traditional conceptions of morals. They continue to use such words as *merit, blame, praise*, and *desert*, but they so divest them of their meanings as to finish by talking about things entirely different, sometimes without themselves realizing that they are no longer on the subject. An ordinary person will hardly understand that anyone can possess merit or vice and be deserving of moral praise or blame as a result of traits that he has or of behavior arising from those traits, once it is well understood that he could never have avoided being just what he is and doing just what he does.

We are happily spared going into all this, however, for the question whether determinism is true of human nature is not a question of ethics at all but of metaphysics. There is accordingly no hope of answering it within the context of ethics. One can, to be sure, simply *assume* an answer to it—assume that determinism is true, for instance—and then see what are the implications of this answer for ethics; but that does not answer the question. Or one can *assume* some theory or other of ethics—assume some version of "the greatest happiness" principle, for instance—and then see whether that theory is consistent with determinism. But such confrontations of theories with theories likewise make us no wiser, so far as any fundamental question is concerned. We can suppose at once that determinism is consistent with some conceptions of morals, and inconsistent with others, and that the same holds for indeterminism. We shall still not know what theories are true; we shall only know which are consistent with another.

We shall, then, eschew all considerations of ethics as having no real bearing on our problem. We want to learn, if we can, whether determinism is true, and this is a question of metaphysics. It can, like all good questions of philosophy, be answered only on the basis of certain data; that is, by seeing whether or not it squares with certain things that everyone knows, or believes himself to know, or with things everyone is at least more sure about than the answer to the question at issue.

Now I could, of course, simply affirm that I am a morally responsible being, in the sense in which my responsibility for my behavior implies that I could have avoided that behavior. But this would take us into the nebulous realm of ethics, and it is, in fact, far from obvious that I am responsible in that sense. Many have doubted that they are responsible in that sense, and it is in any case not difficult to doubt it, however strongly one might feel about it.

There are, however, two things about myself of which I feel quite certain and that have no necessary connection with morals. The first is that I sometimes deliberate, with the view to making a decision; a decision, namely, to do this thing or that. And the second is that whether or not I deliberate about what to do, it is sometimes up to me what I do. This might all be an illusion, of course; but so also might any philosophical theory, such as the theory of determinism, be false. The point remains that it is far more difficult for me to doubt that I sometimes deliberate, and that it is sometimes up to me what to do, than to doubt any philosophical theory whatever, including the theory of determinism. We must, accordingly, if we ever hope to be wiser, adjust our theories to our data and not try to adjust our data to our theories.

Let us, then, get these two data quite clearly before us so we can see what they are, what they presuppose, and what they do and do not entail.

DELIBERATION

Deliberation is an activity, or at least a kind of experience, that cannot be defined, or even described, without metaphors. We speak of weighing this and that in our minds, of trying to anticipate consequences of various possible courses of action, and so on, but such descriptions do not convey to us what deliberation is unless we already know.

Whenever I deliberate, however, I find that I make certain presuppositions, whether I actually think of them or not. That is, I assume that certain things are true, certain things which are such that, if I thought they were not true, it would be impossible for me to deliberate at all. Some of these can be listed as follows:

First, I find that I can deliberate only about my own behavior and never about the behavior of another. I can try to guess, speculate, or figure out what another person is going to do; I can read certain signs and sometimes infer what he will do; but I cannot deliberate about it. When I deliberate I try to decide something, to make up my mind, and this is as remote as anything could be from speculating, trying to guess, or inferring from signs. Sometimes one does speculate on what he is going to do, by trying to draw conclusions from certain signs or omens—he might infer that he is going to sneeze, for instance, or speculate that he is going to become a grandfather—but he is not then deliberating whether to do things or not. One does, to be sure, sometimes deliberate about whether another person will do a certain act, when that other person is subject to his command or otherwise under his control; but then he is not really deliberating about another person's acts at all, but about his own namely, whether or not to have that other person carry out the order.

Second, I find that I can deliberate only about future things, never things past or present. I may not know what I did at a certain time in the past, in case I have forgotten, but I can no longer deliberate whether to do it then or not. I can, again, only speculate, guess, try to infer, or perhaps try to remember. Similarly, I cannot deliberate whether or not to be doing something now; I can only ascertain whether or not I am in fact doing it. If I am sitting I cannot deliberate about whether or not to be sitting. I can only deliberate about whether to remain sitting—and this has to do with the future.

Third, I cannot deliberate about what I shall do if I already know what I am going to do. If I were to say, for example, "I know that I am going to be married tomorrow and in the meantime I am going to deliberate about whether to get married," I would contradict myself. There are only two ways that I could know now what I am going to do tomorrow; namely, either by inferring this from certain signs and omens or by having already decided what I am going to do. But if I have inferred from signs and omens what I am going to do, I cannot deliberate about it—there is just nothing for me to decide; and similarly, if I have already decided. If, on the other hand, I can still deliberate about what I am going to do, to that extent I must regard the signs and omens as unreliable, and the inference uncertain, and I therefore do not know what I am going to do after all.

And finally, I cannot deliberate about what to do, even though I may not know what I am going to do, unless I believe that it is up to me what I am going to do. If I am within the power of another person, or at the mercy of circumstances over which I have no control, then, although I may have no idea what I am going to do, I cannot deliberate about it. I can only wait and see. If, for instance, I am a serviceman, and regulations regarding uniforms are posted each day by my commanding officer and are strictly enforced by him, then I shall not know what uniforms I shall be wearing from time to time, but I cannot deliberate about it. I can only wait and see what regulations are posted; it is not up to me. Similarly, a woman who is about to give birth to a child cannot deliberate whether to have a boy or a girl, even though she may not know. She can only wait and see; it is not up to her. Such examples can be generalized to cover any case wherein one does not know what he is going to do but believes that it is not up to him, and hence no matter for his decision and hence none for his deliberation.

"IT IS UP TO ME"

I sometimes feel certain that it is, at least to some extent, up to me what I am going to do; indeed, I must believe this if I am to deliberate about what to do. But what does this mean? It is, again, hard to say, but the idea can be illustrated, and we can fairly easily see what it does *not* mean.

Let us consider the simplest possible sort of situation in which this belief might be involved. At this moment, for instance, it seems quite certain to me that, holding my finger before me, I can move it either to the left or to the right, that each of these motions is possible for me. This does not mean merely that my finger can move either way, although it entails that, for this would be true in case nothing obstructed it, even if I had no control over it at all. I can say of a distant, fluttering leaf that it can move either way, but not that I can move it, since I have no control over it. How it moves is not up to me. Nor does it mean merely that my finger can be moved either way, although it entails this too. If the motions of my finger are under the control of some other person or of some machine, then it might be true that the finger can be moved either way, by that person or machine, though false that I can move it at all.

If I say, then, that it is up to me how I move my finger, I mean that I can move it in this way and I can move it in that way, and not merely that it can move or be moved in this way and that. I mean that the motion of my finger is within my direct control. If someone were to ask me to move it to the right, I could do that, and if he were to ask me to move it to the left, I could do that too. Further, I could do these simple acts without being asked at all, and having been asked, I could move it in a manner the exact opposite of what was requested, since I can ignore the request. There are, to be sure, some motions of my finger that I cannot make, so it is not *entirely* up to me how it moves. I cannot bend it backward, for instance, or bend it into a knot, for these motions are obstructed by the very anatomical construction of the finger itself; and to say that I can move my finger at all means at least that nothing obstructs such a motion, though it does not mean merely this. There is, however, at this moment, no obstruction, anatomical or otherwise, to my moving it to the right, and none to my moving it to the left.

This datum, it should be noted, is properly expressed as a conjunction and not as a disjunction. That is, my belief is that I can move my finger in one way *and* that I can also move it another way; and it does not do justice to this belief to say that I can move it one way *or* the other. It is fairly easy to see the truth of this, for the latter claim, that I can move it one way or the other, would be satisfied in case there were only one way I could move it, and *that* is not what I believe. Suppose, for instance, that my hand were strapped to a device in such a fashion that I could move my finger to the right but not to the left. Then it would still be entirely true that I could move it either to the left *or* to the right—since it would be true that I could move it to the right. But that is not what I now believe. My finger is not strapped to anything, and nothing obstructs its motion in either direction. And what I believe, in this situation, is that I can move it to the right *and* I can move it to the left.

We must note further that the belief expressed in our datum is not a belief in what is logically impossible. It is the belief that I now *can* move my finger in different ways but not that I can move it in different ways at once. What I believe is that I am now able to move my finger one way and that I am now equally able to move it another way, but I do not claim to be able now or at any other time to move it both ways simultaneously. The situation here is analogous to one in which I might, for instance, be offered a choice of either of two apples but forbidden to take both. Each apple is such that I may select it, but neither is such that I may select it together with the other.

Now, are these two data—the belief that I do sometimes deliberate, and the belief that it is sometimes up to me what I do—consistent with the metaphysical theory of deteminism? We do not know yet. We intend to find out. It is fairly clear, however, that they are going to present difficulties to that theory. But let us not, in any case, try to avoid those difficulties by just denying the data themselves. If we eventually deny the data, we shall do so for better reasons than this. Virtually everyone is convinced that beliefs such as are expressed in our data are sometimes true. They cannot be simply dismissed as false just because they might appear to conflict with a metaphysical theory that hardly anyone has ever really thought much about at all. Almost anyone, unless his fingers are paralyzed, bound, or otherwise incapable of movement, believes sometimes that the motions of his fingers are within his control, in exactly the sense expressed by our data. If consequences of considerable importance to him depend on how he moves his fingers, he sometimes deliberates before moving them, or at least he is convinced that he does or that he can. Philosophers might have different notions of just what things are implied by such data, but there is in any case no more, and in fact considerably less, reason for denying the data than for denying some philosophical theory.

CAUSAL VERSUS LOGICAL NECESSITY

Philosophers have long since pointed out that causal connections involve no logical necessity, that the denial of a particular causal connection is never self-contradictory, and this is undoubtedly true. But neither does the assertion or the denial of determinism involve any concept of what is and what is not logically necessary. If determinism is true, then anything that happens is, given the conditions under which it occurs, the only thing possible, the thing that is necessitated by those conditions. But it is not the only thing that is logically possible, nor do those conditions logically necessitate it. Similarly, if one denies the thesis of determinism by asserting, for instance, that each of two bodily motions is possible for him under identical conditions, he is asserting much more than that each is logically possible, for that would be a trivial claim.

This distinction, between logical necessity and the sort of necessity involved in determinism, can be illustrated with examples. If, for instance, a man is beheaded, we can surely say that it is impossible for him to go on living, that his being beheaded necessitates his death, and so on; but there are no logical necessities or impossibilities involved here. It is not logically impossible for a man to live without his head. Yet no one will deny that a man cannot live under conditions that include his being headless, that such a state of affairs is in a perfectly clear sense impossible. Similarly, if my finger is in a tight and fairly strong cast, then it is impossible for me to move it in any way at all, though this is not logically impossible. It is logically possible that I should be vastly stronger than I am, and that I should move my finger and, in doing so, break the cast, though this would ordinarily not be possible in the sense that concerns us. Again, it is not logically impossible that I should bend my finger backward, or into a knot, though it is, in fact, impossible for me to do either or, what means the same thing, necessary that I should do neither. Certain conditions prohibit my doing such things, though they impose no logical barrier. And finally, if someone—a physician, for example—should ask me whether I can move my finger, and I should reply truthfully that I can, I would not merely be telling her that it is logically possible for me to move it, for this she already knows. I would be telling her that I am able to move it, that it is within my power to do so, that there are no conditions, such as paralysis or whatnot, that prevent my moving it.

It follows that not all necessity is logical necessity, nor all impossibility logical impossibility, and that to say that something is possible is sometimes to say much more than that it is logically possible. The kind of necessity involved in the thesis of determinism is quite obviously the nonlogical kind, as is also the kind of possibility involved in its denial. If we needed a *name* for these nonlogical modalities, we could call them *causal* necessity, impossibility, and possibility, but the concepts are clear enough without making a great deal of the name.

FREEDOM

To say that it is, in a given instance, up to me what I do is to say that I am in that instance *free* with respect to what I then do. Thus, I am sometimes free to move my finger this way and that, but not, certainly, to bend it backward or into a knot. But what does this mean?

It means, first that there is no *obstacle* or *impediment* to my activity. Thus, there is sometimes no obstacle to my moving my finger this way and that, though there are obvious obstacles to my moving it backward or into a knot. Those things, accordingly, that pose obstacles to my motions limit my freedom. If my hand were strapped in such a way as to permit only a leftward motion of my finger, I would not then be free to move it to the right. If it were encased in a tight cast that permitted no motion, I would not be free to move it at all. Freedom of motion, then, is limited by obstacles.

Further, to say that it is, in a given instance, up to me what I do, means that nothing *constrains* or *forces* me to do one thing rather than another. Constraints are like obstacles, except that while the latter prevent, the former enforce. Thus, if my finger is being forcibly bent to the left—by a machine, for instance, or by another person, or by any force that I cannot overcome—then I am not free to move it this way and that. I cannot, in fact, move it at all; I can only watch to see how it is moved, and perhaps vainly resist: Its motions are not up to me, or within my control, but in the control of some other thing or person.

Obstacles and constraints, then, both obviously limit my freedom. To say that I am free to perform some action thus means at least that there is no obstacle to my doing it, and that nothing constrains me to do otherwise.

Now if we rest content with this observation, as many have, and construe free activity simply as activity that is unimpeded and unconstrained, there is evidently no inconsistency between affirming both the thesis of determinism and the claim that I am sometimes free. For to say that some action of mine is neither impeded nor constrained does not by itself imply that it is not causally determined. The absence of obstacles and constraints is a mere negative condition, and does not by itself rule out the presence of positive causes. It might seem, then, that we can say of some of my actions that there are conditions antecedent to their performance so that no other actions were possible, and also that these actions were unobstructed and unconstrained. And to say that would logically entail that such actions were both causally determined, and free.

SOFT DETERMINISM

It is this kind of consideration that has led many philosophers to embrace what is sometimes called "soft determinism." All versions of this theory have in common three claims, by means of which, it is naively supposed, a reconciliation is achieved between determinism and freedom. Freedom being, furthermore, a condition of moral responsibility and the only condition that metaphysics seriously questions, it is supposed by the partisans of this view that determinism is perfectly compatible with such responsibility. This, no doubt, accounts for its great appeal and wide acceptance, even by some people of considerable learning.

The three claims of soft determinism are (1) that the thesis of determinism is true, and that accordingly all human behavior, voluntary or other, like the behavior of all other things, arises from antecedent conditions, given which no other behavior is possible—in short, that all human behavior is caused and determined; (2) that voluntary behavior is nonetheless free to the extent that it is not externally constrained or impeded; and (3) that, in the absence of such obstacles and constraints, the causes of voluntary behavior are certain states, events, or conditions within the agent himself; namely, his own acts of will or volitions, choices, decisions, desires, and so on.

Thus, on this view, I am free, and therefore sometimes responsible for what I do, provided nothing prevents me from acting according to my own choice, desire, or volition, or constrains me to act otherwise. There may, to be sure, be other conditions for my responsibility—such as, for example, an understanding of the probable consequences of my behavior, and that sort of thing—but absence of constraint or impediment is, at least, one such condition. And, it is claimed, it is a condition that is compatible with the supposition that my behavior is caused—for it is, by hypothesis, caused by my own inner choices, desires, and volitions.

THE REFUTATION OF THIS

The theory of soft determinism looks good at first—so good that it has for generations been solemnly taught from innumerable philosophical chairs and implanted in the minds of students as sound philosophy—but no great acumen is needed to discover that far from solving any problem, it only camouflages it.

My free actions are those unimpeded and unconstrained motions that arise from my own inner desires, choices, and volitions; let us grant this provisionally. But now, whence arise those inner states that determine what my body shall do? Are they within my control or not? Having made my choice or decision and acted upon it, could I have chosen otherwise or not?

Here the determinist, hoping to surrender nothing and yet to avoid the problem implied in that question, bids us not to ask it; the question itself, he announces, is without meaning. For to say that I could have done otherwise, he says, means only that I *would* have done otherwise, *if* those inner states that determined my action had been different; if, that is, I had decided or chosen differently. To ask, accordingly, whether I could have chosen or decided differently is only to ask whether, had I decided to decide differently or chosen to choose differently, or willed to will differently, I *would* have decided or chosen or willed differently. And this, of course, is unintelligible nonsense.

But it is not nonsense to ask whether the causes of my actions—my own inner choices, decisions, and desires—are themselves caused. And of course they are, if determinism is true, for on that thesis everything is caused and determined. And if they are, then we cannot avoid concluding that, given the causal conditions of those inner states, I could not have decided, willed, chosen, or desired other than I, in fact, did, for this is a logical consequence of the very definition of determinism. Of course we can still say that, *if* the causes of those inner states, whatever they were, had been different, then their effects, those inner states themselves, would have been different, and that in this hypothetical sense I could have decided, chosen, willed, or desired differently but that only pushes our problem back still another step. For we will then want to know whether the causes of those inner states were within my control, and so on *ad infinitum*. We are, at each step, permitted to say "could have been otherwise" only in a provisional sense—provided, that is, that something else had been different—but must then retract it and replace it with "could not have been otherwise" as soon as we discover, as we must at each step, that whatever would have to have been different could not have been different.

EXAMPLES

Such is the dialectic of the problem. The easiest way to see the shadowy quality of soft determinism, however, is by means of examples.

Let us suppose that my body is moving in various ways, that these motions are not externally constrained or impeded, and that they are all exactly in accordance with my own desires, choices, or acts of will and whatnot. When I will that my arm should move in a certain way, I find it moving in that way, unobstructed and unconstrained. When I will to speak, my lips and tongue move, unobstructed and unconstrained, in a manner suitable to the formation of the words I choose to utter. Now, given that this is a correct description of my behavior, namely, that it consists of the unconstrained and unimpeded motions of my body in response to my own volitions, then it follows that my behavior is free, on the soft determinist's definition of "free." It follows further that I am responsible for that behavior; or at least, that if I am not, it is not from any lack of freedom on my part.

But if the fulfillment of these conditions renders my behavior free—that is to say, if my behavior satisfies the conditions of free action set forth in the theory of soft determinism—then my behavior will be no less free if we assume further conditions that are perfectly consistent with those already satisfied.

We suppose further, accordingly, that while my behavior is entirely in accordance with my own volitions, and thus "free" in terms of the conception of freedom we are examining, my volitions themselves are caused. To make this graphic, we can suppose that an ingenious physiologist can induce in me any volition he pleases, simply by pushing various buttons on an instrument to which, let us suppose, I am attached by numerous wires. All the volitions I have in that situation are, accordingly, precisely the ones he gives me. By pushing one button, he evokes in me the volition to raise my hand; and my hand, being unimpeded, rises in response to that volition. By pushing another, he induces the volition in me to kick, and my foot, being unimpeded, kicks in response to that volition. We can even suppose that the physiologist puts a rifle in my hands, aims it at some passerby, and then, by pushing the proper button, evokes in me the volition to squeeze my finger against the trigger, whereupon the passerby falls dead of a bullet wound.

This is the description of a man who is acting in accordance with his inner volitions, a man whose body is unimpeded and unconstrained in its motions, these motions being the effects of those inner states. It is hardly the description of a free and responsible agent. It is the perfect description of a puppet. To render someone your puppet, it is not necessary forcibly to constrain the motions of his limbs, after the fashion that real puppets are moved. A subtler but no less effective means of making a person your puppet would be to gain complete control of his inner states, and ensuring, as the theory of soft determinism does ensure, that his body will move in accordance with them.

The example is somewhat unusual, but it is no worse for that. It is perfectly intelligible, and it does appear to refute the soft determinist's conception of freedom. One might think that, in such a case, the agent should not have allowed himself to be so rigged in the first place, but this is irrelevant; we can suppose that he was not aware that he was and was hence unaware of the source of those inner states that prompted his bodily motions. The example can, moreover, be modified in perfectly realistic ways, so as to coincide with actual and familiar cases. One can, for instance, be given a compulsive desire for certain drugs, simply by having them administered over a course of time. Suppose, then, that I do, with neither my knowledge nor consent, thus become a victim of such a desire and act upon it. Do I act freely, merely by virtue of the fact that I am unimpeded in my quest for drugs? In a sense I do, surely, but I am hardly free with respect to whether or not I shall use drugs. I never chose to have the desire for them inflicted upon me.

Nor does it, of course, matter whether the inner states that allegedly prompt all my "free" activity are evoked in me by another agent or by perfectly impersonal forces. Whether a desire that causes my body to behave in a certain way is inflicted upon me by another person, for instance, or derived from hereditary factors, or indeed from anything at all, matters not the least. In any case, if it is in fact the cause of my bodily behavior, I cannot help but act in accordance with it. Wherever it came from, whether from personal or impersonal origins, it was entirely caused or determined, and not within my control. Indeed, if determinism is true, as the theory of soft determinism holds it to be, all those inner states that cause my body to behave in whatever ways it behaves must arise from circumstances that existed before I was born; for the chain of causes and effects is infinite, and none could have been the least different, given those that preceded.

SIMPLE INDETERMINISM

We might at first now seem warranted in simply denying determinism, and saying that, insofar as they are free, my actions are not caused; or that, if they are caused by my own inner states—my own desires, impulses, choices, volitions, and whatnot— then these, in any case, are not caused. This is a perfectly clear sense in which a person's action, assuming that it was free, could have been otherwise. If it was uncaused, then, even given the conditions under which it occurred and all that pre- ceded, some other act was nonetheless possible, and he did not have to do what he did. Or if his action was the inevitable consequence of his own inner states, and could not have been otherwise, given these, we can nevertheless say that these inner states, being uncaused, could have been otherwise, and could thereby have produced different actions.

Only the slightest consideration will show, however, that this simple denial of de- terminism has not the slightest plausibility. For let us suppose it is true, and that some of my bodily motions—namely, those that I regard as my free acts—are not caused at all or, if caused by my own inner states, that these are not caused. We shall thereby avoid picturing a puppet, to be sure—but only by substituting something even less like a human being; for the conception that now emerges is not that of a free person, but of an erratic and jerking phantom, without any rhyme or reason at all.

Suppose that my right arm is free, according to this conception; that is, that its motions are uncaused. It moves this way and that from time to time, but nothing causes these motions. Sometimes it moves forth vigorously, sometimes up, some- times down, sometimes it just drifts vaguely about—these motions all being wholly free and uncaused. Manifestly I have nothing to do with them at all; they just hap- pen, and neither I nor anyone can ever tell what this arm will be doing next. It might seize a club and lay it on the head of the nearest bystander, no less to my astonish- ment than his. There will never be any point in asking why these motions occur, or in seeking any explanation of them, for under the conditions assumed there is no expla- nation. They just happen, from no causes at all.

This is no description of free, voluntary, or responsible behavior. Indeed, so far as the motions of my body or its parts are entirely uncaused, such motions cannot even be ascribed to me as my behavior in the first place, since I have nothing to do with them. The behavior of my arm is just the random motion of a foreign object. Behavior that is mine must be behavior that is within my control, but motions that occur from no causes are beyond the control of anyone. I can have no more to do with, and no more control over, the uncaused motions of my limbs than a gambler has over the motions of an honest roulette wheel. I can only, like him, idly wait to see what happens.

Nor does it improve things to suppose that my bodily motions are caused by my own inner states, so long as we suppose these to be wholly uncaused. The result will be the same as before. My arm, for example, will move this way and that, sometimes up and sometimes down, sometimes vigorously and sometimes just drifting about, always in response to certain inner states, to be sure. But since these are supposed to be wholly uncaused, it follows that I have no control over them and hence none over their effects. If my hand lays a club forcefully on the nearest bystander, we can indeed say that this motion resulted from an inner club-wielding desire of mine; but we must add that I had nothing to do with that desire, and that it arose, to be followed by its inevitable effect, no less to my astonishment than to his. Things like this do, alas, sometimes happen. We are all sometimes seized by compulsive impulses that arise we know not whence, and we do sometimes act upon these. But because they are far from being examples of free, voluntary, and responsible behavior, we need only to learn that the behavior was of this sort to conclude that it was not free, voluntary, or responsible. It was erratic, impulsive, and irresponsible.

DETERMINISM AND SIMPLE INDETERMINISM AS THEORIES

Both determinism and simple indeterminism are loaded with difficulties, and no one who has thought much on them can affirm either of them without some embarrassment. Simple indeterminism has nothing whatever to be said for it, except that it appears to remove the grossest difficulties of determinism, only, however, to imply perfect absurdities of its own. Determinism, on the other hand, is at least initially plausible. People seem to have a natural inclination to believe in it; it is, indeed, almost required for the very exercise of practical intelligence. And beyond this, our experience appears always to confirm it, so long as we are dealing with everyday facts of common experience, as distinguished from the esoteric researches of theoretical physics. But determinism, as applied to human behavior, has implications that few can casually accept, and they appear to be implications that no modification of the theory can efface.

Both theories, moreover, appear logically irreconcilable to the two items of data that we set forth at the outset; namely, (1) that my behavior is sometimes the outcome of my deliberation, and (2) that in these and other cases it is sometimes up to me what I do. Because these were our data, it is important to see, as must already be quite clear, that these theories cannot be reconciled to them.

I can deliberate only about my own future actions, and then only if I do not already know what I am going to do. If a certain nasal tickle warns me that I am about to sneeze, for instance, then I cannot deliberate whether to sneeze or not; I can only prepare for the impending convulsion. But if determinism is true, then there are always conditions existing antecedently to everything I do, sufficient for my doing just that, and such as to render it inevitable. If I can know what those conditions are and what behavior they are sufficient to produce, then I can in every such case know what I am going to do and cannot then deliberate about it.

By itself this only shows, of course, that I can deliberate only in ignorance of the causal conditions of my behavior; it does not show that such conditions cannot exist. It is odd, however, to suppose that deliberation should be a mere substitute for clear knowledge. Ignorance is a condition of speculation, inference, and guesswork, which have nothing whatever to do with deliberation. A prisoner awaiting execution may not know when he is going to die, and he may even entertain the hope of reprieve, but he cannot deliberate about this. He can only speculate, guess—and wait.

Worse yet, however, it now becomes clear that I cannot deliberate about what I am going to do, if it is even *possible* for me to find out in advance, whether I do in fact find out in advance or not. I can deliberate only with the view to deciding what to do, to making up my mind; and this is impossible if I believe that it could be inferred what I am going to do from conditions already existing, even though I have not made that inference myself. If I believe that what I am going to do has been rendered inevitable by conditions already existing, and could be inferred by anyone having the requisite sagacity, then I cannot try to decide whether to do it or not, for there is simply nothing left to decide. I can at best only guess or try to figure it out myself or, all prognostics failing, I can wait and see; but I cannot deliberate. I deliberate in order to *decide* what *to* do, not to *discover* what it is that I am *going* to do. But if determinism is true, then there are always antecedent conditions sufficient for everything that I do, and this can always be inferred by anyone having the requisite sagacity; that is, by anyone having a knowledge of what those conditions are and what behavior they are sufficient to produce.

This suggests what in fact seems quite clear, that determinism cannot be reconciled with our second datum either, to the effect that it is sometimes up to me what I am going to do. For if it is ever really up to me whether to do this thing or that, then, as we have seen, each alternative course of action must be such that I can do it; not that I can do it in some abstruse or hypothetical sense of "can"; not that I could do it if only something were true that is not true; but in the sense that it is then and there within my power to do it. But this is never so, if determinism is true, for on the very formulation of that theory whatever happens at any time is the only thing that can then happen, given all that precedes it. It is simply a logical consequence of this that whatever I do at any time is the only thing I can then do, given the conditions that precede my doing it. Nor does it help in the least to interpose, among the causal antecedents of my behavior, my own inner states, such as my desires, choices, acts of will, and so on. For even supposing these to be always involved in voluntary behavior—which is highly doubtful in itself—it is a consequence of determinism that these, whatever they are at any time, can never be other than what they then are. Every chain of causes and effects, if determinism is true, is infinite. This is why it is not now up to me whether I shall a moment hence be male or female. The conditions determining my sex have existed through my whole life, and even prior to my life. But if determinism is true, the same holds of anything that I ever am, ever become, or ever do. It matters not whether we are speaking of the most patent facts of my being, such as my sex; or the most subtle such as my feelings, thought, desires, or choices. Nothing could be other than it is, given what was; and while we may indeed say, quite idly, that something—some inner state of mind, for instance—*could* have been different, had only something *else* been different, any consolation of this thought evaporates as soon as we add that whatever would have to have been different could not have been different.

It is even more obvious that our data cannot be reconciled to the theory of simple indeterminism. I can deliberate only about my own actions; this is obvious. But the random, uncaused motion of any body whatever, whether it be a part of my body or not, is no action of mine and nothing that is within my power. I might try to guess what these motions will be, just as I might try to guess how a roulette wheel will behave, but I cannot deliberate about them or try to decide what they shall be, simply because these things are not up to me. Whatever is not caused by anything is not caused by me, and nothing could be more plainly inconsistent with saying that it is nevertheless up to me what it shall be.

THE THEORY OF AGENCY

The only conception of action that accords with our data is one according to which people—and perhaps some other things too—are sometimes, but of course not always, self-determining beings; that is, beings that are sometimes the causes of their own behavior. In the case of an action that is free, it must not only be such that it is caused by the agent who performs it, but also such that no antecedent conditions were sufficient for his performing just that action. In the case of an action that is both free and rational, it must be such that the agent who performed it did so for some reason, but this reason cannot have been the cause of it.

Now, this conception fits what people take themselves to be; namely, beings who act, or who are agents, rather than beings that are merely acted upon, and whose behavior is simply the causal consequence of conditions that they have not wrought. When I believe that I have done something, I do believe that it was I who caused it to be done, I who made something happen, and not merely something within me, such as one of my own subjective states, which is not identical with myself. If I believe that something not identical with myself was the cause of my behavior—some event wholly external to myself, for instance, or even one internal to myself, such as a nerve impulse, volition, or whatnot—then I cannot regard that behavior as being an act of mine, unless I further believe that I was the cause of that external or internal event. My pulse, for example, is caused and regulated by certain conditions existing within me, and not by myself. I do not, accordingly, regard this activity of my body as my action, and would be no more tempted to do so if I became suddenly conscious within myself of those conditions or impulses that produce it. This is behavior with which I have nothing to do, behavior that is not within my immediate control, behavior that is not only not free activity, but not even the activity of an agent to begin with; it is nothing but a mechanical reflex. Had I never learned that my very life depends on this pulse beat, I would regard it with complete indifference, as something foreign to me, like the oscillations of a clock pendulum that I idly contemplate.

Now this conception of activity, and of an agent who is the cause of it, involves two rather strange metaphysical notions that are never applied elsewhere in nature. The first is that of a *self* or *person*—for example, a man—who is not merely a collection of things or events, but a self-moving being. For on this view it is a person, and not merely some part of him or something within him, that is the cause of his own activity. Now, we certainly do not know that a human being is anything more than an assemblage of physical things and processes that act in accordance with those laws that describe the behavior of all other physical things and processes. Even though he is a living being, of enormous complexity, there is nothing, apart from the requirements of this theory, to suggest that his behavior is so radically different in its origin from that of other physical objects, or that an understanding of it must be sought in some metaphysical realm wholly different from that appropriate to the understanding of nonliving things.

Second, this conception of activity involves an extraordinary conception of causation according to which an agent, which is a substance and not an event, can nevertheless be the cause of an event. Indeed, if he is a free agent then he can, on this conception, cause an event to occur—namely, some act of his own—without anything else causing him to do so. This means that an agent is sometimes a cause, without being an antecedent sufficient condition; for if I affirm that I am the cause of some act of mine, then I am plainly not saying that my very existence is sufficient for its occurrence, which would be absurd. If I say that my hand causes my pencil to move, then I am saying that the motion of my hand is, under the other conditions then prevailing, sufficient for the motion of the pencil. But if I then say that I cause my hand to move, I am not saying anything remotely like this, and surely not that the motion of my self is sufficient for the motion of my arm and hand, since these are the only things about me that are moving.

This conception of the causation of events by things that are not events is, in fact, so different from the usual philosophical conception of a cause that it should not even bear the same name, for "being a cause" ordinarily just means "being an antecedent sufficient condition or set of conditions." Instead, then, of speaking of agents as *causing* their own acts, it would perhaps be better to use another word entirely, and say, for instance, that they *originate* them, *initiate* them, or simply that they *perform* them.

Now this is, on the face of it, a dubious conception of what a person is. Yet it is consistent with our data, reflecting the presuppositions of deliberation, and appears to be the only conception that is consistent with them, as determinism and simple indeterminism are not. The theory of agency avoids the absurdities of simple indeterminism by conceding that human behavior is caused, while at the same time avoiding the difficulties of determinism by denying that every chain of causes and effects is infinite. Some such causal chains, on this view, have beginnings, and they begin with agents themselves. Moreover, if we are to suppose that it is sometimes up to me what I do, and understand this in a sense that is not consistent with determinism, we must suppose that I am an agent or a being who initiates his own actions, sometimes under conditions that do not determine what action I shall perform. Deliberation becomes, on this view, something that is not only possible but quite rational, for it does make sense to deliberate about activity that is truly my own and that depends in its outcome upon me as its author, and not merely upon something more or less esoteric that is supposed to be intimately associated with me, such as my thoughts, volitions, choices, or whatnot.

One can hardly affirm such a theory of agency with complete comfort, however, and not wholly without embarrassment, for the conception of agents and their powers which is involved in it is strange indeed, if not positively mysterious. In fact, one can hardly be blamed here for simply denying our data outright, rather than embracing this theory to which they do most certainly point. Our data—to the effect that we do sometimes deliberate before acting, and that, when we do, we presuppose among other things that it is up to us what we are going to do—rest upon nothing more than fairly common consent. These data might simply be illusions. It might, in fact, be that no one ever deliberates but only imagines that he does, that from pure conceit he supposes himself to be the master of his behavior and the author of his acts. Spinoza has suggested that if a stone, having been thrown into the air, were suddenly to become conscious, it would suppose itself to be the source of its own motion, being then conscious of what it was doing but not aware of the real cause of its behavior. Certainly we are *sometimes* mistaken in believing that we are behaving as a result of choice deliberately arrived at. A man might, for example, easily imagine that his embarking upon matrimony is the result of the most careful and rational deliberation, when in fact the causes, perfectly sufficient for that behavior, might be of an entirely physiological, unconscious origin. If it is sometimes false that we deliberate and then act as the result of a decision deliberately arrived at, even when we suppose it to be true, it might always be false. No one seems able, as we have noted, to describe deliberation without metaphors, and the conception of a thing's being "within one's power" or "up to him" seems to defy analysis or definition altogether, if taken in a sense that the theory of agency appears to require.

ACTIONS, REASONS, AND CAUSES*

Donald Davidson

What is the relation between a reason and an action when the reason explains the action by giving the agent's reason for doing what he did? We may call such explanations *rationalizations*, and say that the reason *rationalizes* the action.

In this paper I want to defend the ancient—and common-sense—position that rationalization is a species of ordinary causal explanation. The defense no doubt requires some redeployment, but not more or less complete abandonment of the position, as urged by many recent writers.[1]

I

A reason rationalizes an action only if it leads us to see something the agent saw, or thought he saw, in his action—some feature, consequence, or aspect of the action the agent wanted, desired, prized, held dear, thought dutiful, beneficial, obligatory, or agreeable. We cannot explain why someone did what he did simply by saying the particular action appealed to him; we must indicate what it was about the action that appealed. Whenever someone does something for a reason, therefore, he can be characterized as (*a*) having some sort of pro attitude toward actions of a certain kind,

*From Donald Davidson, 'Actions, Reasons, and Causes,' *The Journal of Philosophy*, LX, No. 23 (November 7, 1963), 685–700. Reprinted with the kind permission of Professor Davidson.

and (*b*) believing (or knowing, perceiving, noticing, remembering) that his action is of that kind. Under (*a*) are to be included desires, wantings, urges, promptings, and a great variety of moral views, aesthetic principles, economic prejudices, social conventions, and public and private goals and values in so far as these can be interpreted as attitudes of an agent directed toward actions of a certain kind. The word 'attitude' does yeoman service here, for it must cover not only permanent character traits that show themselves in a lifetime of behavior, like love of children or a taste for loud company, but also the most passing fancy that prompts a unique action, like a sudden desire to touch a woman's elbow. In general, pro attitudes must not be taken for convictions, however temporary, that every action of a certain kind ought to be performed, is worth performing, or is, all things considered, desirable. On the contrary, a man may all his life have a yen, say, to drink a can of paint, without ever, even at the moment he yields, believing it would be worth doing.

Giving the reason why an agent did something is often a matter of naming the pro attitude (*a*) or the related belief (*b*) or both; let me call this pair the *primary reason* why the agent performed the action. Now it is possible to reformulate the claim that rationalizations are causal explanations, and give structure to the argument as well, by stating two theses about primary reasons:

1. For us to understand how a reason of any kind rationalizes an action it is necessary and sufficient that we see, at least in essential outline, how to construct a primary reason.
2. The primary reason for an action is its cause.

I shall argue for these points in turn.

II

I flip the switch, turn on the light, and illuminate the room. Unbeknownst to me I also alert a prowler to the fact that I am home. Here I do not do four things, but only one, of which four descriptions have been given.[2] I flipped the switch because I wanted to turn on the light, and by saying I wanted to turn on the light I explain (give my reason for, rationalize) the flipping. But I do not, by giving this reason, rationalize my alerting of the prowler nor my illuminating of the room. Since reasons may rationalize what someone does when it is described in one way and not when it is described in another, we cannot treat what was done simply as a term in sentences like 'My reason for flipping the switch was that I wanted to turn on the light'; otherwise we would be forced to conclude, from the fact that flipping the switch was identical with alerting the prowler, that my reason for alerting the prowler was that I wanted to turn on the light. Let us mark this quasi-intensional[3] character of action descriptions in rationalizations by stating a bit more precisely a necessary condition for primary reasons:

> C1. *R* is a primary reason why an agent performed the action *A* under the description *d* only if *R* consists of a pro attitude of the agent toward actions with a certain property, and a belief of the agent that *A*, under the description *d*, has that property.

How can my wanting to turn on the light be (part of) a primary reason, since it appears to lack the required element of generality? We may be taken in by the verbal parallel between 'I turned on the light' and 'I wanted to turn on the light.' The first clearly refers to a particular event, so we conclude that the second has this same event as its object. Of course it is obvious that the event of my turning on the light can't be referred to in the same way by both sentences, since the existence of the event is required by the truth of 'I turned on the light' but not by the truth of 'I wanted to turn on the light.' If the reference were the same in both cases, the second sentence would entail the first; but in fact the sentences are logically independent. What is less obvious, at least until we attend to it, is that the event whose occurrence makes 'I turned on the light' true cannot be called the object, however intensional, of 'I wanted to turn on the light.' If I turned on the light, then I must have done it at a precise moment, in a particular way—every detail is fixed. But it makes no sense to demand that my want be directed at an action performed at any one moment or done in some unique manner. Any one of an indefinitely large number of actions would satisfy the want, and can be considered equally eligible as its object. Wants and desires often are trained on physical objects. However, 'I want that gold watch in the window' is not a primary reason, and explains why I went into the store only because it suggests a primary reason—for example, that I wanted to buy the watch.

Because 'I wanted to turn on the light' and 'I turned on the light' are logically independent, the first can be used to give a reason why the second is true. Such a reason gives minimal information: it implies that the action was intentional, and wanting tends to exclude some other pro attitudes, such as a sense of duty or obligation. But the exclusion depends very much on the action and the context of explanation. Wanting seems pallid beside lusting, but it would be odd to deny that someone who lusted after a woman or a cup of coffee wanted her or it. It is not unnatural, in fact, to treat wanting as a genus including all pro attitudes as species. When we do this and when we know some action is intentional, it is empty to add that the agent wanted to do it. In such cases, it is easy to answer the question 'Why did you do it?' with 'For no reason,' meaning not that there is no reason but that there is no *further* reason, no reason that cannot be inferred from the fact that the action was done intentionally; no reason, in other words, besides wanting to do it. This last point is not essential to the present argument, but it is of interest because it defends the possibility of defining an intentional action as one done for a reason.

A primary reason consists of a belief and an attitude, but it is generally otiose to mention both. If you tell me you are easing the jib because you think that will stop the main from backing, I don't need to be told that you want to stop the main from backing; and if you say you are biting your thumb at me because you want to insult me, there is no point in adding that you think that by biting your thumb at me you will insult me. Similarly, many explanations of actions in terms of reasons that are not primary do not require mention of the primary reason to complete the story. If I say I am pulling weeds because I want a beautiful lawn, it would be fatuous to eke out the account with 'And so I see something desirable in any action that does, or has a good chance of, making the lawn beautiful.' Why insist that there is any *step*, logical or psychological, in the transfer of desire from an end that is not an action to the actions one conceives as means? It serves the argument as well that the desired end explains the action only if what are believed by the agent to be means are desired.

Fortunately, it is not necessary to classify and analyze the many varieties of emotions, sentiments, moods, motives, passions, and hungers whose mention may answer the question 'Why did you do it?' in order to see how, when such mention rationalizes the action, a primary reason is involved. Claustrophobia gives a man's reason for leaving a cocktail party because we know people want to avoid, escape from, be safe from, put distance between themselves and, what they fear. Jealousy is the motive in a poisoning because, among other things, the poisoner believes his action will harm his rival, remove the cause of his agony, or redress an injustice, and these are the sorts of things a jealous man wants to do. When we learn a man cheated his son out of greed, we do not necessarily know what the primary reason was, but we know there was one, and its general nature. Ryle analyzes 'he boasted from vanity' into 'he boasted on meeting the stranger and his doing so satisfies the lawlike proposition that whenever he finds a chance of securing the admiration and envy of others, he does whatever he thinks will produce this admiration and envy' (*The Concept of Mind*, 89). This analysis is often, and perhaps justly, criticized on the ground that a man may boast from vanity just once. But if Ryle's boaster did what he did from vanity, then something entailed by Ryle's analysis is true: the boaster wanted to secure the admiration and envy of others, and he believed that his action would produce this admiration and envy; true or false, Ryle's analysis does not dispense with primary reasons, but depends upon them.

To know a primary reason why someone acted as he did is to know an intention with which the action was done. If I turn left at the fork because I want to get to Katmandu, my intention in turning left is to get to Katmandu. But to know the intention is not necessarily to know the primary reason in full detail. If James goes to church with the intention of pleasing his mother, then he must have some pro attitude toward pleasing his mother, but it needs more information to tell whether his reason is that he enjoys pleasing his mother, or thinks it right, his duty, or an obligation. The expression 'the intention with which James went to church' has the outward form of a description, but in fact it is syncategorematic and cannot be taken to refer to an entity, state, disposition, or event. Its function in context is to generate new descriptions of actions in terms of their reasons; thus 'James went to church with the intention of pleasing his mother' yields a new, and fuller, description of the action described in 'James went to church.' Essentially the same process goes on when I answer the question 'Why are you bobbing around that way?' with 'I'm knitting, weaving, exercising, sculling, cuddling, training fleas.'

Straight description of an intended result often explains an action better than stating that the result was intended or desired. 'It will soothe your nerves' explains why I pour you a shot as efficiently as 'I want to do something to soothe your nerves,' since the first in the context of explanation implies the second; but the first does better, because, if it is true, the facts will justify my choice of action. Because justifying and explaining an action so often go hand in hand, we frequently indicate the primary reason for an action by making a claim which, if true, would also verify, vindicate, or support the relevant belief or attitude of the agent. 'I knew I ought to return it,' 'The paper said it was going to snow,' 'You stepped on my toes,' all, in appropriate reason-giving contexts, perform this familiar dual function.

The justifying role of a reason, given this interpretation, depends upon the explanatory role, but the converse does not hold. Your stepping on my toes neither explains nor justifies my stepping on your toes unless I believe you stepped on my toes, but the belief alone, true or false, explains my action.

III

In the light of a primary reason, an action is revealed as coherent with certain traits, long- or short-termed, characteristic or not, of the agent, and the agent is shown in his role of Rational Animal. Corresponding to the belief and attitude of a primary reason for an action, we can always construct (with a little ingenuity) the premises of a syllogism from which it follows that the action has some (as Miss Anscombe calls it) 'desirability characteristic.'[4] Thus there is a certain irreducible—though somewhat anemic sense in which every rationalization justifies: from the agent's point of view there was, when he acted, something to be said for the action.

Noting that nonteleological causal explanations do not display the element of justification provided by reasons, some philosophers have concluded that the concept of cause that applies elsewhere cannot apply to the relation between reasons and actions, and that the pattern of justification provides, in the case of reasons, the required explanation. But suppose we grant that reasons alone justify in explaining actions; it does not follow that the explanation is not also—and necessarily—causal. Indeed our first condition for primary reasons (C1) is designed to help set rationalizations apart from other sorts of explanation. If rationalization is, as I want to argue, a species of causal explanation, then justification, in the sense given by C1, is at least one differentiating property. How about the other claim: that justifying is a kind of explaining, so that the ordinary notion of cause need not be brought in? Here it is necessary to decide what is being included under justification. Perhaps it means only what is given by C1: that the agent has certain beliefs and attitudes in the light of which the action is reasonable. But then something essential has certainly been left out, for a person can have a reason for an action, and perform the action, and yet this reason not be the reason why he did it. Central to the relation between a reason and an action it explains is the idea that the agent performed the action *because* he had the reason. Of course, we can include this idea too in justification; but then the notion of justification becomes as dark as the notion of reason until we can account for the force of that 'because.'

When we ask why someone acted as he did, we want to be provided with an interpretation. His behavior seems strange, alien, outré, pointless, out of character, disconnected; or perhaps we cannot even recognize an action in it. When we learn his reason, we have an interpretation, a new description of what he did which fits it into a familiar picture. The picture certainly includes some of the agent's beliefs and attitudes; perhaps also goals, ends, principles, general character traits, virtues or vices. Beyond this, the redescription of an action afforded by a reason may place the action in a wider social, economic, linguistic, or evaluative context. To learn, through learning the reason, that the agent conceived his action as a lie, a repayment of a debt, an insult, the fulfillment of an avuncular obligation, or a knight's gambit is to grasp the point of the action in its setting of rules, practices, conventions, and expectations.

Remarks like these, inspired by the later Wittgenstein, have been elaborated with subtlety and insight by a number of philosophers. And there is no denying that this is true: when we explain an action, by giving the reason, we do redescribe the action; redescribing the action gives the action a place in a pattern, and in this way the action is explained. Here it is tempting to draw two conclusions that do not follow. First, we can't infer, from the fact that giving reasons merely redescribes the action and that causes are separate from effects, that therefore reasons are not causes. Reasons, being beliefs and attitudes, are certainly not identical with actions; but, more important, events are often redescribed in terms of their causes. (Suppose someone was burned. We could redescribe this event 'in terms of a cause' by saying he was burned.) Second, it is an error to think that, because placing the action in a larger pattern explains it, therefore we now understand the sort of explanation involved. Talk of patterns and contexts does not answer the question of how reasons explain actions, since the relevant pattern or context contains both reason and action. One way we can explain an event is by placing it in the context of its cause; cause and effect form the sort of pattern that explains the effect, in a sense of 'explain' that we understand as well as any. If reason and action illustrate a different pattern of explanation, that pattern must be identified.

Let me urge the point in connection with an example of Melden's. A man driving an automobile raises his arm in order to signal. His intention, to signal, explains his action, raising his arm, by redescribing it as signaling. What is the pattern that explains the action? Is it the familiar pattern of an action done for a reason? Then it does indeed explain the action, but only because it assumes the relation of reason and action that we want to analyze. Or is the pattern rather this: the man is driving, he is approaching a turn; he knows he ought to signal; he knows how to signal, by raising his arm. And now, in this context, he raises his arm. Perhaps, as Melden suggests, if all this happens, he does signal. And the explanation would then be this: if, under these conditions, a man raises his arm, then he signals. The difficulty, is, of course, that this explanation does not touch the question of why he raised his arm. He had a reason to raise his arm, but this has not been shown to be the reason why he did it. If the description 'signaling' explains his action by giving his reason, then the signaling must be intentional; but, on the account just given, it may not be.

If, as Melden claims, causal explanations are 'wholly irrelevant to the understanding we seek' of human actions (184) then we are without an analysis of the 'because' in 'He did it because . . . ,' where we go on to name a reason. Hampshire remarks, of the relation between reasons and action, 'In philosophy one ought surely to find this . . . connection altogether mysterious' (166). Hampshire rejects Aristotle's attempt to solve the mystery by introducing the concept of wanting as a causal factor, on the grounds that the resulting theory is too clear and definite to fit all cases and that 'There is still no compelling ground for insisting that the word 'want' *must* enter into every full statement of reasons for acting' (168). I agree that the concept of wanting is too narrow, but I have argued that, at least in a vast number of typical cases, some pro attitude must be assumed to be present if a statement of an agent's reasons in acting is to be intelligible. Hampshire does not see how Aristotle's scheme can be appraised as true or false, 'for it is not clear what could be the basis of assessment, or what kind of evidence could be decisive' (167). Failing a satisfactory alternative, the best argument for a scheme like Aristotle's is that it alone promises to give an account of the 'mysterious connection' between reasons and actions.

IV

In order to turn the first 'and' to 'because' in 'He exercised *and* he wanted to reduce and thought exercise would do it,' we must, as the basic move,[5] augment condition C1 with:

> C2. A primary reason for an action is its cause.

The considerations in favor of C2 are by now, I hope, obvious; in the remainder of this paper I wish to defend C2 against various lines of attack and, in the process, to clarify the notion of causal explanation involved.

A.   The first line of attack is this. Primary reasons consist of attitudes and beliefs, which are states or dispositions, not events; therefore they cannot be causes.

It is easy to reply that states, dispositions, and conditions are frequently named as the causes of events: the bridge collapsed because of a structural defect; the plane crashed on takeoff because the air temperature was abnormally high; the plate broke because it had a crack. This reply does not, however, meet a closely related point. Mention of a causal condition for an event gives a cause only on the assumption that there was also a preceding event. But what is the preceding event that causes an action?

In many cases it is not difficult at all to find events very closely associated with the primary reason. States and dispositions are not events, but the onslaught of a state or disposition is. A desire to hurt your feelings may spring up at the moment you anger me; I may start wanting to eat a melon just when I see one; and beliefs may begin at the moment we notice, perceive, learn, or remember something. Those who have argued that there are no mental events to qualify as causes of actions have often missed the obvious because they have insisted that a mental event be observed or noticed (rather than an observing or a noticing) or that it be like a stab, a qualm, a prick or a quiver, a mysterious prod of conscience or act of the will. Melden, in discussing the driver who signals a turn by raising his arm, challenges those who want to explain actions causally to identify 'an event which is common and peculiar to all such cases' (87), perhaps a motive or an intention, anyway 'some particular feeling or experience' (95). But of course there is a mental event; at some moment the driver noticed (or thought he noticed) his turn coming up, and that is the moment he signaled. During any continuing activity, like driving, or elaborate performance, like swimming the Hellespont, there are more or less fixed purposes, standards, desires, and habits that give direction and form to the entire enterprise, and there is the continuing input of information about what we are doing, about changes in the environment, in terms of which we regulate and adjust our actions. To dignify a driver's awareness that his turn has come by calling it an experience, much less a feeling, is no doubt exaggerated, but whether it deserves a name or not, it had better be the reason why he raises his arm. In this case, and typically, there may not be anything we would call a motive, but if we mention such a general purpose as wanting to get to one's destination safely, it is clear that the motive is not an event. The intention with which the driver raises his arm is also not an event, for it is no thing at all, neither event, attitude, disposition, nor object. Finally, Melden asks the causal theorist to find an event that is common and peculiar to all cases where a man intentionally raises his arm, and this, it must be admitted, cannot be produced. But then neither can a common and unique cause of bridge failures, plane crashes, or plate breakings be produced.

The signaling driver can answer the question 'Why did you raise your arm when you did?', and from the answer we learn the event that caused the action. But can an actor always answer such a question? Sometimes the answer will mention a mental event that does not give a reason: 'Finally I made up my mind.' However, there also seem to be cases of intentional action where we cannot explain at all why we acted when we did. In such cases, explanation in terms of primary reasons parallels the explanation of the collapse of the bridge from a structural defect: we are ignorant of the event or sequence of events that led up to (caused) the collapse, but we are sure there was such an event or sequence of events.

B. According to Melden, a cause must be 'logically distinct from the alleged effect' (52); but a reason for an action is not logically distinct from the action; therefore, reasons are not causes of actions.[6]

One possible form of this argument has already been suggested. Since a reason makes an action intelligible by redescribing it, we do not have two events, but only one under different descriptions. Causal relations, however, demand distinct events.

Someone might be tempted into the mistake of thinking that my flipping of the switch caused my turning on the light (in fact it caused the light to go on). But it does not follow that it is a mistake to take 'My reason for flipping the switch was that I wanted to turn on the light' as entailing, in part, 'I flipped the switch, and this action is further describable as having been caused by my wanting to turn on the light.' To describe an event in terms of its cause is not to identify the event with its cause, nor does explanation by redescription exclude causal explanation.

The example serves also to refute the claim that we cannot describe the action without using words that link it to the alleged cause. Here the action is to be explained under the description: 'my flipping the switch,' and the alleged cause is 'my wanting to turn on the light.' What possible logical relation is supposed to hold between these phrases? It seems more plausible to urge a logical link between 'my turning on the light' and 'my wanting to turn on the light,' but even here the link turned out, on inspection, to be grammatical rather than logical.

In any case there is something very odd in the idea that causal relations are empirical rather than logical. What can this mean? Surely not that every true causal statement is empirical. For suppose 'A caused B' is true. Then the cause of $B = A$; so, substituting, we have 'The cause of B caused B,' which is analytic. The truth of a causal statement depends on *what* events are described; its status as analytic or synthetic depends on *how* the events are described. Still, it may be maintained that a reason rationalizes an action only when the descriptions are appropriately fixed, and the appropriate descriptions are not logically independent.

Suppose that to say a man wanted to turn on the light *meant* that he would perform any action he believed would accomplish his end. Then the statement of his primary reason for flipping the switch would entail that he flipped the switch—'straightway he acts,' as Aristotle says in this case there would certainly be a logical connection between reason and action, the same sort of connection as that between 'It's water-soluble and was placed in water' and 'It dissolved.' Since the implication runs from description of cause to description of effect but not conversely, naming the cause still gives information. And, though the point is often overlooked, 'Placing it in water caused it to dissolve' does not entail 'It's water-soluble'; so the latter has additional explanatory force. Nevertheless, the explanation would be far more interesting if, in place of solubility, with its obvious definitional connection with the event to be explained, we could refer to some property, say a particular crystalline structure, whose connection with dissolution in water was known only through experiment. Now it is clear why primary reasons like desires and wants do not explain actions in the relatively trivial way solubility explains dissolvings. Solubility, we are assuming, is a pure disposition property: it is defined in terms of a single test. But desires cannot be defined in terms of the actions they may rationalize, even though the relation between desire and action is not simply empirical; there are other, equally essential criteria for desires—their expression in feelings and in actions that they do not rationalize, for example. The person who has a desire (or want or belief) does not normally need criteria at all—he generally knows, even in the absence of any clues available to others, what he wants, desires, and believes. These logical features of primary reasons show that it is not just lack of ingenuity that keeps us from defining them as dispositions to act for these reasons.

C. According to Hume, 'we may define a cause to be an object, followed by another, and where all the objects similar to the first are followed by objects similar to the second.' But, Hart and Honoré claim, 'The statement that one person did something because, for example, another threatened him, carries no implication or covert assertion that if the circumstances were repeated the same action would follow' (52). Hart and Honoré allow that Hume is right in saying that ordinary singular causal statements imply generalizations, but wrong for this very reason in supposing that motives and desires are ordinary causes of actions. In brief, laws are involved essentially in ordinary causal explanations, but not in rationalizations.

It is common to try to meet this argument by suggesting that we do have rough laws connecting reasons and actions, and these can, in theory, be improved. True, threatened people do not always respond in the same way; but we may distinguish between threats and also between agents, in terms of their beliefs and attitudes.

The suggestion is delusive, however, because generalizations connecting reasons and actions are not—and cannot be sharpened into—the kind of law on the basis of which accurate predictions can reliably be made. If we reflect on the way in which reasons determine choice, decision, and behavior, it is easy to see why this is so. What emerges, in the *ex post facto* atmosphere of explanation and justification, as *the* reason frequently was, to the agent at the time of action, one consideration among many *a* reason. Any serious theory for predicting action on the basis of reasons must find a way of evaluating the relative force of various desires and beliefs in the matrix of decision; it cannot take as its starting point the refinement of what is to be expected from a single desire. The practical syllogism exhausts its role in displaying an action as falling under one reason; so it cannot be subtilized into a reconstruction of practical reasoning, which involves the weighing of competing reasons.

The practical syllogism provides a model neither for a predictive science of action nor for a normative account of evaluative reasoning.

Ignorance of competent predictive laws does not inhibit valid causal explanation, or few causal explanations could be made. I am certain the window broke because it was struck by a rock—I saw it all happen; but I am not (is anyone?) in command of laws on the basis of which I can predict what blows will break which windows. A generalization like 'Windows are fragile, and fragile things tend to break when struck hard enough, other conditions being right' is not a predictive law in the rough—the predictive law, if we had it, would be quantitative and would use very different concepts. The generalization, like our generalizations about behavior, serves a different function: it provides evidence for the existence of a causal law covering the case at hand.

We are usually far more certain of a singular causal connection than we are of any causal law governing the case; does this show that Hume was wrong in claiming that singular causal statements entail laws? Not necessarily, for Hume's claim, as quoted above, is ambiguous. It may mean that 'A caused B' entails some particular law involving the predicates used in the descriptions 'A' and 'B' or it may mean that 'A caused B' entails that there exists a causal law instantiated by some true descriptions of A and B.[7] Obviously, both versions of Hume's doctrine give a sense to the claim that singular causal statements entail laws, and both sustain the view that causal explanations 'involve laws.' But the second version is far weaker, in that no particular law is entailed by a singular causal claim, and a singular causal claim can be defended, if it needs defense, without defending any law. Only the second version of Hume's doctrine can be made to fit with most causal explanations; it suits rationalizations equally well.

The most primitive explanation of an event gives its cause; more elaborate explanations may tell more of the story, or defend the singular causal claim by producing a relevant law or by giving reasons for believing such exists. But it is an error to think no explanation has been given until a law has been produced. Linked with these errors is the idea that singular causal statements necessarily indicate, by the concepts they employ, the concepts that will occur in the entailed law. Suppose a hurricane, which is reported on page 5 of Tuesday's *Times*, causes a catastrophe, which is reported on page 13 of Wednesday's *Tribune*. Then the event reported on page 5 of Tuesday's *Times* caused the event reported on page 13 of Wednesday's *Tribune*. Should we look for a law relating events of these *kinds*? It is only slightly less ridiculous to look for a law relating hurricanes and catastrophes. The laws needed to predict the catastrophe with precision would, of course, have no use for concepts like hurricane and catastrophe. The trouble with predicting the weather is that the descriptions under which events interest us—'a cool, cloudy day with rain in the afternoon'—have only remote connections with the concepts employed by the more precise known laws.

The laws whose existence is required if reasons are causes of actions do not, we may be sure, deal in the concepts in which rationalizations must deal. If the causes of a class of events (actions) fall in a certain class (reasons) and there is a law to back each singular causal statement, it does not follow that there is any law connecting events classified as reasons with events classified as actions—the classifications may even be neurological, chemical, or physical.

D. It is said that the kind of knowledge one has of one's own reasons in acting is not compatible with the existence of a causal relation between reasons and actions: a person knows his own intentions in acting infallibly, without induction or observation, and no ordinary causal relation can be known in this way. No doubt our knowledge of our own intentions in acting will show many of the oddities peculiar to first-person knowledge of one's own pains, beliefs, desires, and so on; the only question is whether these oddities prove that reasons do not cause, in any ordinary sense at least, the actions that they rationalize.

You may easily be wrong about the truth of a statement of the form 'I am poisoning Charles because I want to save him pain,' because you may be wrong about whether you are poisoning Charles—you may yourself be drinking the poisoned cup by mistake. But it also seems that you may err about your reasons, particularly when you have two reasons for an action, one of which pleases you and one which does not. For example, you do want to save Charles pain; you also want him out of the way. You may be wrong about which motive made you do it.

The fact that you may be wrong does not show that in general it makes sense to ask you how you know what your reasons were or to ask for your evidence. Though you may, on rare occasions, accept public or private evidence as showing you are wrong about your reasons, you usually have no evidence and make no observations. Then your knowledge of your own reasons for your actions is not generally inductive, for where there is induction, there is evidence. Does this show the knowledge is not causal? I cannot see that it does.

Causal laws differ from true but nonlawlike generalizations in that their instances confirm them: induction is, therefore, certainly a good way to learn the truth of a law. It does not follow that it is the only way to learn the truth of a law. In any case, in order to know that a singular causal statement is true, it is not necessary to know the truth of a law; it is necessary only to know that some law covering the events at hand exists. And it is far from evident that induction, and induction alone, yields the knowledge that a causal law satisfying certain conditions exists. Or, to put it differently, one case is often enough, as Hume admitted, to persuade us that a law exists, and this amounts to saying that we are persuaded, without direct inductive evidence, that a causal relation exists.[8]

E. Finally I should like to say something about a certain uneasiness some philosophers feel in speaking of causes of actions at all. Melden, for example, says that actions are often identical with bodily movements, and that bodily movements have causes; yet he denies that the causes are causes of the actions. This is, I think, a contradiction. He is led to it by the following sort of consideration: 'It is futile to attempt to explain conduct through the causal efficacy of desire—all *that* can explain is further happenings, not actions performed by agents. The agent confronting the causal nexus in which such happenings occur is a helpless victim of all that occurs in and to him' (128, 129). Unless I am mistaken, this argument, if it were valid, would show that actions cannot have causes at all. I shall not point out the obvious difficulties in removing actions from the realm of causality entirely. But perhaps it is worth trying to uncover the source of the trouble. Why on earth should a cause turn an action into a mere happening and a person into a helpless victim? Is it because we tend to assume, at least in the arena of action, that a cause demands a causer, agency an agent? So we press the question; if my action is caused, what caused it? If I did, then there is the absurdity of infinite regress; if I did not, I am a victim. But of course the alternatives are not exhaustive. Some causes have no agents. Among these agentless causes are those states and changes of state in persons which, because they are reasons as well as causes, constitute certain events free and intentional actions.

NOTES

1. Some examples: G.E.M. Anscombe, *Intention*, Oxford, 1959; Stuart Hampshire, *Thought and Action*, London, 1959; H. L. A. Hart and A. M. Honoré, *Causation in the Law*, Oxford, 1959; William Dray, *Laws and Explanation in History*, Oxford, 1957; and most of the books in the series edited by R. F. Holland. *Studies in Philosophical Psychology*, including Anthony Kenny, *Action, Emotion and Will*, London, 1963, and A. I. Melden, *Free Action*, London, 1961. Page references in parentheses will all be to these works.

2. We would not call my unintentional alerting of the prowler an action, but it should not be inferred from this that alerting the prowler is therefore something different from flipping the switch, say just its consequence. Actions, performances, and events not involving intention are alike in that they are often referred to or defined partly in terms of some terminal stage, outcome, or consequence.

The word 'action' does not very often occur in ordinary speech, and when it does it is usually reserved for fairly portentous occasions. I follow a useful philosophical practice in calling anything an agent does intentionally an action, including intentional omissions. What is really needed is some suitably generic term to bridge the following gap: suppose '*A*' is a description of an action, '*B*' is a description of something done voluntarily, though not intentionally, and '*C*' is a description of something done involuntarily and unintentionally; finally, suppose $A = B = C$. Then *A*, *B*, and *C* are the same—what? 'Action,' 'event,' 'thing done,' each have, at least in some contexts, a strange ring when coupled with the wrong sort of description. Only the question 'Why did you (he) do *A*?' has the true generality required. Obviously, the problem is greatly aggravated if we assume, as Melden does (*Free Action*, 85), that an action ('raising one's arm') can be identical with a bodily movement ('one's arm going up').

3. "Quasi-intensional" because, besides its intensional aspect, the description of the action must also refer in rationalizations; otherwise it could be true that an action was done for a certain reason and yet the action not have been performed. Compare 'the author of *Waverley*' in 'George IV knew the author of *Waverley* wrote *Waverley*.'

4. Miss Anscombe denies that the practical syllogism is deductive. This she does partly because she thinks of the practical syllogism, as Aristotle does, as corresponding to a piece of practical reasoning (whereas for me it is only part of the analysis of the concept of a reason with which someone acted), and therefore she is bound, again following Aristotle, to think of the conclusion of a practical syllogism as corresponding to a judgment, not merely that the action has a desirable characteristic, but that the action is desirable (reasonable worth doing, etc.).

5. I say 'as the basic move' to cancel the suggestion that C1 and C2 are jointly *sufficient* to define the relation of reasons to the actions they explain. I believe C2 can be strengthened to make C1 and C2 sufficient as well as necessary conditions, but here I am concerned only with the claim that both are, as they stand, necessary.

6. This argument can be found, in one or more versions, in Kenny, Hampshire, and Melden, as well as in P. Winch. *The idea of a Social Science*, London, 1958, and R. S. Peters, *The Concept of Motivation*, London, 1958. In one of its forms, the argument was of course inspired by Ryle's treatment of motives in *The Concept of Mind*.

7. We could roughly characterize the analysis of singular causal statements hinted at here as follows: '*A* caused *B*' is true if and only if there are descriptions of *A* and *B* such that the sentence obtained by putting these descriptions for '*A*' and '*B*' in '*A* caused *B*' follows from a true causal law. This analysis is saved from triviality by the fact that not all true generalizations are causal laws; causal laws are distinguished (though of course this is no analysis) by the fact that they are inductively confirmed by their instances and by the fact that they support counterfactual and subjunctive singular causal statements.

8. My thinking on the subject of this section, as on most of the topics discussed in this paper, has been greatly influenced by years of talk with Professor Daniel Bennett, now of Brandeis University.

MENTAL EVENTS*

Donald Davidson

Mental events such as perceivings, rememberings, decisions, and actions resist capture in the nomological net of physical theory. How can this fact be reconciled with the causal role of mental events in the physical world? Reconciling freedom with causal determinism is a special case of the problem if we suppose that causal determinism entails capture in, and freedom requires escape from, the nomological net. But the broader issue can remain alive even for someone who believes a correct analysis of free action reveals no conflict with-determinism. *Autonomy* (freedom, self-rule) may or may not clash with determinism; *anomaly* (failure to fall under a law) is, it would seem, another matter.

*Originally published in *Experience and Theory* ed. L. Foster and J. Swanson (Amherst, MA: University of Massachusetts Press, 1970). Reprinted with the kind permission of Professor Davidson.

I start from the assumption that both the causal dependence, and the anomalousness, of mental events are undeniable facts. My aim is therefore to explain, in the face of apparent difficulties, how this can be. I am in sympathy with Kant when he says,

> it is as impossible for the subtlest philosophy as for the commonest reasoning to argue freedom away. Philosophy must therefore assume that no true contradiction will be found between freedom and natural necessity in the same human actions, for it cannot give up the idea of nature any more than that of freedom. Hence even if we should never be able to conceive how freedom is possible, at least this apparent contradiction must be convincingly eradicated. For if the thought of freedom contradicts itself or nature . . . it would have to be surrendered in competition with natural necessity.[1]

Generalize human actions to mental events, substitute anomaly for freedom, and this is a description of my problem. And of course the connection is closer, since Kant believed freedom entails anomaly.

Now let my try to formulate a little more carefully the 'apparent contradiction' about mental events that I want to discuss and finally dissipate. It may be seen as stemming from three principles.

> **The first principle asserts that at least some mental events interact causally with physical events. (We could call this the Principle of Causal Interaction.)**

Thus for example if someone sank the *Bismarck*, then various mental events such as perceivings, notings, calculations, judgements, decisions, intentional actions, and changes of belief played a causal role in the sinking of the *Bismarck*. In particular, I would urge that the fact that someone sank the *Bismarck* entails that he moved his body in a way that was caused by mental events of certain sorts, and that this bodily movement in turn caused the *Bismarck* to sink.[2] Perception illustrates how causality may run from the physical to the mental: if a man perceives that a ship is approaching, then a ship approaching must have caused him to come to believe that a ship is approaching. (Nothing depends on accepting these as examples of causal interaction.)

Though perception and action provide the most obvious cases where mental and physical events interact causally, I think reasons could be given for the view that all mental events ultimately, perhaps through causal relations with other mental events, have causal intercourse with physical events. But if there are mental events that have no physical events as causes or effects, the argument will not touch them.

> **The second principle is that where there is causality, there must be a law: events related as cause and effect fall under strict deterministic laws. (We may term this the Principle of the Nomological Character of Causality.) This principle, like the first, will be treated here as an assumption, though I shall say something by way of interpretation.[3]**
> **The third principle is that there are no strict deterministic laws on the basis of which mental events can be predicted and explained (the Anomalism of the Mental).**

The paradox I wish to discuss arises for someone who is inclined to accept these three assumptions or principles, and who thinks they are inconsistent with one another. The inconsistency is not, of course, formal unless more premises are added. Nevertheless it is natural to reason that the first two principles, that of causal interaction and that of the nomological character of causality, together imply that at least some mental events can be predicted and explained on the basis of laws, while the principle of the anomalism of the mental denies this. Many philosophers have accepted, with or without argument, the view that the three principles do lead to a contradiction. It seems to me, however, that all three principles are true, so that what must be done is to explain away the appearance of contradiction; essentially the Kantian line.

The rest of this paper falls into three parts. The first part describes a version of the identity theory of the mental and the physical that shows how the three principles may be reconciled. The second part argues that there cannot be strict psychophysical laws; this is not quite the principle of the anomalism of the mental, but on reasonable assumptions entails it. The last part tries to show that from the fact that there can be no strict psychophysical laws, and our other two principles, we can infer the truth of a version of the identity theory, that is, a theory that identifies at least some mental events with physical events. It is clear that this 'proof' of the identity theory will be at best conditional, since two of its premises are unsupported, and the argument for the third may be found less than conclusive. But even someone unpersuaded of the truth of the premises may be interested to learn how they can be reconciled and that they serve to establish a version of the identity theory of the mental. Finally, if the argument is a good one, it should lay to rest the view, common to many friends and some foes of identity theories, that support for such theories can come only from the discovery of psychophysical laws.

I

The three principles will be shown consistent with one another by describing a view of the mental and the physical that contains no inner contradiction and that entails the three principles. According to this view, mental events are identical with physical events. Events are taken to be unrepeatable, dated individuals such as the particular eruption of a volcano, the (first) birth or death of a person, the playing of the 1968 World Series, or the historic utterance of the words, 'You may fire when ready, Gridley.' We can easily frame identity statements about individual events; examples (true or false) might be:

> The death of Scott = the death of the author of *Waverley*;
> The assassination of the Archduke Ferdinand = the event that started the First World War;
> The eruption of Vesuvius in A.D. 79 = the cause of the destruction of Pompeii.

The theory under discussion is silent about processes, states, and attributes if these differ from individual events.

What does it mean to say that an event is mental or physical? One natural answer is that an event is physical if it is describable in a purely physical vocabulary, mental if describable in mental terms. But if this is taken to suggest that an event is physical, say, if some physical predicate is true of it, then there is the following difficulty. Assume that the predicate '*x* took place at Noosa Heads' belongs to the physical vocabulary; then so also must the predicate '*x* did not take place at Noosa Heads' belong to the physical vocabulary. But the predicate '*x* did or did not take place at Noosa Heads' is true of every event, whether mental or physical.[4] We might rule out predicates that are tautologically true of every event, but this will not help since every event is truly describable either by '*x* took place at Noosa Heads' or by '*x* did not take place at Noosa Heads.' A different approach is needed.[5]

We may call those verbs mental that express propositional attitudes like believing, intending, desiring, hoping, knowing, perceiving, noticing, remembering, and so on. Such verbs are characterized by the fact that they sometimes feature in sentences with subjects that refer to persons, and are completed by embedded sentences in which the usual rules of substitution appear to break down. This criterion is not precise, since I do not want to include these verbs when they occur in contexts that are fully extensional ('He knows Paris,' 'He perceives the moon' may be cases), nor exclude them whenever they are not followed by embedded sentences. An alternative characterization of the desired class of mental verbs might be that they are psychological verbs as used when they create apparently nonextensional contexts.

Let us call a description of the form 'the event that is *M*' or an open sentence of the form 'event *x* is *M*' a *mental description* or a *mental open sentence* if and only if the expression that replaces '*M*' contains at least one mental verb essentially. (Essentially, so as to rule out cases where the description or open sentence is logically equivalent to one or not containing mental vocabulary.) Now we may say that an event is mental if and only if it has a mental description, or (the description operator not being primitive) if there is a mental open sentence true of that event alone. Physical events are those picked out by descriptions or open sentences that contain only the physical vocabulary essentially. It is less important to characterize a physical vocabulary because relative to the mental it is, so to speak, recessive in determining whether a description is mental or physical. (There will be some comments presently on the nature of a physical vocabulary, but these comments will fall far short of providing a criterion.)

On the proposed test of the mental, the distinguishing feature of the mental is not that it is private, subjective, or immaterial, but that it exhibits what Brentano called intentionality. Thus intentional actions are clearly included in the realm of the mental along with thoughts, hopes, and regrets (or the events tied to these). What may seem doubtful is whether the criterion will include events that have often been considered paradigmatic of the mental. Is it obvious, for example, that feeling a pain or seeing an after-image will count as mental? Sentences that report such events seem free from taint of nonextensionality, and the same should be true of reports of raw feels, sense data, and other uninterpreted sensations, if there are any.

However, the criterion actually covers not only the havings of pains and after-images, but much more besides. Take some event one would intuitively accept as physical, let's say the collision of two stars in distant space. There must be a purely physical predicate '*Px*' true of this collision, and of others, but true of only this one at the time it occurred. This particular time, though, may be pinpointed as the same time that Jones notices that a pencil starts to roll across his desk. The distant stellar collision is thus the event x such that Px and x is simultaneous with Jones's noticing that a pencil starts to roll across his desk. The collision has now been picked out by a mental description and must be counted as a mental event.

This strategy will probably work to show every event to be mental; we have obviously failed to capture the intuitive concept of the mental. It would be instructive to try to mend this trouble, but it is not necessary for present purposes. We can afford Spinozistic extravagance with the mental since accidental inclusions can only strengthen the hypothesis that all mental events are identical with physical events. What would matter would be failure to include bona fide mental events, but of this there seems to be no danger.

I want to describe, and presently to argue for, a version of the identity theory that denies that there can be strict laws connecting the mental and the physical. The very possibility of such a theory is easily obscured by the way in which identity theories are commonly defended and attacked. Charles Taylor, for example, agrees with protagonists of identity theories that the sole 'ground' for accepting such theories is the supposition that correlations or laws can be established linking events described as mental with events described as physical. He says, 'It is easy to see why this is so: unless a given mental event is invariably accompanied by a given, say, brain process, there is no ground for even mooting a general identity between the two.'[6] Taylor goes on (correctly, I think) to allow that there may be identity without correlating laws, but my present interest is in noticing the invitation to confusion in the statement just quoted. What can 'a given mental event' mean here? Not a particular, dated, event, for it would not make sense to speak of an individual event being 'invariably accompanied' by another. Taylor is evidently thinking of events of a given *kind*. But if the only identities are of kinds of events, the identity theory presupposes correlating laws.

One finds the same tendency to build laws into the statements of the identity theory in these typical remarks:

> When I say that a sensation is a brain process or that lightning is an electrical discharge, I am using 'is' in the sense of strict identity . . . there are not two things: a flash of lightning and an electrical discharge. There is one thing, a flash of lightning, which is described scientifically as an electrical discharge to the earth from a cloud of ionized water molecules.[7]

The last sentence of this quotation is perhaps to be understood as saying that for every lightning flash there exists an electrical discharge to the earth from a cloud of ionized water molecules with which it is identical. Here we have an honest ontology of individual events and can make literal sense of identity. We can also see how there could be identities without correlating laws. It is possible, however, to have an ontology of events with the conditions of individuation specified in such a way that any identity implies a correlating law. Kim, for example, suggests that Fa and Gb 'describe or refer to the same event' if and only if $a = b$ and the property of being F = the property of being G. The identity of the properties in turn entails that (x) $(Fx \leftrightarrow Gx)$.[8] No wonder Kim says:

> If pain is identical with brain state B, there must be a concomitance between oc-
> currences of pain and occurrences of brain state B. . . . Thus, a necessary condi-
> tion of the pain-brain state B identity is that the two expressions 'being in pain'
> and 'being in brain state B' have the same extension. . . . There is no conceiv-
> able observation that would confirm or refute the identity but not the associated
> correlation.[9]

It may make the situation clearer to give a fourfold classification of theories of the
relation between mental and physical events that emphasizes the independence of
claims about laws and claims of identity. On the one hand there are those who assert,
and those who deny, the existence of psychophysical laws; on the other hand there
are those who say mental events are identical with physical and those who deny this.
Theories are thus divided into four sorts: *nomological monism*, which affirms that
there are correlating laws and that the events correlated are one (materialists belong
in this category); *nomological dualism*, which comprises various forms of paral-
lelism, interactionism, and epiphenomenalism; *anomalous dualism*, which combines
ontological dualism with the general failure of laws correlating the mental and the
physical (Cartesianism). And finally there is *anomalous monism*, which classifies
the position I wish to occupy.[10]

Anomalous monism resembles materialism in its claim that all events are physical, but rejects the thesis, usually considered essential to materialism, that mental
phenomena can be given purely physical explanations. Anomalous monism shows
an ontological bias only in that it allows the possibility that not all events are mental,
while insisting that all events are physical. Such a bland monism, unbuttressed by
correlating laws or conceptual economies, does not seem to merit the term 'reductionism'; in any case it is not apt to inspire the nothing-but reflex ('Conceiving the
Art of the Fugue was nothing but a complex neural event', and so forth).

Although the position I describe denies there are psychophysical laws, it is consistent with the view that mental characteristics are in some sense dependent, or su-
pervenient, on physical characteristics. Such supervenience might be taken to mean
that there cannot be two events alike in all physical respects but differing in some
mental respect, or that an object cannot alter in some mental respect without altering
in some physical respect. Dependence or supervenience of this kind does not entail
reducibility through law or definition: if it did, we could reduce moral properties to
descriptive, and this there is good reason to *believe* cannot be done; and we might be
able to reduce truth in a formal system to syntactical properties, and this we *know*
cannot in general be done.

This last example is in useful analogy with the sort of lawless monism under
consideration. Think of the physical vocabulary as the entire vocabulary of some language L with resources adequate to express a certain amount of mathematics, and its
own syntax L' is L augmented with the truth predicate 'true-in-L', which is 'mental'.
In L (and hence L') it is possible to pick out, with a definite description or open sentence, each sentence in the extension of the truth predicate, but if L is consistent there
exists no predicate of syntax (of the 'physical' vocabulary), no matter how complex,
that applies to all and only the true sentence of L. There can be no 'psychophysical
law' in the form of a biconditional, '(x) (x is true-in-L if and only if x is φ)' where 'φ'
is replaced by a 'physical' predicate (a predicate of L). Similarly, we can pick out

each mental event using the physical vocabulary alone, but no purely physical predicate, no matter how complex, has, as a matter of law, the same extension as a mental predicate.

It should now be evident how anomalous monism reconciles the three original principles. Causality and identity are relations between individual events no matter how described. But laws are linguistic; and so events can instantiate laws, and hence be explained or predicted in the light of laws, only as those events are described in one or another way. The principle of causal interaction deals with events in extension and is therefore blind to the mental-physical dichotomy. The principle of the anomalism of the mental concerns events described as mental, for events are mental only as described. The principle of the nomological character of causality must be read carefully: it says that when events are related as cause and effect, they have descriptions that instantiate a law. It does not say that every true singular statement of causality instantiates a law.[11]

II

The analogy just bruited, between the place of the mental amid the physical, and the place of the semantical in a world of syntax, should not be strained. Tarski proved that a consistent language cannot (under some natural assumptions) contain an open sentence 'Fx' true of all and only the true sentences of that language. If our analogy were pressed, then we would expect a proof that there can be no physical open sentence 'Px' true of all and only the events having some mental property. In fact, however, nothing I can say about the irreducibility of the mental deserves to be called a proof; and the kind of irreducibility is different. For if anomalous monism is correct, not only can every mental event be uniquely singled out using only physical concepts, but since the number of events that falls under each mental predicate may, for all we know, be finite, there may well exist a physical open sentence coextensive with each mental predicate, though to construct it might involve the tedium of a lengthy and uninstructive alternation. Indeed, even if finitude is not assumed, there seems no compelling reason to deny that there could be coextensive predicates, one mental and one physical.

The thesis is rather that the mental is nomologically irreducible: there may be *true* general statements relating the mental and the physical, statements that have the logical form of a law; but they are not *lawlike* (in a strong sense to be described). If by absurdly remote chance we were to stumble on a nonstochastic true psychophysical generalization, we would have no reason to believe it more than roughly true.

Do we, by declaring that there are no (strict) psychophysical laws, poach on the empirical preserves of science—a form of *hubris* against which philosophers are often warned? Of course, to judge a statement lawlike or illegal is not to decide its truth outright, relative to the acceptance of a general statement on the basis of instances, ruling it lawlike must be a priori. But such relative apriorism does not in itself justify philosophy, for in general the grounds for deciding to trust a statement on the basis of its instances will in turn be governed by theoretical and empirical concerns not to be distinguished from those of science. If the case of supposed laws linking the mental and the physical is different, it can only be because to allow the possibility of such laws would amount to changing the subject. By changing the subject I mean here: deciding not to accept the criterion of the mental in terms of the vocabulary of the propositional attitudes. This short answer cannot prevent further ramifications of the problem, however, for there is no clear line between changing the subject and changing what one says on an old subject, which is to admit, in the present context at least, that there is no clear line between philosophy and science. Where there are no fixed boundaries only the timid never risk trespass.

It will sharpen our appreciation of the anomological character of mental-physical generalizations to consider a related matter, the failure of definitional behaviourism. Why are we willing (as I assume we are) to abandon the attempt to give explicit definitions of mental concepts in terms of behavioural ones? Not, surely, just because all actual tries are conspicuously inadequate. Rather it is because we are persuaded, as we are in the case of so many other forms of definitional reductionism (naturalism in ethics, instrumentalism and operationalism in the sciences, the causal theory of meaning, phenomenalism and so on—the catalogue of philosophy's defeats), that there is system in the failures. Suppose we try to say, not using any mental concepts, what it is for a man to believe there is life on Mars. One line we could take is this: when a certain sound is produced in the man's presence ('Is there life on Mars?') he produces another ('Yes'). But of course this shows he believes there is life on Mars only if he understands English, his production of the sound was intentional, and was a response to the sounds as meaning something in English; and so on. For each discovered deficiency, we add a new proviso. Yet no matter how we patch and fit the non-mental conditions, we always find the need for an additional condition (provided he *notices, understands*, etc.) that is mental in character.[12]

A striking feature of attempts at definitional reduction is how little seems to hinge on the question of synonymy between definiens and definiendum. Of course, by imagining counterexamples we do discredit claims of synonymy. But the pattern of failure prompts a stronger conclusion: if we were to find an open sentence couched in behavioural terms and exactly coextensive with some mental predicate, nothing could reasonably persuade us that we had found it. We know too much about thought and behaviour to trust exact and universal statements linking them. Beliefs and desires issue in behaviour only as modified and mediated by further beliefs and desires, attitudes and attendings, without limit. Clearly this holism of the mental realm is a clue both to the autonomy and to the anomalous character of the mental.

These remarks apropos definitional behaviourism provide at best hints of why we should not expect nomological connections between the mental and the physical. The central case invites further consideration.

Lawlike statements are general statements that support counter-factual and subjunctive claims, and are supported by their instances. There is (in my view) no non-question-begging criterion of the lawlike, which is not to say there are no reasons in particular cases for a judgement. Lawlikeness is a matter of degree, which is not to deny that there may be cases beyond debate. And within limits set by the conditions of communication, there is room for much variation between individuals in the pattern of statements to which various degrees of nomologicality are assigned. In all these respects nomologicality is much like analyticity, as one might expect since both are linked to meaning.

'All emeralds are green' is lawlike in that its instances confirm it, but 'all emeralds are grue' is not, for 'grue' means 'observed before time t and green, otherwise blue', and if our observations were all made before t and uniformly revealed green emeralds, this would not be a reason to expect other emeralds to be blue. Nelson Goodman has suggested that this shows that some predicates, 'grue' for example, are unsuited to laws (and thus a criterion of suitable predicates could lead to a criterion of the lawlike). But it seems to me the anomalous character of 'All emeralds are grue' shows only that the predicates 'is an emerald' and 'is grue' are not suited to one another: grueness is not an inductive property of emeralds. Grueness *is* however an inductive property of entities of other sorts, for instance of emerires. (Something is an emerire if it is examined before t and is an emerald, and otherwise is a sapphire.) Not only is 'All emerires are grue' entailed by the conjunction of a lawlike statements 'All emeralds are green' and 'All sapphires are blue,' but there is no reason, as far as I can see, to reject the deliverance of intuition, that it is itself lawlike.[13] Nomological statements bring together predicates that we know a priori are made for each other—know, that is, independently of knowing whether the evidence supports a connection between them. 'Blue,' 'red', and 'green' are made for emeralds, sapphires, and roses; 'grue', 'bleen', and 'gred' are made for sapphalds, emerires, and emeroses.

The direction in which the discussion seems headed is this: mental and physical predicates are not made for one another. In point of lawlikeness, psychophysical statements are more like 'All emeralds are grue' than like 'All emeralds are green.

Before this claim is plausible, it must be seriously modified. The fact that emeralds examined before t are grue not only is no reason to believe all emeralds are grue; it is not even a reason (if we know the time) to believe *any* unobserved emeralds are grue. But if an event of a certain mental sort has usually been accompanied by an event of a certain physical sort, this often is a good reason to expect other cases to follow suit roughly in proportion. The generalizations that embody such practical wisdom are assumed to be only roughly true, or they are explicitly stated in probabilistic terms, or they are insulated from counterexample by generous escape clauses. Their importance lies mainly in the support they lend singular causal claims and related explanations of particular events. The support derives from the fact that such a generalization, however crude and vague, may provide good reason to believe that underlying the particular case there is a regularity that could be formulated sharply and without caveat.

In our daily traffic with events and actions that must be foreseen or understood, we perforce make use of the sketchy summary generalization, for we do not know a more accurate law, or if we do, we lack a description of the particular events in which we are interested that would show the relevance of the law. But there is an important distinction to be made within the category of the rude rule of thumb. On the one hand, there are generalizations whose positive instances give us reason to believe the generalization itself could be improved by adding further provisos and conditions stated in the same general vocabulary as the original generalization. Such a generalization points to the form and vocabulary of the finished law: we may say that it is a *homonomic* generalization. On the other hand there are generalizations which when instantiated may give us reason to believe there is a precise law at work, but one that can be stated only by shifting to a different vocabulary. We may call such generalizations *heteronomic*.

I suppose most of our practical lore (and science) is heteronomic. This is because a law can hope to be precise, explicit, and as exceptionless as possible only if it draws its concepts from a comprehensive closed theory. This ideal theory may or may not be deterministic, but it is if any true theory is. Within the physical sciences we do find homonomic generalizations, generalizations such that if the evidence supports them, we then have reason to believe they may be sharpened indefinitely by drawing upon further physical concepts: there is a theoretical asymptote of perfect coherence with all the evidence, perfect predictability (under the terms of the system), total explanation (again under the terms of the system). Or perhaps the ultimate theory is probabilistic, and the asymptote is less than perfection; but in that case there will be no better to be had.

Confidence that a statement is homonomic, correctible within its own conceptual domain, demands that it draw its concepts from a theory with strong constitutive elements. Here is the simplest possible illustration; if the lesson carries, it will be obvious that the simplification could be mended.

The measurement of length, weight, temperature, or time depends (among many other things, of course) on the existence in each case of a two-place relation that is transitive and asymmetric: warmer than, later than, heavier than, and so forth. Let us take the relation *longer than* as our example. The law or postulate of transitivity is this:

(L) $L(x,y)$ and $L(y,z) \rightarrow L(x,z)$

Unless this law (or some sophisticated variant) holds, we cannot easily make sense of the concept of length. There will be no way of assigning numbers to register even so much as ranking in length, let alone the more powerful demands of measurement on a ratio scale. And this remark goes not only for any three items directly involved in an intransitivity: it is easy to show (given a few more assumptions essential to measurement of length) that there is no consistent assignment of a ranking to any item unless (L) holds in full generality.

Clearly (L) alone cannot exhaust the import of 'longer than'—otherwise it would not differ from 'warmer than' or 'later than'. We must suppose there is some empirical content, however difficult to formulate in the available vocabulary, that distinguishes 'longer than' from the other two-place transitive predicates of measurement and on the basis of which we may assert that one thing is longer than another. Imagine this empirical content to be partly given by the predicate '$O(x,y)$'. So we have this 'meaning postulate':

(M) $O(x, y) \rightarrow L(x, y)$

that partly interprets (L). But now (L) and (M) together yield an empirical theory of great strength, for together they entail that there do not exist three objects a, b, and c such that $O(a,b)$, $O(b,c)$, and $O(c,a)$. Yet what is to prevent this happening if '$O(x,y)$' is a predicate we can ever, with confidence, apply? Suppose we *think* we observe an intransitive triad; what do we say? We could count (L) false, but then we would have no application for the concept of length. We could say (M) gives a wrong test for length; but then it is unclear what we thought was the *content* of the idea of one thing being longer than another. Or we could say that the objects under observation are not, as the theory requires, *rigid* objects. It is a mistake to think we are forced to accept some one of these answers. Concepts such as that of length are sustained in equilibrium by a number of conceptual pressures, and theories of fundamental measurement are distorted if we force the decision, among such principles as (L) and (M): analytic or synthetic. It is better to say the whole set of axioms, laws, or postulates for the measurement of length is partly constitutive of the idea of a system of macroscopic, rigid, physical objects. I suggest that the existence of lawlike statements in physical science depends upon the existence of constitutive (or synthetic a priori) laws like those of the measurement of length within the same conceptual domain.

Just as we cannot intelligibly assign a length to any object unless a comprehensive theory holds of objects of that sort, we cannot intelligibly attribute any propositional attitude to an agent except within the framework of a viable theory of his beliefs, desires, intentions, and decision.

There is no assigning beliefs to a person one by one on the basis of his verbal behaviour, his choices, or other local signs no matter how plain and evident, for we make sense of particular beliefs only as they cohere with other beliefs, with preferences, with intentions, hopes, fears, expectations, and the rest. It is not merely, as with the measurement of length, that each case tests a theory and depends upon it, but that the content of a propositional attitude derives from its place in the pattern.

Crediting people with a large degree of consistency cannot be counted mere charity: it is unavoidable if we are to be in a position to accuse them meaningfully of error and some degree of irrationality. Global confusion, like universal mistake, is unthinkable, not because imagination boggles, but because too much confusion leaves nothing to be confused about and massive error erodes the background of true belief against which alone failure can be construed. To appreciate the limits to the kind and amount of blunder and bad thinking we can intelligibly pin on others is to see once more the inseparability of the question what concepts a person commands and the question what he does with those concepts in the way of belief, desire, and intention. To the extent that we fail to discover a coherent and plausible pattern in the attitudes and actions of others we simply forego the chance of treating them as persons.

The problem is not bypassed but given centre stage by appeal to explicit speech behaviour. For we could not begin to decode a man's sayings if we could not make out his attitudes towards his sentences, such as holding, wishing, or wanting them to be true. Beginning from these attitudes, we must work out a theory of what he means, thus simultaneously giving content to his attitudes and to his words. In our need to make him make sense, we will try for a theory that finds him consistent, a believer of truths, and a lover of the good (all by our own lights, it goes without saying). Life being what it is, there will be no simple theory that fully meets these demands. Many theories will effect a more or less acceptable compromise, and between these theories there may be no objective grounds for choice.

The heteronomic character of general statements linking the mental and the physical traces back to this central role of translation in the description of all propositional attitudes, and to the indeterminacy of translation.[14] There are no strict psychophysical laws because of the disparate commitments of the mental and physical schemes. It is a feature of physical reality that physical change can be explained by laws that connect it with other changes and conditions physically described. It is a feature of the mental that the attribution of mental phenomena must be responsible to the background of reasons, beliefs, and intentions of the individual. There cannot be tight connections between the realms if each is to retain allegiance to its proper source of evidence. The nomological irreducibility of the mental does not derive merely from the seamless nature of the world of thought, preference, and intention, for such interdependence is common to physical theory, and is compatible with there being a single right way of interpreting a man's attitudes without relativization to a scheme of translation. Nor is the irreducibility due simply to the possibility of many equally eligible schemes, for this is compatible with an arbitrary choice of one scheme relative to which assignments of mental traits are made. The point is rather that when we use the concepts of belief, desire, and the rest, we must stand prepared as the evidence accumulates, to adjust our theory in the light of considerations of overall cogency: the constitutive ideal of rationality partly controls each phase in the evolution of what must be an evolving theory. An arbitrary choice of translation scheme would preclude such opportunistic tempering of theory; put differently, a right arbitrary choice of a translation manual would be of a manual acceptable in the light of all possible evidence, and this is a choice we cannot make. We must conclude, I think, that nomological slack between the mental and the physical is essential as long as we conceive of man as a rational animal.

III

The gist of the foregoing discussion, as well as its conclusion, will be familiar. That there is a categorial difference between the mental and the physical is a commonplace. It may seem odd that I say nothing of the supposed privacy of the mental, or the special authority an agent has with respect to his own propositional attitudes, but this appearance of novelty would fade if we were to investigate in more detail the grounds for accepting a scheme of translation. The step from the categorial difference between the mental and the physical to the impossibility of strict laws relating them is less common, but certainly not new. If there is a surprise, then, it will be to find the lawlessness of the mental serving to help establish the identity of the mental with that paradigm of the lawlike, the physical.

The reasoning is this. We are assuming, under the Principle of the Causal Dependence of the Mental, that some mental events at least are causes or effects of physical events; the argument applies only to these. A second Principle (of the Nomological Character of Causality) says that each true singular causal statement is backed by a strict law connecting events of kinds to which events mentioned as cause and effect belong. Where there are rough, but homonomic, laws, there are laws drawing on concepts from the same conceptual domain and upon which there is no improving in point of precision and comprehensiveness. We urged in the last section that such laws occur in the physical sciences. Physical theory promises to provide a comprehensive closed system guaranteed to yield a standardized, unique description of every physical event couched in a vocabulary amenable to law.

It is not plausible that mental concepts alone can provide such a framework, simply because the mental does not, by our first principle constitute a closed system. Too much happens to affect the mental that is not itself a systematic part of the mental. But if we combine this observation with the conclusion that no psychophysical statement is, or can be built into, a strict law, we have the Principle of the Anomalism of the Mental: there are no strict laws at all on the basis of which we can predict and explain mental phenomena.

The demonstration of identity follows easily. Suppose m, a mental event, caused p, a physical event; then, under some description m and p instantiate a strict law. This law can only be physical, according to the previous paragraph. But if m falls under a physical law, it has a physical description; which is to say it is a physical event. An analogous argument works when a physical event causes a mental event. So every mental event that is causally related to a physical event is a physical event. In order to establish anomalous monism in full generality it would be sufficient to show that every mental event is cause or effect of some physical event; I shall not attempt this.

If one event causes another, there is a strict law which those events instantiate when properly described. But it is possible (and typical) to know of the singular causal relation without knowing the law or the relevant descriptions. Knowledge requires reasons, but these are available in the form of rough heteronomic generalizations, which are lawlike in that instances make it reasonable to expect other instances to follow suit without being lawlike in the sense of being indefinitely refinable. Applying these facts to knowledge of identities, we see that it is possible to know that a mental event is identical with some physical event without knowing which one (in the sense of being able to give it a unique physical description that brings it under a relevant law). Even if someone knew the entire physical history of the world, and every mental event were identical with a physical, it would not follow that he could predict or explain a single mental event (so described, of course).

Two features of mental events in their relation to the physical—causal dependence and nomological independence—combine, then, to dissolve what has often seemed a paradox, the efficacy of thought and purpose in the material world, and their freedom from law. When we portray events as perceivings, rememberings, decisions and actions, we necessarily locate them amid physical happenings through the relation of cause and effect; but as long as we do not change the idiom that same mode of portrayal insulates mental events from the strict laws that can in principle be called upon to explain and predict physical phenomena.

Mental events as a class cannot be explained by physical science; particular mental events can when we know particular identities. But the explanations of mental events in which we are typically interested relate them to other mental events and conditions. We explain a man's free actions, for example, by appeal to his desires, habits, knowledge and perceptions. Such accounts of intentional behaviour operate in a conceptual framework removed from the direct reach of physical law by describing both cause and effect, reason and action, as aspects of a portrait of a human agent. The anomalism of the mental is thus a necessary condition for viewing action as autonomous. I conclude with a second passage from Kant:

> It is an indispensable problem of speculative philosophy to show that its illusion respecting the contradiction rests on this, that we think of man in a different sense and relation when we call him free, and when we regard him as subject to the laws of nature. . . . It must therefore show that not only can both of these very well co-exist, but that both must be thought *as necessarily united* in the same subject. . . [15]

NOTES

1. *Fundamental Principles of the Metaphysics of Morals,* 75–6.

2. These claims are defended in Essays I and 3.

3. In Essay 7. I elaborate on the view of causality assumed here. The stipulation that the laws be deterministic is stronger than required by the reasoning, and will be relaxed.

4. The point depends on assuming that mental events may intelligibly be said to have a location; but it is an assumption that must be true if an identity theory is, and here I am not trying to prove the theory but to formulate it.

5. I am indebted to Lee Bowie for emphasizing this difficulty.

6. Charles Taylor, 'Mind—Body Identity, a Side Issue?', 202.

7. J. J. C. Smart, 'Sensations and Brain Processes'. The quoted passages are on pages 163–5 of the reprinted version in *The Philosophy of Mind,* ed. V. C. Chappell (Englewood Cliffs, N.J., 1962). For another example, see David K. Lewis, 'An Argument for the Identity Theory'. Here the assumption is made explicit when Lewis takes events as universals (p. 17, footnotes 1 and 2). I do not suggest that Smart and Lewis are confused, only that their way of stating the identity theory tends to obscure the distinction between particular events and kinds of events on which the formulations of my theory depends.

8. Jaegwon Kim, 'On the Psycho-Physical Identity Theory', 231.

9. Ibid., 227—S. Richard Brandt and Jaegwon Kim propose roughly the same criterion in 'The Logic of the Identity Theory'. They remark that on their conception of event identity, the identity theory 'makes a stronger claim than merely that there is a pervasive phenomenal-physical correlation', 518. I do not discuss the stronger claim.

10. Anomalous monism is more or less explicitly recognized as a possible position by Herbert Feigl, 'The "Mental" and the "Physical" '; Sydney Shoemaker, 'Ziff's Other Minds'; David Randall Luce, 'Mind—Body Identity and Psycho-Physical Correlation'; Charles Taylor, op. cit., 207. Something like my position is tentatively accepted by Thomas Nagel, 'Physicalism', and endorsed by P. F. Strawson in *Freedom and the Will,* 63–7.

11. The point that substitutivity of identity fails in the context of explanation is made in connection with the present subject by Norman Malcolm, 'Scientific Materialism and the Identity Theory', 123–4. Also see Essays 1 and 8.

12. The theme is developed in Roderick Chisholm, *Perceiving.* Ch. 2.

13. The view is accepted by Richard C. Jeffrey, 'Goodman's Query', John R. Wallace, 'Goodman, Logic, Induction', and John M. Vickers, 'Characteristics of Projectible Predicates'. Goodman, in 'Comments', disputes the lawlikeness of statements like 'All emerires are grue.' I cannot see, however, that he meets the point of my 'Emeroses by Other Names'. This short paper is printed as an appendix to the present essay.

14. The influence of W. V. Quine's doctrine of the indeterminacy of translation, as in Ch. 2 of *Word and Object,* is, I hope, obvious. In sect. 45 Quine develops the

connection between translation and the propositional attitudes, and remarks that 'Brentano's thesis of the irreducibility of intentional idioms is of a piece with the thesis of indeterminacy of translation', 221.

15. Op. cit., 76.

SELF-UNDERSTANDING
AND RATIONALIZING EXPLANATIONS*

Jaegwon Kim

I

I want to approach the question of the nature of rationalizing explanations—the question of *how* reasons explain actions—from the point of view of "psychological anomalism". By psychological anomalism I have in mind the thesis that there are not, and cannot be, precise predictive-explanatory laws formulated in terms of *intentional psychological* concepts such as belief, desire, and intention. This thesis is equivalent to the claim that there cannot be a law-based psychological theory couched in the vocabulary of intentional psychological expressions, that is terms expressing contentful attitudes and relations such as "believe", "want", "hope", and "regret". The doctrine is silent on the question whether there can be laws about non-intentional psychological phenomena (if there are such). By a "reason for an action" I mean, roughly, what Donald Davidson means by a "primary reason"[1]: something is a "primary reason" (or "reason" for short) for an action if it consists of a desire for a certain state of affairs and the belief that doing that action will secure, or has a reasonable chance of securing, the desired state of affairs. Are there reasons that are not primary reasons? For the limited purposes of this paper it is sufficient to assume that whenever there is a reason for an action there is also a primary reason.

    The question how reasons are connected with the actions they rationalize, we recall, was one of the dominant questions in philosophy of mind and philosophical psychology from the late 1950's to the early 70's.[2] The specific form of this question around which much of the controversy centered was whether this connection is

*Originally published in *Philosophia Naturalis* 21 (1984): 309–320. Reprinted with the kind permission of the journal and Professor Kim.

causal and empirical, or in some sense conceptual and a priori. This issue, like so many others in philosophy, was never satisfactorily resolved before receding from center stage; discussions in philosophy of mind turned to other matters such as the nature of consciousness, functionalism, the nature of cognitive psychology, mental representation and imagery, and so on. However, the issue has never disappeared; it has only lost its status as a conspicuous philosophical issue of the day. Current debates concerning the nature of cognitive psychology have a direct bearing on this issue, and the recent developments in philosophy of mind provide us with a fresh and richer context in which to consider the problem anew.

One of these developments is the doctrine of psychological anomalism. There has been a long tradition of skepticism about the prospects of a "science of the mind", a nomological-predictive theory of mental phenomena that will do for the realm of the mind what modern physical theory has done for the realm of matter. Recently, however, there has been a new pressure to consider this doctrine seriously and rethink various issues in philosophy of mind in its light. The pressure has come mainly from two quarters: first, there have been arguments, due primarily to Davidson and Quine[3], to the effect that the fundamental a priori constraints on intentional psychological concepts preclude their entering into nomological relationships, whether with other intentional concepts or with physical ones. Second, there are philosophers (e.g., Paul Churchland[4], Stephen Stich[5]) who, while accepting the idea of a scientific psychology, argue that intentional psychological concepts will have no place in the increasingly sophisticated and theoretical psychology that is in store for us. It is not my concern in this paper to discuss, or review, reasons for endorsing or rejecting the doctrine of psychological anomalism.[6] My question here is a conditional one: If we accept this doctrine, how should we understand the explanatory function of reasons vis-a-vis the actions they rationalize?

II

In order to bring our question into sharper focus, consider the following principle (we will call it the "Desire-Belief-Action Principle", or "DBA" for short):

> **DBA: If a person desires that *p*, and believes that doing *A* will secure *p*, then *ceteris paribus* he will do *A*.**

As it stands, DBA is very rough and in need of much refinement; however, the precise form of DBA is not important for us. One of the issues that dominated the discussion in philosophical psychology in the '60's was whether DBA is a contingent empirical law about belief, desire, and action, or whether it is an a priori truth grounded wholly in a conceptual relationship among the three interdependent notions of belief, desire, and action. Now, it is obvious that if psychological anomalism is true, DBA cannot be an empirical law, for there would be no psychological laws at all. (By "psychological" here, and hereafter, I mean "intentional psychological".) And this means that psychological anomalism excludes all accounts of rationalizing explanations that take DBA as an empirical law. One such account is the well-known account of Carl G. Hempel[7] which attempts to fit rationalizing explanations into the standard "covering-law" models. If psychological anomalism is true, there are no laws to do the covering.

Closely related to Hempel's nomological model is Davidson's causal model.[8] At first blush the causal model, which takes reasons to be *causes* of the actions they rationalize, may appear to be consistent with psychological anomalism and entirely home free. This is no surprise; for after all Davidson is also a principal source and defender of psychological anomalism. However, I think the matter is a bit more complicated. The attraction of the causal model consists in the following fact: to sustain the claim that reasons are causes of actions we need not be able to invoke laws that are formulated in *terms* of reasons and actions—in particular, we need not invoke DBA as an empirical law of intentional psychology. For to show that a particular primary reason R is a cause of action A it is only necessary that there are descriptions of R and A, perhaps in physical or physiological terms, which instantiate a law. Thus, the laws subsuming reasons and actions need not speak of belief and desire, or any other psychological states; for all we know, they could be physiological laws about neurons and muscle fibers. Psychological anomalism claims only that there can be no laws about beliefs and desires as *described* or *conceptualized* as such. The claim that a concrete event is a cause of another involves no specific requirement as to the kind of description under which the two events are brought into a nomological relationship. Thus, beliefs and desires can be causes of actions without there being laws *about* beliefs, desires, and actions.

The general account of singular causal judgments that underlies this argument has a great deal of plausibility. When we say, "The accident was caused by Harry's dumb practical joke", we do not believe that there are laws formulated in terms of "accidents" and "dumb practical jokes". What we expect is rather that the two individual events picked out as "the accident" and "Harry's dumb practical joke" can be appropriately redescribed, perhaps as "a fire in the kitchen" and "the soaking of the dish towels in gasoline". Under these descriptions there may well be a law that can be brought to bear on the situation. Davidson's view is that we should view the case of rational causation of behavior in the same way: reasons and actions must be given redescriptions in terms that are better suited for the formulation of empirical laws.

Davidson's causal model, coupled with his account of singular causal statements, is consistent with psychological anomalism. However, I believe the model fails to give a satisfactory account of the "reasons for which" an action is done—it fails as an account of the explanatory nature of reasons. As I see it, the principal cause of the failure is this: Under Davidson's account, the fact that a given primary reason consists of a certain belief and desire—that it *is* a primary reason of a certain sort—is entirely irrelevant to its being a cause of the action it rationalizes. Just as the fact that a cause-effect pair is described as "Harry's dumb practical joke" and "the accident" has no intrinsic relationship to the fact that the first is a cause of the second, the fact that some event is a primary reason, on Davidson's account, has no essential relationship to the fact that it caused the given action. Rather, the event's being a neurophysiological process of a certain type is what makes it a cause of the behavior in question. The fact that we can also pick it out by the description "the belief that . . . and the desire that . . . " is no more relevant to the explanatory connection than the fact that we can pick it out by such descriptions as "the first thing that occurred to Harry that Sunday morning as a fun thing to do", "the event reported in the *Ann Arbor News* on p. 11 yesterday", "the only imaginative thing Harry did since graduation from college", etc. On Davidson's account, reasons *qua* reasons play no explanatory role.[9]

According to some philosophers, both the causal and the nomological models fail because they construe the explanatory connection between reasons and actions as contingent and empirical, whereas, they argue, the connection is in reality conceptual and a priori. Georg von Wright[10] is one of the leading advocates of this "intentionalist" position. According to him, the following schema of practical inference is the principal form of rationalizing explanations:

> **(W) Agent *A* intends to bring about *p*.**
> **   *A* considers that unless he does *a* he cannot bring about *p*.**
> **   Therefore, *A* sets himself to do *a*.**

Although, unlike DBA, this schema is formulated in terms of intention rather than desire, this difference will not affect our main points. Now, von Wright claims, though with some minor conditions and caveats, that (W) is "logically valid", and this corresponds to the claim, which others have made, that DBA is logically or a priori true. But how does (W) fare as a model of action explanation? I think it can be seen that merely saying that the belief and intention (i.e., the premises of (W)) logically entail the action leaves untouched the question of how, or why, they explain the action. For suppose (W) is logically valid. The following would be an acceptable action explanation fitting (W):

> **(1) I intend to attend the 7th International Congress.**
> **   I consider that unless I go to Salzburg I cannot attend the 7th**
> **   International Congress.**
> **   Therefore, I set myself to go to Salzburg.**

It occurs to me that I will need a place to stay while in Salzburg; I write to the local convention bureau, and am given a reservation at Hotel Wolf Dietrich. The premises of the following instance of (W) are all true:[11]

> **(2) I intend to stay at Hotel Wolf Dietrich in Salzburg.**
> **   I consider that unless I go to Salzburg, I cannot stay at Hotel**
> **   Wolf Dietrich.**
> **   Therefore, I set myself to go to Salzburg.**

There can be no dispute, I take it, about whether (2) is explanatory; it is not. However, if (1) is logically valid, so must (2) be. Notice also that (2) *could* be explanatory, in another situation; e.g. one in which my purpose in going to Salzburg is to stay at that hotel. This shows that the logical validity of (2) is not at issue. Thus, both (1) and (2) are logically valid; (1) is explanatory and (2) is not. Therefore, the logical validity of (1) cannot be the reason why it is explanatory. And it will be easy to construct analogues of (1) and (2) with "desire" replacing "intend". Thus, even if desire (intention) and belief logically entail action, *that* cannot be the reason why the former explain the latter.

III

Thus, all three major accounts of rationalizing explanations fail. Hempel's account takes DBA as an empirical law of behavior of rational agents; Davidson's account takes it as a summary of contingent singular causal statements; von Wright's approach views DBA as an a priori conceptual truth. What other possibilities are there?

I suggest we reject the assumption that DBA is a *descriptive* statement representing some existing state of affairs, whether this is some nomological connection between types of events or some logical connection among concepts. Rather, we should look at it as a *normative* or *regulative* rule specifying rational constraints on decision-making and intention-formation. It is a normative principle that tells us the conditions under which a given action is rationalizable as an appropriate thing to do. Equally, it could be considered a regulative rule that places the constraint of coherence and appropriateness on our beliefs, desires, and volitions, helping make the entire system of cognition and attitudes coherent and intelligible. What is required is a shift in our perspective: we should try looking at DBA, and other similar principles, not as mere descriptive statements about how we think, will, and act, or about how these concepts are related to each other, but rather as normative rules that govern our choice of courses of action, and help us evaluate the appropriateness of our actions to our beliefs and desires. They are part of the system of rules and norms that are constitutive of our notion of *rationality*. Here "rationality" must be broadly understood as a certain property, or set of properties, pertaining to the system of propositional attitudes that characterize a person; not only his beliefs, but also his desires, volitions, actions, hopes, regrets, puzzles and wonderments, and all the rest. All these states are characterized in terms of their *propositional contents*, and if the entire system of propositional attitudes is to be "rational"—that is, exhibits a certain degree of coherence, harmony, and mutual appropriateness—then the contents of these states must be in certain required relationships to one another. Thus, the consistency of beliefs is one desideratum but clearly not the only one. We also require that desires be coherent among themselves and in relation to beliefs; for example, if one has the desire that p and believes that q is necessary to secure p, then *ceteris paribus* it is appropriate for the person to desire that q. The escape clause indicates that there are exceptions to the rule; however, too many exceptions would lead us to question the coherence of the person's system of preferences, and its coherence with his beliefs. Similarly for DBA: as we know, desires do not always lead to actions; some desires may be just too weak, and more importantly there may be other desires that override them; and so on. But again, a consistent violation of DBA would lead us to question the coherence and rationality of the subject's desire-belief system. In fact, it is not clear that we would *permit* a consistent violation of DBA: before we admit such violations we might very well decide to review and revise the desires and beliefs that have been attributed to the agent. A minimum of rationality and coherence must be present in a person, that is, in his system of propositional attitudes, before we can treat him as a person, an agent capable of such attitudes. I do not, however, want to dwell on these points; my main purpose here is to point to the normative-evaluative character of DBA and other similar principles and the special holistic constraints they impose on the ascription of intentional states. There are perhaps also non-normative readings of DBA; that is not my concern. My concern is to stress the crucial normative aspect of DBA, and try to construct an account of rationalizing explanations that takes the normativity of DBA seriously.

The account of rationalizing explanations that I shall sketch below in very rough and programmatic outlines may be called a "normative model". As many have noticed, "explanation" has a double meaning, especially as regards human behavior: sometimes it simply concerns the causal provenance of the thing to be explained, a recounting of why and how it has come to pass, but sometimes it carries the sense of "justification". "Explain why you did *A*" uttered by the boss to a subordinate in a certain tone of voice is not a request for a causal explanation of *A*; it is a request for a justification or defense—a "rationalization" of what was done, presumably in terms of the goals to be achieved and the available information. The term "rationalizing explanations" captures this dual aspect of explanation: to rationalize in this sense *is* also to explain, to make sense of what was done, and why it was done.

Let us now get to the substance of the normative account. I shall set forth below the elements of the approach I have in mind in the form of six theses, with explanatory remarks for each. My goal is this: to sketch the outlines of an account of the nature of rationalizing explanations as a mode understanding actions which is not *causal-predictive*, and which is not based on empirical causal laws of psychology but rather on normative-evaluative principles of rationality governing decision making and intention formation.

> *Thesis 1:* Each of us has a need to understand, make sense of, our own actions. In fact, it is an essential part of our nature as reflective rational agents that we need to render our own actions and decisions intelligible to ourselves.

I think one could argue for this thesis on two fronts: first, that the requirement of self-understanding in this sense is a necessary consequence of the very concept of a "reflective rational agent", and second, that there is psychological evidence to show that we, or most of us, are "reflective rational agents" in the intended sense—that is, we do as a matter of psychological fact have a need of self-understanding. The first part of the argument would be a complex philosophical enterprise, something I am not prepared to undertake here. Instead, I would like to point to some psychological studies that would support the second part of the argument. Here I would chiefly mention work in social psychology, especially on people's perception of the causes of their own actions. Work on this topic is usefully reviewed and summarized in a monograph by Richard Nisbett and Stuart Valins entitled "Perceiving the Causes of One's Own Behavior".[12] The psychological work in this area is fascinating; it shows the extent to which subjects are willing to go in modifying their pre-existing beliefs and desires, often unconsciously, so that their actions and decisions may be rationalized. In surveying this literature one cannot fail to be impressed by the strength and pervasiveness of our need to make sense of what we do, even at the cost of fairly serious revisions to our cognitive system.

Let me give you as an example a study done by Festinger and Carlsmith as reported by Nisbett and Valins. Some subjects were offered $1 to tell another person that a dull task they had just completed had been interesting; other subjects were offered $20 to do the same. It was found that the $1 subjects were appreciably more prone to have changed their minds about the dull nature of the task (many of them came to believe that the task was not so boring after all) than the $20 subjects. The psychologist Daryl Bern's explanation of this phenomenon goes like this: the subject offered only $1 to lie realizes that he doesn't like to tell lies, that he had no particular reason to do so (only $1 was offered), and therefore that he must not have particularly disliked the task, and must not have told a lie when he said it was interesting. On the other hand, the subject offered $20 does not re-evaluate the task and change his mind about it because while he knows he doesn't like to tell lies, he is willing to tell them if given sufficient compensation. It is clear that the subject's saying of what was believed to have been a dull task that it was interesting put a pressure on his cognitive system to produce a rationalization, and the two subjects offered $1 and $20 respectively, respond to this pressure in expected ways: each constructs a distinct rationalization that is consistent with the further given that he was offered so many dollars to tell the lie. As a result the apparent "dissonance" has been removed from his system of beliefs, desires, and other attitudes, and an equilibrium has been restored.

David Velleman[13] has argued that we in fact choose our actions in such a way that they are intelligible to ourselves; that the requirement of intelligibility itself works as a constraint on what courses of action are chosen by us. One might argue that not to understand our own actions, not to be able to make sense of them by rationalizing them in terms of our wants and beliefs, how they cohere within our overall system of cognitions and attitudes, is a form of self-alienation; we become alienated from our own actions, and come to view them from the third-person perspective; to recognize them as our own requires that they be seen to cohere within our system of beliefs and attitudes.

> *Thesis 2:* One central way in which we understand and make sense of explaining our own actions is to know how to construct primary reasons (in Davidson's sense) for them. When we know the primary reason of an action of our own, we understand the action.

We may also say that we understand an action that we did when we can construct for it an appropriate instance of practical inference, of the kind we discussed in connection with von Wright. This is not the only way we understand our own actions; sometimes we rationalize something we did in terms of external compulsion; that we were forced to do it, that it was beyond our control, etc. But in the latter sort of case, what was done may not need to be counted as a full-fledged action in need of "rationalization". Thus, it is possible that Thesis 2 could be strengthened to this: an agent understands an action of his own if and only if he is able to construct a practical inference for it. But the more limited Thesis 2, as stated, is sufficient for my purposes here. But why are "primary reasons" important? Why are beliefs and desires, cognitions and preferences, important in understanding our actions? Since this is important to the normative account of rationalizing explanation, I shall set down as a supplement to Thesis 2:

> *Thesis 2a:* The primary reason for an action explains it because it is the reason for which we *chose*, or *would have chosen*, to perform that action. Understanding an action in terms of its primary reason is to reconstruct or recapitulate the practical inference leading to the decision or intention to do it.

That is, to locate for action *A* its primary reason is to come into possession of ingredients out of which we can construct a practical inference that led, or would have led, to an intention to do *A*. Prospectively, this is a process of deliberation and decision-making. Retrospectively, it is a process of rationalizing and explaining. I believe that the retrospective process of rationalizing and explaining is dependent on, and derives from, the prospective process of deliberation and intention formation. As rational agents we necessarily deliberate and decide. The basis of the deliberation consists of the beliefs we have about ourselves and the world, and the goals that we want to achieve. As *reflective* agents, we need to understand why we decide the way we do, and we gain this understanding when we know the practical inference that led to it, or that would have led to it. Understanding is a recapitulation of the actual or possible decision-making.

> *Thesis 3:* The role of DBA, and other such principles, is to place constraints on what counts as a primary reason for an action. It sets forth the normative constraint on decision-making and intention-formation. It is in this sense that DBA, and similar principles, are constitutive of our concepts of rationality and rational action.
>
> DBA tells us what primary reasons are, and what it is to have a primary reason for an action. And since a full-fledged intentional action is one for which a primary reason exists, it can be thought of as telling us what such an action is; broadly speaking, DBA states a constraint on the concept of rational action; a rational action, an intelligible action, is one for which a primary reason in the form of a fitted pair of belief and desire exists. Similar comments apply to von Wright's model of practical inference.

> *Thesis 4:* The purpose of this mode of understanding is not *predictive*; nor is it aimed at acquiring *knowledge* of the causal mechanism leading from our desires and beliefs to actions.

I take this to be evident from the earlier theses and comments. When we deliberate in order to reach a decision about a course of action, we are not engaged in a predictive endeavor—we are not trying to predict our decision will be or how we will act; we do not look upon our goals and information about the world as data upon which to base a prediction, but rather as data upon which to base a decision. This is what makes them "reasons for which" we decide as we do. The fact that decisions are made from the first-person point of view is important; from the third-person perspective it makes sense to try to predict how another agent will decide and act, and such a prediction may be based on a variety of data including the agent's beliefs and desires (but also, and more importantly, the agent's character, habits and dispositions, the patterns of his past decision-making, subliminal influences not evident to the agent, his current mood, etc.). And it is perhaps possible for us to take a third-person view of ourselves. The point, though, is that taking that point of view is *ipso facto* not to be engaged in deliberation. Deliberation by its nature is from the first-person perspective.

> *Thesis 5:* [The projection thesis] Third-person rationalizing explanations are projections of self-understanding.

When we are trying to frame a rationalizing explanation, rather than a causal-predictive explanation, for another agent, we are trying to look at the given action or decision from that agent's point of view—what the deliberations and calculations might have been from his perspective. We could *also* formulate a causal-predictive explanation for what he did; but that is not the point of rationalizing explanations. Our interest in such explanations for other persons is our interest in understanding their actions and decisions as rational, and is part of our interest in them as fellow rational agents.

> *Thesis 6:* [The autonomy thesis] Actions explained by rationalizing explanations are not actions in the sense of overt physical or bodily movement, or in the sense in which such movement is involved. Rather, they are *intentions* and *decisions.*

Lawrence Davis[14] has argued, persuasively and skillfully, for a "volitional theory" of action, according to which actions are *volitions*. I think this is fundamentally right, and can be motivated from another direction. Briefly, the rationale of the autonomy thesis is this: psychology in the sense of "rational psychology" or "intentional psychology" needs to go—in fact, it can go—only as far as our decisions and intentions. What actual physical movement takes place, whether or not our actions succeed, etc. are beyond its purview; this is something it is not able to do, and is not in its province to do. Psychology stops at decisions, and beyond that physics takes over. The so-called commonsense psychology, which often goes beyond decisions and reaches bodily movement, is a mixture of psychology (strictly speaking) and commonsense physics. Whether or not my decision turns out to result in an appropriate movement of my body, and whether this in turn leads to the realization of the intended goal, is a matter beyond my control; nature may or may not cooperate. The rationality of an agent, or an action, depends solely on the decisions the agent makes, and on the decision that underlies the action. The expression "autonomy thesis" is taken from Stephen P. Stich;[15] the substance of the thesis is closely related to the "supervenience thesis" I have discussed elsewhere,[16] and the principle of "methodological solipsism" formulated and defended by J. A. Fodor.[17] These theses provide another way to defend Thesis 6; from the point of view of rational psychology, the defense is direct and perhaps more obvious. As noted before, actions qua decisions and intentions, not actions qua bodily movement, are the proper objects of assessment with regard to rationality and intelligibility.

These six propositions are the ingredients of what I am proposing here as a "normative model" of rationalizing explanations of actions. They obviously require more extensive elaboration and development; I hope, however, to have provided enough details to make clear its main outlines and the kinds of considerations and arguments that could be invoked in its support.

NOTES

1. In: Davidson, Donald, *Actions, Reasons, and Causes*, in: Davidson, Donald, 1980, Essays on Actions and Events", Clarendon Press, Oxford.

2. In addition to the items cited in this paper by Donald Davidson and G. H. von Wright, the following could be mentioned as some of the influential works on Action theory from this period: Anscombe, G. E. M., 1957, "Intention", Blackwell, Oxford; Dray, William, 1957, "laws and Explanations in History", Oxford University Press, Oxford; Hempel, Carl G., *Rational Action*, in: Proceedings and Addresses of the American Philosophical Association 35 (1962–63), 5–23; Melden, A. 1., 1961, "Free Action", Humanities Press, London; Taylor, Richard, 1966, "Action and Purpose", Prentice-Hall, Englewood Cliffs, N.J.; Goldman, Alvin 1., 1970, "A Theory of Human Action", Prentice-Hall, Englewood Cliffs, NJ. See also the anthology, "The Nature of Human Action", Brand, Miles, ed., Scott, Foresinan & Co., Glenview, IL 1970. For a comprehensive bibliography of action theory to the late 1960's see Binldey, Richard Bronaugh and Marras, Ausonio, eds., 1971, "Agent, Action, and Reason", Blackwell, Oxford.

3. The proximate source of the current debates over psychological anomalism is Davidson's *Mental Events* in his "Essays on Actions and Events"; Davidson closely associates his arguments with Quine's much discussed doctrine of translational indeterminacy. I reconstruct and give a qualified defense of Davidson's central argument in *Psychological Laws* (forthcoming). There are also arguments deriving from Wittgensteinian considerations; ace, for example, Goldberg, Bruce, *The Correspondence Hypothesis*, in: Philosophical Review 77 (1968), 438–454, and Malcolm, Norman, 1977, "Memory and Mind", Cornell University Press, Ithaca.

4. See "Scientific Realism and the Plasticity of Mind", Cambridge University Press, Cambridge 1979.

5. See "From Folk Psychology to Cognitive Science: The Case Against Belief", MIT Press, Cambridge, Mass. 1983.

6. For further discussion and references see my *Psychological Laws*.

7. See Hempel, *Rational Action*.

8. Persuasively presented in his *Actions, Reasons, and Causes*.

9. I find essentially similar criticisms of Davidson's account in: Stoutland, Frederick, Oblique Causation and Reasons for Action, in: Synthese 43 (1980), 351–367, and Honderich, Ted, *The Argument for Anomalous Monism*, in: Analysis 42 (1982), 59–64. See Smith, Peter, *Bad News for Anomalous Monism*, in: Analysis 42 (1982), 220–224 for a discussion of Honderich.

10. See von Wright, "Explanation and Understanding", Cornell University Press, Ithaca 1971.

11. This example was suggested by Nicholas Sturgeon of Cornell.

12. General Learning Press, New York 1971.

13. In: "Moral Curiosity" (doctoral dissertation), Princeton University 1982; also *Reflective Reasoning* (in preparation).

14. In: "Theory of Action', Prentice Hall, Englewood Cliffs, N. I. 1979; also see Hornsby, Jennifer, 1980, "Actions", Routledge & Kegan Paul, London.

15. In: *Autonomous Psychology and the Belief-Desire Thesis*, in: The Monist 61 (1978), 573–591.

16. In e.g. *Psychological Supervenience, in*: Philosophical Studies 41 (1982), 51–70.

17. In: Methodological Solipsism Considered as a Research Strategy in Cognitive Psychology, in: Fodor, 1981, "Representations", MIT Press, Cambridge, Mass.

DECISION, CHOICE, PREDICTION AND THE VOLUNTARY*

A. I. Melden

In Chapter 11, I discussed very briefly the question whether or not explanations of action in terms of the character of the agent are causal explanations and in particular whether or not actions that are out of character can be explained in terms of interfering causal factors. It will be remembered that I quickly turned the discussion to an inquiry into the nature of the actions which such allegedly causal accounts are designed to explain. In the argument just concluded I have attempted to show that it is a fundamental mistake to suppose that the causal model employed in the natural sciences will fit the everyday explanations of actions in terms of intentions, interests, desires, etc. It is not even our concern, in asking how someone did such-and-such, to inquire into the natural history of his action, to probe, as it were, behind the scene of human action itself, to discover events in an area that constitutes the general causal condition of action. For the answer to the question 'How did . . . ?', does not remove us from the scene of human conduct; it specifies, rather, an action in the performance of which the agent was able to do what he did. Indeed, the action specified in the answer may even be the very same action as the one explained. Thus if I am asked, how I signalled (or how I got into the house without a key), the reply that I did so by raising my arm (or by climbing through the window) refers the questioner to an action which in the given circumstances is the very same action as the one for which an explanation was sought. In any case, whether the question is 'Why?' or 'How?', the concern is not with logically self-contained events which stand in some empirically discovered causal relation to one another, but with human events. It is hardly necessary at this point to into the logical features of our descriptions of the character of persons. Their logical connection with action, the interests, desires, motives, habits, etc., of agents is surely evident.

---

*A. I. Melden, *Free Action* chap: 14 (London: Routledge and Kegan Paul, 1961). 199–224. Reprinted with the kind permission of the estate of Professor Melden.

It follows that there is a radical disparity between these two modes of explanation: causal explanations of events and our familiar explanations of human actions.

It is this radical disparity that accounts for the characteristic ambivalences and contradictions in current psychological discussions. Insofar as psychologists are obsessed with the desire to establish their inquiry on a parallel footing with the natural sciences, the search is on for mechanisms in terms of which explanations of conduct are to be given. Conduct: viewed in this way becomes 'overt behaviour', an ambiguous term that effectively obscures the important distinction between bodily movements or happenings and actions. As bodily movements, items of overt behaviour are physiological occurrences for which physiological occurrences would appear to be sufficient causal conditions. In that case psychology reduces to physiology, and the alleged explanations of human action have succeeded only in changing the subject, in substituting explanations of bodily movements for explanations of action. For absolutely nothing about any matter of human conduct follows logically from any account of the physiological conditions of bodily movement. If this gap between matters of physiological fact and matters of human action is to be bridged, at least some token concessions must be made to our everyday discourse about persons and their actions. Some mental terms must be retained in the speculations about the mechanism of human conduct. Not infrequently, however, and precisely in order to maintain the fiction of the application of the causal model, homely terms like 'desire', 'person', etc., are eschewed and instead the talk is about 'organism', 'drive', etc. And, not unexpectedly, fatal stresses and strains appear in the uses to which this jargon is put. The word 'drive' is a notorious example: as an interior movement—some sort of causal factor—a drive is blind, fully intelligible without reference to anything to which it might give rise; as something telic it is logically essential that it refer us to that to which the agent is driven—his action.

Does the rejection of the causal model imply that actions are uncaused, that freedom is to be purchased at the expense of a capricious indeterminism, or of a libertarianism that misrepresents every responsible action as an heroic effort that somehow thwarts the causal order? Quite the contrary, the argument is designed to show the logical incoherence involved in the supposition that actions, desires, intentions, etc., stand in causal relations, either in the Humean sense or in any sense in which the term 'causal' is employed in the natural sciences. And if the argument is correct, determinism, if it employs this sense of cause, is not false but radically confused. So it is with indeterminism and libertarianism which grant to determinism the intelligibility of employing the causal model these seek to avoid the conclusion that each of us is the hapless victim of events, in the former case by viewing actions as causally indeterminate happenings, in the latter by viewing actions for which a person is responsible as events produced by extraordinary and mysterious self-exertions. The trouble in all these cases is that the applicability in principle of the causal model is taken for granted. Given this fatal blunder, actions degenerate into mere bodily happenings, produced or not as each of these doctrines would have it; and once this conceptual mistake has been made the way is open to a radical misunderstanding of desires, intentions, decisions, etc., as internal events that can operate in some sort of mechanism of the mind.

Notorious in this connection is the all too frequent talk about the causality of decision and choice, as if a decision or choice were some sort of inner 'oomph' that sparked something (but what?—an action, or a bodily movement?) into being. Surely it would be absurd to attempt to make out the distinction between bodily movement and action by reference to either decision or choice. For it is not true that agents decide or choose to do everything they do. If, for example, I go to the corner grocer to purchase a dozen eggs, it may well be that I have decided to do just that. But do I, when I pick up each egg and place it in a bag, then go on to make one decision or twelve—one for each egg? And if I pick up two eggs at a time, do I make one or two decisions? Must I, once I have decided to go to the grocer to purchase eggs, make any further decisions in the matter? Often, at least, I simply go to the grocer, and as a matter of course without giving the matter any further thought, pick up the eggs I see and put them in a bag. And if, say, I scratch my head or blow my nose, do I decide to do such things? So with choosing must I choose to do everything I do? Perhaps I choose to purchase eggs rather than meat. But must I choose this egg rather than that egg when I pick up the former and not the latter? I might if I were selecting eggs for size; but often at least I do nothing of the sort—I just pick up each egg as it comes to hand. If I give my wallet to someone who holds a pistol to my head, must I have decided to do so, chosen to do so? It would be a priorism at its worst to say that, even when I am terrified—as indeed I would be in such a case and act as I do, there must have been choice or decision. And, finally, deciding cannot possibly be an interior Humean cause of doing (and so too with choosing) for reasons that parallel precisely those given for the case of desire. If I decide to do X, the decision is intelligible only as the decision to do X. The reference to the doing is logically essential to the very thought of the decision. So too with choice, when in choosing between objects A and B, I choose to take A. Far from carrying us behind the scenes of action to events that somehow produce action, decisions and choices are intelligible only within the arena of action. By reference to them we may characterize, not bodily movements as actions (for that they are actions we already know when we ask whether a person has decided or chosen to act as he does), but actions as those the agent has decided or chosen to do and hence actions for which reasons of one sort or another can be given. It is, therefore, essential to decision and choice—no mere logical accident as it were—that there be agents, actions and reasons for doing.

Granted all this, do we not speak of the causes of a person's action? Do we not predict what persons will do, and if one can predict precisely and exactly what a person will do, must there not be causes of his doing which would justify such predictions? Again, some actions are voluntary, others involuntary; we say, as circumstances warrant, that a person could or could not have done otherwise; we recognize that some have and others do not have much will-power; and that some acts are and others are not performed of the agent's own free will. How can we avoid the irresistible conclusion that in various ways causal conditions of doings are applicable to human conduct?

It is certainly true that we use 'cause' in speaking about the actions of agents, but we can no more infer from this verbal consideration that actions are the Humean effects of events than we can from the etymological derivation of the term 'motive'. Earlier I discussed the impropriety in general of supposing that a motive is a Humean cause, but I examined in detail only the case of intention. 'Motive' covers a variety of items, not only the intention a person may have in doing something but also such items as anger, jealousy, revenge, etc. Consider the most likely candidate for Humean cause: the sudden flare-up of anger that causes a man to spank his child. Even here the Humean model will not fit in the way in which it fits the case of a blow on the patella which causes a man's leg to jerk up. In the latter case the person, his thoughts, his concerns, his intentions, reasons, etc., are wholly irrelevant to the occurrence thus produced. It is not that the blow causes him to jerk his leg, but rather that the blow caused, not something the man did, but a happening, the jerking of the leg. In the case of the angry man, the anger caused the man to act as he does. Anger indeed is no mere Humean impression of reflection; for it is logically essential to the concept of anger that the anger be about or over something. It is no more possible for a person to be angry about nothing than for a person to have a desire that is not a desire for something. And even here it is not causal knowledge that enables a man to say that he spanked his child because he was angry as it is in the case of one who explains the movement of the leg by a 'Because it was struck in the patellar region'. It is rather that the reference to his anger explains the action as that of an angry man— it enables us to describe what he did. And this by no means ends the matter, for anger may be justified or unjustified and the person in giving way to it may be blameable on account of it. Nothing of this sort applies to the jerk of the leg that results from the blow on the patella. Here we do not have an action of an agent but the action of the leg, namely, a bodily movement.

'Cause', then, is one of the snare words in both ordinary and philosophical speech, and here every attention to the precise manner in which it is employed is essential. For even in cases in which we have an immediate response (e.g. the startled jump of a person when a fire-cracker suddenly explodes behind him, or the scream of terror at the sight of the apparition on the stairs, or the sudden withdrawal of the hand from the hot object one has touched), in which there is neither calculation nor any of the other evidences of reasoned or intentional conduct, the question is not 'What caused the action?' but 'What caused him (or her) to do . . . (to jump, scream, or withdraw the hand)?' Here the reference to the agent is essential in the way in which it is not in the case of the reflex jerk of the leg, the twitch of a muscle or the movement of the intestines. And here we have extreme cases which shade almost imperceptibly (when we consider the broad and varied spectrum of cases to which the question 'What caused him (or her) to . . . ?' is applicable) into the cases in which there is calculated and reasoned behaviour, in which the agent is getting what he wants for good and sufficient reasons. The important thing is not to be blinded by the fact that 'cause' may be used in all cases but to recognize just how it is applied and in what varied ways to cases that range from instinctive responses to reasoned, rational transactions of agents with one another. In none of these cases, varied though they may be, is causation in the sense in which this term applies to physical events applicable to the actions of agents. But a detailed inquiry into these uses of 'cause' is not possible within the limits of this essay.

Equally treacherous is the term 'prediction'. Granted that to predict is to say what will be the case what does this mean? I can be said to say what will be by promising that I shall do such-and-such. By declaring that I shall hit the target, I can be said to say what will be, and then proving it by exhibiting my skill. I can be said to say what will be by contradicting someone's expression of intention, e.g. 'I won't let you harm that child!' and succeeding. I can be said to say what will be by saying that the coin will fall heads and having my guess come true. I can be said to say what will be by predicting the villainous act of someone I know to be a villain. I can be said to say what will be by predicting the path of a comet from its known velocity, direction of motion, etc. And so on. Here someone may object that after all there must be something common to all of these cases—saying what will be—whatever the differences between them might be. Certainly, in all of these and other cases of prediction this is common: something is said about the future. But to say this is only to say that these words apply. It is not to say that there is a common ingredient so that promising, for example, is saying what will be plus something else that makes the saying a promise and not, say, an expression of my resolution. What makes the promise a promise is not that there is one item—saying what will be—together with some other item. It is, rather, as I have argued elsewhere, that the saying what will be when it is done by an agent under such-and-such circumstances (and here it is no matter what goes on in the mind of the person speaking) is the very same thing, as, and not part of, promising.[1] The formula 'saying what will be' is singularly unhelpful. It would be just as unilluminating to say that in all cases in which we use the term 'cause', whether in speaking about the causes of the contractions of muscles or in speaking about the actions of agents (what caused him to do), there is something common to which we are referring—but of what and in what sense of 'cause' is the crucially important question. And if I predict that someone I know and fully understand—for I know the kind of person he is, the sorts of character traits he has, the things he wants and the goods with which he is concerned—will in such-and-such circumstances act in such-and-such a way, this is not at all like predicting the path of a satellite; nor does the reliability of my prediction rest upon hidden causal factors that operate in such a way as to make true what I say will be the case. For here the reliability of my prediction rests upon my understanding of the person—he is like an open book to me—not upon hidden Humean causal factors about which, if they were at all relevant, I can at best only speculate. Here nothing is hidden; it is because I understand him, not because I am aware of events transpiring in some alleged mechanism of his mind or body, that I am able to say what he will do.

Such predictions sometimes go wrong. Suppose, however, it were possible in principle to predict with perfect accuracy, how could one then maintain that the agent could do anything other than what he does, that his behaviour is not subject to causal factors in precisely the way in which this is admittedly true of the motions of some heavenly body, that a human, being is not a helpless victim of circumstances within and without him? Here we have the picture of a human being reacting to stimuli from without in accordance with the precise character of his constitution—the pattern of events within his nervous system—an extraordinarily complex mechanical or electronic system no different in principle, but only in degree of complexity, from some of the self-regulating mechanisms of the laboratory which perform their perfectly predictable operations when suitably programmed.

This picture wholly misrepresents the character of agents and their actions. What would one predict—actions or bodily movements? Certainly, if one knew the state of the nervous system and musculature, then one could predict, given such-and-such stimulation, that, say, the arm would rise in the air. But our concern is not with the rising of the arm but with the person's raising of his arm; and with raising his arm, say, in order to signal, to get what he wants, and so on. Let it be that the nervous system of one who has been trained to drive and to give the signal that he is about to make a turn has been suitably 'conditioned'—that there are characteristic brain patterns present in these and only these cases at the time the arm is raised in order to give the signal—farther conditions are required for the raising of the arm, and what can these be? It is no good saying that these conditions are the appropriate visual and auditory stimuli, the nervous excitation of the end-organs in the eye or ear. For so far all that such stimulations of the appropriately conditioned bodily mechanism can produce is the movement of the arm. In order that one might predict that the person will raise his arm in order to give the signal, one needs not only a knowledge of the central nervous system and of the appropriate stimulation of the endorgans, but also of the circumstances in which the *agent*—not the bodily mechanism—is placed and of what, in these circumstances, he will do. We need to know, in short, that we have an agent, a motorist, who is driving and whose action of raising the arm is to be understood in terms of the appropriate rule of the road as a case of signalling a turn as the crossroad comes into view. But in that case we have left behind all reference to hypothetical occurrences in the nervous system, for now we are back to the scene of human action. And the circumstances to which we must now attend, if we are to predict that he will raise his arm to signal, are not Humean causal conditions of his doing. They are rather circumstances in the context of which the bodily movement that does occur, and however it may be that it is produced, is understood as the specific action it is.

'Condition' is in fact the source of a great deal of confusion in the philosophical literature. Sometimes it refers to a legal requirement or stipulation; sometimes to an event related to that of which it is a condition by some fact of causation or by some law of nature; sometimes to an action (*e.g.* as in 'I shall *do* such-and-such on condition that you do . . . '); sometimes to the circumstance in which a matter of fact is also a reason for doing (*e.g.* my wanting food is the condition in which 'There is a restaurant across the street' is a reason for my going there), and so on. In the present case, the conditions or circumstances in which the bodily movement occurs—an agent who is a motorist and who is executing his intention, guided by the rules of the road and a variety of considerations as the turn in the road approaches—*constitute* or *define* the bodily movement as the action it is.

Here someone may object: granted that there is no one central nuclear experience that constitutes the intention of an agent, and similarly in the case of a desire or a decision or a choice, still these do make a difference to the character of a man's thoughts and feelings, *i.e.* to his inner mental state. And if so, there must be corresponding sorts of neural events, however complex these may be, in each of these cases. So too with the circumstances in which a motorist finds himself and to which he attends as he performs his various actions. If he attends to these, if he has been trained, if he executes his skilful performances, there are characteristic states of the nervous system and characteristic exciting stimuli. Now if one knew enough about the nervous system, could we not 'interpret' or 'decode' such states and stimuli as the states and stimuli of such-and-such an agent doing such-and-such in the given sort of circumstances? And given a knowledge of the future stimuli, similarly 'decoded', could we not infallibly predict such-and-such bodily movements, similarly decipherable as the bodily movements performed by the given sort of agent in doing such-and-such? No doubt such predictability would depend on our own status as agents who can understand cases of bodily movements as cases of actions and who

can recognize that in given circumstances the actions in question would be ⸱
sort; but we could, given this understanding that would enable us to interprₑ
data in the appropriate way, predict on the basis of such data what any given ₗ
will do. If so, could we still insist that any agent, even when he attends carefuₗ
what he is doing, even when his behaviour is as calculated and as deliberate as it ₗ
be, could possibly have done otherwise? And since he in turn, equipped with tₗ
same ability, could discover, predict and interpret the neural data in *our* nervous systems, are we not equally helpless in all that we do—even in discussing these very
matters? And if so, we seem to be on the brink of insanity—it is as if computing machines were to be programmed and decoded only by other machines of like sorts, as
if work were being done in a laboratory without any person doing it.

What we know about the nervous system and the events transpiring in it as we
think, feel and do is extraordinarily little, but the reply need not rest on such an appeal
to our manifest ignorance. Indeed, one should hope and pray that it may be possible
one day to know enough about the mechanism of the body to enable qualified persons
to cure mental disorders by introducing the necessary changes in the central nervous
system, perhaps by means of surgery. One may grant, in fact, that the development of
the central nervous system goes hand-in-hand with the maturation of human beings
as they acquire the varied skills which they exhibit in their reasoned and responsible
thoughts and actions, that the latter is in some way dependent upon the former. But
none of this implies the forbidding picture painted by the epiphenomenalist in which
the status of a person reduces to the vaporous after-effects of physiological processes.
For even if we could do the decoding, we should still have the central nervous system
of a person who reasons, justifies, decides, chooses, intends, wants, and conducts
himself as he does with other persons about him. Indeed, what our speculation implies is the requirement, for the thoughts and actions of such persons, of requisite
states of the nervous system and this, far from reducing persons to hapless mechanisms, is only a more radical representation of the familiar view that persons are not
disembodied spirits but persons who can be seen and touched and hurt, who use their
arms, legs, etc. in the actions they perform, and who require for such employment of
their limbs and other bodily parts certain general conditions and particular states of
their nervous systems. Indeed, the alleged conclusion that each of us is a helpless
victim of the events transpiring in the central nervous system is simply a logical
howler. 'Could have done' and 'could not have done', 'helpless', etc.—these are expressions employed not with respect to events occurring in the mechanism of the
body, nor to mental events, whether or not these are regarded as mere by-products of
bodily processes—Humean effects of neural events—but to *persons*. We do not say
that an itch or twitch, a feeling, thought or desire, however we understand these, is
helpless. Neither do we say that the body is helpless in any sense in which we say this
about a person. It is *persons* who are able or unable to do or to refrain from doing; to
think or to refrain from thinking, etc. We need, in short, to recognize the necessary
starting point for any elucidation of expressions of these sorts—persons who act,
think, feel, in their commerce with the things about them and with each other. This is
the language-game in which expressions like 'could have done', 'could not have
done', 'helpless', etc., are employed, in any sense in which they bear upon questions
of the freedom of human action. To suppose that they can be employed, without radical distortion or change, in the account of the events within the body, or in any

effects, is the confusion upon which the apparently disas-
speculative assumption rests.

ion about the decoding were granted, would it not be
how human beings would behave, but also and with-
ntrol them by altering the neural conditions within their
point of fact, other devices are currently employed by politi-
oncerned to manipulate, human beings—the difference is only one
the success of the results; the methods currently employed are fortu-
y crude and frequently in efficacious. And if by introducing an electrode
the brain of a person, I succeed in getting him to believe that he is Napoleon,
that surely is not a rational belief that he has, nor is he responsible for what he does
in consequence of this belief, however convinced he may be that he is fully justified
in acting as he does. There would be no virtue in any philosophical doctrine which
ruled out the possibility that human beings may be controlled, that by virtue of what
we do to them we may render them incompetent, insane, devoid of responsibility.
But here as before, we can understand terms like 'competence', 'control', 'responsible' only by keeping clearly in mind the contexts appropriate to their employment—
human beings who are rational in and attentive to what they are doing in their
transactions with one another and in their dealings with the things about them.

In short, even on our speculative assumption, nothing disastrous to our common
beliefs about the freedom of human action would follow. Such knowledge might be
dangerous—it might open the way to abuses in the management of human beings.
But even if this knowledge were achieved, we should still employ our familiar discourse in describing persons and their conduct. Far from it being the case that the
possibility of such knowledge implies the helplessness of human beings in all of
their thoughts and actions, the achievement of such knowledge would enable us to
understand, in a two-fold sense, why human beings think, desire, choose, decide and
do as in fact they do. For one thing, we should have a knowledge of the neural conditions under which such human events occur; and, for another, since the neural
states and events would be 'decoded', these would be understood in terms that go
beyond the purview of the physiologist. In effect, then, the knowledge of such decoded neural states and events would indeed give us a fuller understanding of the actions of responsible persons and hence a better basis for prediction than we now
have; but it would do this *only* by revealing more fully their characters, interests, desires, hopes, social and moral roles, choices, intentions, etc.—just those sorts of
items in terms of which we do in fact explain and predict the actions of human beings. We should then be able, for one thing, to understand, explain and predict the
quite rational, responsible actions of free agents; and we should then be able to understand and to predict that such agents would decide not to perform actions of various sorts, in circumstances to which they were attending, and which they could then
and there have done, for this or that reason.

What needs to be emphasized again and again is the fact that there are contexts
appropriate to the use of expressions like 'could have done' and 'could not have
done'. In his justly celebrated 'Ifs and Cans', J. L. Austin has exposed some of the
confusions that surround these and other locutions—confusions that are the immediate consequence of the failure to recognize the relevant details of the circumstances in which such locutions are familiarly employed.[2] Here I can only repeat

that these locutions are intelligibly employed only in the context of huma... this, not events in the nervous system or bodily movements in which the... is the language-game in which they are intelligibly employed.

But what of the distinction between the voluntary and the involuntary? S... this is one of the most central matters that requires comment and explanation eve... a preliminary study, such as this one, of matters that are basic to the concept of a fr... and responsible action—one of the very first items on the agenda of any discussion... of this concept! I want to say, on the contrary, that it must be one of the last, impor- tant as the distinction between the voluntary and the involuntary in fact is. Here in- deed is one of the most gravely misunderstood pairs of terms in the philosophical vocabulary.

The familiar view is that the distinction is to be made in terms of the order of the causes of action: a voluntary action is one that is somehow produced by the will— acts of volition; an involuntary action is one that proceeds from other events. So prevalent and insistent has this view been that it has seeped into some dictionary ac- counts of these terms. But if by 'will' is intended the causal agency that consists in the occurrence of such acts of volition, then there is no will and, as I argued earlier in Chapter V, there cannot possibly be any since the conception of acts of volition or willings, by means of which actions allegedly are performed, is self-contradictory. Yet 'will' can be used quite unobjectionably; for we do speak of a person's will in such-and-such a matter, of a person of good will, of a person with a will of iron, of persons who do or refrain from doing of their own free will, and so on. So, too, with the term 'volition'—this does not refer us to interior acts of volition hidden in the re- cesses of the mind which are the alleged effective agents in the production of ac- tions, but to perfectly familiar items in the lives of human beings. A man's will in such-and-such a matter may be simply what he wants or wishes. A person of good will is one who is a morally estimable agent who is concerned in his thought and ac- tion with the well-being of others no less than with his obligations towards them. A man with a will of iron is one who is unusually steadfast in executing his intentions, undeterred by considerations that would distract or prevent most people from achieving their goals. And if we are to understand what is involved in the idea of someone doing something of his own free will we must look to the centrally impor- tant and fully enriched cases in which a rational, indeed a moral, agent chooses and decides to act as he does for reasons he considers good and proper. This is not to say that every action done of one's own free will is one chosen or decided; or that every such action is one performed for a moral reason. It is rather that 'free will' is not as- cribed to any agent other than a moral agent capable of rational choice and decision. Just as it is logically impossible for someone always to want something for no reason whatsoever, so it is logically impossible for someone always to act of his own free will without rational and moral choice and decision. It is only by reference to such cases of persons who act as they do on the basis of the rational, and indeed moral, choices and decisions they make for reasons they consider good and sufficient that the conception of free will can be fully elucidated.

Once we recognize the diversity of items that come under the term 'will'—rea- sons, desires, decisions, choices, intentions, etc., each of which in the requisite sense explains an agent's conduct—it is possible to understand some of the otherwise per- plexing features of some of the uses of 'voluntary' and 'involuntary'. For one thing,

austive terms; that is to say, it is not every action that is ei-
⟨...⟩y. If, for example, I rub my nose, this is not something I
⟨...⟩ntention in doing it, or a desire to do so; nor need I de-
⟨...⟩ do it—period. Hence with respect to this action, the
⟨...⟩ry or involuntary?' is correctly given by saying 'Nei-
⟨...⟩ the absurdity of asking 'Which is it?' is by no means due
⟨...⟩erms 'voluntary' and 'involuntary' apply, as some have sug-
⟨...⟩ctions that are objectionable, untoward or unusual. It is rather that in
⟨...⟩ is manifest that I have no intention, desire or reason for doing it that
⟨...⟩ serve to reveal its import in any transaction in which I engage—none of the
⟨...⟩ems covered by the term 'the will' serves to explain it. I simply do, and that is all.
In the second place, the terms 'voluntary' and 'involuntary' are not even mutually
exclusive. Suppose, for example, a young man has committed some crime, which so
far has not been charged to him. But instead of waiting to be discovered, tracked
down and arrested, he goes to the police and gives himself up. Certainly the police
would consider this action to be voluntary—he gives himself up not because he is ordered to do so by an arresting officer, but for reasons which have nothing to do with
any of the functions of the police. But suppose, further, that our youth does this, not
by choice but under the threat of his father to disinherit him if he does not do so, and
let us suppose, further, that the crime is a minor one which nonetheless carries with
it a disagreeable punishment. In this case, he gives himself up against his will and
only in order to avoid the far more disagreeable prospect of disinheritance. Surely
we would distinguish this involuntary action from the voluntary action of one who,
having committed a crime, gives himself up because he has chosen to submit to the
punishment which he recognizes he deserves.

Now there is no difficulty in understanding how the same action—appearing at
the police station to give oneself up—can be characterized in these two distinct
ways: as voluntary by the arresting police officer, as involuntary both by the agent
and by those aware of the further circumstances with which the police officer is un-
acquainted. For the action of giving oneself up is, in these further circumstances, the
further action of submitting to the pressure exerted by the father. There is no difficulty, then, in seeing how it is that the same action—walking into the police station
and announcing that one has committed such-and-such a crime—may be characterized as voluntary when understood in one way and as involuntary when understood in quite a different way. Here everything depends upon *what* the action of
walking into the police station is; and what it is is determined by his intention in
doing this, his reasons, his desires, in short, just those items that come under the general heading of the term 'will'.

But how does this establish that the terms 'voluntary' and 'involuntary' are not
mutually exclusive? All that has been shown is that the action of walking into the police station can be understood further in two quite different ways—in the one case as
the action of submitting to the authority of the police, in the other as submitting to
the threat of one's father—as two quite distinct actions. But given that the action of
giving oneself up has been *properly* understood, is it not then settled which of the
two—voluntary or involuntary—it must be?

Here, however, we need to recognize the import of the terms 'voluntary' and 'involuntary' and the ways in which these reflect our interests in conduct. As moral

agents surveying the scene, our concern may well be with the moral ch[...]
young man and his conduct. Given this interest, we do need to know [...]
wanted to do the legally and morally required thing and hence whether, [...]
himself up in order to accept the legal consequences of his crime, he was do[...]
in order to save his precious inheritance or in order to receive his just deserts. [...]
whether an action is voluntary is, in effect, to ask whether further questions abou[...]
intentions, his desires, his reasons, are relevant. But such a question is never ask[...]
out of the blue, but only in a context in which the questioner has a quite particular interest in the action. And since, as moral agents, our interest in an action is the interest we have in affixing the measures of praise or blame appropriate to it, we do need
to know something more about the agent's further intentions, his further reasons,
etc., than appear on the surface and which enable us to understand the moral features
of what the person has done. But our interests are not always moral. A policeman's
concern with the action of one who has committed a crime may be quite circum-
scribed by the legal responsibility, determined by the character of his office, which
he has in dealing with him. It is quite irrelevant to his legal office that our young man
has been led to come into the police station for this or that morally commendable
reason. All that he need be concerned with is the fact that our young man has submitted to the authority of the police without having set into motion by his crime the
usual operations of the police in tracking him down and compelling him to surrender. From this point of view, giving himself up as he has is submitting himself to the
authority of the police. Whether or not he wants to do this because it is right or because he wants to save his inheritance is of no matter to the policeman's interest in
the affair insofar as it is determined by his office; the action of giving himself up,
which our young man does for whatever reason he may have, is from the point of
view of the policeman's interest in the action voluntary. It may be that the policeman
in seeing the young man give himself up has not *fully* understood the action, that failing to appreciate that he is doing it in order to avoid disinheritance he fails to recognize that he is submitting to the pressures of his father and that he is in this way
providing for his own future; nonetheless he has most certainly *properly* understood
it. For this is not at all like the case of a criminal who absentmindedly or inadvertently walks into a police station while on his way to cash a check—here one would
have neither a full nor a proper understanding if one supposed that he was giving
himself up even if it led to his being marched into a cell. In our example, giving oneself up is submitting to the authority of the police and *this* action, so described, can
be characterized either as voluntary or as involuntary, depending upon one's interest
in the action and hence upon what knowledge of the agent's interests, desires, reasons, etc., is relevant to one's proper understanding of the action. The fact that the
same action, properly understood, may be correctly characterized as either voluntary
or involuntary depends upon the fact that different features of the agent's will may or
may not be relevant to the different interests a person may have in the action.

Generally, it is impossible, in the abstract and without reference to those features of an action that reflect the quite particular interests one may have in it, to answer the question 'Voluntary or involuntary?' This question is never asked out of the
blue, as it were, but only within the context of some interest we have in appraising
the action. There are limiting cases, of course. We do speak of the voluntary and the
involuntary movements of parts of the body (for example, of the arm and of the heart

...use such movements can occur in actions performed by
...ny interest to him or to anyone else in the ordinary cir-
...The centrally important uses of 'voluntary' and 'invol-
...s to the scene of social and moral conduct, where
...ave a bearing upon the lives and actions of others.
...nflicting interests are involved, it is not surprising
...ould be characterized as voluntary by one person, as in-
...Consider how complex are the issues involved in deciding
...on of a soldier is voluntary or involuntary when, for example, it
...rm of obeying the order of one's commanding officer to shoot at random
...ozen inhabitants of a hostile village, and where it is done without hesitation and
even with satisfaction! A great deal hinges upon whether we decide the action to be
voluntary. Shall we be led in our judgment to consider only the military propriety,
perhaps necessity, of obeying one's commanding officer? If our interest is moral,
shall we say that his brutish satisfaction marks the voluntary character of the action,
that it cannot be involuntary since that would serve to absolve the soldier of all moral
responsibility? Shall we say that the soldier's action is voluntary whether or not he
derived satisfaction from it? Can we demand of a soldier that he risk court martial
and even death by refusing to obey an order? Here the issues become exceedingly
complex—our judgment that the action is voluntary or involuntary as the case may
be is bound up with important and difficult issues that reflect not only diverse and
even diverge interests but difficult matters of moral principles, legal rules, political
and social policies.

NOTES

1. Cf. 'On Promising', *Mind*, January 1956.

2. The Annual Philosophical Lecture, Henriette Herz Trust, *Proceedings of the British Academy, Vol*. XLII, London: Oxford University Press.

Index